a history of instructional technology

paul saettler

Sacramento State College

mcgraw-hill book company

New York   St. Louis   San Francisco   Toronto   London   Sydney

a history of instructional technology

a history of instructional technology

Library of Congress Catalog Card Number: 67–21599
54410

1 2 3 4 5 6 7 8 9 0   M A M M   7 4 3 2 1 0 6 9 8 7

I enthusiastically dedicate this book to Dr. F. Dean McClusky, in recognition of his generosity, his friendship, and his monumental contributions to instructional technology.

foreword

Philosophers, commentators, schoolteachers, industrialists, and songwriters all have, in the course of time, commented on the value and usefulness of history. History has been considered as a philosophy, as a technique, as an aesthetic experience, as a sure guide to the future, as an account of the crimes of mankind, as a tissue of lies, as "bunk."

With so much comment on historical writing existing as a vast literature of its own, it is difficult to compose a foreword to Dr. Saettler's work which, in any new way, might suggest the value of his contribution. Perhaps one of the earliest historians, Thucydides, in commenting on his own work, stated my general feelings. Speaking of his history of the Peloponnesian War, Thucydides said, "But if he who desires to have before his eyes a true picture of the events which have happened, and of the like events which may be expected to happen thereafter in the order of human things, shall pronounce what I have written to be useful, then I shall be satisfied." An accurate, generalizable account of the past which may serve, at least in part, as a guide to the future is what we want from history. In this pioneering work on the history of instructional technology, Paul Saettler has given us such a tool.

The history of technology (and of science, for that matter) is a relatively new professional area for historians that, with the great explosion in technology occurring in this century, has become increasingly popular. In a large sense, Paul Saettler's work is in this new tradition. The history of technology is a difficult area to work in, as Lynn White, Jr., one of the leading historians in this field, has pointed out. Knowledge in the general area of the history of technology is as yet so sketchy that some of the existing compilations have been referred to as the "codification of error." Historical work in all aspects of technology is badly needed. Hence, the present book is especially valuable in adding to our knowledge of technology in education.

In tracing the history of instructional technology up to the present time, Dr. Saettler has had to deal with this development in the context of American education. This is especially important when American education is considered, technically, as a bureaucracy. For, as Charles Hoban has recently pointed out, we know very little about the processes of innovation within a bureaucracy. All aspects of instructional media—the *Orbus Pictus*, the Keystone slide sets, the sound motion picture or television—have represented innovations thrusting into the context of a very special kind of bureaucracy. Hence, the accounts of committees, commissions, organization plans, and departments of various kinds, which are all, in the correct sense of the term, technological in nature, give us some insight into this little-understood process.

The result of Dr. Saettler's hard work is the book before you. We can do no better, in conclusion, than return to the quotation of Thucydides. For American education is either in the midst of, or on the verge of, a great technological revolution that has penetrated from the industrial, scientific, and military sectors of our culture. The changes are sure to be great; they may be so great that the past will not prove too sound a basis upon which to predict the future; nonetheless, such insight as we can get from the past is perhaps the major path to the "like events which may be expected to happen hereafter in the order of human things." Paul Saettler has helped us a long way down that path.

James D. Finn
University of Southern California

preface

This book was written because no history of instructional technology existed. Moreover, no history brought into focus the theoretical and methodological foundations or the interrelationships of the audiovisual/radio/television/ programed instruction complex within the field of instructional technology. This task seemed essential not only to provide a basis for historical sophistication in a barren area of historical research, but for an adequate assessment of the past and for the intelligent direction of the rapidly developing man-machine systems approach to instruction.

The nucleus for this history was formed some years ago with the encouragement and guidance of Dr. James D. Finn, professor of education at the University of Southern California, to whom the author is grateful for his continued interest as well as for his delightful Foreword. The history of the audiovisual movement within the field of instructional technology could not have been written without the invaluable help of Dr. F. Dean McClusky, professor emeritus of education at the University of California at Los Angeles, who opened his library and personal files to the author and gave unstintingly of his time and counsel. Professor McClusky has also contributed the Introduction to Part 2.

The first chapter of this work serves as general introduction to the field of instructional technology. Part 1 traces its significant theoretical and methodological foundations. Part 2 is a systematic treatment of the development of a technology of instruction in American education, from the late nineteenth century to the present. Part 3 is a history of experimental research on instructional media. The final chapter in Part 3 contains a prospective view of instructional technology.

Much of the data for this history was gathered from interviews with pioneers in instructional technology, many of whom are now deceased, from personal letters, and from unpublished and published material. From the various sources, a consensus of the basic postulates was drawn and interpreted whenever it was deemed necessary for exposition.

The author also wishes to express his particular appreciation to the following individuals whose contributions of historical data, materials, or ideas aided greatly in the preparation of the manuscript: William H. Allen, B. A. Aughinbaugh, Floyde E. Brooker, W. W. Charters, E. Winifred Crawford, Edgar Dale, Ellsworth C. Dent, John Dewey, Anna V. Dorris, Franklin Dunham, Don Carlos Ellis, Donald P. Ely, Frank N. Freeman, Graham H. Friese-Greene, Elizabeth Golterman, William M. Gregory, Eric H. Haight, G. E. Hamilton, Charles F. Hoban, Jr., Rita Hocheimer, E. Burton Holmes, H. V. Kaltenborn, Harold W. Kent, Robert Kissack, Daniel Knowlton, Cline M. Koon, L. C. Larson, Paul F. Lazarsfeld, William Lewin, Mark A. May, Joy Amelia Meissner, Arch Mercey, Elmer Morgan, Mario Montessori, Lorraine Noble, Paul C. Reed, Alexander Stoddard, Elmer G. Sulzer, Edward L. Thorndike, I. Keith Tyler, Tracy F. Tyler, Levering Tyson, Alexander Victor, Judith Waller, G. D. Wiebe, and Dennis Williams. Many others who made important contributions cannot be listed, unfortunately, because of space limitations. For permission to reproduce illustrations and quotations from periodicals and books, grateful acknowledgment is made to the authors and publishers whose names appear in footnotes throughout this book.

Appreciation for the most significant contribution is reserved for my wife, Rosalind Saettler. Without her constant encouragement, patience, and editorial help, the book could not possibly have been completed. Despite the considerable aid of friends and colleagues, errors unquestionably persist in the manuscript. The author assumes sole responsibility for the product.

Paul Saettler

contents

the meaning of instructional technology

Any definition of instructional technology must be subject to the concept held by the definer, and this involves consideration of at least two distinct concepts: the physical science, or media, concept and the behavioral science concept. Although often functionally interrelated, each is an outgrowth of different theoretical notions, and each viewpoint holds important implications for learning and instruction. The physical science (media) concept predates the behavioral science concept by several decades and continues to have the strongest influence on contemporary educational practice. Behavioral science–oriented instructional technology is of more recent origin and holds great promise for the ultimate development of a mature science and technology of instruction.

Physical science concept of instructional technology

The physical science concept of instructional technology usually means the application of physical science and engineering technology, such as motion picture projectors, tape recorders, television, teaching machines, for group presentation of instructional materials. Characteristically, this concept views the various media as aids to instruction and tends to be preoccupied with the effects of devices and procedures, rather than with the differences of individual learners or with the selection of instructional content.

The historical development of the physical science concept of instructional technology seems to have been relatively little influenced by educational needs or psychological theory in relation to the design of instructional messages or experimental media research. Comenian-Pestalozzian-Herbartian concepts [1] of educational practice, however, may have had some influence on the use of visual aids to instruction.

The most influential theoretical notion embodied within the physical science concept of instructional technology is that which casts materials (audiovisual) and machines (still and motion picture projectors, etc.) in nonverbal roles and some of the more traditional media (lectures, books) in verbal roles. The assumption underlying this view is that nonverbal media

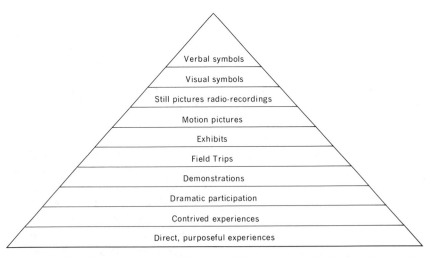

Fig. 1.1   The "Cone of Experience." (From Edgar Dale, Audio-Visual Methods in Teaching, rev. ed., New York, The Dryden Press, Inc., 1954. By permission of the publishers.)

[1] See Chapters 2 and 3 of this book for a discussion of the educational theories of Comenius, Pestalozzi, and Herbart.

are more concrete and effective, and that the perennial villain in the teaching-learning process is "verbalism." [2]

This rationale has led to an abstract-concrete dichotomy which is, in fact, no dichotomy at all, since both verbal and nonverbal media and/or signs vary along an abstract-concrete continuum. It is not true, for example, that the pictorial is inevitably "real" or "concrete." It can be highly abstruse and abstract. What is more, whether we speak with words or pictures, we must abstract if we are to generalize or develop concepts about the world in which we live.

Many of those who support the abstract-concrete theoretical notion do not always make it sufficiently clear that in denouncing verbalism they are not necessarily claiming to have found a superior alternative to verbal communication. A few extremists have, in fact, expressed the hope that audiovisual specialists might develop a completely nonverbal language for the purposes of exact communication. The very idea reflects the assumption that nonverbal media offer a true alternative to either written or spoken communication and can, therefore, be used as a substitute method of instructional communication. Some of those on the other side of the fence have unwittingly supported the same assumption, attacking nonverbal media on the grounds that they may hinder or serve as a substitute for the development of reading or other language skills.

The physical science concept of instructional technology has been accepted quite generally by practitioners in the audiovisual movement and by the electronic communications industry. Since the early 1900s, such terms as visual aids, teaching aids, audiovisual aids, visual instruction, audiovisual instruction, audiovisual materials, audiovisual communication, audiovisual technology, and many more have been used to designate a group of machines and materials. Yet as early as 1926, Nelson L. Greene, a notable pioneer in the audiovisual movement, pointed out that use of the term *visual education* was as undescriptive and meaningless as would be the adoption of the terms "tactual education," "gustatory education," "olfactory education," or "aural education." [3] Still another audiovisual pioneer, Joseph J. Weber, flatly stated in 1930 that the term visual education was "unscientific." [4]

In recent years, a number of individuals in the audiovisual movement have voiced increasingly their dissatisfaction with the physical science, or

[2] It is interesting to observe that Brown, Lewis, and Harcleroad recently recognized the twin villain of verbalism, whose name is "pictorialism." See James W. Brown, Richard B. Lewis, and Fred F. Harcleroad, *A-V Instruction: Materials and Methods*, 2d ed. New York, McGraw-Hill Book Company, 1964, pp. 11–12.

[3] Nelson L. Greene, "Motion Pictures in the Classroom," *The Annals*, vol. 128 (November, 1926), p. 122.

[4] Joseph J. Weber, *Visual Aids in Education*. Valparaiso, Ind., Valparaiso University, 1930, p. 2. (Mimeographed.)

media, concept of instructional technology.[5] The first formal steps toward redefinition were taken in the monograph "The Changing Role of the Audiovisual Process in Education: A Definition and a Glossary of Related Terms." [6] The evident uneasiness within the audiovisual movement makes it seem quite likely that the prevailing physical science concept of instructional technology will be progressively modified in the years ahead.

Behavioral science concept of instructional technology

The use of the term *behavioral science* is so recent that it may be helpful to summarize its history and explain its meaning. This approach to the study of human behavior, focused on the fields of anthropology, sociology, and psychology (now designated as the behavioral sciences), did not really get started until the latter half of the nineteenth century. It began with the British development of social anthropology by E. B. Tylor (1832–1917) and J. B. Frazier (1854–1941); the first experimental psychological laboratory of Wilhelm Max Wundt (1832–1926) in Leipzig, Germany, in 1879; the antecedent of the modern intelligence test by Alfred Binet (1857–1911) in France; the beginning of child study by G. Stanley Hall (1846–1924); and the first large-scale sociological investigations stemming from early twentieth-century reform movements in the United States.

World War I gave psychology a forward impetus in the United States in the areas of intelligence tests and statistical measurements. Growth of the behavioral sciences in the period between the two world wars was stimulated largely by university research. Great expansion occurred during World War II, which created an increased demand for behavioral scientists in connection with the American war effort. Behavioral science growth then continued at such an accelerated rate that the United States emerged as the leading practitioner—with the result that many observers feel there is an American version of behavioral science.[7] The term behavioral science first began to be widely accepted in the 1950s when the Ford Foundation supported a Behavioral Science Program with several millions of dollars. The Federal gov-

[5] See, for example, James D. Finn, "Technology and the Instructional Process," *AV Communication Review,* vol. 8, no. 1 (Winter, 1960).

[6] See *AV Communication Review,* vol. 11, no. 1, supplement 6 (January–February, 1963). (Prepared by the Commission on Definition and Terminology as Monograph 1 of the Technological Development Project of the NEA.)

[7] European versions of the behavioral sciences have tended to be primarily historical, theoretical, and philosophical and have been considered a part of scholarship rather than a part of science. The American version, on the other hand, is considered to be primarily a part of science. In this view, the behavioral sciences must deal with human behavior in a scientific manner. The ultimate aim is to establish generalizations about human behavior, supported by empirical data, which may enable us to understand, explain, and predict human behavior. Typically, American teams of technicians do research projects on specific subjects and report experimental findings.

ernment, through the National Science Foundation and research offices in various departments, is now providing a major part of the support.

Today there is an emerging *Zeitgeist* that an applied behavioral science approach to the problems of learning and instruction is fundamental to instructional technology. Thus the basic view of the behavioral science concept of instructional technology is that educational practice should be more dependent on the methods of science as developed by behavioral scientists in the broad areas of psychology, anthropology, sociology, and in the more specialized areas of learning, group processes, language and linguistics, communications, administration, cybernetics, perception, and psychometrics. Moreover, this concept includes the application of engineering research and development (including human factors engineering) and branches of economics and logistics related to the effective utilization of instructional personnel, buildings (learning spaces), and such new computerized machine systems as data processing and information retrieval.

The word "technology" (the Latin form is *texere*, to weave or construct)

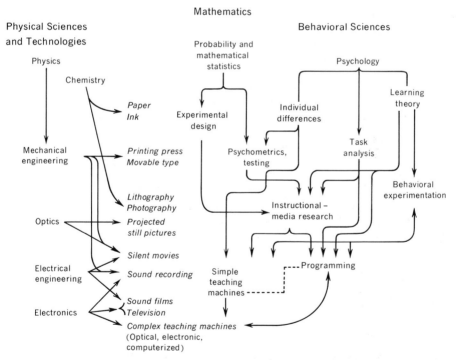

Fig. 1.2 *Diagrammatic representation of the interrelationships in physical and behavioral sciences related to instructional technology. (From E. R. Hilgard (ed.), Theories of Learning and Instruction, The Sixty-third Yearbook of the National Society for the Study of Education, part I. Chicago, The University of Chicago Press, 1964. By permission of the publishers.)*

does not necessarily imply the use of machines, as many seem to think, but refers to any practical art using scientific knowledge. The French sociologist Ellul says that "it is the machine which is now entirely dependent upon technique, and the machine represents only a small part of technique." [8] Not only is the machine the result of a certain technique, but also its instructional applications are made possible by technique. Consequently, the relation of behavioral science to instructional technology parallels that of the physical sciences to engineering technology or the biological sciences to medical technology.

In recent years, the behavioral science concept of instructional technology has been elaborated by a number of individuals. Glaser, for example, has described it in the following words:

> The design of instructional procedures will be modified as behavioral science and educational practice begin to be related in a mutually helpful way—a way not atypical of science and practice in other fields. As this occurs, it is hypothesized that four main areas of the educational process will be influenced: (a) the setting of instructional goals will be recast in terms of observable and measurable student behavior including achievements, attitudes, motivations, and interests; (b) the diagnosis of the learner's strengths and weaknesses prior to instruction will become a more definitive process so that it can aid in guiding the student along a curriculum specially suited for him; (c) the techniques and materials employed by the teacher will undergo significant change; and (d) the ways in which the outcomes of education are assessed, both for student evaluation and curriculum improvement, will receive increasingly more attention. [9]

Other significant expressions of the behavioral science concept of instructional technology can be found in the literature of the behavioral sciences as well as education. [10]

The concept of instructional technology held by the author of this book is congruent with the behavioral science meaning of instructional technology. However, since the application of behavioral science to educational practice constitutes a relatively brief history, the historical focus in this book necessarily reflects the more traditional instructional technology embodied in the

[8] Jacques Ellul, *The Technological Society*. New York, Alfred A. Knopf, Inc., 1964, p. 4.
[9] Robert Glaser (ed.), *Teaching Machines and Programed Learning, II*. Washington, D.C., Department of Audiovisual Instruction, NEA, 1965, p. 804.
[10] See, for example, Robert Glaser (ed.), *Training Research and Education*. Pittsburgh, The University of Pittsburgh Press, 1962. Arthur W. Melton, "The Science of Learning and the Technology of Educational Methods," *Harvard Educational Review*, vol. 29 (Spring, 1959), pp. 96–105. *The American Behavioral Scientist* (Nov. 6, 1962). Robert M. Gagne (ed.), *Psychological Principles in System Development*. New York, Holt, Rinehart and Winston, Inc., 1962. E. R. Hilgard (ed.), *Theories of Learning and Instruction*, The Sixty-third Yearbook of the National Society for the Study of Education, part I. Chicago, The University of Chicago Press, 1964.

applications of physical science and the engineering arts to instructional resources.

Organization of the book

The materials of this book are organized in parts, around three aspects of instructional technology. Each part can be read or studied more or less independently of the others.

Part 1 focuses on the theoretical and methodological foundations of instructional technology from the last half of the fifth century B.C. to the present time.

Part 2 focuses on the emergence of the formative patterns of instructional technology in American educational practice. This section includes a comprehensive history of the first systematic applications of media for instructional purposes and the first approaches toward a technology of instruction. Attention is directed, specifically, to the professional developments in the applications of the newer instructional media. One chapter in this section is devoted to a case study of the development of instructional technology in industry and in the military during World War II—a significant landmark in the history of the field. Part 2 concludes with a discussion of programed instruction and the systems' approach to learning and instruction.

Part 3 focuses on the institutional background of instructional media research and the development of historical phases of research on instructional media. The final chapter in Part 3 surveys the problems and prospects of instructional technology.

part 1

theoretical and methodological foundations of instructional technology:
450 B.C. to the present

Introduction

Our purpose in Part 1 is twofold: (1) to survey selected theoretical and methodological antecedents of contemporary instructional technology (Chapters 2 and 3) and (2) to provide a broad review of developing concepts of a science and technology of instruction (Chapter 4).

It is not our purpose here to provide a comprehensive historical account of the antecedents or earlier movements of instructional technology. Our intent is, rather, to provide a broad historical perspective so that the reader may be able to evaluate the significance of new instructional developments as well as the impact of technological changes on instructional practices.

chapter 2

**early forerunners
of instructional technology:
until 1700**

Instructional theory and method have an ancient heritage
that can be traced to the time when tribal priests systematized bodies of knowledge and early cultures invented
pictographs or sign writing to record, preserve, transmit,
and reproduce information. There is even good reason to
believe that the first makers and users of tools, living more
than a million years ago, systematically taught their children many kinds of skills, attitudes, and concepts thought
too complicated for mastery by unsupervised imitation.[1]

In every age, one can find a technique or a set of procedures intended to implement a particular cultural value
system which is based on specific philosophical conceptions of the nature of man and the world. The more
advanced the culture, the more complex becomes the

[1] Mark Hanna Watkins, "The West African 'Bush School,'" *American Journal of Sociology*, vol. 48, no. 6 (1943), pp. 666–675.

devising of a method or methods of instruction for the purpose of incorporating the results of learning into ways of thinking, acting, speaking, and feeling. The aim of each age or society is to find the basic skills or subject matter which offer promise of transfer to learner behavior. Each significant shift in cultural values or perceptions over the centuries has led to new theories of knowledge and learning and to new methods of instruction.

Methods foreshadowing modern instructional technology

Although historic instructional methods were not based on science as we understand it, they embodied many concepts which exerted an important influence on the thinking, language, method, research, and development of subsequent methods or technologies of instruction. For example, there were certain early educators (the Sophists) who were aware of the problems associated with perception, motivation, individual differences, and evaluation and who recognized that different instructional strategies were required for different behavioral outcomes. What is more, they analyzed modes of effective instruction and made hypotheses to take into account the factors disclosed by their analyses, just as contemporary researchers are doing today.

The relationship, therefore, between the early unscientific approaches to instruction examined in this chapter and modern instructional technology is not only historical but genetic. The major difference between such early inquiries and those of contemporary research lies in the invention and refinement of modern research instruments and scientific design. Even today, however, with these advances, we have taken only the first tentative steps toward the development of a mature science and technology of instruction.

Criteria used for selection of instructional technology antecedents

The choice of theoretical and methodological antecedents of instructional technology for this and the following chapters in this part was guided mainly by two broad criteria. First, selection was made among the theories and methods of those who actually made teaching their principal vocation, thus automatically eliminating a number of religious figures known as "great teachers," and nonteaching philosophers like Rousseau and Locke who, nevertheless, influenced the educational practices of others.

The second, and most important, criterion was to select from among the many historic antecedents the most distinctive instructional techniques whose characteristics clearly place them in the mainstream of influence and identify them as the key precursors of a modern science and technology of instruction.

With these preliminary words, we now turn to a brief examination of those forerunners selected for our purpose.

The Elder Sophists: ancestors of instructional technology

There is good reason to believe that a small group of peripatetic teachers known as Elder Sophists,[2] drawn to Athens from all corners of ancient Hellas during the last half of the fifth century B.C., were probably the first instructional technologists. We know that there were five Elder Sophists, although the dates of their birth and death are uncertain. Chronologically, Protagoras (ca. 500–410 B.C.) of Abdera is usually regarded as the eldest; Gorgias of Leontini lived from about 485 to 380 B.C.; the youngest are thought to be Prodikos of Ceos, Hippias, and Thrasymachus.

The Sophists never formed a school in the institutional sense, but operated as free-lance teachers in competition with each other, for fees.[3] Since it was not customary to accept payment for teaching in those days, they had to go out and persuade the public to purchase their skills, resorting frequently to publicity stunts such as donning purple robes or making proclamations from a raised throne. Such stage effects aroused sarcasm from conservatives. Plato referred to a Sophist's function as that of "paid hunter of the young . . . a sort of trader in intellectual disciplines of the soul"; yet Plato, in his dialogue *Protagoras,* attests to the Sophists' fame in a scene in which young Hippocrates rouses Socrates from sleep to tell him that Protagoras has just arrived in Athens and that the great Sophist teacher must be visited without delay and that he must be persuaded to accept him as a student.[4]

[2] During the century between 450 and 350 B.C., the Greek title *sophist* or *sophistes* was used to describe any man of science or learning. But by the time of the Peloponnesian War (431–404 B.C.), the name began to acquire an equivocal ring because the conservative fathers of Athens suspected the Sophist teachers of ruining the city by leading the youth from the traditional Homeric virtues and the old religion. The later denigration of the Sophists by Plato accentuated the prejudices against them. We must, however, go beyond Plato's prejudices to assess the educational role of the Elder Sophists. In this effort, we are indebted to the technical scholarship of Eric A. Havelock and his *The Crucifixion of Intellectual Man,* as well as his *The Liberal Temper in Greek Politics,* in which he endeavors to put Sophist thought and practice into proper historical perspective.

[3] Although the widespread prejudice against the Sophists was partly due to their acceptance of fees, Protagoras was quite unashamed of his profession and of the fact that he accepted payment for his teaching. His fees, indeed, seem to have been high. He demanded 10,000 drachmas for a two- or three-year course of instruction at a time when a drachma was a skilled worker's daily wage. By 350 B.C., however, the price of such a course had fallen to about 1,000 drachmas. It is clear from the high cost of instruction that only aristocrats could afford the services of the Sophists, despite their liberal, democratic concepts.

[4] Eric A. Havelock, *The Liberal Temper in Greek Politics.* New Haven, Conn., Yale University Press, 1957, p. 161.

Typically, the Sophist demonstrations took three forms: the delivery of a carefully prepared lecture; or the delivery of an extemporized lecture on some subject suggested by a member of the audience; or free debate with another Sophist or some other person on a subject chosen by the audience. Thus began the public lecture.

Having obtained students and made a contract, the Sophists taught by a modified tutorial system.[5] For the first time, it was no longer a relationship between a tutor and his one disciple, but between the teacher and a group of pupils. In this may be seen the beginnings of mass instruction.

Sophist Theory. The Elder Sophists belonged to the pre-Socratic-Promethean liberal tradition in Greek thought of which the basic tenets are:

1 An evolutionary view of man in which man can evolve through technology and social organization to a state of civilization in which he can learn to guide his affairs effectively.
2 This evolutionary process is continuous. Morality and law are aspects of this process, evolved and accepted because they have survival value, and deriving their sanction from social consensus and not from a priori absolute principles or from divine authority.
3 History is viewed as a slow, but continuously forward progress in the management of human affairs rather than as cyclical or regressive.
4 The general societal attitude is democratic and egalitarian.
5 The theory of knowledge is progressive, pragmatic, empirical, and behavioristic.[6]

Not every Sophist necessarily expounded all these views, but as a theoretical frame of reference for their educational practice, all of them had this common liberal tradition which was condemned by Plato in his dialogues.

The Sophist view was that all men had the potential for intelligent, socially responsible self-rule and dominion over nature but that they could not achieve this potential without education. Plato, on the other hand, believed that all men were destined for either a low or high social position, for subservience or for leadership. In contrast to Plato's belief that virtue could not be taught and that only aristocrats ("the rich, the wise, and the well-born," as Plato's student, Aristotle, was later to describe them) might be depended upon for right action, the Sophists believed in the positive value of teaching virtue, which included identifying and defending a just cause.

Plato also differed with the Sophists on the value of *techne* (technology). The Sophists honored all technology, which included both statecraft and

---

[5] The period of instruction seems to have lasted generally for three or four years.
[6] Havelock, *op. cit.,* pp. 30, 80, *et passim.*

handicraft, whereas Plato believed that technology was unworthy of gentle-men and had no place in their education. Plato insisted on universal abso-lutes in knowledge and ethics, whereas the basic teaching of the Sophists was the relativity or contingency of experience, knowledge, and values—perhaps best expressed in the formula attributed to Protagoras: "Man is the measure of all things." Thus, the beginnings of the rift between culture and religion in ancient Greek education can be located in the age of the Sophists.

Instructional Method.   The Sophists undertook to teach the art of politics and to develop political *arete*—that is, the excellence of the individual human being in relation to an ideal that could be realized in a political, democratic community. This *arete,* for them, consisted primarily in intellectual power and oratorical ability. To develop these skills was

> . . . clearly the systematic expression of the principle of shaping the intellect, because it begins by instruction in the form of language, the form of oratory, and the form of thought. This educational technique is one of the greatest discoveries which the mind of man has ever made: it was not until it explored these three of its activities that the mind apprehended the hidden law of its own structure.[7]

Although the instructional methods of individual Sophists varied, they seem to have had in common the use of the expository lecture, often using mythology as a vehicle for the expression of ideas. A "Sophistic dialogue"[8] or group discussion method (probably invented by Protagoras) of finding solutions to problems was another approach employed by the Sophists. The lecture and group discussion techniques were combined by Protagoras into a third method, applicable specifically in political activities but which can be considered an instructional technique in the wider use of the term. This technique is defined by Havelock as "the antithetical formulation of public positions and the setting of party lines which took place in any parliament or assembly where power was at stake and public policy was made."[9]

The Sophists probably first invented and developed the technique of analysis in the teaching of rhetoric. By analyzing the works of poets and other exemplary models of writing and speaking, they formulated rules for effective writing and speaking. Protagoras is given credit for developing rules for distinguishing the tenses of verbs and for classifying modes of dis-

---

[7] Werner Jaeger, *Paideia: The Ideals of Greek Culture,* tr. from the 2d German ed. by Gilbert Highet. Fair Lawn, N.J., Oxford University Press, 1939, vol. I, pp. 311ff.
[8] In contrast to the so-called Socratic method, the Sophistic dialogue provided both flexi-bility and creativity in its free conversational exchange of ideas. Students were not ex-pected merely to answer "Yes" or "No" to questions or, in effect, to separate one syllogism from another. The theory of Sophistic dialogue viewed the student as an active, inquiring individualist who could lead the discussion down new, divergent paths.
[9] Havelock, *op. cit.,* p. 216.

course. Prodikos studied synonyms and attempted to clarify the meanings of words. Gorgias, the master of rhetoric and historically as important as Protagoras, influenced subsequent oratory and prose style with his three "Gorgiac figures" of antithesis, balance of clauses, and final assonance.

Rhetoric was the chief subject of Sophistic instruction for two reasons: in ancient Greece the spoken word, or oral tradition, reigned supreme; and the Sophists found rhetoric to be the most effective instructional technique for transmitting practical knowledge in a condensed, systematic manner. In teaching rhetoric, they followed a basically similar method which combined theory and application. First, the Sophist teacher instructed his students in the rules (theory) of the spoken and written word. Then he prepared a model speech for them to copy, analyze, discuss, and duplicate in actual spoken practice—especially in the earlier stages of instruction. The model discourse was often on a poetic, moral, or political subject. Plato showed us Protagoras improvising on the myth of Prometheus and Epimetheus; in another dialogue there are references to a eulogy of the city of Elis by Gorgias. Sometimes a fantastic subject was used to demonstrate pure virtuosity and the result might be a eulogy of mice or peacocks. The final objective, however, was not precise imitation of the model but the development of virtuosity and the skill to choose alternative formulas and accurately judge the relative merits of each model in terms of the differing demands of each communication situation (application).

It should be emphasized that Sophist instruction was not confined to formal aspects of rhetoric. Their ideal was what they termed a "polymath" (today the equivalent phrase is "general education"), a man whose competence was universal and whose knowledge extended over every kind of specialized study. Consequently, Sophistic instruction did not consist merely in imitating forms but in gaining a mastery of relevant and necessary content. What is more, the Sophist technique of analysis applied to the teaching of rhetoric was extended to other instructional content. Whole bodies of cognitive rules were formulated in every field they sought to teach: geography, natural history, logic, history, painting, drawing, music, religion, sculpture, and athletics. They also evolved a branch of rhetoric devoted to the invention and discovery of ideas. Here again their analytical approach to instruction enabled them to develop a rather sophisticated technology of instruction for extracting every possible topic from any given case—a technology which combined rhetoric with eristic (the art of disputation).

Because Sophist instructional procedures were inherently systematic, the student always knew what was expected of him, how he might achieve his goals, and how well he was progressing. And although Sophist methods have often been considered formal and rigid, they possessed a certain amount of flexibility since the student usually had an opportunity to choose from a variety of formulas or modes of action for application to practical situations.

Influence of the Sophists.   The influence of the Sophists on subsequent instruction and courses of study has been enormous. Their use of rhetoric, dialectic, and grammar dominated the design of the *quadrivium* and the *trivium* (the seven liberal arts, as they came to be called) which made up the curriculum of European education for a thousand years to come.[10]

Before the influence of Plato [11] overthrew the educational success of the Sophists and became the chief influence in the Western world, the Sophists offered a bold solution of a difficult problem which has still not been satisfactorily resolved. It is the contemporary problem explored by Snow in his *The Two Cultures and the Scientific Revolution:* One separate culture is presumed to be inhabited by men of science, another by men of letters. Yet as Snow shows, science and technology do not necessarily deny art any more than art, or any of the humanities, denies science.[12]

The Sophist solution was to reconcile the two cultures by combining both in a single concept, *techne,* or technology. Thus the Sophist legacy is an old formula for our modern endeavor to reconcile the humanities and science (and within science, to reconcile pure science with technology).

The Socratic method

Socrates (470–399 B.C.) left no writings and all we know of his teaching is through the works of his students, Plato and Xenophon. In contrast to the relativism of the Sophists, Socrates sought to attain universally valid knowledge of the nature of virtue which should serve as a guide and motivation to moral conduct. Perhaps his most important educational contribution was the so-called Socratic method of instruction. This method aimed to teach by inquiry into what might be accepted as valid knowledge. The inquiry was carred on through the give-and-take of conversation, which Socrates guided by a series of leading questions. It was essential that the questions lead to a definite point.

A second element in the Socratic method was the use by the questioner of only those facts already known to his pupil. If the pupil had to collect

[10] The favorite subjects of the Sophists, grammar and rhetoric, occupy two-thirds of the *trivium,* in which Plato is not even represented.
[11] In contrast to the democratic viewpoint of the Sophists, the practical consequences which Plato drew from his philosophy included an antidemocratic, totalitarian government in which a ruling and military elite of "supermen" were to rule a lower-class majority who were considered to be inferior and motivated by gross appetites. Such doctrines supported authoritarian tendencies and control throughout the history of the Western world. In the teaching of the Church, these doctrines were wedded with the will of God as revealed in Scripture. Therefore, the influence of Plato (427–347 B.C.) and his student and successor, Aristotle (384–321 B.C.), along with religious revelation, built up a complete identification of Platonism with Christianity.
[12] See C. P. Snow, *The Two Cultures and the Scientific Revolution.* New York, Cambridge University Press, 1959.

data before he could reach a new conclusion, the teacher had introduced a factor not included in the original Socratic technique.

A dramatic example of the Socratic method is described in Plato's *Meno*. Socrates, at random, selected a boy off the street and by clever questioning led him to demonstrate a geometrical theorem despite the fact that the boy had had no previous mathematical training. Because of this story, some contemporary leaders in the programed instruction movement have mistakenly claimed Socrates as their educational forefather. His method was predicated, however, on the principle that knowledge is inborn and that it can be withdrawn by means of skillful questioning. Since the reinforcement schedule of the programed text or machine is usually based on an entirely different principle (stimulus-response associationism), it is obviously incorrect to claim Socrates as the forerunner of programed instruction.

Abelard: precursor of scholastic method of instruction

Scholasticism, an intellectual movement which flourished in Europe during the twelfth and thirteenth centuries, could never have sustained its vitality had it not been productive and effective as a method of instruction. Its name was derived from the term *doctor scholasticus*, applied during the medieval period to authorized teachers in monastic or cathedral schools. For it was among these teachers, best exemplified by Pierre Abelard,[13] that the distinctive tendencies and methods of philosophical speculation associated with scholasticism began to develop. This intellectual awakening ultimately transformed some of these schools into universities, especially in the north of Europe.

Abelard Shapes the Pattern of Scholastic Instructional Method. The basic characteristics of the scholastic method of instruction were established by Abelard when he taught at the Notre Dame cathedral school (which became the University of Paris in 1180) at various periods between 1108 and 1139. By training his theological students in Aristotelian logical analysis, Abelard helped to transform theology from the mere citing of authorities to the interpretation of Scripture. His method was best represented by his famous book *Sic et Non* (*Yes and No*), wherein his general approach was to present the pros and cons of certain theological or philosophical propositions, furnishing no final answers, but leaving the formulation of conclusions to his students. Abelard also made the assumption that any subject or thought can be reasonably examined for the purpose of understanding, verification, or qualification. Not all of his theological colleagues imitated this

[13] Pierre Abelard (1079–1142) was born of noble stock in Brittany and died in the Priory of St. Marcel, near Chalons, France.

method of instruction. Many were shocked that Abelard gave his students the freedom to arrive at heretical conclusions.

Elements of Abelard's Method of Instruction.   In *Sic et Non,* Abelard formulated 158 questions about the Trinity, Redemption, and the Sacraments. He placed the "Yes" answers from the authorities in one column; in an opposite column he placed the "No" answers. His instructional procedure in reaching reconciliation was as follows:

1. The contradictory statements were first read and studied in context to determine if they continued to be contradictory. Before the contexts could be finally considered, some type of historical scholarship would probably have to be undertaken either by the teacher or by other scholars.
2. Next, textual distortions were to be discovered and corrected. The necessary textual-criticism skills demanded were a knowledge of etymology, grammatical form, and linguistic knowledge.
3. The third stage was to make a judgment as to the real meaning of each of the statements cited. Authorities could be used in making this judgment.
4. A final check was to be made to ensure that there was no retraction of the cited passages on record.
5. Finally, a search or inquiry was to be made concerning the circumstances that led to the writing of the statements.
6. If certain contradictions still remained, the student could then make one of two conclusions: (a) this was a mystery to be believed, or (b) a theory was needed which could encompass both views, each of which was but a partial aspect of the truth.[14]

Influence of Abelard on Lombard and Aquinas.   Abelard's method had a direct influence on Peter Lombard (1100–1160) and on St. Thomas Aquinas (1225–1274), his successors at Paris. Lombard, a former student of Abelard, modeled his famous textbook *The Sentences* on the *Sic et Non;* but for every question he posed, he was careful to supply the correct, orthodox response. The result was that Lombard's method came to be more generally accepted because of its less controversial aspects.

The final technique of instruction, one to be widely employed by many generations of scholars, was the scholastic method as developed by St. Thomas Aquinas. According to Aquinas, the proper instructional approach was to teach the student how he might acquire knowledge for himself through the logical demonstration of the syllogism. In his *Summa Theologiae,* Aquinas, like Abelard, introduced material in the form of questions, then proceeded in a series of logical syllogisms to propose the correct solutions.

[14] Adapted from Harry S. Broudy and John R. Palmer, *Exemplars of Teaching Method.* Chicago, Rand McNally & Company, 1965, pp. 62–63.

A thesis was proposed; the proof was given; objections were raised and refuted; the whole proposition was treated in a minutely logical procedure.

Influence of the Scholastic Method.   Without question, Abelard deserves an important place among the forerunners of modern instructional technology. His greatest achievement was the development and popularization of his method of instruction—the unique instructional technique created during the medieval period of history.[15]

It may be argued that Abelard's methodological offspring, the scholastic method, degenerated into a cumbersome formalism in which Aristotelian logic became hopelessly ossified. But unless we consider its historical origin and climate, we may miss its close and important relationship to the rise of European universities and its role in laying the groundwork for scientific inquiry and experimentation. Confronted with a mass of traditional and irrational doctrines, the medieval teacher used the scholastic method as his only means of considering them in a systematic, rational manner.

A method of instruction according to Comenius

Johann Amos Comenius (1592–1670), born of modest, Protestant (Moravian Brethren) parents in Moravia (now a part of Czechoslovakia), attended the Protestant universities of Herborn and Heidelberg in Germany.[16] As a Moravian pastor and teacher, Comenius spent a long, itinerant life in Poland, Hungary, Sweden, England, and Holland—due primarily to the disruptions of the Thirty Years' War (1618–1648) between the Catholics and the Protestants.

His period of greatest educational productivity began in 1627 at the Polish town of Lissa where, as a teacher of Latin and rector of the Moravian gymnasium, he began writing a series of remarkable textbooks.[17] Later he directed curricular reforms in Holland and Sweden and organized a model school in Hungary.

Educational Theory.   The *Great Didactic*,[18] the most important theoretical treatise written by Comenius, dealt with every phase of instruction.

[15] Abelard may have found the model for his method in the work of such men as Ivo of Chartres, who in the tenth century had undertaken to reconcile contradictory statements.
[16] The closer University of Prague was then controlled by the Utraquists, a Hussite sect opposed to the Moravians.
[17] Among them was the *Janua linguarum reserata* (*The Gate of Languages Unlocked*), published in 1631, in which Comenius selected 8,000 of the commonest words and used them in 1,000 graded sentences.
[18] Comenius's ideas for his system of instruction were first formulated at Leszne, Poland, where he wrote his *Great Didactic*. His later texts were elaborations of this basic work. The *Great Didactic*, written in Czech, was first published in German in 1633 and in Latin in 1657.

One of its recurrent themes was his idea of *pansophia*,[19] or system of universal knowledge in which a methodical procedure could be applied to all problems of mankind. This was manifest in his goal of teaching the rudiments of all things to everyone in a systematic manner. Further, he recommended the establishment of a college of pansophy, or scientific research.

According to Comenius, Christian philosophy should not prevent an examination of the human mind by methodical and empirical observation. Thus the theory underlying the instructional system of Comenius consisted in this: the goal of education was to be derived deductively from Christian philosophy; the instructional process had to be analyzed and improved inductively, according to science.

Comenius's educational aims were knowledge, morality, and piety. He regarded education as a means of preparing men to live as human beings rather than to fit them into a predetermined occupation or station. Moreover, he wanted to end the custom of educating according to social status rather than ability. To achieve these broad aims, Comenius proposed a system of education open to all, one which led from the kindergarten through the university—a proposal some three centuries ahead of his time.

Principles of Instructional Method.   Among the great mass of instructional principles advocated by Comenius, we have selected the following:

1 Instructional method should follow the order of nature. Content should be studied according to the developmental stage of each learner.

2 Instruction should begin at infancy and should be designed for the age, interest, and capacity of each learner.

3 Whatever is to be taught should be taught as being of practical application to life and should possess some value for the learner.

4 Subject matter should be organized according to its difficulty. Instruction should proceed by the inductive process from the simple to the complex.

5 A graduated series of textbooks and illustrative materials should be correlated with instruction.

6 Sequence is important. For example, it is irrational to teach a foreign language before the mother language has been learned.

7 General principles should be explained and examples given before

[19] The Moravians, who had suffered severely from the Catholics during the Thirty Years' War, were in secret sympathy with the Protestant Swedes during their invasion of Poland. After peace was declared, Comenius openly published a letter of congratulation to the Swedish king, Charles Gustavus. In retaliation, the Poles attacked and plundered Leszne, the town where Comenius was living. He barely escaped with his life and lost his entire family and his collection of pansophic materials on which he had worked most of his life. Since he was then in his sixty-fifth year, he lacked the enthusiasm and strength to pursue the dream further.

rules are learned; nothing should be memorized until it is understood.

8   Reading and writing should be taught together; subjects should be correlated whenever possible.

9   Learning is to be approached through the senses; actual objects and things should be studied and associated with words.

10   Content should first be presented orally by the teacher and pictorially illustrated wherever possible.

11   All parts of an object (or subject matter) must be learned with reference to their order, position, and connection with one another, and not more than one thing should be taught at any one time. (Comenius suggested outlining all the texts specified for use on the walls of the classroom so that the learner could see the entire content to be studied.)

12   Corporal punishment should not be used for failure in learning.

13   Schools must be cheerful, equipped with real and illustrative materials, and staffed with sympathetic teachers. (Something of the monitorial plan was latent in Comenius's system. He believed that it was possible for one teacher to instruct several hundred children at one time. After the general presentation by the teacher, the large group was to be divided into sections of ten for further drilling and reciting to small-group student leaders.)

It is evident from the instructional principles enumerated above that Comenius was the first real forerunner of modern instructional technology. By applying Bacon's inductive method to education, he laid the foundation of a systematic understanding of the teaching-learning process and anticipated, to a remarkable extent, the modern concept of instructional technology as applied science in support of the practical arts. It is unfortunate that during his lifetime he was never in a position to test most of his own pioneering principles in any sustained situation.

The Orbus Pictus: Application of the Method of Cómenius.   Perhaps the best published example of an application of Comenius's method of instruction was his own *Orbus Pictus* (*The World in Pictures*), published in Nuremburg in 1658. This illustrated, thoroughly planned, "visual aid" textbook was written specifically for children who were studying Latin and sciences. Although it has often been referred to erroneously as the first illustrated book of its kind, it has been without question the most popular illustrated textbook ever written for children.[20] The book was still being purchased in the United States as late as 1810.

[20] Peter Canisius, one hundred years before, had issued a child's catechism with marginal pictures and woodcuts illustrating the lives of Christ and the saints, as well as church ceremonies.

Organized in a series of topics (e.g., God, world, air, trees, man, flowers, vegetables, metals, birds), the *Orbus Pictus* was illustrated by 150 pictures, each serving as a topic for one lesson. Thus the teaching of Latin and the sciences was accomplished by associating objective reality, or its pictorial representations, with abstract cognate word symbols.

Influence of Comenius. For nearly two centuries Comenius was generally unknown and had little direct effect on instructional theory or practice, except through his language methods texts. The *Orbus Pictus*, for example, went through an almost unlimited number of editions in many languages and became the sole link to his work. When his other works were finally rediscovered in the middle of the nineteenth century, it became clear that he had been the greatest educator of his century. Many of his ideas have since been incorporated into contemporary instructional method.

Recapitulation and analysis

Our completed survey of the early forerunners of instructional technology has various implications. The Elder Sophists appear to be the classical ancestors of modern instructional technology because they were probably the first professional teachers, who, by their systematic analyses of subject matter and organization of teaching materials, laid the groundwork for a technology of instruction. What is more important, when teaching was not commonly considered a profession, the Sophists viewed it as *techne*—in the old Greek sense—or a technology in which the theoretical is combined with the practical.

With Abelard and the scholastic method, some of the techniques of the Elder Sophists, together with the rules of logic and the content of philosophical, theological, and other writings were used to produce a distinctive method of instruction suited to the historic moment. The primary emphasis was on developing an attitude toward knowledge.

For Comenius, nature offered the key to biological, cognitive, and moral development whereby learners would be led inductively to generalized knowledge by working with natural objects and studying practical things. On the basis of these convictions, Comenius devised a system of instruction which anticipated many of the modern principles of learning.

In the learning theory underlying the methods of the early forerunners, faculty psychology has been implicit or openly advocated. Faculty psychology assumes the human mind to be of such a nature that, with adequate cultivation, it can know the objective reality of the world. Man, being a rational animal, is free, within limits, to act as he chooses in the light of what he understands. Instead of being a creature of instinct, he enjoys a complex and delicate faculty of "knowing" whose basic aspect is reason. This frame of reference in an educational context also assumes that the character of knowledge is a fixed body of true principles which are handed down as the heritage of the race in the form of great books or basic content. Thus, specific subject matter can lend itself to the exercise or training of the faculty of reason.[21]

Abelard, as well as later medieval Scholastics, also accepted faculty psychology as a theory of learning. The emphasis on the role of intellect in learning at the expense of the senses was generally stressed even more in the medieval world, because knowledge derived from sense impression was considered to be highly variable and unreliable, while that of the intellect was thought to be stable and dependable.

The first educator to restore the educational balance between intellect and sensory knowledge was Comenius. Nevertheless, it is notable that he also accepted the faculty psychology current in his day. However, predicating his instructional method, as we have seen, on the priority of the senses, he anticipated the theoretical ideas of Locke.

From the foregoing analysis, it appears as if the primary function of exercising the faculties was believed to be that of acquiring knowledge. There are, however, repeated references in educational literature from Plato onward which illustrate the psychological viewpoint that instruction consists in the exercise of these faculties for their own sake. According to this viewpoint, exercise or strengthening of the faculties is of prime importance, rather than the acquisition of knowledge and the development of understanding.

In the next chapter, we shall continue our survey with an examination of the theories and methods of later forerunners of modern instructional technology.

---

[21] Plato and his student successor, Aristotle, refined and formulated the theory of faculty psychology. Plato's entire educational structure was based on faculty psychology, directed toward producing leaders by means of rigid choice of subject matter. He believed that training the faculties through mathematics and philosophy was the best preparation for the conduct of public affairs. Having trained his mental faculties, a philosopher-king was considered ready to solve all problems. Aristotle was in agreement with Plato regarding faculty psychology, contending that faculties which man had once trained by mastery of specific subject matter would enable him to transfer his power to the mastery of other subjects. He described at least five different faculties, the greatest, and the one unique to man, being that of reason.

chapter 3

later forerunners
of instructional technology:
1700-1900

In this chapter, we continue our survey of selected theories and methods of instruction begun in Chapter 2. The period here covered is marked by the evolution of new scientific outlooks, by the development of new theories of learning, and by the founding of experimental psychology—which increasingly challenged the influence of earlier educational theorists and prepared the way for the formulation of a scientific technology of instruction.

Status of instructional method in American schools: before 1800

Before we begin our survey of the later forerunners of instructional technology, we will briefly examine instructional method in American schools just prior to the emergence of the theories and methods we shall be discussing.

Before 1800, instruction at both the elementary and secondary levels was predominantly individual. The principal method of the village schoolmaster consisted in calling one or several pupils to his desk to hear individual, memorized recitations. Procedures of developing understanding through inductive group discussions were unknown. When teaching writing, the teacher's primary concern was with whittling goose-quill pens and "setting copies" for pupils. Much of the instruction was superficial and impractical, and the school term was of short duration (one to six months). Children sometimes attended school for years without progressing beyond a smattering of reading and writing. Since the teachers were generally incompetent, it is not surprising that they relied on fear to motivate learners and keep order in the classroom.[1]

The buildings and equipment of the early American schools, not to mention their instructional materials, were primitive. The typical one-room schoolhouse prior to 1800 was a log building, often situated at some undesirable location—at the intersection of two roads, or even adjoining a cemetery or an animal slaughter yard. One end of the schoolroom was usually occupied by a fireplace, and at the opposite end was the room's only window. Equipment and furniture were very crude. Sticks inserted between the logs which formed the walls were used to hold boards which served as desks. Backless benches made of split logs ran the entire length of the board desks. These benches were of such a height that the feet of the smaller pupils could never rest on the floor.

The beginning of the nineteenth century brought little improvement in these conditions. Public and free schools were generally lacking outside the New England area, and even there conditions and facilities were wretched. Illiteracy prevailed everywhere among children of the poor. This condition became intensified with the development of industry, the breakdown of the apprenticeship system, and the rapid growth of American cities. "Free school societies" (such as the Public School Society of New York) were organized in some of the larger cities to try to cope with the problems of ignorance, poverty, and crime. These semipublic, philanthropic organizations later came to regard the so-called Lancasterian system as ideal for their purposes, since it offered mass education at low cost. What is more, as the public became increasingly aware of the desperate need for mass education, legislators saw in monitorial schools a solution to the school-financing problem which had to be found before adequate public schools could be established. The intro-

[1] The teachers included ministers, college students, indentured servants, mechanics, physicians, and even ex-convicts and tramps. In many areas, the summer sessions catered to young children who were not needed in the fields for work. Women and girls as young as sixteen were often employed to teach these sessions, since the problems of discipline were not too severe. In the winter term, men generally taught the older children.

duction of the Lancasterian system, in fact, provided the basis for the eventual support of free public schools in the United States.

Lancasterian monitorial instruction

The wide success of a monitorial system of instruction in the first half of the nineteenth century was chiefly due to Joseph Lancaster (1778–1838) [2] of England, whose unique manuals of instruction included details of classroom organization and economic management, as well as subject matter organized according to a graded plan for group instruction. To aid in the implementation of his method, Lancaster studied the construction of special classrooms which would make the most effective use of instructional media and student grouping. He also explored the techniques of motivation. Although it appears questionable that Lancaster's method had its roots in any systematic theory of learning, he was probably influenced by Locke's conception of learning, which prevailed at the time. [3]

Economy of the Lancasterian System.　　Much of the popularity of the Lancasterian system was due, as we have said previously, to its low cost. For example, during the period (1806–1853) when the Lancasterian plan was in operation in New York City, the annual cost of instruction, per child, ranged from $1.37 in 1822 to a maximum of $5.83 in 1852. The Lancasterian system was also adopted in Pennsylvania where the legislators were unwilling to appropriate money for free education, except for the children of paupers. A particular means of Lancasterian economy may be noted in the ratio of pupils to teachers. In Philadelphia in 1819, there were ten public Lancasterian schools with 10 teachers and 2,845 pupils, or 1 teacher to 284 pupils.

School buildings were constructed to accommodate hundreds of children in a series of large, undivided rooms, with careful attention paid to lighting, ventilation, slant of floor, seating, and acoustics. One 50- by 100-foot room could accommodate as many as five hundred pupils, a space of 10

[2] A Scot, Andrew Bell (1753–1832), simultaneously and independently developed the monitorial method. In the matter of details, Lancaster elaborated more than Bell; he also toured both Europe and the United States. The method, however, was not original with either Bell or Lancaster. It was used by the Hindus; it had formed part of the Jesuit method; and it had been recommended by Comenius in his *Great Didactic*. Bell was primarily concerned with religious instruction while Lancaster was generally animated by secular motives. In time, laymen and educators began referring to the monitorial system as "the Lancasterian method."

[3] In the seventeenth century, John Locke (1632–1704) challenged the whole notion of innate faculties or ideas, as well as the conception of learning as development of innate faculties. He developed his *tabula rasa* (blank tablet) theory, which held that the mind is empty at birth and that any ideas a person subsequently holds must have come to him originally through his senses. Locke's theory opened the way for psychologists to place their emphasis on environment rather than on heredity. In the classroom, teachers were to develop a systematic instructional method for training the senses rather than the faculties.

square feet being allotted to each. The use of slates, sand tables, wall charts, and blackboards saved paper, ink, and pens, and made fewer books necessary. By establishing the principle of mass instruction at low cost, the Lancasterian schools provided the only kind of instruction that could be hoped for in what were to become free schools during the latter part of the nineteenth century.

The Lancasterian Monitorial Method of Instruction.   The Lancasterian plan provided a detailed, systematic method in the following six areas: instruction (memoriter and drill) and a body of content; monitor training; control; grouping; testing; and administration. Under an efficient scheme of classroom management, one teacher taught a group of fifty head pupils, or monitors, who in turn each drilled ten pupils. Thus, one teacher was able to take charge of five hundred or more students at one time.[4] In the teaching of arithmetic, for example, Lancaster had the following plan: the basis of progress was founded on a thorough knowledge of the multiplication tables. As each new rule was introduced, the examples were at first short and easy, then increased in length and difficulty as the ability of the learner increased. Each class had a definite number of sample problems to be worked over and over until they could be solved with facility. When teaching a new rule, the monitor first dictated an example, then worked it out while the pupils copied the process on their slates. Afterward, the slates were cleaned and examples were written on the blackboard, each pupil, in turn, taking part in the operation. This process was repeated until the method of problem solving was understood.[5]

The results of the Lancasterian method, contrasted with the earlier one-room-school method of individual recitation, were revolutionary. Salmon relates an incident in which an anxious parent protested to his pastor against the practices of the monitorial school, because he was convinced that the rapid progress of his son in arithmetic resulted from an evil magic being employed by the school.[6]

The pupils were grouped according to ability, which made it possible

---

[4] Schools which used the monitor method soon experienced difficulties because of competition for clerical and other kinds of literate workers in the cities. Of those pupils mature enough to become monitors, few could be induced to remain after their parents discovered that they could earn more money in other occupations. About 1827, women replaced boy monitors, but at a salary of $25 for the first year. These untrained women could not be relied upon to provide even the low-level, standardized instruction which the trained boy monitors had assumed. To improve this situation, some cities, such as New York, established Saturday classes for new women teachers. The normal schools, which developed after 1840, became the major teacher training ground. However, these training schools were so influenced by the Lancasterian method that the adults who would replace the boy monitors were given essentially the same intrapersonal, authoritarian perspective. This was a simple process of insisting on obedience within a hierarchical chain of command, which made rote learning the only practicable type of instruction.

[5] John Gill, *Systems of Education*. Boston, D. C. Heath and Company, 1887, pp. 192–193.

[6] David Salmon, *Joseph Lancaster*. New York, Longmans, Green & Co., Inc., 1904, p. 12.

for a pupil to recite with a group at one stage of advancement in reading or spelling, while he might recite with a group at a different stage of development in some other subject. Economy of time was also important in the Lancasterian school routine. For example, to avoid calling the roll of the entire school in order to discover who was absent, each pupil was given a fixed number, and corresponding numbers were printed in a row on the wall. The class was marched into position, each pupil took his place beneath his own number, and the vacant numbers immediately indicated the absentees. Another timesaving device was in the disposition of hats (not an inconsiderable problem in a room which seated several hundred pupils). Each pupil wore a hat attached to a string, so that when he removed it, it hung down his back. At a given signal, all the pupils tossed their hats into suspended position, and by this means all headgear was simultaneously disposed of.

Use of Instructional Materials. Ingenuity was refreshingly displayed in the use of instructional media. For example, a thin layer of sand was spread on each desk for writing practice. The learner wrote with a pointed stick and made erasures by passing a long straight stick across the sand writing. This procedure was designed to save ink and paper. The text of a speller or some other book was sometimes printed in large letters and suspended from the schoolroom wall, in order that one volume could serve an entire class. Through the use of slates, hundreds of learners wrote and spelled the same word at the same time, and when reciting, groups of ten gathered around the monitors.

Assessment of the Lancasterian System. As we have seen, the Lancasterian schools were not only economical but also effective, when the prevailing primitive instructional conditions of the times are taken into consideration. Through the influence of the methods of Lancaster, American schools began to adopt centralized management practices, improve instructional media, develop more systematic approaches to instruction, and recognize the need for trained teachers. Viewed in this light, we can understand why such men as Governor DeWitt Clinton of New York; Governor Wolcott, of Connecticut; William Russell, editor of the first *American Journal of Education;* and John Griscom, noted scientist and educator, praised the system. For example, Governor Clinton stated in 1809:

> When I perceive that many boys in our school have been taught to read and write in two months, who did not before know the alphabet, and that even one has accomplished it in three weeks—when I view all the bearings and tendencies of this system—when I contemplate the habits of order which it forms, the spirit of emulation which it excites, the rapid improvement which it produces, the purity of morals which it inculcates—when I behold the extraordinary union of celerity in instruction and economy of expense—and when I perceive one great assembly of a thousand children, under the eye of a single teacher,

marching with unexampled rapidity and with perfect discipline to the goal of knowledge, I confess that I recognize in Lancaster the benefactor of the human race. I consider his system as creating a new era in education, as a blessing sent down from heaven to redeem the poor and distressed of this world from the power and dominion of ignorance.[7]

Likewise, a prominent educator of the time, William Russell, strongly favored the system and even edited a *Manual of Mutual Instruction* (1826), which contained directions for organizing instruction according to the Lancasterian plan and encouraged its adoption in the colleges.

The monitorial method met a great educational emergency in the United States, but it was clearly mechanical and lacked a systematic psychology of learning. Furthermore, it encouraged the development of narrow, supposedly practical rules of thumb, which were to be used as instructional method for teacher education in the newly established normal schools. Under the monitorial influence, method became a set of standardized techniques for handling large numbers of children at one time. Such a practice-centered approach lacked a theoretical unity and was utterly separated from a recognizable theory of learning. In all fairness to the Lancasterian schools, however, they deserve to be called forerunners of modern instructional technology because they were the first to introduce order and system in instructional method in American schools.[8] Indeed, their impact on subsequent educational practices, although negative in many respects, would be difficult to overemphasize. For example, in 1891, Gordy pointed out two misconceptions of the monitorial method which had not yet disappeared from teacher training: (1) that teaching consists in imparting knowledge; and (2) that all that is necessary to impart this knowledge is simply to know as much as is to be imparted.[9] Even today one can discover this viewpoint in much of the rationale voiced by such contemporary critics of teacher education as Rickover, Bestor, and Koerner,[10] and implied in such legislation as the

[7] W. O. Bourne, *History of the Public School Society of New York City.* Baltimore, Wood and Company, 1870, p. 19.
[8] Those who support the idea of using master teachers, assisted by monitors, to instruct large groups with such instructional media as television, for the purpose of saving time and money, might well study the Lancasterian scheme.
[9] J. P. Gordy, *The Rise and Growth of the Normal-School Idea in the United States.* U.S. Bureau of Education Circular of Information 8, 1891, p. 24.
[10] See H. G. Rickover, *Education and Freedom.* New York, E. P. Dutton & Co., Inc., 1959; Arthur E. Bestor, *Educational Wastelands.* Urbana, Ill., The University of Illinois Press, 1953; and James D. Koerner, *The Case for Basic Education.* Boston, Little, Brown and Company, 1959. We generally agree with these critics that teachers have often been poorly educated, but this should not imply that strengthening the background of teachers in the liberal arts and sciences will necessarily increase their effectiveness as teachers in the classroom. It is surprising that, in the contemporary teacher education controversy, the nature of instruction has not been analyzed in specific terms nor has the discussion led to a careful description and examination of the relevance of various proposals and practices to what teachers actually are confronted with and what they actually do in the process of instructing groups of learners.

Licensing of Certificated Personnel Law (known as the Fisher Bill), recently enacted in California.

The practice and influence of the Lancasterian system began to wane by the middle of the nineteenth century as increased financial resources enabled the people to provide support for free public education. Moreover, the inherent defects of the Lancasterian method became more fully apparent as the psychological conceptions of Pestalozzi, and later, Froebel and Herbart, became more widely known and implemented.

Pestalozzi and his "psychologizing" of instructional method

Johann Heinrich Pestalozzi (1746–1827) was the first to develop a comprehensive system of instruction based on the educational theories expounded by Jean Jacques Rousseau (1712–1778) in his *Emile*.[11] Born in Zurich, Switzerland, Pestalozzi attended the university there to prepare himself first for the pulpit and later for law. Then, discouraged by legal conservatism, and profoundly influenced by the social and educational ideas of Rousseau, he decided to undertake what was to become a historic series of educational experiments. These began with waifs he gathered at his home (Neuhof), near the village of Birrfield (1774–1780), and continued in his experimental schools at Stanz (1798), Burgdorf (1799–1804), and Yverdon (1805–1825), where he did his most significant work.

Educational Theory. The underlying principle of the method evolved by Pestalozzi was best formulated in his own statement, "I wish to psychologize instruction." By this, he meant the harmonizing of instruction with what he believed to be the laws of orderly, harmonious development. He felt that the moral, intellectual, and physical powers of each learner would unfold, according to natural laws, in successively widening circles of experience and that each succeeding level of experience would have to be mastered before the learner could enter the next stage of development. To Pestalozzi, this organic unfolding of the individual learner was the supreme objective of instruction, to be accomplished by constant emphasis on sense impression: "The most essential point from which I start is this: Sense impression of Nature is the only foundation of human instruction, because it is the only true foundation of human knowledge." [12]

[11] Rousseau's central theme in *Emile* was that education should be in accordance with the natural interests of the child. He also made a sharp division of the learner's development into definite stages and prescribed a distinct program of education for each successive period. His outlook stems from the viewpoint that man is naturally good and is at the same time active in relation to his environment. Since man is naturally good, the teacher should let the learner develop in a natural environment, free from corruption. Pestalozzi used this same principle under the name of "organic development" as a basis for his own educational theory and practice.

[12] J. H. Pestalozzi, *How Gertrude Teaches Her Children*, tr. by L. E. Holland and F. C. Swan. Syracuse, N.Y., Bardeen's Inc., 1874, p. 200.

In accordance with this principle, Pestalozzi believed it vital that instruction proceed with increasing sensitivity to knowledge of how children grow and develop. What is more, it must begin with the simplest elements, advancing gradually in a series of steps psychologically connected with the learner's development. Thus Pestalozzi recognized the principle of individual differences and the necessity for methods of instruction which would function with the learner as an organically structured whole. Although learning through the senses became the chief medium of instruction for Pestalozzi, he accepted the theory of separate faculties. As we have seen, the process of exercising the faculties was often considered more important than the acquiring of knowledge. Even Pestalozzi seems to have thought that exercise of the faculties was supposed to have transfer value. Ironically, the followers of Pestalozzi began to concentrate on the formal exercise or discipline of the senses, similar to the formal training of the faculties undertaken by the classicists.

Instructional Method. The reform of instructional method had been anticipated by Comenius, who predicated his method on nature and the senses and who insisted on going from concrete to abstract concepts. But with the exception of Comenius's instructional methods, Francke's *Realschule,* and Basedow's *Philanthropinum,* little had been done to implement these insights in the classroom until Pestalozzi began his educational experiments.[13] Briefly, Pestalozzi's method focused on providing content to ideas through firsthand experience or giving significance to individual expression by means of ideas. He simplified the complicated process of cognition by giving learners threefold instruction: (1) in the elements of number (arithmetic); (2) in the elements of form (drawing, leading to writing); and (3) in names and the ideas they connote (language). According to Pestalozzi, such a method of instruction would lead toward *Anschauung,* or the development of insight.

For example, a lesson in which the learner sees, handles, or otherwise makes direct contact with an object illustrates Pestalozzi's idea of an *Anschauung* lesson. *Anschauung* enters into a geography lesson when the learner sees real things or real places for himself, instead of merely hearing about them or seeing them on maps or in drawings. Insight is achieved when instruction is designed to follow the order of the mind's growth, or proceeds by gradual steps from the simple to the complex.

Pestalozzi elaborated his concept of learning sequence in what he called the ABC of *Anschauung.* His object was to analyze content into its simplest

---

[13] August Herman Francke (1663–1727) founded the first *Realschule* at Halle, Germany, where he and his fellow teachers employed "real things" to facilitate instruction. Johann Bernard Basedow (1723–1790) established his *Philanthropinum* at Dessau, Germany, where he attempted to put Rousseau's theories into practice.

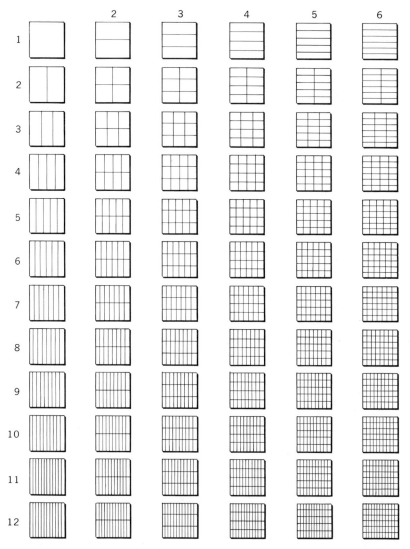

Fig. 3.1   Part of a chart for teaching fractions. (From H. Pestalozzi, How Gertrude Teaches Her Children, p. 329.)

elements and to develop graded exercises based as far as possible on the study of objects, rather than words. For example, the right approach to arithmetic was to have the learner count the things around him—the number of steps across the room, the number of plies in the thread he was weaving, etc.—and to come to know what each number meant. Pestalozzi devised arithmetic boards divided into squares on which were placed dots or lines concretely representing each unit up to 100. By means of this table of units, the learner received a clear concept of the meaning of digits and the process of addition. In the study of form, objects such as sticks were placed in different directions; then lines representing them were drawn until all elementary forms, lines, or angles had been mastered and could be combined into the drawing of more complex figures.

In the study of names (language), the fundamental units were the elementary sounds. From their articulation, the learner progressed to the reading of syllables, words, and sentences. Pestalozzi developed graduated "syllabaries" whereby his pupils examined the number, form, position, and color of the designs, holes, and rents in the wallpaper of the school and expressed their observations in increasingly complex sentences. Language was taught, not by abstract rules, but by conversation concerning objects, since speaking was held to precede grammar, reading, spelling, and composition.

Like the Lancasterian system, the Pestalozzian instructional method changed the old recitation method by which the teacher called children to his desk, a few at a time, to hear them recite their lessons. Under Pestalozzi's method, the teacher taught the whole class as a group, framing questions in accordance with the understanding reflected in their answers to previous questions. This method challenged the resourcefulness of the teacher, since it demanded knowledge of subject matter as well as competence in skillful questioning and group management.

Influence of Pestalozzi.   Although Pestalozzi experimented without the aid of science or an empirical method, he did anticipate a science of instruction. By a process of introspection, he sought to understand what he should do and then attempted to use the insights of such thinking to improve his method. Those observers who visited Pestalozzi's experimental schools reported a program of studies that brought life closer to the learner, replaced drill with observation and learner motivation, respected the individuality of each learner, and supplanted fear of punishment with mutual cooperation.

Since the instructional principles set forth earlier by Comenius had not yet been rediscovered or were not generally known, Pestalozzi's ideas seemed unique for his age and found champions in Europe and in the United States. His greatest contribution, however, was not his own instructional methodology but, rather, his inspiration in stimulating others to find better methods.

Pestalozzi's major influence in Europe was in Germany, where the philosopher Johann Gottlieb Fichte (1762–1814) provided the greatest impetus to Pestalozzian method. In the course of his famous *Addresses to the German Nation* (1807–1808), in which he emphasized the regeneration of the German nation following the defeat by Napoleon, Fichte declared: "To the course of instruction which has been invented and brought forward by Heinrich Pestalozzi, and which is now being successfully carried out under his direction, must we look for our regeneration." [14] As a result, German schools became models of Pestalozzianism, and were observed by many educators from other countries.

Pestalozzi also exerted an important influence on the German educator Friedrich Wilhelm Froebel, the founder of the kindergarten. As will be shown in the next section, Froebel incorporated Pestalozzian object teaching into his own methodology by means of his now-well-known "gifts and occupations."

Pestalozzianism in the United States.   Pestalozzianism made its debut in the United States as early as the first decade of the nineteenth century. It was introduced indirectly, in the form it had in Germany, France, England, and other European countries. The earliest development in the United States was in 1809, when William MacClure (1763–1840) brought an assistant of Pestalozzi, Joseph Neef (1770–1854), to Philadelphia, where he opened the first of a series of schools. Although Neef's schools were not significant in their influence, competing as they were with the Lancasterian system at the time of its rising popularity, they did represent the earliest American interpretation of Pestalozzi's teachings. Pupils learned by inquiry and investigation and through oral discussion. Drawing preceded writing, and books were not used until the pupil had acquired some understanding, through conversation, of the material at hand. In the study of geography, the pupils measured gardens and fields and drew plans to scale. They collected minerals and plants on long field excursions. Arithmetic was taught in short steps by the use of objects.[15]

Another variation of Pestalozzi's methodology was exemplified in the industrial feature which came into vogue quite early in the United States. Philip von Fellenberg (1771–1844), a Swiss nobleman and educator, had developed a school where the objects of instruction were the tools and materials of shop and farm. Transplanted to the United States, Fellenberg's ideas swept the country between the years of 1825 and 1835. In New York City in 1831, the Society for Promoting Manual Labor in Literary Institutions was formed for the purpose of collecting and diffusing information. By 1860, the movement had come full circle, and there was little respect for manual-labor instruction in academic quarters.

Another Pestalozzian influence in the United States was effective only regionally, in Westfield, Massachusetts, where W. H. Wells established a

---

[14] *Die Reden an die Deutsche,* fourteen in all. The endorsement of Pestalozzi's principles occurs in the tenth.
[15] Neef published his *Sketch of a Plan and Method of Education* (1808), and employed object teaching in his later schools at Village Green, Pennsylvania (1813), Louisville, Kentucky (1816), and New Harmony, Indiana (1825), as well as at Philadelphia.

school (1855) and demonstrated the practicality of teaching all subjects by the object teaching method. In the meantime, Pestalozzian principles had been widely spread by early educational journals, professional textbooks, and official reports of Pestalozzian schools in Europe. For example, Albert Picket's *Academian* (1818–1820), William Russell's *American Journal of Education* (1826–1830), and Henry Bernard's *Connecticut Common School Journal* (1838–1842), were among those presenting Pestalozzi's ideas. The official reports of such men as Calvin Stowe (1802–1886), Victor Cousin (1792–1867), and Horace Mann (1796–1859) reported Pestalozzi's methods in even greater detail, and such men as Louis Agassiz (1807–1873) and Herman Krusi, Jr. (1817–1903) supplied firsthand knowledge of the effectiveness of Pestalozzi's methods.

Meanwhile, Warren Colburn (1793–1833) published his *First Lessons in Arithmetic on the Plan of Pestalozzi* (1821); [16] David P. Page (1810–1848), director of New York State Normal School at Albany, condemned mere book learning; [17] Warren Burton (1800–1866), in his charming little book, *The District School as It Was* (1833),[18] spoke of the abstract moral sentences presenting but faint meaning to the child; Henry Barnard anticipated that educational efficiency might be increased "ten-fold" by the use of "some simple apparatus so as to employ the eye in the acquisition of knowledge"; [19] and Charles W. Eliot (1834–1926), president of Harvard University (1869–1909), in his later years dwelt on the thought that the absence of sense training was "the greatest defect in the kind of education which has come down upon us from the middle ages." [20]

After precariously maintaining itself for almost six decades, Pestalozzian object teaching received its first widespread acceptance in the United States through the work of Edward A. Sheldon (1823–1897), superintendent of schools in Oswego, New York. Sheldon was first inspired to adopt new classroom methods after visiting an educational museum in Toronto, Canada, in 1859. There an appealing display of pictures, color charts, models, and other object-teaching materials previously used by Charles Mayo (1792–1846) and Elizabeth Mayo (1793–1865) of the Home and Colonial Training School, in London, induced him to purchase these "objects" so that he might show them to his own board of education. Returning to Oswego, Sheldon obtained approval for their use and immediately began revising the curriculum and

[16] Colburn's book ranks with the *New England Primer* and Webster's *Speller* in historical importance because it was the first to emphasize sense objects in achieving mental arithmetic.

[17] David P. Page, *Theory and Practice of Teaching*. New York, A. S. Barnes and Co., Inc., 1893.

[18] Warren Burton, *The District School as It Was*, ed. by Clifton Johnson. New York, Thomas Y. Crowell Company, 1928, p. 52.

[19] Henry Barnard, *Connecticut Common School Journal*, vol. 3 (Dec. 15, 1840), p. 61.

[20] Charles W. Eliot, *The Tendency to the Concrete and Practical in Modern Education*. Boston, Houghton Mifflin Company, 1913, p. 11.

classroom procedures of the Oswego schools to conform to the English Pestalozzian pattern.

In 1860, at Oswego, the object lesson plan became the first major effort of American educators to psychologize instruction. From London, Sheldon brought a teacher familiar with Pestalozzian principles and methods; shortly thereafter, he engaged Herman Krusi, Jr., son of one of Pestalozzi's helpers at Yverdun. Within a few years, the Oswego system, along with the Oswego State Normal School (1867), became the great proponent of object teaching and progressive instructional methods in the United States.[21]

The Oswego method soon assumed a formalism of its own and sometimes became as verbal and mechanistic as the classical methods it was trying to reform. Many teachers shifted from the traditional concept that everything could be learned by reading to the new extreme that everything should be taught exclusively by the object method. Even Krusi observed that the lessons at Oswego sometimes had no connection with each other and failed to follow some general plan. Furthermore, in the object lessons, the objects chosen were not always used effectively.

As Oswego declined, a new variation of American Pestalozzianism was being introduced in 1875 by Francis W. Parker (1837–1902), superintendent of schools at Quincy, Massachusetts. Although the so-called Quincy methods were similar to the Oswego method in the use of concrete or object materials, they were actually a new form of object teaching that employed a wider variety of materials from everyday life and the sciences. To illustrate erosion, for example, the children formed hills in a sandbox and poured water on them. In an introduction to botany, they planted seeds in a box filled with earth. Local geography assumed more importance than the study of foreign lands, and the solving of common life problems was of more consequence than learning abstract rules and principles.

Quincy parents soon began to criticize Parker for changing their schools into "natural history museums" and "mud-pie factories." To settle the issue, the Massachusetts State Board of Education gave the Quincy children an examination in traditional subject matter and found them to be superior to those educated by traditional methods. Ultimately, the Quincy methods exerted a wide influence on instructional method throughout the country.[22]

Object teaching made a brief, transformed reappearance in the nature study movement of the 1880s and early 1900s when a group of educators saw how it could be applied to the firsthand study of animals, insects, minerals, plants, and geographic features. L. H. Bailey of Cornell University said that the nature study movement was an effort to put the child in contact with his

---

[21] For a comprehensive account, see Ned H. Dearborn, *Oswego Movement*. New York, Teachers College Press, Columbia University, 1925.

[22] See Lelia E. Patridge, *The Quincy Methods Illustrated*. New York, E. L. Kellogg and Company, 1886.

own environment, and insisted that "education should always begin with objects and phenomena" instead of books and museums.[23] He also insisted that nature study was a new method rather than a subject.

There had always been a few teachers who took their pupils on excursions or brought natural objects and specimens into the classroom for the children to study. The father of nature study, as a movement in the United States, was probably Louis Agassiz, the great naturalist and professor at Harvard. As early as 1847, when lecturing at teachers' institutes, he would appear with a jar of live grasshoppers and explain their structure and habits as each teacher, personally, examined one of the specimens. He helped his wife, also a teacher, prepare *A First Lesson in Natural History* (1859), and gave daily lectures illustrated with specimens, drawings, and models to her school pupils. Agassiz and his students were also instrumental in the creation of many natural history museums, among them the American Museum of Natural History in New York City, for which one of his students, Albert Smith Bickmore, created the design.

H. H. Straight (1846–1886), a disciple of both Agassiz and Nathaniel Shaler (1841–1906), another early leader in the nature study movement, was regarded by some as the real founder of the movement.[24] These men all denounced textbooks, dispensed with lectures, and ridiculed questions on assigned readings. They were convinced that the most effective method of studying nature was to catch or find a specimen and study it until it was understood.[25]

Object teaching achieved its greatest popularity in the 1860s.[26] Something of its philosophy and method became part of the kindergarten movement in the 1870s and of the learning-by-doing movement, which reached its height in the 1880s. By the end of the nineteenth century, object teaching had gone into a decline and began increasingly to give way to Herbartian principles of teaching. There was no doubt, however, that Oswego had made a lasting contribution to the development of instructional technology. Under the Oswego program wherein experts demonstrated how methods worked and gave a philosophic rationale underlying their practice, there occurred the first synthesis of theory and practice in both action and word. Before we examine the next step in the evolution of a technology of instruction, we turn first to an examination of the ideas of Froebel—sometimes called "the metaphysician of the object method."

[23] *National Education Association Proceedings* (1903), pp. 109–116.
[24] In his annual report for 1871, William T. Harris (1835–1909), superintendent of schools of St. Louis, reported that *A Syllabus in Nature Study* had been published.
[25] Wilbur S. Jackson carried on the work of H. H. Straight by publishing a teachers' guide entitled *Nature Study for the Common Schools* (1891).
[26] In post-Civil War years, the spread of Oswego graduates throughout normal schools all over the United States developed the first unified theoretical viewpoint in teacher training.

A method of instruction according to Froebel

Friedrich Wilhelm Froebel (1782–1852) was born in Oberweissbach, Germany, and, after a haphazard education, spent several years groping for a career until Herr Gruner, headmaster of a Pestalozzian model school in Frankfort, persuaded him to become a teacher there. More significant, however, was Froebel's later experience of living and working with Pestalozzi at Yverdon.[27] There he developed a keen interest in young children, which culminated in his greatest educational achievement—the kindergarten.

Educational Theory.   Detailed discussion of the complicated metaphysical framework of Froebel's educational theory as laid out in his *The Education of Man* (1826) is not within the scope of this chapter. A few words with regard to some of his key ideas are necessary, however, in order to understand his method.

The dominant idea underlying Froebel's whole view of education was the organic unity of all things in God. The forming crystal, the growing tree, the developing child—all reflect God's plan of creation. The purpose of the educator was to control the growth of a child into a man, just as the purpose of the gardener was to control the growth of a plant into its full flowering. Thus, according to Froebel, instruction had to be controlled development by which the learner came into realization of the life in the all-encompassing unity of which he was a part.

Froebel was also devoted to the recapitulation theory. According to this theory, cultural epochs were relived by each learner in his transition from infancy to adulthood, as he progressed to increasingly higher levels of development. He believed history could provide a timetable for the natural interests and activities of learners. Thus, on the basis of the recapitulation theory, the literary history of the culture could be scanned and used as a resource for materials specifically appropriate for every stage of development, with each stage preparing for the next.

As basic components in the education of the child, Froebel embodied in his mystical philosophy doctrines of (1) free self-activity; (2) creativeness; (3) social participation; and (4) motor expression. He contended that free self-activity directed the growth of the learner and allowed him active creativeness and social participation to merge his personality with the spirit of humanity. To Froebel, motor expression meant to learn a thing by doing, not through verbal communication alone. What is more, individual educative

---

[27] Froebel first spent two weeks with Pestalozzi at Yverdon, in 1805, and later taught there from 1807 to 1809. Thereafter he pursued a university career, first at Göttingen, then at Berlin. He founded his first school at Keilhau in 1817 and established the first kindergarten at Blankenburg in 1837.

activity was to take place only when the learner had a felt need for it. This readiness he believed to be a condition of man's inner nature, not a mere result of curiosity, interest, or past experience.

Perhaps most important to Froebel's instructional method was his notion of opposites. According to this opinion, a plant or animal or child grew by the twofold process of impressing the form of its own life on some external material and by developing its own nature in doing so; or, as Froebel put it, by making the inner outer and the outer inner. Growth was the process of overcoming differences by finding a connection between things which appeared at first opposed. The complement of the law of opposites was the law of connection, which was really a law of trinity, since it brought together two contrasted things by means of reconciling a third.

Instructional Method.   The most notable application of Froebel's theoretical principles was his system of early education in the kindergarten. The central feature of the plan was to present itself to the child as play. The system, although not rigid, was systematic. It consisted of three aspects: (1) games and songs; (2) construction; and (3) gifts and occupations. The games and songs, perhaps the finest expression of the kindergarten spirit, were chiefly for the purpose of acquainting the child with the inner life of animals and humanity. Froebel was the first educator to grasp the value of socialization as a basic method of teaching. The "morning circle" in his kindergarten, where the teacher and the children stood in a ring and joined hands for song and play, affords an excellent example of this method. A visitor to almost any kindergarten almost anywhere may still observe a Froebelian activity in which a dozen children might be singing in a circle while going through a pantomime of planting, watering, weeding, plucking, or smelling flowers.[28]

Construction was undertaken in such pursuits as drawing, paper cutting, pasteboard work, modeling, etc.—all familiar activities in a contemporary kindergarten. To implement his instructional method, Froebel devised a series of materials which he called *gifts and occupations.* The occupations represented activities, while the gifts provided ideas for them. Gifts were of two types: geometric shapes, and the basic materials for modeling, drawing, sewing, and coloring. The first gift was a ball, the most universal plaything, symbolic of the unity of the universe. The second consisted of a ball, a cube, and a cylinder, symbolizing thesis, antithesis, and synthesis. The third gift was formed by dividing a cube into various forms. Building blocks were

---

[28] Froebel published *Mother Play and Nursery Songs* in 1843. This work consisted of an organized series of songs, games, and pictures intended to direct the educational role of the mother. Each song contained three parts: (1) a motto for the guidance of the mother; (2) a verse with the accompanying music, to sing to the child; and (3) a picture illustrating the verse.

specifically designed to illustrate certain relationships and to teach form, number, and measurement. They also led children to compare, examine, arrange, and analyze. Today's modern school has adapted Froebel's concept of gifts by providing materials and games, miniature industrial processes, and mechanical models from the world with which the child is in active contact.

Froebel used objects (gifts) in a uniquely different way than Pestalozzi. While Pestalozzi used a great variety of objects and expected the learner to exercise his sensory powers to become acquainted with them, Froebel, on the other hand, used fewer formal objects and seemed to be more interested in the symbolic knowledge suggested by the quality of the object rather than in the immediate knowledge yielded by a sensory experience (observation) of them.

Influence of Froebel. Although a reactionary Prussian government closed all kindergartens in 1851,[29] a year before Froebel's death, his influence spread rapidly throughout Europe and the United States—reaching its height in the United States about 1880. The kindergarten movement in the United States was led by Mrs. Carl Schurz (a former student of Froebel), who established the first American kindergarten (German-speaking) at Watertown, Wisconsin, in 1855. By the end of the nineteenth century, there were about 1,400 English-speaking public kindergartens in the United States, enrolling more than 95,000 pupils.[30]

The manual-training movement (not to be confused with the manual-labor movement last mentioned in connection with Pestalozzian influence) also owes much to Froebelian ideas of motor expression, that is, learning by doing. It was brought influentially to the attention of American educators during the Centennial Exposition in Philadelphia in 1876, where it was shown as it was then being practiced in postkindergarten schools in Finland and Russia.[31]

Although superficial defects of Froebel such as his mysticism and the

[29] Prussian kindergartens were suspected of reflecting socialistic and liberal viewpoints dangerous to the existing government. The effects of their closing were felt in Prussia for a decade. Elsewhere, this educational movement, in which women took a major part, received impetus from Baroness von Marenholtz-Bülow in Germany and spread to England, France, Italy, and the Netherlands. Henry Barnard, an American educator, witnessed a kindergarten demonstration at the Great Exhibition in London in 1854 and his description inspired Elizabeth Peabody to start a kindergarten in Boston in 1860.

[30] Nicholas Murray Butler, *Education in the United States*. New York, American Book Company, 1900, pp. 41–42.

[31] Uno Cygnaeus (1810–1888) introduced the manual-training concept into Finnish schools in 1886. John D. Runkle, president of the Massachusetts Institute of Technology, after seeing a display of the Imperial Technical School of Moscow, recommended the establishment of manual-training workshops in the United States. His idea was further developed by Calvin M. Woodward and others. The manual-training vogue continued until about 1910.

crudity of his materials [32] may seem obvious, his basic doctrines have proven to be psychologically and socially sound. Through his emphases on motor expression and on the social aspects of instruction, along with his advocacy of a school without set tasks, Froebel made a distinctive contribution to instructional method. His experiments led not only to the establishment of kindergartens, but his principles of instruction were applied in later years.

The Herbartian method of instruction

It is appropriate to conclude this chapter in our survey with an examination of Johann Friedrich Herbart (1776–1841), in whom trends developing since the time of Comenius came to fruition. Both Comenius and Pestalozzi, as we have seen, were sensitive to the need of beginning with sense perception to develop clear conceptualization. Herbart built on this heritage and proceeded to show how the teacher could assimilate new concepts with old ones. Herbart's emphasis on moral development as the primary aim of education, and his use of historical materials for the realization of these ends, reflects the influence of Froebel. Perhaps not since the time of the Elder Sophists had instruction become so highly systematized, nor had such a sophisticated formula been devised for the teaching of virtue.

Brilliant son of a distinguished middle-class family of Oldenburg, Germany, Herbart entered the University of Jena, at Bremen, to prepare for a law career. However, he left before graduation to spend two years (1797–1799) as private tutor to the sons of the governor of Interlaken, Switzerland.[33] During this period, he visited Pestalozzi's school at Burgdorf, which impressed him. Later, after completing his university doctoral studies, Herbart focused his interest on education. From 1802 to 1809, he lectured on education and philosophy at the University of Göttingen, Germany, where he published his *Science of Education* (1806). For the next twenty-four years, he held the chair of philosophy (formerly occupied by Immanuel Kant) at the University of Königsberg, Germany. Here he founded an educational seminar and a practice school for teacher education and experimentation in method teaching. In 1833, he returned to Göttingen, where in 1835 he published his famous *Outlines of Educational Doctrine*.

[32] In *Mother Play and Nursery Songs,* the pictorial illustrations are rough and poorly drawn, the music is crude, and the verses are lacking in rhythm, poetic spirit, and diction. The arrangement of verses is awkward and seems at times to lack consistency.

[33] Herbart's tutoring experience proved to be a most valuable practical experience as well as an important influence on his educational thinking. He was required by his patron to make a bimonthly written report of his methods and his students' progress. Five of these letters are still extant and reveal the germs of an educational system. At this early date, Herbart recognized individual differences in learners and attempted to adapt his instruction to their individual needs. He afterward maintained that a careful study of the development of a few children was the best preparation for a teaching career.

Educational Theory.   In contrast to any of his predecessors, Herbart rooted his method in a systematic psychology of learning. His was the first modern psychology of learning to harmonize with the *tabula rasa* (blank tablet) theory of mind which had been formulated by Locke.[34] Not only did he negate the idea of inborn faculties, prevalent since classical times and held by most of his predecessors, but he denied that the mind itself existed at birth. Minds, according to Herbart, were simple battlegrounds and storehouses of ideas, and ideas, he thought, had an active quality of their own. On the basis of this concept, Herbart developed a systematic psychology of learning and instruction.[35]

To Herbart, all perception was apperception, or a process of relating new ideas to old ones and of assimilating them into a totality of an apperceptive mass. Within this apperceptive process, Herbart recognized three levels of learning: the first level of predominantly sense activity; the second level wherein previously formed ideas were reproduced; and the third, or highest, level in which conceptual thinking or understanding occurred.

The implication of Herbart's theory was that the primary task of instruction involved the formation of an apperceptive mass by the proper presentation of the right sequence of ideas. Psychologically, learners were formed by the world of ideas presented to them from without. Thus the problem of instruction became one of selecting the correct ideas and materials for developing manysidedness of interests and forming a large, apperceptive mass. Herbart was particularly convinced that the history and great literature of the world, when properly selected and arranged, would develop the interests and understanding of learners at their successive periods of growth.

Instructional Method.   Herbart implemented his conception of mind and his theory of apperception by formulating a systematic method with four logical steps:

1 *Clearness.* The first stage concentrated on the absorption of new ideas by the learner. The objects to be studied had to be broken up into their elements so that the learner might focus on each fact or detail in isolation from the rest.

2 *Association.* When the object or idea had been kept before the mind as long as necessary for a sufficient knowledge of it, it had to be associated with related objects already known. This could be done

[34] See footnote 3 for note on Locke's *tabula rasa* theory.
[35] Herbart's psychology was the last great system of metaphysical psychology. Although he maintained that his system was based on "metaphysics, empiricism and mathematics," no empirical studies were conducted by Herbart, and his entire system was based on introspection. He felt that it was appropriate for a science like physics to be experimental but equally appropriate that psychology be introspective and metaphysical.

by free conversation or by sensory experiences, when these would help in the foundation of generalization and abstraction.

3 *System.* When the facts were seen in their proper relationship, they would become arranged into a unity. At this stage, a clear distinction took place between the essential and the irrelevant, thereby completing the process of apperception.

4 *Method.* In this stage, the system was to be put to a test by seeing the relationship of each fact in it. For example, once an arithmetical rule had been established (system), the learner needed to test himself in his knowledge of it with reference to new problems (method). The new experience, in this process, would then become part of the unity of the mind.[36]

In essence, the four steps of Herbart are the transfer of Pestalozzi's method of sensory impressions to the intellectual level of learning. While Pestalozzi felt the need of beginning with sense impressions, he had neither the time nor the scholarship to construct a psychology of learning beyond the faculty psychology of the time. Herbart, on the other hand, developed a system of learning that, while purely speculative and mechanical, provided a logical theoretical framework for educational practice.

Influence of Herbart.   The ideas of Herbart had surprisingly little impact on European educational practice until about a quarter of a century after his death. In Germany, Tuiskon Ziller (1817–1882) did much to popularize Herbartian principles by applying his methods to elementary school instruction,[37] by organizing a pedagogical seminar at the University of Leipzig, and by founding the Association for the Scientific Study of Education. Wilhelm Rein (1847–1929), a student of Ziller who became head of the pedagogical seminar and practice schools at the University of Jena, further spread the influence of Herbart by making Jena a great center of German Herbartianism.

Next to Germany, the United States has been more influenced by Herbartianism than any other country. Before 1880, little mention had been made of Herbart in American educational literature. The American movement was fostered largely by a few enthusiastic American teachers who studied with Rein at Jena and then brought back with them the new science of instructional method. They included Charles De Garmo, who published *The Essentials of Method* in 1889; and Charles A. McMurry, who published

[36] Herbart's four steps were later expanded to five by American Herbartians. Clearness became (1) preparation and (2) presentation; association became (3) comparison and abstraction; system became (4) generalization; and method became (5) application.

[37] Ziller elaborated the Herbartian principles of correlation and concentration, which unified all subjects around one or two central studies such as literature or history. Ziller also formulated the culture epochs theory, which held that materials for a course of study should be selected to parallel the development of the individual and the race.

his *General Method* in 1892, and who, with Frank M. McMurry, his brother, published books on the special methods of teaching various subjects stressed by the Herbartians.

Simultaneously, Herbartians began to penetrate the entire structure of American public education. In 1892, the National Herbart Society [38] was organized at the Saratoga Springs meeting of the National Education Association for the purpose of translating the works of Herbart and various German Herbartians. Also, most of the normal schools—particularly in the Midwest —were soon advocating Herbartian principles and, through the teachers they sent to every section of the country, greatly influenced the practices of the schools. For some twenty years after 1895, the Herbartians wrote most of the educational texts and dominated several educational journals, as well as the professional discussions and debates. Nevertheless, it was clearly evident, as early as 1901, that Herbartianism was waning in the United States.

In his book of 1901, *Talks to Teachers on Psychology*, William James (1842–1910) made a distinction between the art and science of education and proceeded to demolish the Herbartians' key concept of apperception by revealing its empty verbalism and the mystical origins of its generalizations. James was joined in his attacks on Herbartianism by philosophers John Dewey, Wilhelm Dilthy, and Josiah Royce, all of whom pointed out the anachronisms of Herbartian rational science. More important, perhaps, than the criticisms based on the abstruse features of Herbart's theoretical system were criticisms of the instructional practices to which they appeared to lead. For example, Herbartianism seemed to commit teachers to a program of indoctrination whereby they determined precisely what their pupils were to be taught. Each lesson plan included, in addition to the questions, all the answers as well, which the learners were to arrive at through a largely mechanical process completely dominated by the teacher. Thus, learning was conceived as a process similar to the filling of a storage container.

Despite its limitations, no other system of instruction, except that of Pestalozzi, has ever had so wide an influence on American instructional method as well as on teacher thinking. It has made important contributions to instructional technology by emphasizing a psychological and scientific, if not experimental, approach to instruction and learning.

Recapitulation and analysis

Our survey just completed is intended to provide only a set of concepts selected from historic instructional theory and method, which may be

[38] Predecessor of the National Society for the Scientific Study of Education, which was organized in 1895. However, the NSSS never seemed comfortable with the word "Scientific." In 1910, the official title became the National Society for the Study of Education.

considered as precursors to modern instructional technology. It is not, as we have said before, a history of instructional method in any definitive sense.

There are few tendencies in contemporary instructional practice that cannot be traced back to Lancaster, Pestalozzi, Froebel, and Herbart. The Lancasterian method segmented instruction into separate classroom packages and thus introduced a type of lockstep instruction which still dominates educational organizational patterns of today. The prevailing conception that instructional method consists principally in developing techniques of transmitting information and of controlling learner behavior was reinforced and elaborated in the monitorial system.

Viewing the instructional task in more complicated terms than the monitorial method, object teaching, as developed by Pestalozzi and Froebel, went beyond mere practice and shifted talk to theoretical considerations and to things of a less immediately practical nature. In Herbart, there was a more advanced return to methods similar to those of the Elder Sophists. Instruction became highly systematized, and cognitive elements once again came into central focus in the instructional process. It was a new formula for virtue through knowledge, to be acquired from the intellectual resources of the race. Moreover, Herbart developed a rational science of learning which pointed the way to a science of instruction.

In the next chapter, we will begin our examination of the formative concepts which have led toward the development of a modern science and technology of instruction.

chapter 4

beginnings of a
science and technology
of instruction:
1900 to the present

It would be futile to designate any particular event or
date to mark the beginning of a science and technology
of instruction. Yet it is clear that at the beginning of the
twentieth century there occurred a series of related events
which, together, might be interpreted as the beginning of
a science of instruction.

William James, for example, in his book of 1901,
Talks to Teachers on Psychology, made one of the first
distinctions between the art and science of teaching, calling for a scientific approach to instruction. Similarly, in
1901, John Dewey (1859–1952) so interpreted the method
of empirical science in educational terms as to make the
classroom an experimental laboratory. In 1902, Edward
Thorndike (1874–1949) offered the first course in educational measurements at Columbia University and
became the first to apply the methods of quantitative

research to instructional problems.[1] G. Stanley Hall (1846–1924) published his *Adolescence* (1904), a landmark in the scientific study of the child. In 1905, the French psychologist Alfred Binet (1857–1911) and Theodore Simon, his collaborator, published *A Method of Measuring the Intelligence of Young Children.* Moreover, a true science of behavior, and especially of learning theory, began to emerge (not based primarily on metaphysical or philosophical speculations, as previously), from which applications to a technology of instruction might be anticipated.

In this chapter, our attention will be focused on a few selected educators whose theories and methods produced or fostered a modern science and technology of instruction. Among them were two who dominated much of the thought and practice of American education during the first half of this century—Edward L. Thorndike and John Dewey. Both Thorndike and Dewey rose to eminence during roughly the same period and, for a time, both were arrayed against those who still clung to the unscientific modes of thinking then prevalent. Dewey, as a philosopher, developed a comprehensive theoretical system, ranging from the nature of man and learning to ethical and logical theory. Thorndike, as an educational psychologist, fashioned the first scientific learning theory and established empirical investigation as the basis for a science of instruction.

By the early twenties, it was apparent that Thorndike's and Dewey's theories of instruction were incompatible. Dewey, the pragmatist, founder of the experimentalist school, built a system that had little basis in empirical data and whose hypotheses, to this day, have not been subjected to experimental investigation, despite his warnings to inquire, test, and to criticize. On the other hand, Thorndike was the exemplar of what might be done by empirical theorizing and investigation. His theories, however, were rejected by many educational leaders who were attracted by Dewey's more democratic approaches to instruction and learning, although these approaches were untested.

[1] Sometimes called the "father of educational measurements," Thorndike cannot be credited with initiating the measurement movement in the United States. This happened in 1895, when J. M. Rice, editor of *The Forum*, undertook a ten-month study to show teacher effectiveness in teaching spelling. His general aim in testing nearly thirty-three thousand children was expressed as follows: "I endeavor to prove that the first step toward placing elementary schools on a scientific basis must necessarily lie in determining what results may reasonably be expected at the end of a given period of instruction." See J. M. Rice, "The Futility of the Spelling Grind," *The Forum*, vol. 23 (March–August, 1887), p. 163. Rice was a physician who, after a brief medical practice, had left for a two-year visit to Europe where he had studied pedagogy and psychology at the Universities of Jena and Leipzig. Upon his return to the United States, he had begun to devote his efforts to educational reform, through publication and by undertaking research studies of instructional practices. Professional educators of the time paid scant attention to his work, and little reference is found to him in the educational literature of the period. Yet today one finds that most of the reforms toward which he directed his efforts have been implemented in modern educational practices.

Thorndike and the science of instruction

The contributions of the American educational psychologist Edward L. Thorndike to a science and technology of instruction were monumental. The most remarkable aspect of Thorndike's work is that he dealt with every major psychological conception of his time, either demonstrating their inadequacies experimentally or incorporating them into his own system. It is well known, for example, how he demolished the validity of the mental discipline theory as a psychology of learning, as well as the recapitulation theory of psychological development.[2] Thorndike was not an ivory-tower theorist. He shuttled back and forth between his laboratory at Columbia University and countless classrooms in the public schools, tackling the relevant instructional problems of his day.

Thorndike began his psychological career with laboratory studies of learning in various animal species while he was a student of William James, at Harvard, and of James McKeen Cattell (1860–1944), at Columbia.[3] His doctoral dissertation on *Animal Intelligence* (1898) remains a landmark in the history of psychology. Thorndike joined the faculty of Teachers College, Columbia University, in 1899, where, at the suggestion of Cattell, he shifted his emphases from animal learning to what was to be a lifetime concern with a science of human learning and a technology of instruction.

Thorndike's Theory of Connectionism. Out of Thorndike's studies with animals had come the first scientific theory of learning, his theory of connectionism. Whereas previous theories had emphasized practice or repetition, Thorndike gave equal consideration to reward or punishment, success or failure, and satisfaction or annoyance to the learner. Building on the idea

[2] See Edward L. Thorndike and R. S. Woodworth, "The Influence of Improvement in One Mental Function upon the Efficiency of Other Functions," *Psychological Review*, vol. 8 (May, 1901), pp. 247–261; (July, 1901), pp. 384–395; (November, 1901), pp. 553–564. For a refutation of G. Stanley Hall's recapitulation theory, see Edward L. Thorndike, *Educational Psychology*, vol. I, *The Original Nature of Man*. New York, Teachers College Press, Columbia University, 1913.

[3] Both James and Cattell had an important influence on Thorndike. Thorndike comments in an autobiographical piece that he had "no memory of having heard or seen the word psychology" until his junior year at Wesleyan University (1893–1894). During his first year at Harvard, Thorndike dropped literature in favor of psychology for his doctoral subject, after the impact of a psychology course with James. Although James was not an experimentalist, he started to conduct informal psychological experiments about 1875 and contributed to the growth and development of psychology through his ability to synthesize psychological principles. His definitive work in psychology was the famous, two-volume *Principles of Psychology* (1890). Cattell probably influenced Thorndike to an even greater extent through his pioneer work in the promotion of mental tests and his interest in individual differences. As a result of his own work with Wilhelm Wundt (the founder of the first psychological laboratory) at the University of Leipzig, Cattell had founded a psychological laboratory at Columbia, in 1891.

Fig. 4.1   Photograph of Thorndike at his desk. (Scott, Foresman and Company. Courtesy of the publishers.)

of the reflex arc, which connected the brain and neural tissue with the total behavior of the organism, he ended the search for mind by eliminating it as a separate entity, placing it in the total response of the learner to his environment. Moreover, Thorndike discarded the earlier views that man is either sinful or good and that he is completely modifiable. Human nature, Thorndike maintained, is simply a mass of "original tendencies" that can be exploited for good or evil, depending on what learning takes place.[4]

Thorndike formulated laws of learning which provided basic principles leading to a technology of instruction. We describe here only his three primary laws:

1   *The law of exercise or repetition.* According to this law, the more times a stimulus-induced response is repeated, the longer it will be retained.

2   *The law of effect.* The law of effect states the pleasure-pain principle. A response is strengthened if it is followed by pleasure and weakened if followed by displeasure.

[4] Thorndike, *Educational Psychology*, vol. I, *op. cit.*, Chap. 17.

3 *The law of readiness.* Thorndike assumed that, because of the structure of the nervous system, certain conduction units, in a given situation, are more predisposed to conduct than others.[5]

Thorndike based these laws on the stimulus-response hypothesis that a neural bond would be established between the stimulus and the response when a given stimulus produced a satisfying response within a given environment.[6] Learning would result from formation of these bonds into patterns of behavior.

Thorndike's Technology of Instruction.   According to the connectionist conception, the instructional task of the teacher would be guided by two broad rules: (1) to put together what should go together, and (2) to reward desirable connections and make undesirable connections produce discomfort.[7] In his classic three-volume work, *Educational Psychology*, Thorndike formulated the basic principles underlying his technology of instruction as (1) self-activity; (2) interest (motivation); (3) preparation and mental set; (4) individualization; and (5) socialization. To implement these principles, a teacher would have to control the activity of the learners in the desired direction, without ignoring the learners' own interests and individual responses to stimulation. Since the nature of the learning response, according to Thorndike, depended on past experience and the mental set of the learners, it was important that the stimuli presented by the teacher be adapted to the experience and mental set of the learners and that their individual differences be taken into consideration in the design or arrangement of situations and in the use of instructional media so that desirable connections could be established. Finally, every response had its social implications, and all learning responses had to be developed in natural social settings.

[5] In later writings, Thorndike disavowed his law of exercise and modified his law of effect. However, through implication, he continued to emphasize repetition in learning and though he shifted his emphasis to pleasure in his law of effect, the pain aspect was not completely discarded.

[6] Thorndike developed the most complete system of psychology yet developed along associationist lines. Since associationism has its roots in philosophy, its history extends back to Aristotle. Associationism as a doctrine was developed by British empiricists during the seventeenth and eighteenth centuries. For John Locke (1632–1704), ideas were the units of a mind, and associations consisted of combinations of ideas. David Hartley (1705–1757) developed Locke's concepts still further and established associationism as a systematic doctrine. Such men as James Mill (1773–1836), John Stuart Mill (1806–1873), and Herbert Spencer also postulated associationist positions. The experimental work of Hermann Ebbinghaus (1850–1909), Ivan P. Pavlov (1849–1936), and Vladimir M. Bekterev (1857–1927) during the nineteenth century replaced the association of ideas by association of stimuli and responses. This shift was related to the transition of psychology into an empirical and natural science in its own right.

[7] Edward L. Thorndike, *Educational Psychology*, vol. II, *The Psychology of Learning*. New York, Teachers College Press, Columbia University, 1913, p. 4.

Thorndike's studies on the design of instructional media, the organization of instruction, individual differences, and methods of evaluation were both extensive and original. For example, he anticipated programed instruction when he wrote, in 1912:

> If, by a miracle of mechanical ingenuity, a book could be so arranged that only to him who had done what was directed on page one would page two become visible, and so on, much that now requires personal instruction could be managed by print. Books to be given out in loose sheets, a page or so at a time, and books arranged so that the student only suffers if he misuses them, should be worked in many subjects.[8]

He commented further on the misuse of textbooks, as follows:

> On the whole, the improvement of printed directions, statements of facts, exercise books and the like is as important as the improvement of the powers of teachers themselves to diagnose the condition of pupils and to guide their activities by personal means. Great economies are possible by printed aids, and personal comment and question should be saved to do what only it can do. A human being should not be wasted in doing what forty sheets of paper or two phonographs can do. . . . The best teacher uses books and appliances as well as his own insight, sympathy, and magnetism.[9]

Thorndike's impressive demonstration of what could be accomplished by empirical-inductive means in the development of a science and technology of instruction unquestionably marked him as the first modern instructional technologist. Nevertheless, by the time many educators began to believe in the imminence of a science of instruction, his influence was eclipsed by that of the great educational philosopher John Dewey. Thorndike was criticized by Dewey and by prominent members of the Progressive Education Movement in America for his frequent use of such terms as "habit," "repression," and "systematic practice," and for his conservative social ideas.[10] Perhaps part of the waning influence of Thorndike's ideas, near the first quarter of this century, can be attributed to the fact that his psychology of learning seemed less adequate than the new, emerging systems of behaviorism [11] and gestalt psychology.

[8] Edward L. Thorndike, *Education.* New York, The Macmillan Company, 1912, pp. 164–166.

[9] *Ibid.,* p. 167.

[10] Many of Thorndike's major conceptions went counter to the prevailing social and intellectual ideas current in early twentieth-century America. For a comprehensive account of the social implications of Thorndike's ideas, see Merle Curti, *The Social Ideas of American Educators.* Paterson, N.J., Littlefield, Adams, 1961, pp. 323–324.

[11] John B. Watson (1878–1958) published *Behavior* (1914) and championed a new school of psychology which came to be known as behaviorism. Watson claimed that environment (stimuli or conditioning) makes the organism and that any child could be reared to be a thief or a professional man. The behavioristic theory of learning, a logical extreme of Thorndike's connectionism, assumed that learning was simply a matter of what happened to the learner.

Thorndike's contributions to modern instructional technology cannot be overestimated: he began the first systematic laboratory investigation of animal learning; produced the first scientific learning theory; made a comprehensive analysis of human learning; made extensive scientific studies of mental tests, scales of achievement, and textbooks; pioneered in the application of quantitative measures to certain sociopsychological problems; and invented new techniques in the field of lexicography. Today his influence can be seen in a contemporary viewpoint—that of B. F. Skinner of Harvard University.[12] Indeed, Thorndike is the historic starting point for any study or analysis of modern instructional technology.

Theories of instruction according to Dewey and Kilpatrick

John Dewey's importance in instructional technology stems primarily from his vast influence on American education and, particularly, from his analysis of thinking in reflective, problem-solving terms. Dewey studied with G. Stanley Hall [13] at Johns Hopkins University where he took his doctorate. He then taught at the Universities of Michigan, Minnesota, and Chicago, before joining the Columbia University faculty in 1904. More than anyone, Dewey was responsible for the application of pragmatism to education—the notion that education *was* life. However, Dewey cannot be held responsible for the frequent misinterpretations of his ideas nor for the excesses of many of his followers who were in the Progressive Education Movement.

Dewey's Psychology of Learning. A comprehensive analysis of John Dewey's psychology of learning has yet to be accomplished, and we present here only a few of the most significant ideas underlying his view of instruction.

In contrast to Thorndike, Dewey believed that stimulus and response were not to be sharply distinguished but were to be seen always as organically related. In a short paper that is now regarded as a psychological classic,[14] he attacked the widely held reflex arc concept, contending that learning involved interaction or two-way action between the learner and his environment.[15] The environment supplied learners with cues and prob-

[12] B. F. Skinner's system of instruction is discussed in this chapter.

[13] Hall received, in 1878, the first American doctorate in psychology under William James at Harvard. He then went to Germany, where he did two years of postdoctorate work under Wilhelm Wundt at Leipzig. In 1883, he founded, at Johns Hopkins, the first psychological laboratory in the United States. Hall developed a number of new areas in psychology, proceeding from child psychology—where he popularized the use of the questionnaire as a research tool—through adolescent psychology to the psychology of old age. He was also one of the leaders in developing the field of educational psychology.

[14] For Dewey's criticism of reflex arc psychology, see "The Reflex Arc Concept in Psychology," *Psychological Review*, vol. 3 (1896), pp. 357–370.

[15] Dewey anticipated this gestalt-field viewpoint twenty years before it was first formulated.

Fig. 4.2   Portrait of John Dewey. (Courtesy of Teachers College, Columbia University.)

lems, and the human nervous system functioned to interpret the cues effectively so that problems could be evaluated and satisfactory solutions found. Moreover, Dewey explained that the experiences which learners undergo within their environment become the materials out of which they make meanings and on which they base their goals and actions.

Dewey's Experimental Laboratory School.   In 1896, while at the University of Chicago, Dewey decided to establish a Laboratory School for the purpose of testing his educational theories and their sociological implications. Beginning with 16 pupils and 2 teachers, it grew by 1902 to 140 children, 23 teachers, and 10 assistants. Dewey served as director; his wife was principal; Ella Flagg Young, later to be Chicago's first woman superintendent of schools, was supervisor of instruction. The Laboratory School closed in 1903, and the next year Dewey left Chicago to teach philosophy at Columbia University.

During the seven years of its existence, the Laboratory School became the most interesting experimental endeavor in American education. An observer found none of the conventional arrangements, routines, or activities.

Desks and benches were not arranged in rows; the traditional teacher's desk with bell and ruler was missing; drills and recitations were not to be heard. Subject matter could no longer be clearly identified. Some children might be busily engaged with books; others, with pen and paper; and some might be painting or using hammers. The teacher could usually be found mingling with the children, offering counsel and guidance as the pupils proceeded in their activities.

From the time Dewey established this experimental school, he was hailed as the guiding light of the Progressive Education Movement. But, as Dewey himself observed, the school was overweighted on the "individualistic" side so that he might obtain data. More importantly, Dewey sought to substitute a newer curriculum that was better planned, better designed, and more effectively organized than the conventional curriculum of which he was a pointed critic. Although the evidence is clear that his instructional approaches at the school were effective, he did not consider his innovations as final, but only as the first step in developing a science of instruction. He was, however, destined for disappointment; a quarter of a century later he declared progressive education a failure because it had too hastily destroyed the traditional instructional pattern without replacing it with something better.[16]

The Reflective Method of Instruction.   Dewey's only lasting contribution to a technology of instruction was probably his conception of instruction in terms of scientific method, defined in its broadest sense. To him, all worthwhile thinking was reflection, or the "active, persistent, and careful consideration of any belief or supposed form of knowledge in the light of the grounds that support it and the further conclusions to which it tends." The essence of this reflective method of Dewey's was contained in his little book *How We Think* (1910), which described reflection as psychological movement through the following steps:

1   The learner sensed and recognized a problem. Preferably, he had to become aware of some goal and feel blocked by an intervening obstacle so that he would feel a need in restoring continuity.
2   After having sensed a problem or felt discrepancy in known data, he would formulate hypotheses for the purpose of providing tentative answers or generalizations which might offer possible solutions.
3   Once the problematic situation had been surveyed or deductive ob-

[16] The published records of the Dewey Laboratory School are voluminous. See especially the nine monographs published monthly through 1900 as *The Elementary School Record* and successive issues of *The Elementary School Teacher* for 1901 and 1902. The entire June, 1903, issue of *The Elementary School Teacher* was devoted to the Laboratory School. Also, for firsthand accounts of the school, see Katherine Camp Mayhew and Anna Camp Edwards, *The Dewey School*. New York, D. Appleton-Century Company, Inc., 1936.

servations made and checked against present knowledge or experiments designed to test hypotheses, steps could be taken to restore the continuity of the learner's activity, or his goal could be more adequately visualized.

4 The learner would test hypotheses and attempt to verify the consequences of logical implications deduced.

5 Finally, the learner would draw conclusions. This might involve the acceptance, modification, or rejection of hypotheses, or it might lead to the conclusion that the available evidence did not provide a basis for action or for making an unqualified statement or taking a firm position.

Dewey did not mean to imply a rigid, mechanical order of steps in this method. All were closely interrelated and a learner would not necessarily go through them in the consecutive fashion in which they are here listed. A learner might move continuously back and forth from problem to hypotheses, to evidence, to conclusions, in varying order. Thus, Dewey's instructional approach resembled that of a scientific investigation in which hypotheses could be formulated and tested.

Many so-called followers of Dewey never understood the full implications of his theory of instruction because they found his writing difficult to understand or because they tended to ignore his insistence on placing the reflective approach at the center of the instructional process. Dewey believed the primary goal of instruction to be the improvement of intelligence, and he attacked much of the formalism inherent in both the mental discipline theory and in the connectionism of Thorndike. Dewey gave teachers a philosophical, theoretical-deductive psychology of learning which made empirical inquiry unnecessary for most educators who accepted his ideas. But though he urged inquiry and experimental investigation, his philosophy tended to block educational research. Thus, until Dewey's hypothesis is tested against predictions made from it, it cannot meet the basic criterion of a scientific technology of instruction.[17]

Kilpatrick: The Popularizer of Dewey.   The man who probably had most to do with popularizing Dewey's educational ideas was William Heard Kilpatrick (1871–1965). After graduation from Mercer University in Macon, Georgia, Kilpatrick taught for a time in the public schools before returning to Mercer, first as a teacher of mathematics, later as vice-president, and then as acting president. In 1906, he resigned and the following year became a graduate student and Dewey disciple at Columbia University. After completing his doctoral dissertation in 1912, he joined Teachers College as a

[17] It should be clear that we are not criticizing Dewey's theoretical model in itself but only the failure to test it and to use the empirical method to revise it.

full-time faculty member, an association which lasted throughout his professional life.

By 1916, Kilpatrick was simplifying and clarifying Dewey's complex thinking and writing, as well as adding his own interpretations. He became known as "the million-dollar professor" because his estimated thirty-five thousand students (drawn mostly from classroom teachers and school administrators) had paid over a million dollars in fees to Columbia University. Kilpatrick was, in fact, a compelling teacher who was extraordinarily successful in making his own disciples. Although acclaimed as the great interpreter of Dewey, in the last analysis it seems clear that Kilpatrick ended by transforming Dewey's ideas into something quite different than Dewey had originally intended.

Kilpatrick's Project Method.   Some of the theoretical differences between Dewey and Kilpatrick come clearly into focus when Kilpatrick's Project Method is examined. In his effort to present a purposeful approach to instruction, Kilpatrick developed the Project Method in the spring of 1918.[18] It was also his purpose to reconcile Thorndike's connectionism with Dewey's theory of instruction. By emphasizing purposeful activity—activity in harmony with the learner's own goals—he sought to take full account of Thorndike's law of effect; by locating this activity in a social environment, he believed he could introduce an ethical outcome, since moral character was for him centered in the welfare of the group. Kilpatrick reorganized the curriculum as a succession of projects suitable to the interests of learners. He summarized the role of the teacher as follows: The teacher helps (1) initiate the activity, (2) plan how to carry the activity forward, (3) execute the plan, (4) evaluate progress, (5) think up and note new leads, (6) formulate the new leads by writing them down for later recall, (7) keep the pupils critical of their thinking en route to the solution, (8) look back over the whole process to pick up and fix important kinds of learning, as well as to draw lessons for the future.

Within this particular technology of instruction, Dewey's problem-solving method became only one special type of project. Other types of projects such as building a boat, presenting a play, or developing a skill might be less scientific or not scientific at all. The other steps of conventional instructional method—presentation, eliciting the trial response, correcting the trial response, and eliciting the test response—were also part of the Kilpatrick instructional approach, in which they assumed a distinctive form. Rather than presenting an instructional task, the teacher assisted the learner in defining it. The object was not to learn something from a book but to

[18] Franklin Ernest Heald (1870–1943), specialist in agricultural education (1914–1918) in the U.S. Department of Agriculture, first used the term "project" in connection with vocational agricultural education.

meet a need or to resolve a difficulty or problem. Trial responses and their correction were automatically resolved during the planning and execution process. The test response constituted the results of the activity and the degree to which such activity had resulted in the attainment of a desired goal.[19]

Comparative Analysis of Dewey and Kilpatrick. On the surface, the Dewey problem-solving method and the Kilpatrick project method seemed to have come out of the same theoretical mold. There were, however, basic differences. Dewey talked about problem solving as central to the instructional process and was also deeply concerned with the interests and purposes of the learner. He also proposed a new body of content, beginning with the learner's experiences and culminating with structured subject matter. Kilpatrick, on the other hand, attacked subject matter fixed in advance and emphasized a child-centered approach which Dewey himself rejected, first in his *The Child and the Curriculum* (1902) and later in his *Experience and Education* (1938). Moreover, Kilpatrick's influential *Foundations of Method* (1926) unequivocally states a Thorndikean, connectionist psychology which Dewey had consistently opposed. For example, one of the slogans popularized by Kilpatrick and other Progressives in education, "Children learn by doing," distinctly implies a connectionist psychology of learning. Finally, Kilpatrick seemed to assume the validity of Rousseau's permissivism, which was incompatible with the Dewey view.

The Montessori method

An important pioneer in nourishing a science of instruction was the remarkable Italian educator, Maria Montessori (1870–1952),[20] the first woman to receive a medical degree from the University of Rome. Her dominating interest in the development and welfare of children soon diverted her from medicine to education, and she was placed in charge of a state school for defectives, a position she held from 1899 to 1901. During this period, Montessori began to develop techniques for teaching mentally deficient children, based on the methods and materials of Edouard Seguin (1812–1880).[21]

[19] See William H. Kilpatrick, *Foundations of Method.* New York, The Macmillan Company, 1926.
[20] Maria Montessori was born at Chiaravalle, in the province of Ancona. Her father, Allessandro Montessori, was descended from a noble family of Bologna; her mother was a niece of Antonio Stoppani, noted philosopher-scientist-priest.
[21] Instructional technology owes much to the French educator Seguin for his ingenious work with idiots. Seguin is one of the forgotten men of education, although his direct influence on the training and testing of children of low ability was very great. Even today,

In 1901, she resigned to reenter the University of Rome for courses in experimental psychology and anthropology, hoping to obtain a scientific foundation for the science of instruction she wished to develop for normal children. By 1907, Montessori was ready to apply her theoretical formulations to the instruction of young culturally deprived children in the first of the Case dei Bambini, or "Children's Houses," which she established in a low-cost housing development in a Roman slum.[22] Montessori trained a resident teacher for each school, selected the instructional materials, and devised techniques derived partly from Seguin, partly from Froebel, and partly from her own experience with teaching mental defectives. She continued this work with extraordinary success for a period of four years, until 1911.

When Montessori published her *Scientific Pedagogy as Applied to Child Education in the Children's Houses* in 1909, people came from all over the world to observe her schools. She devoted herself to two principal lines of activity—acquainting teachers and educational leaders outside of Italy with her methods, and working out an application of those methods to older children.[23] Many prominent Americans became intensely interested in her work. They included such diverse personalities as Alexander Graham Bell, psychologist Dorothy Canfield Fisher (better known for her novels), Arnold Gesell,[24] Howard C. Warren,[25] and Lightner Witmer.[26] S. S. McClure, publisher of the "muckraking" *McClure's Magazine*, helped communicate her methods to the public, and generated an interest that exploded into a social movement.[27]

By 1917, however, American interest in Montessori had already subsided. This was partly due to a false tension that developed between Pro-

---

one finds evidence of his work in kindergartens and first-grade rooms. Although Seguin did not organize the special tests he devised for mental defectives, as did Alfred Binet, his were the first modern tests for the measurement of intelligence. The student of today meets his name mainly in reference to the Seguin Formboard, which is one of the tests in the third year of the Binet Scale.

[22] Montessori worked with children as young as two and one-half years old at a time when American educators were discussing the relevance of her ideas for the four- and five-year-olds in American public school kindergartens.

[23] Montessori established her first training course for teachers in Rome, in 1913. This training program was attended by seventy American teachers. She ultimately set up similar training programs or served as a consultant in England, Spain, Holland, India, and the United States. She did not, however, succeed to any great extent in realizing her goal of applying her methods to older children.

[24] Director of the Yale University Clinic of Child Psychology and pioneer investigator in the scientific study of child behavior.

[25] Howard C. Warren was president of the American Psychological Association (1912).

[26] Lightner Witmer founded the first Psychological Clinic at the University of Pennsylvania (1914).

[27] S. S. McClure offered to build an institution for Montessori in the United States in 1913, but she rejected his offer.

gressivism in American education and Montessori. For example, the basic criticism of Montessori, as offered by William Heard Kilpatrick, centered on her failure to provide for "self-directing adaptation to a novel environment." [28] Also, as Hunt pointed out in his introduction to *The Montessori Method,* she collided with several more of the firmly held psychological beliefs relative to "fixed intelligence" and the "unimportance of early experience." [29]

A second explosion of American interest in Montessori occurred during the middle 1950s, partly because many of her instructional practices seemed justified in the light of new contributions to learning theory. One of the decisive catalysts in the revival of the Montessori movement has been the work of the American Montessori Society, founded in 1956 by Nancy McCormick Rambusch in Greenwich, Connecticut.[30]

Basic Concepts of the Montessori Method. Montessori's genius lay in her ability to anticipate what a learner was attempting to do in his informational interaction with his environment and then to develop for him a plan providing relevant experiences. Her technology of instruction possessed three characteristics: adaptation of schoolwork to the individuality of each learner; provision for freedom in which the teacher did not dominate the learner nor did the learner become overly dependent on the teacher; and emphasis on sensory discrimination, perhaps the most distinguishing feature of the system.

Two of the basic principles of the Montessori method—respect for the learner's individuality and encouragement of his freedom—determined not only the psychological climate and physical arrangement of the classroom, but the relation of teacher and learner, the instructional media, and the nature of instructional procedures. She used, for example, small, light chairs and tables that the children could rearrange as they chose. Each learner selected from a central room those materials he wished to use, took them to a place that suited him, and proceeded to work in his own way. There was no group instruction, although the children sometimes played group games or did their work together on their own initiative. A teacher was always present to observe and guide. If a learner failed to complete an exercise, he received no penalty; his failure indicated to the teacher that he was not yet ready for the work, and she would suggest some other exercise. Whenever possible, the instructional materials used by the children were self-corrective,

---

[28] See William Heard Kilpatrick, *The Montessori System Examined.* Boston, Houghton Mifflin Company, 1914, p. 10.
[29] See introduction by J. McV. Hunt in Maria Montessori, *The Montessori Method.* New York, Schocken Books, 1964.
[30] Largely through the influence of the American Montessori Society, Montessori schools have been organized throughout the United States. The contemporary Montessori movement revives its historic danger of becoming a cult, which could restrict innovation and experimental research, much as did the cult which developed around Dewey despite his own intentions.

so that learners could discover their own mistakes and become progressively more independent of the teacher.[31]

To reinforce the idea that freedom implies independence from the services of others, small children in the Montessori schools were taught how to dress themselves, keep themselves clean, dust the room, care for school equipment, and help serve lunch. The youngest began with exercises in buttoning, hooking, and lacing pieces of cloth together. Later they learned to walk quietly, to move their chairs without noise, and to be able to handle increasingly delicate objects. At first, the younger children were helped by the older children, but they were encouraged to dispense with aid as soon as possible.

Montessori emphasized the senses, individually and in association with one another, working particularly with visual, muscular, tactile, and auditory sensations. Through sight, sound, and touch, the children learned to distinguish shapes, sizes, weights, textures, colors, and pitch. They were also trained to observe and care for plants, birds, and animals. Thus the Montessori technology of instruction was a blend of three somewhat divergent elements: the two fundamental tenets of learner individuality and freedom, and the specific technique of sensory training.

Contributions of Montessori.   A basic consideration of the contributions of Montessori must be the fact that there was often a sharp divergence between her stated theories and their implementation. In general, her theories were derivative, whereas her practices stemmed from her own clinical observation and her special insights. As a consequence, her instructional procedures often either contradicted her stated theoretical principles or had no apparent relation to them. Thus Montessori often did the right things for the wrong theoretical reasons. However, she considered her system to be completely scientific. And despite the fact that she never employed techniques of measurement, statistical design, or analysis, many of her conceptions do suggest that she built a sounder system of instruction than her critics realized. For example, Montessori's emphasis on "sensory learning," based as it was on her careful observation of mentally retarded children, was closer to reality than the theories of those of her critics who held such stress in contempt. Recent evidence appears to indicate that the role of the eyes and the ears, and perhaps the tactile organs, may be much more important in the organism's development than was thought possible.[32]

---

[31] One of Montessori's exercises consisted of a series of wooden blocks with ten holes of different diameters and ten wooden cylinders just fitting the holes. Since a child could not put a cylinder into a hole too small for it or too large, without having a cylinder left at the end of the exercise, the materials automatically informed him of his errors. This can probably be considered the first "teaching machine." Maria Montessori, *The Montessori Method*, tr. by A. E. George. Philadelphia, J. B. Lippincott Company, 1912, 377 pp.

[32] See O. K. Moore, *Automated Responsive Environments*. Film, parts 1 & 2, Hamden, Conn., Basic Education, Inc., 1960.

Another example from recent data which seems to provide an important psychological basis for Montessori's practice was her notion that children have a spontaneous interest in learning and that motivation is inherent within the organism's interaction with the environment.[33] In accordance with this idea, Montessori attempted to grade didactic materials and match them to those standards which the learner had already developed in the course of his past experience. What is more, by having children aged from three to seven years together, she provided the younger children with a graded series of models for imitation and the older ones with an opportunity to learn by teaching. Thus Montessori succeeded in breaking the lockstep and provided an opportunity for the learner to make his own selection of materials and models.[34]

Of particular relevance to contemporary educational problems of "cultural deprivation" was Montessori's contention that the young learner is characterized by self-creating energies that can be sustained and enhanced by the imaginative and controlled use of environmental materials. Her "prepared environment," so successful with the Italian slum children among whom her work began, deserves renewed study. For example, it is well known that the restriction of childhood experiences to a narrow and drab environment may result in serious psychological damage which is often irremediable.

Modern instructional technology suggests many ways in which Montessori's idea of a prepared environment can be extended. For example, her didactic materials can be expanded through programed instruction, or optimum learning environments can be devised for particular groups of learners. What is more important, Montessori has provided an instructional approach which, when supplemented by experimental research, can provide the basis for a scientific technology of instruction.

Individualized instruction according to Burk, Washburne, Parkhurst, and Morrison

Prior to 1800, instruction in American schools, as we have seen, had been predominantly individual. The introduction of blackboards and slates and the invention of steel pens brought about innovations in methods of instruction. The monitorial method, for example, as used in the Lancasterian schools, was a shift from individual to a more systematized group instruction approach. With the evolution of the graded school, graded instructional materials, and even graded teachers in the middle of the nineteenth century,

[33] See, for example, J. McV. Hunt, "Motivation Inherent in Information Processing and Action," in O. J. Harvey (ed.), *Motivation and Social Interaction: Cognitive Determinants.* New York, The Ronald Press Company, 1963, Chap. 3.
[34] In our present state of knowledge about the proper matching of materials to learners, probably the learner is the only one who can make an appropriate selection.

a lockstep educational machine began to be created that has changed little since those days.

However, beginning in the 1880s, there arose what has become an almost continuous interest in individualizing instruction. One of the first attempts to break the lockstep of graded instruction came with the general introduction of the laboratory method about 1885. Each student was encouraged to initiate individual experimental procedures, and the laboratory was made a definitive core of his learning experience. Moreover, a number of individualized instructional materials such as stereographs, scientific apparatus, construction materials, hand tools, study prints, self-checking devices, and diagnostic tests were utilized.

Burk's System of Individualized Instruction.   Frederic Burk (1862–1924) developed one of the first systems of individualized instruction at the San Francisco State Normal School, in 1912.[35] He and his faculty rewrote courses of study to permit learners to advance at their own rate of progress with a minimum of teacher direction. Self-instruction bulletins in arithmetic, geography, grammar, history, language, and phonics were written, published, and distributed throughout the United States and in foreign countries. Over one hundred thousand bulletins were sold without any advertising—or profit to the authors. However, a 1917 ruling of the California attorney general abruptly stopped their publication, as the power to publish textbooks or printed instructional materials was judged to rest entirely with the State Board of Education. As a result of the California ruling, the fruitful work begun by Burk was curtailed. It remained for two of his associates, Carleton W. Washburne and Helen Parkhurst, to develop two of the most outstanding and distinctive plans of individual instruction.

Washburne's Winnetka Plan.   The Winnetka Plan was developed by Carleton W. Washburne (1890–   ) when he was appointed superintendent of the Winnetka, Illinois, public schools in 1919. The plan provided for self-instructional and self-corrective practice materials (workbooks), a simple record system on which each pupil's progress was noted, and prepared materials appropriate to each pupil's particular project and assignment. Thus, the twofold problem of the faculty was to analyze course content into specific objectives and to develop a plan of instruction that would enable the learner to master each of the objectives at his own rate.

[35] A member of Burk's faculty, Mary Ward, deserves the credit for initiating the Burk program. After trying an informal experiment with self-instructional materials with a small group of students, she explained to Burk what she had done and its successful results. Burk was impressed with her approach and proposed that every teacher-supervisor begin with the preparation of self-instructional bulletins in his subject for the classes he supervised. At first, these bulletins were used with existing textbooks, but in time they became complete in themselves.

The Winnetka Plan not only provided for learners to proceed at different rates but also recognized that the learners proceeded at different rates in different subjects. As a result, diagnostic tests were given each learner to determine what goals and tasks he should undertake. When the learner thought he had accomplished his goals, he took a self-administered test to see whether he was ready for testing by the teacher and whether he was prepared to undertake new goals and tasks.[36]

Parkhurst's Dalton Plan.   The Dalton Plan, first developed by Helen Parkhurst (1887–   ) in 1919 in an ungraded school for crippled children, was adopted by the Dalton, Massachusetts, High School in 1920. Its principal features were: differentiation of assignments for different ability levels, self-instructional practice materials, and assistance with individual study difficulties. Under this plan, the teacher made a contract with the student concerning his assignments. Having undertaken it, the student was free to budget his time in completing the contract. His only limitation was that he could not receive another contract until he had completed every phase of the one he had in progress.[37]

Group activities in both the Winnetka and the Dalton Plans were not neglected, but the emphasis was placed on individualized instruction. The Winnetka Plan, however, emphasized group activities more than the Dalton Plan, devoting approximately half of each morning and afternoon to such activities as plays, music, student government, and open forums. In both plans, classrooms became laboratories or conference rooms, and teachers became consultants or guides.[38]

The Morrison Plan.   Another instructional proposal, highly influential from about 1925 to 1935, was that of Henry Clinton Morrison (1871–1945), former director of the University of Chicago High School. His system provided for units [39] in sequence, and guide sheets for lesson assignments. The classroom was viewed as a laboratory where units and assignments were

[36] For a comprehensive report on the Winnetka Plan, see Carleton W. Washburne and Sidney P. Marland, *Winnetka: The History and Significance of an Educational Experiment.* Englewood Cliffs, N.J., Prentice-Hall, Inc., 1963. The Winnetka Plan has continued to be implemented along the pattern established by Washburne. Meanwhile, other schools in various sections of the United States have introduced a compromise between the Winnetka Plan and traditional practice.
[37] See H. H. Parkhurst, *Education on the Dalton Plan.* London, G. Bell & Sons, Ltd., 1922. In this book, Helen Parkhurst refers to her earlier associations with Maria Montessori.
[38] The Dalton Plan has generally been discontinued: too many pupils accepted the freedom but neglected their responsibility. However, the New York City Dalton School still uses the Plan.
[39] Although the term *unit* was employed prior to Morrison, it was Morrison who apparently inaugurated its widespread usage. Today the term is such a standard part of educational terminology that it is not often realized how recent is its origin. What is more, its use today does not usually follow the Morrison pattern but more frequently refers to long-term assignments of two to three weeks or more, in contrast to daily lesson assignments.

differentiated for learners of varying ability. Morrison's formula for mastery was: "Pretest, teach, test the result, adapt procedure, teach and test again to the point of actual learning." [40]

For science-type units or those designed for developing understanding, Morrison devised a five-step procedure reminiscent of Herbart's four-step plan, as follows: exploration, presentation, assimilation, organization, recitation. Exploration was a test to determine how much each learner already knew of the unit or how much understanding he possessed. Presentation usually involved a lecture, which provided an overview or summary of the unit as a whole and explained the principle to be learned. Assimilation represented the achievement of unit understanding. When the learner passed a mastery test, he terminated the assimilation period and reached the organization phase. Morrison referred to the period of organization as the time when the learner provided a written reproduction of a unit in outline form, discussing the logical argumentation supporting the basic understanding or principle embodied in the unit. Recitation was practically the reverse of the first step, presentation: now the learner presented, orally, to the teacher and his classmates, a summary version of the principle learned in the unit.

Morrison's plan called for individualized instruction, but unlike Washburne's Winnetka Plan, each class began and ended each unit together. Moreover, learners tended to remain together through all the steps with the exception of step three, assimilation, when each was on his own. In order to inform each learner what was expected of him, a "guide sheet," or worksheet, was provided. The teacher maintained close supervision as the learners worked, reading their notebooks, conversing with them, or conducting group discussions.

Analysis of Individualized Instructional Plans. The significance of the individualized instructional plans we have discussed lay in their attempt to provide for individual differences in learning and, at the same time, teach for specific objectives. A study of the contemporary programed instruction approach reveals that these early individualized instructional plans anticipated much of what has been termed as today's "major breakthrough" in education.[41]

[40] See Henry C. Morrison, *The Practice of Teaching in the Secondary School.* Chicago, The University of Chicago Press, 1931, p. 81.

[41] Preston W. Search (1853–1932) organized an individualized instructional program as early as 1877 at West Liberty, Ohio. When he became superintendent of the Pueblo, Colorado, public schools in 1888, Search introduced his now fully developed plan which practically dispensed with home study and recitations. Instead, the school day became a working period or a kind of laboratory where pupils mastered their assignments as rapidly as their differing abilities permitted. Although there were inadequate instruments or hardware for recording or checking pupil progress, the results were startling. Some pupils completed their work in half the normal time. This method was discontinued after Search left to become superintendent of schools in Los Angeles where he was unsuccessful in establishing his plan. See P. W. Search, *An Ideal School.* New York, D. Appleton & Company, Inc., 1901.

At this point, it seems relevant to note that the meaning of the phrase "science of education" was expanded by Washburne and others (such as Bobbitt and Charters) [42] to mean not only basing a technology of instruction on scientific principles but also employing statistical analysis of the kind of activities people most frequently perform or of the kinds of information or words most frequently used as a basis for selecting curriculum content.

These individualized instructional plans made an outstanding contribution to instructional technology by breaking the lockstep method of learner progress and substituting mastery learning for partial learning. They opposed the concept of a normal distribution curve or the notion that only a small percentage of learners should complete the period of study with a thorough mastery of the subject. They enabled learners to progress at their own rate but required that each reach an approved level of achievement as a requisite for advancement to another level.

Another contribution of these particular methods to a technology of instruction was their emphasis on careful organization of assignments. The necessity of organizing materials on an individual basis often brought with it a deeper appreciation of the nature of the learning process and the realization that much could be eliminated from courses which had formerly been considered essential. Moreover, the teachers involved in these programs found that they had to analyze their own instructional materials more carefully than when they had employed traditional procedures. Thus individualized instruction led to a technology for organizing the curriculum as well as to a technology of instruction.

Lewin's field theory and a science of instruction

The series of experimental studies directed by Kurt Lewin (1890–1947) at the University of Berlin in the late 1920s, were models of theoretical creativity combined with brilliant experimentation. Although Lewin was associated with an active center of gestalt psychology at Berlin, his theories had little formal relationship to those of the orthodox gestaltists.[43] Lewin's early

---

[42] Franklin Bobbitt (1876–1952), professor of education at the University of Chicago, proposed an "activity analysis" of the broad range of human experience into its major fields in order to arrive at an effective curriculum and sound instructional objectives. See Franklin Bobbitt, *How to Make a Curriculum.* Boston, Houghton Mifflin Company, 1924. Merritt W. Charters (1875–1956), another pioneer in activity or job analysis, contended that educational aims were far too general to be effectively translated into teaching directives. Consequently, by careful analysis, he broke the broad aims down into their constituent parts. This approach met opposition from educational philosophers, especially Boyd H. Bode (1873–1953), who claimed that science was not equipped to determine educational aims.

[43] Max Wertheimer (1880–1943), Kurt Koffka (1886–1941), and Wolfgang Köhler (1887–1967), who had been together as research students at the University of Berlin, founded the gestalt school of psychology about 1912, while working together at the

work on motivational problems led to an interest in personality organization and a wide variety of problems in social psychology, culminating in his development of the group dynamics movement and action research (i.e., research directed at producing social changes). He also concerned himself with the problem of constructing scientific principles of learning as the basis for a science of instruction. In all these diverse areas, Lewin took the same fundamental approach: emphasis on the psychological rather than on the simple, environmental factors in a communication situation or field.

A native of Germany, Lewin received his doctorate at the University of Berlin, where he later became a professor of psychology and philosophy. He came to the United States in 1932 and taught at the universities at Stanford, Cornell, and Iowa. In 1944, he was named director of the Research Center for Group Dynamics at the Massachusetts Institute of Technology, where he remained until his untimely death in 1947.

Lewin's General Theoretical Approach. It is not our purpose here to review the substance of Lewin's field psychology, since excellent expositions of this position are readily available.[44] Our primary concern is, rather, to point to Lewin's general theoretical orientation, so that the reader may have a clearer understanding of the constructs underlying his theory of learning.

Although Lewin began his scientific career as an associationist, he soon became convinced that the associationist concept of learning had to be radically revised. Moreover, he also diverged from the views of the major gestalt psychologists and said: "Psychology cannot try to explain everything with a single construct, such as association, instinct, or gestalt. A variety of constructs has to be used. These should be interrelated, however, in a logically precise manner."[45]

To Lewin, scientific method included not only the processes of observation and classification of data but also those of formulating and testing hypotheses. He stressed the importance of theory by stating that "a science without theory is blind because it lacks that element which alone is able to organize facts and give direction to research."[46] He was also convinced that, in order to understand and predict learner behavior, he had to focus his

---

Psychological Institute in Frankfurt-am-Main. They began by criticizing the analytical methods of connectionism and associationism, contending that learning does not arise from a specific response to a specific stimulus but rather as the individual sees the whole pattern (or gestalt) in a situation and changes his behavior in accordance with the pervading character of the situation. Thus the learner responds as a whole organism and not automatically, or mechanically, through specific reflexes.

[44] For example, see Ernest R. Hilgard, *Theories of Learning*, 2d ed. New York, Appleton-Century-Crofts, Inc., 1956.

[45] Kurt Lewin, "Formalization and Progress in Psychology," *University of Iowa Studies in Child Welfare*, vol. 16, no. 3 (1940), p. 16.

[46] Kurt Lewin, *Principles of Topological Psychology*. New York, McGraw-Hill Book Company, 1936, p. 4.

attention on careful, full descriptions of particular, learner-environmental instructional situations.

In order to portray his conceptualization of psychological processes, Lewin chose topological geometry [47] as the best mathematical model for adequately representing concepts broad enough to be applicable to all kinds of behavior and, at the same time, specific enough to represent a definite person in a concrete situation. Since topology lacked directive concepts, Lewin invented a new hodological (from the Greek *hodos,* translated as "path") space geometry, which he used to represent certain dynamic factors in psychological relationships.

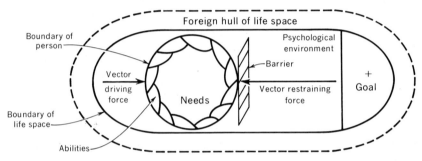

Fig. 4.3   Life space of an individual according to Lewin.

Lewin formulated three key constructs—life space, topology, and vector. He defined life space as the whole of one's psychological reality, or the total pattern of factors or influences which affect behavior at any one time. He also viewed life space as a dynamic series of events in which a person and his environment are in simultaneous, mutual interaction, and are mutually inter-dependent. Topological concepts were used by Lewin to represent the structure of a life space in such a way as to define the range of possible perceptions and actions. He accomplished this by showing the arrangement of the functional parts of a life space in terms of regions and boundaries and indicated that, when an individual structures or makes sense of his life space, he divides it into regions. For example, if the region "eating" is located in a person's life space, the person is either engaging in, or thinking about engaging in, that activity.

[47] Topology is a nonmetrical geometry which encompasses concepts such as inside, outside, and boundary but has no dealings with length, breadth, or thickness. No distances are defined. Rather, topology is concerned with the relative position of the geometric figures being considered. Topologically, things may be next to, inside, or outside one another. Size or shape has no significance in a topological figure. It may be helpful to think of a topological plane figure as being made of a perfectly elastic sheet of rubber which we may stretch, twist, pull, and bend, but the relationships it represents remain the same. See H. Arnold Bradford, *Intuitive Concepts in Elementary Topology.* Englewood Cliffs, N.J., Prentice-Hall, Inc., 1962, p. 24.

Lewin used the concept vector to represent direction and strength as two of the three properties of a force. The third property is its point of application. Thus Lewin saw vectors symbolizing the tendencies of the life space to change or to resist change. For example, both driving and restraining forces may arise from the needs and abilities of a particular learner, from the actions of another person, or from the impersonal aspects of an instructional situation. Lewin's guiding formula, based on a summary of his work, could be written

$$B = f(P,E)$$

Behavior depends on the interaction of the Person and the Environment within a psychological field, or life space.

Lewin's Cognitive-field Theory of Learning.   Lewin's cognitive-field theory of learning often is called merely "field theory." However, "cognitive field" is more truly descriptive, since it describes how a learner comes to know (from the Latin verb *cognoscere,* which means "to know") or gains insights into himself and his environment and how, using his insights or cognitions, he acts in relation to his environment.

Learning, to Lewin, was perceived as problem solving—seeking perceptions to restructure the cognitive field, acting in ways to overcome barriers, and incorporating these understandings (or insights and ways of behaving) into a newly reorganized life space. Within this process, he distinguished four kinds of change, namely: change in cognitive structure (knowledge); change in motivation (learning to like or dislike); changing into group belongingness or ideology; and gain in voluntary control and dexterity of musculature.

Implications of Field Theory for a Technology of Instruction.   Within a field approach to instructional communication, each teacher's unique function is to implement the development of useful insights so as to help students become more adequate or more intelligent in whatever situation they find themselves. To accomplish this, a technology of instruction built around the field concept must provide for analysis of the instructional situation as a whole. According to Lewin,

> A teacher will never succeed in giving proper guidance to a child if he does not learn to understand the psychological world in which the individual child lives. To describe a situation "objectively" in psychology actually means to describe the situation as a totality of those facts, and of only those facts, which make up the field of the individual. To substitute for that world of the individual the world of the teacher, of the physicist, or of anybody else is to be, not objective, but wrong.[48]

[48] See Kurt Lewin, *Field Theory in Social Science.* New York, Harper & Row, Publishers, Incorporated, 1951, p. 62.

The Lewin field theory of learning can be used as a starting point for the technical analysis of instructional communication. One way to accomplish this would be to ask what characteristics would have to be built into a scientific technology of instruction that would symbolically, as well as functionally, represent the following three interrelated aspects in the instructional situation or field: (1) the teacher-communicator and his production and/or manipulation of a body of sign-symbol material with the intent of cognitively structuring the field of specific learners who are perceived in terms of specific needs and demands; (2) the learner-communicant who perceives or cognitively structures a specific body of sign-symbol material produced by specific teacher-communicators in terms of his present pattern of needs, expectancies, and demands; and (3) the nature of the instructional message as part of an organized, planned stimulus field in which sign-symbol materials are produced and utilized with the intent of structuring the cognitive-perceptual fields of both the teacher and the learner via single or multimedia communication channels.

Thus, the central task of the teacher-communicator in the Lewinian theoretical context is essentially creative, because it involves the unique potentialities of signs and symbols, the structuring of content, and a particular relationship with the learner and/or learners in terms of how he or they perceive the instructional communication situation and what he or they want in it.

Contributions of Lewin.   Lewin made historic contributions to the development of psychology as a behavioral science. His particular contributions to instructional technology were in the areas of child psychology and social psychology, exemplified by his early research on behavior in social climates that had been experimentally manipulated.[49] For example, leadership techniques were experimentally varied in boys' clubs (laissez-faire, democratic, autocratic), and various behaviors, such as aggression, were correlated with the different social climates that resulted. These studies not only opened an important new area of social research but have held significant implications for a technology of instruction.

Lewin's contributions to psychological theory were of great scope and originality. He developed concepts and experimental techniques, such as level of aspiration, that have had an important influence on modern instructional technology.

[49] For example, three of the present emphases within motivational theory have direct connections with Lewin's "level of aspiration." One of these is the achievement motivation concept of McClelland and his associates; another is cognitive dissonance, associated with Festinger; the third is cognitive balance, a theory developed by Heider.

A technology of instruction according to Skinner

In essence, B. F. Skinner's (1904–   ) psychology, operant conditioning or behaviorism, is a modern extension of the earlier stimulus-response psychologies—connectionism, as developed by Thorndike, and behaviorism, as developed by Watson. Thorndike dealt with both physical and mental elements but was always mechanistic in his study of man. Watson, too, was mechanistic, but he limited his study to the behavior of biological organisms. Skinner, like both Thorndike and Watson, assumes that man is neutral and passive and that all behavior can be described in mechanistic terms.

A professor at Harvard University since 1947, Skinner was influenced by the research of Pavlov and Watson while attending Harvard as a graduate student in biology. Following several years of postdoctoral fellowships, he taught at the University of Minnesota and at Indiana University before returning to Harvard to join the faculty. Skinner has displayed great breadth of interest and ingenuity in his experimental work.[50] He has concerned himself with an analysis of verbal learning, with "missile-guiding pigeons," with teaching machines, and with the control of behavior by scheduled reinforcement.

His goal is a science of behavior in which the basic order of nature can be discovered, including human nature, for the purpose of achieving predictability and control of human behavior. To Skinner, a science of instruction must be based on operant reinforcement in which sets of learner acts are reinforced, or strengthened, so as to increase the probability of their recurrence in the future. In this process, it is essential that teachers use properly timed and spaced schedules of reinforcement.

Skinner's System of Operant Conditioning.   Skinner's basic thesis is that, since an organism tends in the future to do what it was doing at the time of reinforcement, one can lead it to do much what the experimenter or the teacher wishes it to do. For example, Skinner taught rats to use a marble to obtain food from a vending machine, pigeons to play a modified game of tennis, and dogs to operate the pedal of a refuse can in order to retrieve a bone. He has concentrated his study on lower animals because their behavior is simpler, their surrounding conditions may be more easily controlled, and techniques for observation of them may be less complicated.[51]

[50] His accomplishments include a novel on a utopian theme, *Walden Two* (1948), and the invention of an automatized baby-tending device which has been commercially marketed.

[51] For his animal studies, Skinner invented the "Skinner box," a simple form of puzzle box made to contain a rat, a lever, and a device for delivering a pellet of food each time the rat pressed the lever. Recording devices were set outside the box to record the responses of the rat during the experimenter's absence.

On the basis of many experiments with rats, pigeons, and other animals, Skinner has developed his psychological theory of operant conditioning. However, Skinner considers his methodological approach to be strictly atheoretical, because he has long felt that the state of knowledge in psychology is inadequate to justify elaborate, formal theorizing, particularly physiological speculations. Skinner also insists on a thorough analysis of the behavior of a single organism, rather than of large groups of subjects.

In operant conditioning, the important stimulus is the one immediately following a response, not the one preceding it. Any emitted response which leads to reinforcement is thereby strengthened. According to this viewpoint, it is not the specific response that is strengthened but rather the general tendency to make the response. The law of operant conditioning is that, if the occurrence of an operant is followed by presentation of a reinforcing stimulus, the strength probability is increased.

Translating this concept into instructional terms, it implies that the key to successful instruction is to analyze the effect of reinforcement and design techniques and to set up specific, reinforcing sequences in which a response is followed by a reinforcing stimulus. Thus the implementation of operant conditioning occurs, for example, when a child is taught reading by reinforcing him with "Right" or "Wrong" according to his response to appropriate, visual stimuli. Implicit in operant behaviorism is the conviction that "when all relevant variables have been arranged, an organism will or will not respond. If it does not, it cannot. If it can, it will." [52]

A Technology of Instruction Based on Operant Conditioning.   Skinner is convinced that operant conditioning, so fruitful when applied to animal training, holds great possibilities for more complex instruction. He feels that the most efficient control of human learning requires instrumental aid and that steps should be taken to rectify the shortcomings of traditional instructional practice by developing a scientific technology of instruction.

For example, Skinner has criticized the conventional instructional procedures as being dominated by aversion stimulation and lacking a planned program of serial reinforcement. Thus, according to him, a learner is usually trying to escape from or to keep away from something, or there is an excessive time lapse between behavior and reinforcement, or desirable behavior may not be reinforced at all. Skinner contends that a test taken near the end of a week is too far removed from the behaviors the learners emitted (sent out) while studying the subject matter earlier in the week. Reinforcing stimuli, Skinner says, should follow the response immediately.

According to Skinner, in order to develop a technology of instruction based on operant conditioning, certain specific questions need to be answered: (1) What behavior is to be established? (2) What reinforcers are

[52] B. F. Skinner, *Science and Behavior*. New York, The Macmillan Company, 1953, p. 112.

available? (3) What responses are available? (4) How can reinforcements be most efficiently scheduled? [53] According to this view, the teacher is the builder and architect of behaviors and he must establish specific learner objectives and define them in terms of desired behaviors. Skinner contends, however, that the teacher is out of date as a mere reinforcing mechanism and must use mechanical and electrical devices if there is to be an efficient control of learning in an organism.

In order to schedule reinforcements efficiently, Skinner means to make them contingent on the desired behavior. Here, says Skinner,

> The whole process of becoming competent in any field must be divided into a very large number of very small steps, and reinforcement must be contingent upon the accomplishment of each step. . . . By making each successive step as small as possible, the frequency of reinforcement can be raised to a maximum, while the possibly aversive consequences of being wrong are reduced to a minimum.[54]

This is the purpose of programed instruction, according to the Skinnerian concept. In Skinner's view, teaching machines encourage learners to take an "active" role in the instructional process because they must develop the answers before they can be reinforced. In building a case for teaching machines, Skinner states, "the effect upon each student is surprisingly like that of a private tutor." [55]

Influence of Skinner.   Skinner's influence guided the mainstream of developments in programed instruction during the late fifties and early sixties. Historically, the term *program*, as applied to a sequence of instruction presented by a teaching machine, derived from his 1954 and 1958 papers.[56] In some respects, Skinner represents a renewal of Watsonian behaviorism. Like Watson, he too has attracted to him many young experimenters eager to make behavior study an exact science. These Skinnerians, as they are often called, resenting the orthodox restrictions of the American Psychological Association's journals (particularly the unwritten regulations concerning sample size and statistical tests), established their own journal, *Journal of the Experimental Analysis of Behavior.*

Contemporary status of instructional technology

From our foregoing survey of selected instructional theories and methods, it should be clear that almost every system of instruction we have dis-

---

[53] *Ibid.,* pp. 152–153.
[54] *Ibid.,* p. 153.
[55] B. F. Skinner, "Teaching Machines," *Science,* vol. 128 (Oct. 24, 1958), p. 971.
[56] B. F. Skinner, "The Science of Learning and the Art of Teaching," *Harvard Educational Review,* vol. 24 (1954), pp. 86–97; "Teaching Machines," *op. cit.,* pp. 969–977.

cussed, from the time of Comenius to the present day, has left a residue of theory and technique in contemporary educational practice. The other impressive fact that emerges is the painfully slow rate of development of a scientific technology of instruction. For example, the science-of-education concept advanced by Thorndike in the beginning of this century has still scarcely penetrated the professional educational community, much less the lay world. Moreover, reflective teaching, as a methodology, has developed slowly. Dewey's *How We Think* was highly praised when it first appeared in 1910; yet scientific instructional approaches have never been widely employed. However, the recent efforts of the curriculum-revision commissions, sponsored largely by the National Science Foundation, do emphasize a reflective-scientific instructional orientation, especially in the sciences and mathematics.

Today, a search of the literature reveals (1) a general lack of agreement upon instructional technology concepts and (2) absence of a synthesis of these concepts into a general theory or theories of instruction that might be tested by empirical research. While volumes have been devoted to theories of learning, instruction has been almost completely neglected. What is needed are theories of instruction which *prescribe* what the teacher should do to improve learning, as well as theories of learning which *describe* what the learner does, and theories of communication which *explain* the interaction of teacher and learner. In effect, theories of instruction can serve a mediating function between learning theory and communication theory.

Before a science and technology of instruction can be developed, however, centers for instructional R & D [57] must be established. The major objective would be the development of prototype model instructional systems which could improve and advance instructional practice. Behavioral scientists, instructional technologists, subject-matter specialists, school administrators, teachers, and various skilled craftsmen could work together to develop and introduce instructional innovations (tools, organizational patterns, materials, methods) into the educational system. Within this context there could develop a science of instruction which would serve as a fundamental guide to educational practice.

Certain medical and engineering schools and institutes, as well as military and industrial training R & D centers, suggest patterns for instructional R & D centers. Gilbert, for example, has described a pattern for instructional R & D based on the pattern of an R & D industrial organization [58] (Bell Telephone). He sees the components of such an organization as being (1) ex-

---

[57] Henceforth, the abbreviation R & D will be used in this book to designate research and development.

[58] Thomas F. Gilbert, "A Structure for a Coordinated Research and Development Laboratory," in Robert Glaser (ed.), *Training Research and Education*. Pittsburgh, The University of Pittsburgh Press, 1962, pp. 559–578.

ploratory research (theoretical); (2) fundamental development; (3) specific development; (4) design and proving; and (5) training and follow-through.

Exploratory research, or what is often called basic research, is directed toward the increase of knowledge and is characterized by questioning attitudes and freedom to explore the general problem areas in which the research is focused. The second research function, fundamental development, gives necessary continuity to carrying knowledge from theory to practice and consists of laboratory investigation of instructional variables which may have some potential relevance to exploratory investigations. The next step, specific development, involves the development of prototype instructional models or systems which would serve the purpose of testing preceding research, identifying unsuspected problems, and generally refining the system in anticipation of general use. The fourth step, design and testing, is an extension of the preceding step and involves the demonstration of the effectiveness of the instructional system in a variety of field situations. In the final step of R & D, training and follow-through mean the introduction and application of the method or instructional system into educational practice, and the follow-up of further tests and evaluations in terms of efficiency, design refinement, and suggested problems for experiment.

The shortage of teachers, classrooms, equipment, and the lack of investment for a comprehensive R & D program indicates that the American educational system today is out of technological equilibrium with large sectors of our society. As such, it can be viewed as a relatively primitive or underdeveloped, nontechnological folk culture—technologically isolated from the more sophisticated cultures of industry, business, the military, and the scientific. A historical and cultural analysis of some of the factors contributing to this status has been cogently presented by Travers.[59]

The U.S. Office of Education in recent years has taken the first steps in implementing a comprehensive R & D program by funding R & D centers. The significance of these centers cannot be underestimated. For the first time in the history of American instructional technology, instructional theory and methods will be experimentally investigated, and tested concepts will be embodied in educational practice. Moreover, these centers can provide a model of the research process and can serve to upgrade instructional research as well as to increase its quantity and bring about a wider dissemination of research results. Perhaps, most significantly, this development may set a precedent by making instructional research a matter of national policy and by transforming American instructional technology into an applied behavioral science.

[59] Robert M. W. Travers, "A Study of the Relationship of Psychological Research to Educational Practice," in *ibid.*, pp. 525–558.

part 2

**toward a technology
of instruction**

Introduction

F. Dean McClusky, *Professor Emeritus of Education, University of California, Los Angeles*

Knowledge spread rapidly after the invention, in the fifteenth century, of the printing press which used movable type. The letterpress and the books it produced laid the foundation for education of the masses. But it took nearly four hundred years for the structure of the public school to be built on that foundation in Western Europe and the United States.

As textbooks became the basis of educational content, classroom methodology became formalized. There were those with keen insight who recognized the dangers of memoriter linguistic drills and who spoke out for more meaningful methods in instruction. Their voices were overshadowed at first by the exigencies of keeping pace with the rapid spread of educational opportunities for the many who had to be taught how to read, to write, and to cipher.

In Part 1 of this book, Saettler has made the point that for centuries many educators have advocated systematic technologies of instruction. During the eighteenth and nineteenth centuries, there was a strong trend in educational philosophy toward making instruction less abstract and less formalized. Toward the latter part of the nineteenth century, however, the writings of realists such as Locke, Rousseau, and Pestalozzi began to be heeded and to influence educational methods in Western Europe and America. The coming of the machine age and the realization that all who went to school could not enter white-collar jobs implemented the growing demand for more practical curricula and more functional methodologies. A wholesome distrust of "book learning," as such, was to be found in many quarters. However, educators in general were slow to adopt new techniques of communication as they became available at the close of the nineteenth century. Evolving slowly were ideas on how best to use new media, such as the museum exhibit, the photograph, the projected still picture, and the motion picture, in instruction.

There were pioneers, of course, who experimented with the new media, and they made history. But the impact of their efforts on the broad stream of instruction caused little more than a ripple on the surface. Education is conservative. It takes time to bring about widespread changes in content and methodology. It was twenty-three years after the establishment of the first unit for the administration of visual media in public schools that the first comprehensive book on the use of the new media in schools was published.[1] In fact, the early label "visual education" came into widespread use and acceptance more than a decade after the first educational museums were established at St. Louis (1905), Reading (1908), and Cleveland (1909), and more than twenty-five years after New York State began to collect and distribute lantern slides for the public schools.

One factor which characterized general overall thinking about the use of the new media in education, at top policy-making levels, was specialization in the production and administration of instructional media. At the outset, following the turn of the century, commercial interests producing media for school purposes centered on one or two media. Many companies still do. Certain companies made blackboards, others produced slides, some produced motion pictures, others concentrated on maps and models, one centered on sets of slides and stereographs, others produced slidefilms, and some specialized in recordings.

Parallel with specialization by producers of media there was specialization in the administration of instructional media. For example, New York State's Division of Visual Education collected and distributed lantern slides only. The St. Louis Educational Museum concentrated on exhibits. The University of California's Department of Visual Education in University Extension distributed motion pictures only. In a number of universities, the department of visual instruction was in charge of the distribution of motion pictures and another department was charged with education by radio. During the 1930s, there was at one time a national association of visual educationists, a national association of educators specializing in school excursions, and a national association of those in charge of education by radio. As time went on, there were those who administered audiovisual materials under one central unit and who tried to develop a rationale for the value and place of each device in instruction.[2]

---

[1] Anna Verona Dorris, *Visual Instruction in the Public Schools*. Boston, Ginn and Company, 1928.
[2] St. Louis may be cited as a case in point. In 1943 the name of the Educational Museum was changed to the Division of Audio-Visual Education. The division administered all types of audiovisual media.

The commercial interests competed with each other for the school's dollar and in so doing sold their wares under the overall label "visual education." All this fragmentation was confusing to teachers and administrators. To some, visual education meant the motion picture, and to others, visual education centered in the museum. The competition was between things rather than ideas. As a result, the advancement of instructional technology on the whole suffered.

Two contemporary companies of the early 1920s may be cited to illustrate the point. The Keystone View Company of Meadville, Pennsylvania, specialized in the production and sale of lantern slides and in duplicating stereographs for school use. Its teachers' guide to the famous "Keystone 600 Set" carried the title Visual Education. *Keystone salesmen sold, as visual education, slides and stereographs only. Their sales vocabulary did not include the motion picture or other instructional media.*

A competing company, the Society for Visual Education, Inc., of Chicago, Illinois, produced motion pictures and published a magazine entitled Visual Education. *SVE's salesmen sold motion pictures only, and advocated the use of motion pictures in instruction.*[3] *Both companies, failing to expand as time passed and new concepts developed, have faded into minor roles in the picture.*

Motion pictures, radio broadcasts, lantern slides, objects, models, charts, maps, television, recordings, field trips, exhibits, and teaching machines, like the theater, are media for expression. From the educational point of view it is "that which appears on the screen" [4] *that is important, just as the ideas expressed on the printed page are important, not the paper nor type font. From the standpoint of content for teaching, there are good dramas and bad dramas, good textbooks and bad textbooks, good teaching films and bad teaching films, good field trips and bad field trips, good charts and bad charts, good exhibits and bad exhibits, good pictures and bad pictures, and so on. It goes without saying that even the use of specific instructional media does not always result in effective instruction. There must be a technology of instruction in which men, machines, methods, procedures, and organization are coordinated in the interest of more effective learning.*

[3] Later, when it failed to make ends meet with the motion picture, SVE concentrated on the production of slidefilms and the projectors for them.

[4] "That which appears on the screen" is a generalization intended to apply to all media of expression. It could be written "that which appears on the chart," or "that which appears in the exhibit," or "that which appears on the map," and so on.

Space does not permit us to do more than indicate some guidelines for readers in this introduction to Part 2. It has been stated that educators in general were slow to develop a systematic technology of instruction and that ideas and concepts governing the effective use of media in schools were slow to develop. Aside from the inherent conservatism of education, specialization with certain media by producers and by educators caused confusion. For this reason, progress in the overall development of a rationale for instructional technology was delayed.

Despite the slow pace with which the use of instructional media progressed at first, the growth in acceptance and use of the products of technology has been substantial and has accelerated during the past twenty-five years. This has been particularly true since World War II, during which instructional technology made an immeasurable contribution to the rapid training of millions of people who served in the Armed Forces and in industry. Today the number of educational media administrative units in state, county, city, town, university, college, religious, and industrial categories, spread geographically throughout the United States, is in the hundreds. Instructional media and/or communication specialists are to be numbered in four figures. A comprehensive bibliography of published books, monographs, research reports, and magazine articles would total over ten thousand items.

Instructional technology has not developed to its present status without a struggle. It has had to compete for recognition and financial support in a rapidly growing nationwide educational program, which has been characterized by many administrative innovations and a shortage of funds. To cite a few examples since 1900, consider the rapid growth of senior high schools in number and influence, the coming of the junior high school, the junior college movement, and the growth of the land-grant colleges and universities.

This is not all. During the period from 1900 to the present, we have had two world wars, a major depression, and the advent of the space age. The latter has put pressure on American education to teach more, to teach better, and to teach in less time. Despite the increasing demands on the school dollar, appropriations have increased to support programs and research leading to a science and technology of instruction.

To a historian, the lack of unity in the development of a technology of instruction poses the problem of how to treat the various facets of the field. Thus, an historian writing on the growth *of instructional technology in general as Saettler has, in Part 2 of this book, must blend the development of things and the development of ideas. The fragmented portions of the development of instructional technology must be tied together. This Saettler has done with considerable skill.*

chapter 5

origins of school
museums

Because of their significant role in laying the groundwork for a modern technology of instruction, it seems appropriate to begin Part 2 of this book with the contribution of the school museums. School museums began the first systematic experiments in the preparation of exhibits for instructional purposes. As part of this approach, they developed some of the first instructional system prototypes in which new content, methods, materials, and media were introduced in American education.[1] Thus the school museums were the true antecedents of modern instructional technology in American public schools.

[1] For a comprehensive discussion of the contributions of museums to education, see Grace Fisher Ramsey, *Educational Work in Museums of the United States.* New York, The H. W. Wilson Company, 1938.

Forerunners of school museums

The word "museum" originally meant "a temple of the Muses," and it was applied metaphorically to any place where literature and the arts were cultivated. The most famous example in antiquity was the Museum of Alexander. When this museum was destroyed, the term fell into disuse. The modern practice of forming collections of relics and specimens of natural history probably dates from the secret scientific societies established in Italy during the fifteenth and sixteenth centuries when the Roman Catholic Church was unfriendly to the exponents of experimental science. At the same time, the Renaissance revival of interest in classical antiquities and in the collection of objects led rulers and the wealthy classes to assemble collections of ancient statuary, inscriptions, gems, coins, medals, manuscripts, plants, and minerals, as well as religious relics, magical objects, and paintings.

Great social movements have always been closely tied to the popularization of knowledge, and promoting this diffusion of learning has constituted an important part of museum history. In England, the publication of Chamber's *Cyclopedia* was contemporary with the creation of the British Museum (1753); France opened the doors of the royal collections of Luxembourg at the same time the program of the Encyclopedists was first published.

The two oldest museums in America were both founded by societies. The museum at Charleston, South Carolina (1773), was designed to exhibit the natural resources of the province of South Carolina; in Salem, Massachusetts, the East India Marine Society Museum (now a part of the Peabody Museum) became the repository in 1799 for the collections of ship captains gathered from all portions of the globe.

The first half of the nineteenth century saw the rise of a number of museums supported by learned societies and colleges, among them the Pennsylvania Academy of Fine Arts (1805), Bowdoin College Art Museum (1811), Academy of Natural Sciences of Philadelphia (1812), New York Academy of Sciences (1815), Allegheny College Museum (1820), Boston Society of Natural History (1830), Wesleyan University Museum (1831), and the Portland Society of Natural History (1843). (The New York Academy of Sciences is probably the spiritual parent of the American Museum of Natural History.) This first era of museum development in the United States came to an end with the founding of the United States National Museum in 1846.

The very early establishment of college museums of natural history was a logical consequence of American interest in natural history. The purpose of these museums was unqualifiedly educational, with their primary objective that of impressing students and the visiting public with the order of creation in terms of natural theology. Much of our popular education in natural history has, in fact, been derived from such early college museums as the Dartmouth College Collection, started in 1783; the Mineralogical Collection of the University Museum at Harvard, begun in 1784; the Peabody Museum of Natural History, founded by Yale in 1802; and the University of Ohio Museum (Athens, Ohio), dating from 1823.

Beginning with the Crystal Palace Exposition at London in 1851, followed by a long succession of world's fairs in Europe and the United States, American museums began to assume a new educational role by making the industrial arts and sciences a part of their collections. The many international exhibitions held during this period, although commercial in nature, provided the museums with ideas and models for displays relating to the life of the community. The Centennial Fair in Philadelphia, in 1876, not only gave an impetus to this changed concept through its display of science, art, and industry, but later provided exhibits for a number of educational museums, including the Philadelphia Commercial Museum, the St. Louis Educational Museum, and the Reading (Pennsylvania) Public Museum and Art Gallery.

Among the museums that came into existence during this new period of development were the American Museum of Natural History, New York (1869); Metropolitan Museum of Art, New York (1869); Museum of Fine Arts, Boston (1870); New York State Museum (1870); Pennsylvania Museum (1876); Art Institute of Chicago (1879); Milwaukee Public Museum (1882); Brooklyn Institute of Arts and Sciences (1889); Field Museum of Natural History, Chicago (1894); Worcester (Massachusetts) Art Museum (1896); John Herron Art Institute (1896); and the Carnegie Institute, Pittsburgh (1896). Most of these new-style museums, supported either by private endowments or municipal or state funds, were planned largely for educational purposes.

Instructional role of early museums

Beginning in the latter part of the nineteenth century, the museum increasingly assumed an educational role. Rather than serving merely as a storage house for collections, its role has become one of instruction. This conception had an important influence on the methods of selection and presentation of museum exhibits. There were period rooms, dioramas, and habitat groups for showing one single item—a painting, a model, or a zoological specimen—as part of its environment: a display quite distinct from a loose collection of objects. The increasing fulfillment of the instructional function of American museums was acknowledged as early as 1880 when, at the opening of the new building of the Metropolitan Museum of Art in

New York City, museums were declared to be social instruments for the educational progress of the masses.

Of major importance in the museum movement has been the development of new methods of instruction. Specimens and object collections were made an integral part of the instructional process and were not used as supplementary illustrations of verbal instruction. Operating tools or machines illustrated essential principles of mechanics, and concrete objects, models, drawings, and stuffed animals provided first-hand experiences.

Conducted tours, lectures, and cooperative instructional programs with the public schools were organized by many museums. Temporary loans, in the form of collections or single specimens, were made to libraries, schools, associations, individuals, or to other museums.

Early Museum Instructional Programs.   As early as 1878, the Davenport (Iowa) Academy of Sciences arranged a cooperative instructional program with the Davenport public schools. In 1904, the school board of Davenport paid for half of the time of the curator for his educational work. At this same time, the science teachers of Buffalo, New York, were encouraged to bring their classes to the Buffalo Society of Natural Sciences in order to utilize the collections and rooms for instruction. Other educational efforts of the Buffalo museum included the preparation of lantern slides and specimens for illustration.[2]

The Children's Museum was established in 1899 as a branch of the Central Museum of the Brooklyn Institute of Arts and Sciences so as ". . . to form an attractive resort for children, with influences tending to refine their tastes and elevate their interests; to create an attractive center of daily assistance to pupils and teachers in connection with school work; and to offer new subjects of thought for pursuit in leisure hours."[3] Anna Billings Gallup, the first curator of this museum, described the original plan as including (1) the preparation of collections which children can enjoy, understand, and use; (2) an arrangement of material pleasing to the eye and expressive of a fundamental truth; (3) briefly descriptive labels expressed in simple language and printed in clear, readable type; and (4) a system of instruction which children will voluntarily employ.[4] A direct influence of the Children's Museum was the establishment of a similar children's museum in the Smithsonian Institution at Washington, D.C., in 1900.

Museums of Arts and Sciences.   Art museums and museums of science made an early contribution to instructional technology by their develop-

[2] *Proceedings of the American Association of Museums,* vol. 2 (1908), p. 65.
[3] *Proceedings of the American Association of Museums,* vol. 3 (1909), p. 75.
[4] Anna Billings Gallup, "The Work of a Children's Museum," *Proceedings of the American Association of Museums,* vol. 1 (1907), p. 144.

ment of a number of instructional programs in cooperation with public schools, colleges, and universities. The Fogg Art Museum of Cambridge, Massachusetts, began working very closely with Harvard University in the early 1900s. The Field Museum of Natural History in Chicago began a system of museum service to the Chicago public schools in 1911. This system was based on the assumption that city-born boys and girls are complete strangers to the natural world. Therefore, nature study collections were emphasized and sent to all Chicago schools for a year. The schedule was arranged so that each school could have five deliveries of three cases of natural objects—one each of zoology, botany, and geology.[5]

American Museum of Natural History.   An outstanding example of museum instruction rendered to the public schools is that provided by the American Museum of Natural History of New York City. From its inception in 1869, the guiding motto of this museum has been, "For the people, for education, for science." Beginning in 1880, Albert S. Bickmore inaugurated his illustrated lectures for teachers, and in 1904, nature study collections were first distributed to the schools. One of the more useful services provided to the schools by this museum has been its distribution of lantern slides, films, filmstrips, study prints, and the establishment of its outdoor museums for school children in the Adirondack State Park (New York).

Within the museum's halls themselves, mammals, birds, reptiles, amphibia, and fishes are mounted or modeled in lifelike attitudes, grouped as in nature, and shown in a setting consisting of a pictorial background, reproducing realistically the natural environment, with trees, shrubbery, and other objects faithfully modeled to simulate nature. A similar method is followed with the lower forms of life, such as the marine and freshwater invertebrates. The beautiful, natural coloration and translucent quality of many soft-bodied creatures are modeled in glass, wax, and other materials, tinted with translucent colors of the living animal through which light filters. Actual specimens, including real trees, bushes, and rocks, are included in the terrestrial group displays. These lifelike exhibits are in turn supplemented by arresting explanatory labels and well-written, pictorial handbooks as a guide to interpretation.

Philadelphia Commercial Museum.   Edward Brooks, superintendent of the Philadelphia schools, on his return from the 1893 Chicago Columbian Exposition, conceived the idea of a new and expanded museum service for the schools as follows:

> During my visit last summer at the World's Fair I was naturally impressed with the great benefits accruing to teachers in having the

[5] Charles E. Skinner, "Museums and Visual Education," *Educational Screen*, vol. 3 (October, 1924), p. 308.

opportunity of seeing and studying representative school work. In reflecting upon the matter I formed the purpose of establishing on a small scale a Pedagogical Museum for the use of teachers of Philadelphia. My plan was to take some of the best of our own work as a nucleus and combine with it some of the best representative work from several other leading cities of the country, and place the whole in one of our unoccupied or partially occupied school buildings for the observation and study of our teachers. This purpose was presented to a special committee of the Board having charge of the educational exhibit, and was cordially approved by them. Soon after making this arrangement I learned that Dr. Wm. P. Wilson, who was representing the Park Commission at Chicago, in securing material for an Economic Museum, had conceived the idea of a large and complete educational museum, and had entered into negotiations with the authorities having charge of the educational exhibits of various foreign countries with a view of securing them for Philadelphia. Realizing the immense value to Philadelphia of such a collection of educational material I immediately directed my representatives at Chicago to turn over all the material, of which they had obtained the promise, to Dr. Wilson, and also sent two other representatives to Chicago to aid in the selection of such other material as might be desirable.[6]

The Dr. Wilson mentioned by Brooks finally secured the entire German exhibit of instructional charts and models, as well as the educational exhibits of Japan, Brazil, Russia, Egypt, Costa Rica, Guatemala, New South Wales, France, and Canada. The Argentine Republic donated 200 photographs of plans of school buildings. The Japanese exhibit, costing some $15,000, and including 1,000 costumes, and valuable statistical maps and charts, required three freight cars to hold it.[7]

This collection was housed in two of the old Philadelphia Centennial (1876) buildings and organized into what became known as the Philadelpha Commercial Museum. Beginning in 1900, this museum

> . . . prepared and presented free of cost to the schools in Pennsylvania 250 collections. Each set contained several hundred specimens of imported commercial products, and from 100 to 200 photographs. These collections were distributed not as a loan, but as a gift so that the specimens were always available. The collections proved to be of great service, furnishing object lessons of much value in the study of geography and commerce.[8]

In 1925–1926, Philadelphia public school teachers were appointed to the museum staff for the purpose of conducting a systematic instructional pro-

[6] *Annual Reports of Superintendents of Philadelphia Public Schools* (1894), p. 90.
[7] The complete material brought from Chicago required fifteen freight cars. The Pennsylvania Railroad supplied the cars free of charge.
[8] Charles R. Toothacker, *The Educational Work of the Commercial Museum of Philadelphia.* U.S. Bureau of Education Bulletin 13, 1920, p. 16.

gram. Attendance for this first year of formal classes was 49,323. By 1926, the total visitations of pupils from the Philadelphia public schools passed 90,000.

The circular announcing the lectures and classes of 1924–1925 is of particular interest because of its reference to visual instruction:

> Museums are the most potent factors of visual education. Exhibits properly displayed stimulate interest in the subject matter of textbooks and tend to a liberal education.
>
> The aim of any museum should be education, not a storehouse of inanimate objects alone, but really a collection of labels illustrated by specimens, for the sole purpose of explaining visually those things, and especially the simple things with which we are brought in daily contact.[9]

In 1905, the Pennsylvania State Legislature recognized the educational value of the Philadelphia Commercial Museum, appropriated $25,000 for its work, and has since continued to support the museum by annual grants.[10]

Beginnings of school museums

As we have seen, museums have either developed instructional programs of their own or worked out a cooperative arrangement with the schools. During the first decade of the twentieth century, a new type of museum began to be established by some public school systems. This museum—known as the educational museum—served as the central administrative unit for visual instruction by its distribution of portable museum exhibits, stereographs, slides, films, study prints, charts, and other instructional materials. The primary function of the educational museum is to supplement and enrich the instructional program of the school system.

Although a number of other educational museums were established in later years, the first three—founded by the city school systems of St. Louis, Missouri; Reading, Pennsylvania; and Cleveland, Ohio, during the short period of 1905–1909—may be selected as typifying the school museum instruction movement because of the extent to which the work of these museums has been correlated with the school curriculum.

St. Louis Educational Museum.   In 1905, the St. Louis Educational Museum became the first administrative unit for instructional media in a public school system. Much of the impetus for this development came from former

---

[9] *Circular Announcement of Commercial Museum Classes,* 1924–1925.

[10] See James G. Sigman, "Origin and Development of Visual Education in the Philadelphia Public Schools." Unpublished doctoral dissertation presented to School of Education, Temple University, Philadelphia, Pa., 1933.

Fig. 5.1   "Bring the World to the Child" symbol of the St. Louis Educational Museum.

United States Commissioner of Education, William Torrey Harris. In 1875, when Harris was superintendent of the St. Louis public schools, he stated in his annual report that, "every lesson should be given in such a way as to draw out the perceptive powers of the pupil by leading him to reflect on what he sees or to analyze the object before him." [11]

The first opportunity to implement this so-called original-instruction conception of education did not come until 1904, when the city of St. Louis played host to the Louisiana Purchase Exposition. As the direct consequence of organizing and managing a "Public Schools Exhibit," Carl G. Rathmann, then assistant superintendent of the St. Louis public schools, became aware of the instructional potential of the many exhibits on display.

On September 13, 1904, the St. Louis Board of Education made its first authorization to Rathmann for the purchase of appropriate instructional materials. Following this action, the school museum dream became a reality.[12]

---

[11] William T. Harris, *Twenty-first Annual Report of the Board of Directors of the St. Louis Public Schools* (1875), p. 164.
[12] *Minutes of the St. Louis Board of Education*, Sept. 13, 1904.

The first art objects and models were soon supplemented by extensive gift collections from national museums and countries around the world. Amelia Meissner, the daughter of a famous horticulturist, was ready to "bring the world to the child." She organized the museum's materials and became its first curator.[13]

On April 11, 1905, the museum opened in an old school building. A short time later, a horse and wagon were acquired to make weekly deliveries of instructional materials to the St. Louis schools. In the 1905–1906 school year, about five thousand such deliveries were made, thus effectively supplementing museum visits by students and their teachers. This delivery service was such an essential part of the museum's function that its collections were designed to supplement rather than supplant the course of study. A catalog, arranged in terms of the course of study, was printed and made accessible to St. Louis teachers.

The museum collections were listed in the teachers' catalog as follows:

(1) food products; (2) materials for clothing; (3) other natural products; (4) industrial products; (5) articles and models illustrating the

Fig. 5.2   First display room of St. Louis Educational Museum.

[13] Amelia Meissner's organizational skill was illustrated in her preparation and direction of the St. Louis Public Schools Exhibit at the 1915 Panama Pacific Exposition in San Francisco, California. In that effort, her work was so well received that she was requested to remain for six months longer in order to help organize the San Francisco public schools' visual instruction department.

Fig. 5.3   *First horse-drawn delivery wagon of the St. Louis Educational Museum, put into operation in 1905.*

life and occupations of the different peoples of the world; (6) plants and models and charts of plants; (7) the animal world; (8) minerals, rocks, and ores; (9) apparatus for illustration of physics and physical geography; (10) charts, colored pictures, maps, and objects illustrating history; (11) collections of art objects and models used by classes in drawing; and (12) photographs, stereoscopic pictures, and lantern slides to accompany the preceding groups.[14]

In 1927, a tornado completely wrecked the museum building and destroyed the bulk of the materials. This could have been the final chapter in the history of the St. Louis Educational Museum, but for the courageous effort made to restore it. Materials which could be salvaged were moved to a bowling alley. With the electricity out, the restoration process proceeded at once by candlelight. In the meantime, Carl Rathmann began a nationwide tour, appealing for aid. Museums and other organizations throughout the country responded quickly by supplying numerous materials which replaced many of the lost objects. The ability to overcome such obstacles is tangible evidence that the St. Louis Educational Museum, which changed its name to the Division of Audio-Visual Education in 1943, will remain an integral part of the St. Louis public school system.

[14] Carl G. Rathmann, *Educational Museum of St. Louis Public Schools.* U.S. Bureau of Education Bulletin 48, 1915, p. 11.

Reading Public Museum and Art Gallery.   The Reading (Pennsylvania) Public Museum was established in 1908 as the second museum designed solely for the purpose of providing instructional materials to the schools. Credit for its founding belongs largely to a teacher in the Reading public schools, Levi W. Mengel. Although the idea for such a museum had occurred to Mengel during his preparation for his science and history classes, he saw the practicality of a school museum when he visited the 1904 St. Louis Louisiana Purchase Exposition.

When Mengel returned to Reading, he secured permission from Charles S. Foos, superintendent of the Reading public schools, to procure such materials from the St. Louis Exposition as could be useful in teaching. At the end of the fair, Mengel had been promised enough material to begin the organization of a museum. However, when it came time to transport this material to Reading, it was found that the foreign exhibitions could not be moved until cleared through United States customs. Meanwhile, the Philadelphia Commercial Museum was also attempting to obtain the release of material it had been promised by exhibitors at the St. Louis Exposition. Since the time required for clearing customs would take months, Superintendent Foos appealed to Dr. William P. Wilson, director of the Philadelphia Commercial Museum, for help in this matter. As a consequence, the museum agreed to clear the material and transport it to the Reading public schools.

Eventually, in 1905, the Reading public schools received nearly two thousand items from the exhibitions of Japan, China, India, Ceylon, the Philippines, and the Central and South American Republics. The bulk of the material was stored in the Reading High School until it could be organized and arranged for instructional use. In 1907, the Reading Board of Education passed a resolution which provided for the organization of these materials and reserved the third floor of the old high school building for a museum. After the considerable work of cleaning, labeling, and arranging—done after school hours, at night, and on holidays—the museum was opened in 1908 to teachers and pupils of all grade levels.

During the 1909–1911 period, illustrated lectures for schoolchilden were established. At first lantern slide sets were borrowed from the Philadelphia Commercial Museum, but within a few years a slide library was established. In 1913, an epoch-making event took place when the Reading Board of Education authorized the addition of an art gallery to the museum. Its name thus became the Reading Public Museum and Art Gallery.

A significant event in the history of the Reading Museum occurred in 1924. A request was made by the Reading School Board for a loan for school buildings, which included provision for a modern museum building. After a campaign in which even the children took part, the loan was passed. However, a bitter controversy ensued over the new location of the museum, ending in a stalemate. Fortunately, a botanical garden was offered as a home for the museum, thus resolving the question of location. Today, the modern building of the Reading Public Museum and Art Gallery, set amid the beauty of a park filled with flowers and birds, makes this school museum one of the most impressive in the country.

Cleveland Educational Museum.   The third school museum was established by the Cleveland public schools in 1909. The influence of the St. Louis Educational Museum is evident from the following statement made by J. M. H. Frederick, former superintendent of the Cleveland public schools: "The schools of St. Louis are supplied with illustrative material from an educational museum which has more than 22,000 cases of materials. Educational authorities of this country have fully approved the St. Louis plan of providing the teacher and pupils with illustrative materials."[15] The first curator of the Cleveland Educational Museum was W. M. Gregory. Following the St. Louis pattern, collections of instructional materials were sent to the teacher as ordered.

School museums as instructional resources

Although the school museums discussed here were founded in the first decade of this century, surprisingly few others have been established since that time, and the utilization of school museums as part of a systematic technology of instruction is still generally unrealized. In many cities, of course, municipal, state, or privately endowed museums are widely used for instructional purposes. However, the reconstruction of the school museum as an integral, functioning component of a modern science and technology of instruction seems essential for the teaching-learning process.

[15] J. M. H. Frederick, *Annual Report of J. M. H. Frederick, Superintendent, for the School Year 1914–15, to the Board of Education,* Cleveland, Ohio, Board of Education (Jan. 24, 1916), p. 62.

chapter 6

**emergence of the
instructional film**

Our purpose in this chapter is to show the historical relationship of the instructional film to the mainstream of
theatrical films and to identify those persons who shaped
the form and content of the first instructional films. It is
also our purpose to describe the early organizations and
agencies which set the patterns for the production and
distribution of instructional films and to assess some of
these efforts. The larger history of the instructional film
concerns its relationship to the developing technology of
instruction in American education. Much of this history
has been treated in other chapters of this book as one
aspect of a broader discussion of instructional technology.

Beginnings of the instructional film

The first films used for instructional purposes were

usually theatrical films. Kleine had this to say about the selections contained in his 1910 educational film catalog:

> In a sense, all subjects are educational, but in classifying a mass of motion picture films for educational purposes the line must be drawn about a reasonable area.
>
> A dramatic or comic tale in motion pictures, laid in some foreign country, is educational in so far as it shows the manners, customs and environment of the people. . . .
>
> The word "educational" is here used in a wide sense and does not indicate that these films are intended for school or college use exclusively. They are intended rather for the education of the adult as well as the youth, for the exhibition before miscellaneous audiences, as well as for more restricted use.[1]

Freeman,[2] in 1923, classified and offered as a working basis the following four types of instructional films: (1) the dramatic, either fictional or historical; (2) the anthropological or sociological, differing from the dramatic in that it is not primarily based on a narrative or story; (3) the industrial or commercial, which shows the processes of modern industry and commerce; and (4) the scientific, which may be classified into subgroups corresponding to the individual sciences such as earth science, nature study, etc.

By the early 1920s there were many who supported a distinct line of demarcation between the entertainment and educational, or instructional, motion picture. Their motives varied. Producers, distributors, and exhibitors of theatrical films wanted to protect box-office receipts and calculated that a potentially powerful source of competition could be eliminated if "educationals" could be typed into a dull illustrated-lecture pattern. Meanwhile, educators fell in with this unflattering concept of instructional films because of the fear of the moral effects of theatrical films on children and their own traditional aversion to entertainment in the classroom.

It was obvious that more and more films originally produced for theatrical purposes possessed educational values as well. For example, very few educators could deny that such documentary films as Pare Lorentz's *The River* and Robert Flaherty's *Nanook of the North* or *Man of Aran* could not contribute to understanding and influence attitudes and perceptions. The rigid classification of films as either educational or entertaining has proved detrimental to the development of a broad, realistic concept of the instructional film.

Early Instructional Films.   Most films used for instructional purposes prior to World War I were a form of salvage for old theatrical, industrial,

---

[1] George Kleine, *Catalogue of Educational Motion Pictures.* New York, George Kleine Company, 1910, p. 1.
[2] Frank N. Freeman, "Requirements of Education with Reference to Motion Pictures," *The School Review*, vol. 31, No. 5 (May, 1923), pp. 340–350.

government, or welfare films. An early evaluation of these films was made by Cohen as follows:

> In some quarters there is an impression that right now we are ready to go ahead with the motion picture as a means of imparting knowledge to those seeking an education. Many schools have already installed motion picture machines and have found them more than valuable along certain lines.
>
> This impression that we are ready to supply just what the schools need in the way of educational pictures, either supplying or supplementing the textbook, is quite general and absolutely erroneous. It is true that we have an array of educational releases which when properly marshalled in a catalogue, appear quite imposing, but it is also true that not one of these pictures represents a systematic effort to supply a definite series of pictures for a definite purpose.[3]

In 1922, Gregory identified and evaluated sources of so-called instructional films as follows:

> Present sources of educational films are: Old commercial films that have been junked and are now reworked into so-called educational pictures.
>
> Advertising films giving an interesting but one-sided story of a particular product.
>
> Government films consisting of: war-propaganda films, distinctly out of date; excellent agricultural films, and a few health films.
>
> Welfare films of large corporations; suitable in only a few cases for general educational purposes.
>
> Health films; some special health films too technical and too costly for general use in schools; a large group of films produced from junk and of no value.
>
> Educational films for schools—comprising stories, technical subjects, travel, geography, history, language, and hygiene. The group of films especially prepared for school use is very small. Most of the so-called educational film consists of material that has been stripped from cast-off commercial film and retitled, and is being offered now for school purposes. Much of the film is shown in schools because of the novelty of the motion picture. In the effort to keep pace with the commercial exhibitor the schools frequently have disregarded quality.
>
> Experienced and skilled educators have given the film material but comparatively little attention. The material has been too often accepted without protest *if it is low priced.*[4]

First Instructional Film Catalog.   Shortly after the turn of the century, there were a number of individuals both in the United States and Europe

[3] M. J. Cohen, "The Evolution of the Motion Picture." Unpublished manuscript, 1918, p. 1.
[4] W. M. Gregory, "Problems concerning the Educational Motion Picture," *Moving Picture Age*, vol. 5, no. 1 (January, 1922), p. 20.

who envisaged the use of motion pictures in education. In a 1907 pamphlet titled *The Cinematograph in Science, Education, and Matters of State,* Charles Urban, working in England, stated that he had "spent the past five years in equipping a qualified staff to provide animated films depicting various manifestations, transformations, and phenomena of nature." By August, 1909, Urban had control of enough educational film footage to publish the second edition of a catalog of educational films titled, *Urbanora.* Not finding a ready market for his films in England or on the continent, Urban moved to the United States and continued his activities in New York City.

The first instructional film catalog to appear in the United States was the *Catalogue of Educational Motion Pictures,* published by George Kleine in New York, in 1910. This catalog contained 330 pages and listed 1,065 titles classified under thirty main topics. It also had a foreword by the anthropologist Frederick K. Starr of the University of Chicago; a quoted statement from P. Chambers, Secretary of the Zoological Society of London, England; and a letter from Thomas A. Edison to Kleine, dated December 20, 1909. Edison became so enthused over the educational possibilities of the motion picture that he was quoted in the New York *Dramatic Mirror*'s issue of July 9, 1913, with the statement, "Books will soon be obsolete in the schools. Scholars will soon be instructed through the eye. It is possible to teach every branch of human knowledge with the motion picture. Our school system will be completely changed in ten years." The enthusiasm of men like Edison for the instructional value of the motion picture served to motivate many individuals, business men and educators alike, to enter the budding field of visual education.

First School Use of Instructional Films.   In 1910, George Kleine undertook the promotion of a school film service, and with this objective, screened selected films at a meeting of the New York City Board of Education. However, despite the impressive presentation, Kleine's plan was not accepted because of a lack of inexpensive, portable motion picture projection equipment. Later the same year, the public schools of Rochester, New York, became the first to adopt films for regular instructional use.[5]

Early commercial instructional film enterprises

When the realization grew that instructional films were different in form and objective from theatrical or religious films, schools became potential

---

[5] Although educational institutions were beginning to realize the value of instructional films, the fire-hazard problem succeeded in hampering the diffusion of the instructional film. For example, in 1910, the Boston schools barred all films in the schools because of the fire menace. The first fireproof booth for projecting motion pictures, built as an integral part of a school, was constructed in Vanderlip Hall at the Scarborough School in New York State in 1916.

markets for projection equipment and for the rental and purchase of films for instructional purposes. As a consequence, a number of commercial organizations were established during the first two decades of this century for the purpose of manufacturing low-priced nonprofessional equipment, producing "educationals," and serving as film distribution centers. An additional impetus to this development was brought about by the special demand for training films during World War I.

Herman DeVry Company.   One of the earliest commercial concerns catering to the needs of the users of instructional films was that founded in Chicago in 1900 by Herman DeVry. By 1913, DeVry began manufacturing his famous E Model DeVry suitcase 35-mm projectors. Subsequently this company built up large collections of films and slides and was among the first to offer short reels for school use.

Bell and Howell Company.   The Bell and Howell Company came into being in Chicago on New Year's Day, 1907, when Don J. Bell, a young in-

BELL & HOWELL "FILMO"   16-mm silent motion picture projector. This is a special model designed to operate on 32-volt direct current in the many then existing locations where utilities power was not available. Regular models ran on 100-12-v. A. C.

Fig. 6.1   Bell and Howell "Filmo" Projector.

ventor, formed a partnership with Albert S. Howell. This company began by specializing in projectors and cameras. Later it added a library of over one thousand 16-mm silent films and some two hundred 16-mm sound-on-film motion pictures. Branch film libraries were established in many parts of the country; users of the Bell and Howell instructional film library were supplied with a projector, a screen, and an operator.

Victor Animatograph Company.   This company was founded by Alexander F. Victor, a former Swedish magician, with Samuel G. Rose, in Davenport, Iowa, in 1910. A year before, Victor had invented the Animatograph, the first portable projector which combined a camera with sound-on-disc. Following this achievement, Victor and his associates continued to make a number of technical contributions. In 1912, the company produced the first portable lantern slide projector and made smaller, lighter slides. Other achievements were the first 16-mm projector and the first spring-driven 16-mm cameras (which dispensed with a tripod). Victor was prominent among those who first proposed the 16-mm film as standard for instructional films.

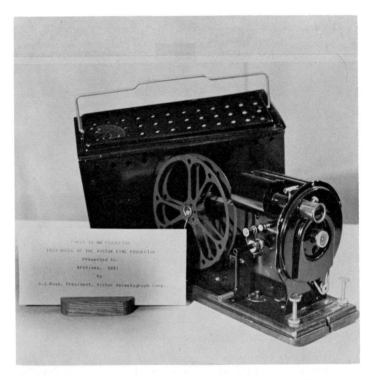

Fig. 6.2   *First 16-mm projector—1923 model of the Victor Cine Projector.*

Charles Urban Company.   Although the Charles Urban Company was not strictly an American company, it did exert an important influence on the development of instructional films in this country. Urban experimented with instructional film production in England as early as 1896, founding the Kinemacolor Company in 1911. He later came to America to help develop an instructional film production company known as the Urban-Kineto Corporation at Lowville, New York.[6]

Kleine Optical Company.   The American distributor of Urban was George Kleine. As we have seen, Kleine developed the first catalog of instructional films and attempted to promote their use in the schools. He also made such film classics as *Julius Caesar* and *Quo Vadis* available to schools at low rentals and was the first to distribute films through the college and university extension divisions on a profit-sharing arrangement. Through the Kleine Optical Company which had been organized in the late nineteenth century by his father, Kleine also sold portable 35-mm projectors.

The Edison Film Library.   In 1911, a notable instructional film effort began: The Edison Company began a series of instructional films known as Edison's Library, on history and on natural and physical science.

The early Edison instructional film production attempts at West Orange, New Jersey, were brought to an abrupt end by two disastrous fires in April and December of 1914, which destroyed much of the Edison Library of negatives and discouraged the continued manufacture of the Edison Kinetoscope home projector. The negatives which were not destroyed were subsequently scattered and lost. Some of the Edison films were, however, being distributed by the Kleine Optical Company as late as 1929. Edison did much to promote films for schools, but his efforts were misunderstood and he was distinctly ahead of his time.

Educational Films Corporation.   This company was formed in New York City in 1915 by Earle W. Hammons. After a period of experimentation, George A. Skinner provided some needed financial support and became president. Skinner had a more advanced understanding of the role of instructional films than most of the producers at this time.[7] He wanted to make films specifically for the schools and objected to the term "educational" as

---

[6] Urban developed the Kinemacolor process which involved revolving discs of red and green filters through which black-and-white film was projected at double speed. The mechanical complexity of the process and patent difficulties hampered its acceptance. Urban encountered his greatest failure on the lyceum circuits because the theaters did not have the necessary special equipment.
[7] Skinner supervised and produced two outstanding early instructional films, titled *The Valley of the Ten Thousand Smokes* and *Unhooking the Hook Worm.*

applied to the typical films of the day. Hammons disagreed, believing that theatrical films possessed sufficient educational content. He later purchased Skinner's interest in the company and developed a cooperative exchange system with the Hudson Bay Company of London.

The Atlas Motion Picture Corporation.   This company was formed in Detroit, Michigan, in 1916, financially backed by Henry Ford. With its large laboratory and extensive equipment, it was soon releasing *The Ford Educational Weekly*. In the summer of 1919, a committee of educators, headed by William H. Dudley of the University of Wisconsin, was invited to the Ford plant to edit fifty-one Ford films for instructional use. This group completed its work, and in 1920 *The Ford Educational Library* was announced as ready for distribution. It is interesting to note that "each film had a complete synopsis or syllabus containing: the title and subtitles, the instructional aim, data suitable to aid the teacher, definite questions for presenting the lesson, problems, questions, and a list of references." The advertising, however, was unsuccessful and even created some antagonism toward the Ford Motor Company and the educators who had served on the selection committee.

The Society for Visual Education, Inc.   Somewhat in the tradition of a medieval guild, Harley L. Clarke, a utilities magnate, together with Forest Ray Moulton, professor of astronomy at the University of Chicago, founded the Society for Visual Education in November, 1919. The officers of the company were Rolin D. Salisbury, president; H. L. Clarke, vice-president; F. R. Moulton, secretary; and Frank A. Vanderlip, chairman, board of directors. Its objective was to produce instructors' films specifically for school use.

It is interesting to note that both Salisbury and Moulton were professors at the University of Chicago and that other directors on the board were associated with such educational institutions as the universities of Harvard, Columbia, and Michigan. There was also a general advisory board of sixty-four members and a host of committees with a membership of eight to fourteen members each. The men and women comprising the board represented the leading educators of the country.[8]

Although the Society for Visual Education began with $400,000 and the best educational consultants available, failure followed less than three years after its founding. Skinner observed that the society "lacked competent producers."[9] It produced the first extensive library of films for school use, but

[8] Many of the educators on the board of the Society for Visual Education had the impression that the company was a nonprofit organization and, as a consequence, allowed their names to be used. However, many also invested their money in this venture.
[9] George A. Skinner, "A Short History of the Educational Motion Picture Organizations Which Have Been Projected during the Past Twenty-five Years." Unpublished manuscript, p. 2, undated.

Fig. 6.3   Picturol projector.

its 110 productions lacked both appeal and technical excellence.[10] The films were not "systematically built to supplement existing courses of study" nor were the educators serving on the various committees consulted regarding the films' educational merits or demerits. The situation was made more untenable by the reported unethical business practices of Clarke, and by tasteless advertising which antagonized many who had supported the society.[11]

Although the society had gone into industrial production and had become affiliated with the Acme Motion Picture Projector Company in bringing out the Acme suitcase projector, it was evident by 1923 that it was not meeting with financial success. As a consequence, Clarke sold the society to Marie Witham, a member of the staff, that same year.

Marie Witham fared far better and continued the society on a smaller scale. In October, 1923, the society manufactured a slidefilm projector known as the Picturol. This led to the production and distribution of slidefilms and slidefilm projection equipment. At the same time, the society started and has since maintained the most complete library of slidefilms in the world.

[10] One of the first films of this series, often credited with being the first true educational motion picture, was *The Story of the Monarch Butterfly.*
[11] A pioneering activity of the Society for Visual Education was the magazine, *Visual Education.* This was an elaborate monthly house organ which first appeared in January, 1920, with Nelson L. Greene as its editor. The journal was later edited by W. C. Bagley and F. R. Moulton. The December, 1924, issue announced the merger of *Visual Education* with *Educational Screen.* In 1926, the society reentered the publishing field when it issued an annual *Visual Review.* This periodical was first edited by Marie Witham.

Chronicles of America Photoplays.   As the result of the publishing success of a series of histories known as the *Chronicles of Canada* and the
Chronicles of America, the Canadian firm of Glasgow and Brook became interested in 1918 in the possibility of producing an educational film series
based on their publications. Accordingly, a material survey was made, a
budget prepared, and theatrical continuity writers began writing the first
scenarios. The plan called for five sequences of eight units each, covering
the history of America from Columbus to Woodrow Wilson, inclusive.

By 1920, Glasgow and Brook were ready to form the Chronicles of
America Picture Corporation. George Parmly Day, head of the Yale Univer-
sity Press and treasurer of Yale University, was made president.[12] Robert
Glasgow became vice-president; Arthur E. Krows, secretary; and Arthur
Brook, treasurer.

Just as film production was to start, a series of unexpected difficulties
arose. First, plans were disrupted because of the death of Glasgow. Then
a distinguished committee of historians, who had been appointed by the
Council of Yale University, began to dispute the various historical and technical details in the scenarios which had been written by theatrical writers.
In order to resolve this impasse, Brook gave production authority to the
historians. They eventually succeeded in putting out a series of films known
as the *Chronicles of America Photoplays.*

Only forty-seven of the one hundred reels originally planned were completed. The initial plan had called for the lease of complete sets of films to
schools on a ninety-nine-year basis for $20,000; but few sets were actually
leased because fifty-three reels were missing! Attempts were made to release
the series for theatrical film distribution so that some of the great financial
investment could be recovered.[13] However, their lack of dramatic appeal and
their factual, academic approach caused them to be rejected.[14]

McClusky gives this appraisal of the *Chronicles of America Photoplays:*

1. The first big effort to produce a systematic series of films on one
    subject.
2. The first time "educators" were, in an official capacity, working
    with "producers."

[12] Arthur E. Krows, secretary of the Chronicles of America Picture Corporation, reveals
that George Parmly Day succeeded in securing the financial support of the Harkness
family which was reputedly worth about $2 million. See Arthur E. Krows, "Motion
Pictures—Not for Theaters," *Educational Screen,* vol. 21 (March, 1924), pp. 104–106.
[13] George Parmly Day, in order to protect the reputation of Yale University, spent nearly
$2 million in liquidating the stock of subscribing alumni and friends of the university.
[14] Daniel C. Knowlton and J. Warren Tilton conducted a study of the *Chronicles of
America Photoplays* to determine their effectiveness as an aid in seventh-grade history
instruction. See D. C. Knowlton and J. W. Tilton, *Motion Pictures in History Teaching.*
New Haven, Conn., Yale University Press, 1929.

3. Planning failed, however, to bring historical experts, teachers, and producers together at the outset.
4. Theatrical continuity writers did not win approval from historians. . . . This cost $50,000.
5. The historians then took charge but failed to produce pictures which made a hit with teachers of American history in elementary and secondary schools.
6. By the time this was discovered, the money was exhausted and the series was only half completed.
7. Theatrical showings failed to reap box office returns because the films were as dead as the historical detail which characterized them.
8. A grand opportunity was wasted because of poor management and lack of harmony in the organization.
9. Had the Yale University Press done some proving ground work, sought the advice of experienced visual educators, teachers, and educational psychologists, this failure might have been avoided. Cost was too high and the episodes took too long to show.[15]

Eastman Teaching Films.   The Eastman Kodak Company formed Eastman Teaching Pictures, Inc., in 1928, with Thomas E. Finegan, former

Fig. 6.4   Eastman Kodascope Model C.

[15] F. Dean McClusky, "Motion Pictures for the Schools." Unpublished report made for the Rockefeller Foundation, 1937, pp. 15–16.

deputy commissioner of education for New York State and superintendent of public instruction for the state of Pennsylvania, as president. The enterprise was capitalized at $1 million and designed as an elaborate research-demonstration project under the direction of Ben D. Wood of Columbia University and Frank N. Freeman of the University of Chicago.[16]

The first Eastman Teaching Films were made in the subject areas of geography, general science, and health. Ultimately, some 250 silent instructional films (mostly one reel in length) were produced, containing much material taken directly from the negatives of industrial films which had been given without cost to the Eastman Company.

The impact of the instructional sound film, the depression of the thirties, and the deaths of George Eastman and Thomas E. Finegan combined to bring an abrupt halt to the Eastman Kodak Company's film production activity in 1932. No attempt was made to replace Finegan, but W. H. Maddock was made sales manager of Eastman Teaching Films, and the sale of films continued. In 1944, the Eastman Kodak Company finally gave the University of Chicago its entire stock of film negatives.

Electrical Research Products, Inc.   The introduction of the educational sound film provided a new impetus for the development of commercial enterprises.[17] The most important of these was Electrical Research Products, Inc. (better known as ERPI and pronounced "urpi").[18]

ERPI was organized as a subsidiary of the Western Electric Company, the manufacturing division of the American Telephone and Telegraph Company. At first ERPI confined itself to supplying Western Electric sound systems to theaters throughout the country. Inevitably the attention of the company turned toward nontheatrical possibilities. Since sound equipment had been in such demand in the theaters, it seemed logical to ERPI that the schools' requirements would be equally urgent. Consequently, ERPI fitted sound-on-disc attachments into approved 35-mm silent models, such as the Holmes and Super-DeVry projectors, and proceeded to establish an elaborate sales organization. ERPI leaders also became convinced that the nontheatrical field would need encouragement and support. To implement this

[16] See Ben D. Wood and Frank N. Freeman, *Motion Pictures in the Classroom.* Boston, Houghton Mifflin Company, 1929.

[17] New companies organized during the thirties included Castle Films, Films Incorporated, Academic Films Corporation, Vocational Guidance Films, Inc., Knowledge Builders, Garrison Films, and the William H. Dudley Visual Education Service, Inc. Dudley, a former director of the Bureau of Visual Instruction of the University of Wisconsin, founded his company primarily for the distribution of educational slides and films. A circuit plan of distribution was used and schools were organized on a commercial basis. By 1937, more than four thousand schools were on his circuit service. Each school paid $50 per year for the service and received 120 reels of film and a projector.

[18] Henceforth, the Electrical Research Products, Inc., will be referred to in this history as ERPI.

thinking a nontheatrical film producing unit was formed as a model for others to follow.

ERPI's first film was devoted to explaining how sound is put on film. Called *Finding His Voice*, it became one of the most popular short subjects of all time and was screened in all important theaters. Max Fleisher did the cartoon showing how the silent motion picture, symbolized by a caricature figure, attempts to become articulate. Carlyle Ellis did the narration.[19]

In January, 1929, the nontheatrical division of ERPI, known as the educational department, was formed with Colonel Frederick L. Devereux as president. Devereux had been an executive for many years in the American Telephone and Telegraph Company, but he was a complete stranger to the nontheatrical film field. Howard Gale Stokes was chosen to assist him.

Shortly after the organization of ERPI, it was announced that they would specialize in the manufacture and sale of portable sound projectors for nontheatrical use. To provide guidance for this venture, a committee of educators was chosen by Devereux, including N. L. Engelhardt, Paul Mort, and Alexander J. Stoddard. Ironically enough, none of these men had experience in motion picture production. Varney C. Arnspiger was selected as the director of educational research. Other research associates were Melvin Brodshaug, Edgar Stover, Howard Gray, Max R. Brunstetter, Laura Krieger Eads, and James A. Brill.

One of the first efforts of the educational committee was to produce a demonstration educational sound film. The scheme was to use excerpts from a series of diverse shots to illustrate a talk by some educator. The choice of the educator narrowed down to Harry Dexter Kitson of Teachers College, Columbia University. The result, in two reels, was entitled *First Experimental Demonstration of Educational Talking Pictures*. The ERPI demonstration film was first publicly exhibited on July 23, 1929, at Macy Hall, Teachers College, Columbia University, to a gathering of 200 members of the Columbia faculty.

During the early months of 1929, William Lewin of Newark, New Jersey, urged Devereux to make a survey of the school market. The plan approved, Lewin embarked on a nationwide tour to show the demonstration film and distribute questionnaires as to the advantages and disadvantages of the new medium, the comparative value of the various parts of the film, and the improvements that might be made. When he returned, he recommended to ERPI that there be a close correlation between textbooks and film production.[20] He further suggested that ERPI purchase the motion picture rights

[19] Bell Laboratories engineers first studied the possibilities of educational sound films for ERPI and concluded that moving graphs and charts would make effective educational films. The problem was next handed to the Carpenter-Goldman Laboratories which had made some of the first animated films for the parent company.

[20] This was the forerunner of the McGraw-Hill Book Company Text-Films which were developed in 1947.

to textbooks. The recommendations of the Lewin report, however, were rejected by Devereux.

The next important undertaking of the ERPI educational division was a four-reel sound film on civics, entitled *Our Government at Work*, produced by Fox Films. Following this, a number of films were produced with the guidance of specialists, particularly in music, science, and teacher education.

Robert Hutchins, then president of the University of Chicago, was a major influence in the continued production of films by ERPI. Hutchins had long contended that film production should be associated with an outstanding university, with freedom to enter any subject-matter field where a contribution to education could be made. In 1932, therefore, ERPI entered into a contract with the University of Chicago to produce a series of instructional sound films under the direction of the university faculty.

A new source of support came to ERPI in 1936 when William M. Benton became vice-president of the University of Chicago. Benton made a detailed analysis of the instructional possibilities of the film medium and recommended expanded production of instructional films. From 1936 on, Benton worked for an ever-closer relationship between the university and ERPI. In 1943, the university acquired the Encyclopedia Britannica and later purchased the ERPI films, with the aid of money furnished by Benton. Thus, ERPI Classroom Films, Inc., became Encyclopedia Britannica Films.

An evaluation of ERPI by McClusky follows:

> ERPI's production has been second and third rate with the exception of the University of Chicago films. Much of ERPI's production has been salvaged from U.F.A. and other sources. ERPI has spent large sums (reputed to have been seven million dollars) for advertising and sales efforts, but few sales resulted. The total gross volume during the first ten years did not exceed $200,000. ERPI's educational talent (except that secured through the Chicago tie-up) has consisted largely of young graduate students taken from Teachers College, Columbia University. The only thing that ERPI can point to with pride is its contract with the University of Chicago. Even there, the production cost of from $8,000 to $10,000 per reel is too high. What does an ex-American Telephone and Telegraph Company accountant know about the needs of American education anyway? [21]

Fox Films Corporation.   Some theatrical film producers have attempted to establish instructional film departments, but these efforts have tended to be rather transitory and not very significant for instructional technology.

Fox Films Corporation constitutes a case history of an early instructional film production effort by a theatrical film producer. William Fox opened an educational division in 1922 under the direction of Herbert Hancock, former head of Fox News. By 1926, the first films for school use had been produced. Part of the Fox plan was to install a sound projector in every classroom and

[21] McClusky, *op. cit.*, p. 25.

in every church. However, by 1930 Fox had become so deeply indebted that he sold his voting control to Harley Clarke, one of the cofounders of the Society for Visual Education.

Once again Clarke dreamed of making educational films. Early in 1931, a group of school superintendents succeeded in interesting him in producing films which would be correlated with the school curriculum at the junior high level. The first, known as The Movietone School Series, were made in May, 1931. Ten films were ready for release by July, 1931, and a public demonstration was held in Washington, D.C. Despite this auspicious beginning, however, Fox Films Corporation ceased educational film production a few years later.[22]

Other Early Enterprises. We have described only a few of the more prominent early companies associated with the production or distribution of instructional films or "educationals." However, there are some others which deserve mention, for example, the John R. Bray Studios, the Bureau of Commercial Economics, the Educational Motion Pictures Bureau, Inc., the Pathescope Company of America, Inc., F. S. Wythe Pictures Corporation, Rowland Rogers Productions, the University Film Foundation (founded at Harvard University in 1927), and the Jamison Handy Company.

Era of crisis for the instructional film

The advent of the sound film in the late twenties introduced a critical period in instructional film history.[23] Just as educators were becoming con-

[22] Ellis and Thornborough quoted an undisclosed theatrical film producer who had produced educational films as saying: "The non-theatrical exhibitor is usually a poor businessman, he is unreliable, far from a steady customer, he does not know what he wants, yet he is dissatisfied with what has been produced, or else he wants us to produce a film according to his ideas to meet the needs of no other user of educational films. In addition, his equipment is often poor, he damages films far more than does his theatrical neighbor, and yet he is willing to pay less than a fifth of the price the theatrical exhibitor expects to pay. It is because the non-theatrical exhibitor wants everything for nothing or practically nothing that we have abandoned, at least for the present, the non-theatrical field." See Don Carlos Ellis and Laura Thornborough, *Motion Pictures in Education*. New York, Thomas Y. Crowell Company, 1923, p. 23.

[23] Sound films have existed since before the close of the nineteenth century. One of Edison's first efforts, after the invention of the Kinetoscope, was to combine his phonograph with film. Leon Gaumont supervised a demonstration of a sound film in New York City in 1913 for which a French patent had been granted him in 1901. Other early variations of the sound film were Whitman's Cameraphone (1904), Powers's Fotofone (1910), and Greenbaum's Synchronoscope (1908). In 1923, Lee De Forest gave a public showing of the Phonofilm in New York City. The first "all-talkie," known as *Oil Films on Water,* was exhibited by the Bell Telephone Laboratories at the Philadelphia sesquicentennial exposition in 1926. The first public sound program was presented by Warner Brothers at the Knickerbocker Theater in New York City on August 7, 1926. The first educational sound film was produced by Don Carlos Ellis for the Western Electric and Manufacturing Company in 1929. This film was titled *Dynamic America.*

vinced of the educational merits of the silent film, the advocates of the sound film realized they had to fight the old battle all over. The first instructional sound films brought mixed reactions. Some educators repudiated the old silent films; others rejected the new sound films; still others refrained from either open approval or disapproval until they became convinced that the addition of sound was not just another technical novelty. Many hesitated to accept the sound film because they feared their silent equipment would become useless.

Aside from the sound crisis, it was clearly evident in the late twenties and the early thirties that commercial educational film enterprises were failing at an alarming rate. Although the depression that was in progress contributed in no small measure to their decimation, it could not account for all the failures. Ironically, too, commercial instructional film producers seemed to fail just when research findings were emphasizing the particular usefulness of the film as a medium of instruction. It was plain that unless there was some permanent corporation to produce acceptable instructional films and also show a financial profit, instructional technology would be hampered in its development. Obviously, too, no commercial educational producer could achieve success without national support, and that support could not be attained until the users of instructional films were convinced that no "special interests" were invading the classroom.

In 1937, David H. Stevens of the Rockefeller Foundation requested F. Dean McClusky to investigate the causes of the failure of commercial educational film producers so that remedial steps might be taken. According to the McClusky study, there had been a general lack of coordination between educational and commercial interests due to the following reasons:

1. Educators have failed to make their problems articulate to the commercial producers, and both educators and business men developed the notion that entertainment, commercialism, and education do not mix.
2. Commercial interests have failed to grasp or to study the nature of instruction and the complexity of educational institutions.
3. Business men dominated by the quick profit motive lost sight of the necessity of gaining the confidence and backing of professional leadership in education.
4. Educational leaders have been critical of the bad taste, stupidity and low moral tone of theatrical motion pictures. As a result, those in whom the control of education rested developed a feeling of opposition to motion pictures in general. They regarded with suspicion all plans and all enterprises which had as their aim the introduction of motion pictures into schools. While leading educators have recognized the potential value of motion pictures in education, they have quietly and continuously opposed all attempts to introduce into broad classroom use motion pictures

which smacked of commercialism, low moral tone, propaganda or controversial issues. The unsatisfactory pictures were found to be so numerous that the good ones suffered from being too frequently found in bad company.

5. The stupidity which has characterized the advertising, propaganda, and sales methods of companies producing and distributing so-called "educational" motion pictures created strong opposition in educational circles to school films, good or bad. Some of this propaganda created a fear in teachers that motion pictures would supplant them and mechanize instruction. The notion expressed in this propaganda that films would be used to supplant textbooks aroused not only the opposition of teachers to visual education, but also the antagonism of the authors and publishers of books.

6. Non-theatrical exhibitors and distributors met vigorous opposition from theatrical distributors and exhibitors who feared that school and church competition would hurt the theatrical box office receipts.

7. Low financial returns to producers and distributors of motion pictures in the non-theatrical field have been caused to some extent by the competition of "free" films and "subsidized" distributors such as state universities and museums.

8. Heads of educational institutions have devoted little time, energy or thought to the organization, supervision and administration of visual education. This resulted in a lack of leadership and guidance needed by sincere producers and distributors of "educational" motion pictures, and by pioneering teachers using this new medium of instruction.

9. The mechanical problems involved in the use of motion pictures in classrooms have been a strong inhibitory factor. Before the safety standard 16 mm. film was perfected, the fire hazard was great, and laws prohibited the use of films in classrooms unless equipped with fire proof booths. Many teachers have been timid about operating the machines. Many, also, would not take the trouble to order films, set up the projector, etc. even when such were available for use.

10. Commercial interests and educators alike have failed to develop definite, agreed upon policies with respect to production and use of motion pictures in education. The resultant confusion was matched only by that created by producers and distributors of visual materials who were competing with each other in their efforts to capture the school market. Slides and stereographs, silent films, sound films, models, and charts have each been sold for the most part by competing companies. This competition between different types of visual materials confused school boards and executives.

11. Many of the failures of commercial efforts in the non-theatrical field have been traced directly to poor management due to in-

competent executives, or unsound business methods or questionable business ethics, or to excessive overhead and/or lack of
planning.[24]

McClusky suggested the following remedies:

1. The production of motion pictures for schools can be successfully
    accomplished only by independent companies working in con-
    junction with educators—not by theatrical producers or by any
    others with whom the production and distribution of motion
    pictures is a side line or medium for propaganda or purely a
    commercial enterprise.
2. In order that coordination between educators and commercial
    interests may be made effective—
    a. Educational leadership would be obtained through advisory
        boards, or committees, each member of which would retain
        his or her professional standing and position.
    b. These educational advisors would blueprint needs, conduct
        research, and validate materials.
    c. They would operate in a non-profit framework.
3. The cooperating commercial producers would manufacture the
    productions outlined by the educational advisory groups and mar-
    ket only those materials which they had validated.
    a. The commercial producers would operate at a profit, but the
        service motive would be dominant.
    b. The object of the commercial producers would be to market
        materials for instruction independent of special interests.[25]

In 1932, Will H. Hays, president of the Motion Picture Producers and
Distributors of America, attempted to deal with the competitive problem
when he called a private conference for the officials of ERPI, Eastman Teaching Films Division, and the representatives of twelve other educational film
producers for the purpose of effecting a merger of their film efforts. None of
the participants came to an agreement.[26]

Early college and university instructional film production

A number of colleges and universities engaged in some form of instructional film production as early as the second decade of this century.[27] One of

---

[24] McClusky, *op. cit.*
[25] *Ibid.*
[26] George A. Skinner had implanted the merger idea in the mind of Hays. F. Dean
McClusky wrote *Visual Instruction: Its Values and Needs* in 1932 with a merger in mind.
Both of these men attended the Hays merger conference.
[27] These included the Universities of Yale, Chicago, Illinois, Indiana, Iowa, Oklahoma,
Michigan, Nebraska, Wisconsin, Utah; Harvard University; and the Massachusetts Institute of Technology.

the first efforts to provide complete film coverage of any subject was that attempted in 1921 and 1922 in the Yale University *Chronicles of America Photoplays* which we have already discussed in this chapter.

In the early thirties, another prominent production effort was made at Arnold Gesell's Clinic of Child Development at Yale University. In 1932, the University of Minnesota established the General College under the leadership of Dean Malcolm McLean. In order to implement the General College program, a Visual Education Service, under the direction of Robert A. Kissack, was organized to collect and classify sources of visual materials, develop a servicing program, and produce instructional films.

Early instructional film distribution agencies

During the 1910–1940 period of this century, a number of instructional film distribution agencies came into existence. Film distribution agencies were organized, for example, in state departments of education,[28] in college and university extension divisions, in local and state museums,[29] in public or city school libraries,[30] and in government departments on a state and federal level.[31] In addition, a number of cooperative and commercial rental libraries were organized throughout the country. There were also a number of national organizations with their own film distributing networks which promoted the effective use of instructional films. The YMCA Motion Picture Bureau, founded in 1914, was one of the earliest of these. Other such important agencies, established during the thirties, were the American Institute of Cinematography, the American Film Center, the International Film Center, the Association of School Film Libraries,[32] and the Psychological Cinema Register.[33]

Founding of Instructional Film Libraries in City School Systems.   The Chicago Bureau of Visual Instruction established the first instructional film library in a city school system in 1917. Newark founded its visual instruction

[28] The Ohio State Department of Education established its Central Slide and Film Exchange in 1926.

[29] The Museum of Modern Art and the American Museum of Natural History of New York City were among the first museums pioneering in the distribution of instructional films.

[30] The first experiment in public library film distribution was made by the Kalamazoo, Michigan, Public Library in 1929.

[31] Such federal agencies as the Department of Agriculture, Department of the Interior, Bureau of Mines, and the Office of Education were early government distributors of educational films.

[32] The Association of School Film Libraries, founded in August, 1938, by the Rockefeller Foundation, made one of the first attempts to decentralize the distribution of educational films, but it succeeded in bringing nothing but frustration to its members.

[33] The Register was founded in 1938 by Adelbert Ford of Lehigh University for the purpose of developing a film library in the field of psychology.

department and film library in 1918; Detroit and Kansas City followed in 1919; and Los Angeles, Buffalo, and New York City formed both their visual instruction departments and film libraries in 1920. The year 1922 marks the beginning of four more film libraries in Atlanta, Pittsburgh, Berkeley,[34] and Sacramento.

Founding of Instructional Film Libraries in Extension Divisions.   An important impetus to the growth of instructional film libraries in extension divisions of colleges and universities, state departments of education, normal schools, and museums came from the distribution of war films to these divisions by the U.S. Bureau of Education Motion Picture Department in 1919. Each extension division received an average of 113 reels and agreed to act as a distributor to its local area. What is more, national advertisers soon followed this example by placing hundreds of reels of advertising film in extension depositories. By 1941, over thirty film libraries had been established in various extension divisions.

The earliest unique development in extension divisions of state departments of education occurred in North Carolina. The North Carolina Bureau of Commercial Service, which later became a division of the State Department of Education, was organized in 1916. The following year, the North Carolina Legislature appropriated $25,000 to the bureau for work "designed to improve social and educational conditions" in rural communities through a series of motion pictures selected by the Department of Public Instruction. The program also included the organization of complete, portable operating units for ten community circuits. In applying for service, a community simply agreed to pay two-thirds of the cost to the one-third paid by the state. To raise their share of the expenses, most communities charged a small admission fee for attendance at monthly meetings. Eventually, this service grew to such proportions that over four hundred community meetings were held each month with an average attendance of 45,000. Ellis and Thornborough reported that "people often walked for either eight or ten miles to attend a meeting." [35]

Films were distributed by extension divisions to all who did not intend using them for personal profit. The only charge was a small service fee or the cost of transportation. This development soon began to have an adverse effect on nontheatrical commercial enterprises which depended on educational film rentals. If they were to successfully compete with extension divisions, they would have to reduce film rentals to such an extent that their profit margin would be critically narrowed. Thus an era of hostility arose between

[34] In 1923, the Berkeley public school system distinguished itself by being the first to publish a graded list of films. Most of the early educational film catalogs listed the available films according to subjects and titles, rather than making any attempt to supply graded lists. See *Visual Instruction*, Curriculum Committee on Visual Education, Course of Study Monographs, no. 7, Berkeley, Calif., The Berkeley Public Schools, 1923.

[35] Ellis and Thornborough, *op. cit.*, p. 29.

nontheatrical producers and distributors and the extension divisions' operating film libraries.

College and university extension division leaders soon realized that the policy of operating a film library on a free basis was not satisfactory and that continued reliance on advertisers for films was not to be condoned if certain educational objectives were to be achieved. By 1923, a movement for selecting only educational films and operating on a sound financial basis, led by W. H. Dudley of the University of Wisconsin, had become so widespread that practically all state bureaus were charging service and rental fees.

Excerpting of theatrical films for instructional purposes

Although the National Education Association Judd Committee [36] had first recommended the excerpting of theatrical films for instructional use in 1923, the first large-scale, systematic excerpting of theatrical films for educational purposes did not take place until 1936. The reason for this long delay was that the Motion Picture Producers and Distributors of America repeatedly refused to approve the release of theatrical films because of their fear that excerpting would destroy the motion picture industry.

Committee for the Study of Social Values in Motion Pictures. The first small-scale excerpting of theatrical films for classroom use came about as the result of the organization of a Committee for the Study of Social Values in Motion Pictures, in September, 1927, by the Payne Fund.[37] A sum of $65,800 was allocated to underwrite a two-year period of activity including a survey of the motion picture field by William H. Short of the Motion Picture Research Council and a series of studies by leading social scientists.

By June, 1928, Short's study was completed and printed for the private use of Payne Fund members in a 400-page volume entitled *A Generation of Motion Pictures.* This preliminary study was next placed in the hands of people selected for their knowledge of education and social science as well as of the history and problems of the motion picture industry. In addition, a conference was organized "to secure factual data regarding motion pictures on the basis of which a national policy, socially constructive in character, may be formulated." [38] As a result, twenty-one studies were proposed, of which twelve served as a basis for the subsequent Payne Fund studies of motion pictures.[39]

[36] See Chap. 7 of this book for details of the Judd Committee activities.
[37] Dean Howard M. LeSourd of Boston University was chairman of the Committee for the Study of Social Values in Motion Pictures.
[38] *The Payne Fund Annual Report* (1928), p. 5.
[39] As a result of the Payne Fund studies of the Committee for the Study of Social Values in Motion Pictures, a Committee on Educational Research was organized under the direction of W. W. Charters of Ohio State University. The Payne Fund studies evolved out of the work of the Committee on Educational Research.

In 1929, the motion picture industry, in order to disarm some of its critics, permitted the Committee for the Study of Social Values in Motion Pictures to excerpt portions of theatrical films for the first time. From these, a 35-mm silent film series entitled *Secrets of Success,* dramatizing certain moral issues, was created and distributed by the committee to schools, churches, and other organizations for character education.[40] This series failed after a few years, largely because of opposition from the motion picture industry, limited projection equipment, and chaotic distribution.

Commission on Human Relations.   The Committee for the Study of Social Values in Motion Pictures secured a grant of $75,000 from the Rockefeller Foundation in 1936 for the Progressive Education Association, so that its work on the excerpting of theatrical films might be continued.[41] A Commission on Human Relations was established under the chairmanship of Alice V. Keliher in July, 1936. This led to the first large-scale excerpting. By 1938, sixty excerpts known as *The Human Relations Series* had been prepared and had begun to be used experimentally in a number of schools as a means of helping adolescents solve their personal problems and develop a better understanding of human relations.[42]

Advisory Committee on the Use of Motion Pictures in Education.   In 1934, Will H. Hays of the Motion Picture Producers and Distributors of

[40] Hugh Hartshorne and Mark A. May had found in their 1928 *Studies in Deceit* that verbal learning of moral codes did not seem to have much effect on behavior. As a result of these studies, May became interested in finding some type of instruction which produced what he called an "emotional punch." It occurred to May, probably as a result of the earlier Judd Committee recommendation, that live situations in the form of filmic stories would be more effective. After attempting to use the *Secrets of Success* series for character education, he found a more systematic approach was necessary.

[41] When the motion picture industry permitted the Committee for the Study of Social Values in Motion Pictures to make excerpts from theatrical films, the first major bulwark had been penetrated. In 1936, Paramount Studios became the first theatrical film producer to release film classics to the schools. Eric Haight of Films Incorporated, a nontheatrical film producer and distributor, deserves much credit for persuading Paramount to consent to this release. As a result of Paramount's action, other studios later joined in this move.

[42] To achieve the objective of the commission, a number of provocative films were used. These included a film called *Fury,* which centered on the behavior of a mob in a lynching; the film, *A Devil Is a Sissy,* which revealed the problems faced by a boy who moves from one community to another; and *An Educating Father,* a film centering on the dispute between father and son over the choice of the son's vocation. Schools participating in the human relations experiment included two New York City high schools, Benjamin Franklin and Washington Irving; two New York City private schools, Dalton and Lincoln; and the following other schools: Bronxville public schools, New York; Freehold public schools, New Jersey; Cambridge School, Massachusetts; Stephens Junior College, Missouri; University High School, Oakland, California; Francis W. Parker School, Chicago; North Shore Country Day School, Winnetka; Western Military Academy, Illinois; Shaker Heights Public School, Cleveland; Oak Lane Country Day School, Philadelphia; George School, Pennsylvania; and the Denver public high schools, Denver, Colorado. Adult and parent groups in Vermont also took part in this experiment. See Commission on Human Relations, Progressive Education Association, *The Human Relations Series of Films,* New York, 1939.

America called in a number of consultants to discuss a plan whereby the motion picture industry could make a contribution to the use of theatrical films in the schools. As a result of this meeting, Hays sent Mark A. May, director of the Institute of Human Relations, Yale University, to Hollywood to further explore the possibilities of excerpting theatrical films with the advice that he avoid the use of two words—"16-mm" and "education." May cautiously probed the attitudes of Hollywood producers without discussing his mission and on his return prepared a memorandum recommending the release of theatrical films for school use. Reluctantly the major producers, with the exception of Metro-Goldwyn-Mayer, agreed to go along with the May recommendation despite the protests of countless exhibitors.

The advisory committee, supported by the Rockefeller Foundation and the Motion Picture Producers and Distributors of America, called in some fifty educators to review 1,800 theatrical shorts, from which 360 were selected and put on 16-mm film for distribution to schools.[43] Moreover, film descriptions were prepared and catalogs printed. The advisory committee was incorporated in the state of New York in 1939 as a nonprofit membership corporation under the name of Teaching Film Custodians, Inc.[44]

An emerging technology for the instructional application of films

We have seen that a clear distinction between the film as an entertainment and informational medium and as a medium of instruction was first made early in this century, although instructional films were usually considered as aids to teaching rather than as self-contained sequences of instruction.

One of the first descriptive technologies for the instructional use of the

---

[43] Somewhat related to this development was the rise of the motion picture appreciation movement in the thirties. Although this movement was generated to a large extent by the provocation of the Payne Fund studies, the increased accessibility of theatrical films for school use had an important influence. William Lewin and Max J. Herzberg of the Newark, New Jersey, public schools were early leaders in this movement. The basic object was to establish courses designed to analyze and discuss theatrical motion pictures for the purpose of influencing the attitudes and behavior of adolescents. See William Lewin, *Photoplay Appreciation in American High Schools*. New York, D. Appleton-Century Company, Inc., 1934.

[44] The first officers of Teaching Film Custodians, Inc., were Mark A. May, chairman and director of research; Carl E. Milliken, general business and financial manager; and Roger Albright, director of educational services. When Teaching Film Custodians was first established, contracts were negotiated with the motion picture industry which provided for three-year contracts to schools. The films were to be used only during school time and not for entertainment. No admission was to be charged, nor were the films to be used for fund raising by school organizations. A number of other restrictive clauses were included in the contract. In effect, the service of the Teaching Film Custodians was not satisfactory for many reasons. Prominent among these was the fact that films were often loaned to certain schools while others were arbitrarily excluded for a variety of reasons.

film came about when the Frederick Stephen Wythe Pictures Corporation of San Francisco, California, produced a series of civics films in 1918, entitled, *Citizens in the Making: A Film Text Composed of Thirty Lessons*. A *Manual of Civics Film Text* by C. A. Stebbins, published by the Wythe Company, contained suggestions to teachers for the use of this "film textbook."

During the twenties, the first books describing a methodology for the film in the classroom were written and the first courses were established for teachers concerning the use of the instructional film. By the late twenties, a definitive methodology had been developed. For example, Weber adapted Johann Herbart's "instructional step" plan by dividing his methodology for film use into six steps: (1) preparation, or a discussion of the synopsis of the film in the light of the learner's previous experience; (2) presentation, or the presentation of the film when the learners' "curiosity is at high pitch and their minds sharpened for the central message of the film"; (3) informal discussion and assignments consisting of readings, problems, or projects; (4) supplementary showings, either running the film again without interruption or, preferably, showing it in parts, followed by more informal discussion; (5) formal recitation, or assimilation of the film's concepts by means of generalization and application, with the teacher having a carefully prepared lesson plan structured as to aim, content, and procedure; and (6) check-up, or oral or written review quizzes or a list of test items in the form of an essay, report, or project.[45]

Much of the theorizing behind the methodology of film use was based on the concept that the pictorial is inevitably "real," "concrete," and "meaningful"; that is, the film medium not only brought visual reality but added concreteness through the quality of motion.

Although the term *visual instruction* was used since the beginning of this century to refer to a variety of visual instructional media, it is not surprising that the instructional film intensified its use and provided a great impetus to the development of the audiovisual instruction movement in American education. For a historical survey of this vital, important facet of instructional technology, we now turn to the next three chapters in this book.

[45] Adapted from Joseph J. Weber, *Visual Aids in Education*. Valparaiso, Ind., Valparaiso University, 1930, pp. 47–50. (Mimeographed.)

chapter 7

**the audiovisual instruction
movement: emergence**

An important new movement in American education
which came to be known as visual instruction (later, audiovisual) first developed from the mainstream of instructional technology during the years 1918–1924. During this
six-year period, these events occurred:

> The first formal credit courses in visual instruc-
> tion were offered for teachers at the college and
> university level.
>
> The first visual instruction professional organiza-
> tions were founded at local and national levels.
>
> The first professional visual instruction journals
> appeared.
>
> The first systematic visual instruction research
> studies were reported.

The first administrative units of visual instruction were organized in the public schools, colleges, universities, and state departments of education.

There is no simple answer to the question of why the visual instruction movement evolved as it did or when it did. A number of factors combined to bring about its emergence. Some of these are as follows:

The long tradition of revolt against formalism and verbalism in educational practice as reflected in the work of men like Comenius, Rousseau, Pestalozzi, Froebel, Herbart, and Dewey.

The growing realization that instructional programs were inadequate to meet the needs of increased school enrollments in the public schools at all levels from 1880 to 1920.

The growing conviction that the film was destined to revolutionize educational practices and that it would simultaneously reduce the costs of instruction.

The development of a theoretical rationale which attached unique qualities of "concreteness" to the use of certain instructional media (i.e., visual materials).

The success and popularity of illustrated lectures on the Lyceum and Chautauqua circuits convinced many educators that this same instructional technique could be used effectively in the schools.

The development of physical science and engineering technology made feasible the use of new, economically mass-producible resources of instruction.

The extensive and effective use of training films during World War I gave an impetus to the new movement.

A sound basis for the movement was established when the U.S. Bureau of Education donated hundreds of reels of surplus war film to thirty-three university extension divisions throughout the United States.

These factors explain in part why educators became interested in the use of specific instructional media and why the visual instruction movement began to develop as it did in the years immediately following World War I.

There does not seem to be any documented evidence that any one individual conceived the term visual instruction. Rather, it is safe to assume that it developed quite spontaneously. With the technological development of projected still and motion pictures, many began to see inherent instructional value in these particular media. These people comprised two groups: one composed of social workers and a few imaginative educators; the other consisting of commercial producers and distributors of such visual media as stereographs, lantern slides, and films, who envisioned an extended market for their wares.

It is easy to see why the commercial promoters soon christened this new movement visual education. This was first done formally when the Keystone View Company of Meadville, Pennsylvania, published *Visual Education* (1908)[1]—a teachers' guide to Keystone's "600 Set" of stereographs and lantern slides. This book consequently achieved the dubious distinction of introducing a term that many have argued is psychologically unsound.

Regardless of its commercial heritage, visual education, or visual instruction, came to be generally accepted by educators. It remained as the primary semantic label of the movement until the Department of Visual Instruction of the National Education Association officially changed its name to the Department of Audiovisual Instruction in 1947. Since this time the terms "audiovisual education" or "audiovisual instruction" have been most frequently used to designate the use of specific equipment for presenting instructional materials of a visual nature. However, a new term was introduced in 1953 when the Department of Audiovisual Instruction of the NEA sponsored the professional journal known as the *AV Communication Review*.[2]

Theoretical rationale underlying the audiovisual instruction movement

The traditional theoretical rationale underlying the audiovisual instruction movement has identified media and machines, use of particular senses (the eye and the ear), and characteristics of materials for learning and instruction on the basis of their concreteness or abstractness. One of the earliest abstract-concrete continuums designed to serve as a guide to instruction appeared in 1886, as follows: (1) object, (2) model, (3) picture, (4) diagram, (5) experiment, (6) language, and (7) printed or written material.[3]

In 1910, Adams wrote *Exposition and Illustration in Teaching* and included the following "order of merit": (1) the real object, for which anything else is a more or less inefficient substitute; (2) a model of the real object; (3) a diagram dealing with some of the aspects of the object; and (4) a mere verbal description of the object.[4]

Adams goes on to explain that "too frequently the above general order

[1] The Keystone View Company published its first guide to the use of its stereographs in 1906. However, this was an untitled, paper-covered booklet of approximately one hundred pages. The title *Visual Education* did not appear on the cover until 1908.
[2] The Department of Audiovisual Instruction sponsored the publication of *Instructional Materials* in 1955, but it was promptly changed to *Audiovisual Instruction* because of loud protests from audiovisualists.
[3] *Proceedings of the National Education Association* (1886), p. 274.
[4] John Adams, *Exposition and Illustration in Teaching*. New York, The Macmillan Company, 1910, p. 319.

of merit is carried over to the purely illustrative field [and there is] an un-warranted glorification of objects." [5]

In 1928, Weber observed that "we can acquire visual experience from situations that are as concrete as reality and as abstract as the scheme of typical visual aids which follows: (1) actual reality, as we find it on a school journey; (2) pseudo-reality, as exemplified by artificial models and exhibits; (3) pictorial realism, as depicted in drawings and photographs; (4) pictorial symbolism, as found in graphs and diagrams; and (5) verbal symbolism—similes, metaphors, and plain language." [6]

Much of this early rationale of audiovisual instruction still persists. Men like Edgar Dale [7] and other leaders in the audiovisual instruction movement later developed other theoretical variations based on these concepts.[8]

Professionalization of visual instruction: development of national organizations

Beginning in 1919, five national visual instruction organizations were established. Two were short-lived; one lost its national status; one served the visual instruction field for twelve years; and one has continued to provide leadership in the visual instruction movement since it was first founded.

First National Visual Instruction Organizations.   The first two organizations of national scope formed in the emerging visual instruction field lasted less than a year. They were (1) the National Academy for Visual Instruction, incorporated in Washington, D.C., in October, 1919; (2) the American Educational Motion Picture Association which began operations in New York City, also in October, 1919. The American Educational Motion Picture Association was formed to provide the active study of school requirements for the classroom use of motion pictures. Allen S. Williams, director of the Reptile Society, was president, and A. D. V. Storey was executive secretary.

The National Academy of Visual Instruction.   This organization (not to be confused with the National Academy for Visual Instruction mentioned in the preceding paragraph that had been formed the previous year) came into existence as the result of a conference of some forty educators during the annual meeting of the Department of Superintendence of the National Education Association at Cleveland, Ohio, in February, 1920. A committee of nine was appointed to take the necessary steps in organizing a national

[5] *Loc. cit.*
[6] Joseph J. Weber, "Picture Values in Education," *Educational Screen*, vol. 7 (1928), p. 126.
[7] See Dale's "Cone of Experience," Fig. 1.1 of this book.
[8] In the main, such theorization seems to have had little effect on the design of instructional materials or hardware.

association. On April 7, 1920, this committee met at the University of Michigan and drew up a constitution and bylaws, adopted a name, and elected temporary officers. The first annual meeting of the National Academy of Visual Instruction was held at Madison, Wisconsin, on July 14, 1920.[9] In the opening address, William H. Dudley, then chief of the Bureau of Visual Instruction at the University of Wisconsin, sensed the historic importance of this meeting when he said:

> It is for us to preempt the field, to plant our standards, to set the pace. We must establish fundamental principles, must work out specific and constructive programs of procedure, must study the needs of the schools and other educational groups and point out definite ways to meet such needs. We must recognize, however, that basic educational principles and policies are already firmly established—that ends to be accomplished are clearly defined, and that hence we are not to attempt ends, but rather to introduce devices that will lead more directly to ends already in view.[10]

The stated purpose of this early visual instruction organization was to promote noninflammable film, distribute suitable reels of educational film, organize state associations, improve subject matter, establish standards, and conduct tests.[11] This organization was merged with the Department of Visual Instruction of the National Education Association in 1932.

The Visual Instruction Association of America.   Two years after the Academy was established, the Visual Instruction Association of America was formally organized at Boston, Massachusetts, on July 6, 1922.[12] It had its beginnings in the New York City Visual Instruction Association, first organized in 1920 for the purpose of offering assistance to the New York City public schools in their experimental use of instructional films.

The particular contribution of the association to the budding visual instruction movement was its active role in initiating visual instruction demon-

---

[9] The first officers elected at the first meeting of the National Academy of Visual Instruction were: president: F. W. Reynolds, University of Utah, Salt Lake City, Utah; vice-president: G. E. Condra, University of Nebraska, Lincoln, Nebraska; secretary: J. V. Ankeney, University of Missouri, Columbia, Missouri; treasurer: Charles Roach, Iowa State College, Ames, Iowa.

[10] *Proceedings of the First Annual Meeting of the National Academy of Visual Instruction,* July 14–16, 1920, Madison, Wis., p. 10.

[11] *Moving Picture Age* (October, 1921), p. 43.

[12] The first president of the Visual Instruction Association was Ernest L. Crandall, director of lectures and visual instruction of the New York City public schools. In addition to Crandall, members of the association included Rita Hochheimer, assistant to Crandall; A. G. Balcom, assistant superintendent of the Newark, New Jersey, public schools; George Zehrung, director of the YMCA. Motion Picture Bureau; Rowland Rogers, Columbia University; Illsley Boone; Don Carlos Ellis of the U.S. Department of Agriculture; Clyde Fisher, American Museum of Natural History; John H. Finley, and George D. Strayer, both of Columbia University.

strations centers at educational conferences held throughout the country. The association, in cooperation with the National Education Association, sponsored the first national visual instruction demonstrations as well as the first national commercial exhibits of visual instructional materials. The association further distinguished itself by accepting, as full voting members, representatives of commercial companies serving the visual instruction field.[13]

When Ernest Crandall, its president and guiding force, retired in the late 1920s, the association lost its national standing and reverted to its original status as the New York City Visual Instruction Association. In 1931, as we shall see, the association became a part of the National Academy of Visual Instruction and changed its name to the Metropolitan New York Branch of the Academy. When the academy merged with the Department of Visual Instruction of the National Education Association in 1932, the Metropolitan New York Branch also joined in the merger.

National Education Association Department of Visual Instruction.   The NEA Department of Visual Instruction (DVI) was established on July 6, 1923, at the Oakland, California, summer convention of the NEA. Two main lines of influence contributed to the development of DVI: (1) the introduction of the idea of creating such a department within the NEA by Dudley Grant Hayes, president of the National Academy of Visual Instruction, and A. W. Abrams, head of the New York State Division of Visual Instruction, at the NEA Boston convention in 1922; and (2) the creation of the Judd Committee. Since the ramifications of the Judd Committee are rather extensive, it is considered in some detail in the next major section of this chapter.

Prior to the establishment of the Department of Visual Instruction, there had been a long-felt need for such an organization. Nelson Greene, editor of *Educational Screen,* was prompted to comment as follows:

> Some thousands of earnest educators, to be sure, have been working along these lines for years, but against fearful odds. The wise action of the NEA will give a strong additional impulse and incentive to their work. In the minds of many other thousands, visual education will now cease to be a "fad"—as they were afraid it might be—because the fiat of the great Association has been set upon it. The visual movement now has its credentials, with the official vise upon them. With such credentials it will travel fast and far.[14]

[13] A complete exhibition and demonstration of slides, films, stereographs, posters, maps, charts, stereopticons, portable and standard projectors, optical instruments, and slidefilm projectors was held. In addition, the Visual Instruction Association of America provided rest and conference rooms as well as a specially equipped projection room. The Visual Instruction Association of America, "Visual Instruction Association of America: Its Origin and Achievements," *Visual Instruction Handbook,* vol. 1 (June, 1924), pp. 39–41.

[14] "The New Department of the NEA," *Educational Screen,* vol. 2 (September, 1923), p. 317.

Since its formation, the Department of Visual Instruction gradually grew in membership and prestige. However, its greatest growth and change did not occur until after World War II.[15]

The Judd Committee and the first formal assessment of the visual instruction movement

The so-called Judd Committee was an important early influence in the professional organization of visual instruction. It also provided the first formal assessment of the visual instruction movement through its investigations.

Will H. Hays, president of the newly formed Motion Picture Producers and Distributors of America, Inc.,[16] appeared before the general assembly of the 1922 summer convention of the NEA in Boston and pledged the resources of the motion picture industry in support of visual instruction. Following the convention, Will Owens, president of the NEA, appointed a committee to cooperate with the MPPDA.[17] The chairman of this committee was Charles

[15] Much of the history of the activities of the Department of Visual Instruction during the 1923–1942 period is related in this chapter. Its more recent history is contained largely in Chapter 9 of this book.

[16] In 1922, the motion picture industry selected Will H. Hays, a member of President Harding's cabinet and an elder in the Presbyterian Church, to head the newly formed Motion Picture Producers and Distributors of America, Inc., in Washington, D.C. Although the purpose of the organization was to create a favorable public image of motion pictures, the public gradually realized that it had been duped; Hollywood productions did not reflect the image Hays was attempting to build. After some five years of parrying criticism and dissatisfaction, Hays found the way out through the formulation of a morals code. At this juncture, he selected two assistants on the basis of the influence they wielded in other fields. They were Carl E. Milliken, who had served two terms as governor of Maine, and who had been for three years a federal officer charged with prohibition enforcement in New England, and Colonel Jason S. Joy, former executive secretary of the American Red Cross. Milliken was put in charge of New York studio relations work; Joy was sent to Hollywood for the same purpose. In 1929, Mrs. Thomas G. Winter, formerly national president of the General Federation of Women's Clubs, was added to the Hays staff. For another three years the motion picture industry used the Hays Office as a smoke screen behind which it continued to do just as it pleased. When it became apparent that further negotiations with the Hays Office were useless, a well-knit Catholic force developed the Legion of Decency, an organized attack upon the motion picture industry at the box-office level. For the first time, the motion picture producers became seriously concerned and proceeded to make adjustments in policies that the public had been led to believe were made some twelve years previously. As a result, a real censorship power became centered in the Hays Office, with Joseph I. Breen as censor, and the long-promised cleanup became a reality. Nevertheless, the Legion was "still sitting outside his door watching for the first false move." See Ruth A. Inglis, *Freedom of the Movies*. Chicago, The University of Chicago Press, 1947.

[17] The Judd Committee was officially known as the Committee on Cooperation with the Motion Picture Producers and Distributors of America, Inc. The original members were Judd, Leonard Ayres of Cleveland, Elizabeth Breckenridge of Louisville, Ernest L. Crandall of New York City, Susan Dorsey of Los Angeles, Elizabeth Hall of Minneapolis, and Payson Smith of Boston.

H. Judd of the University of Chicago. His committee immediately received a grant of $5,000 from the Hays Office.

Subcommittees Formed.   Upon receipt of the MPPDA grant, two sub-committees were appointed: the first, headed by Ernest L. Crandall of the New York City schools and president of the Visual Instruction Association of America, reviewed old theatrical films to determine which films or portions had educational value;[18] the second subcommittee, under the chairmanship of F. Dean McClusky of the University of Illinois, made a nationwide survey of the administration of visual instruction.[19]

The Judd Committee Summary Report.   After the subcommittees had reported to the Judd Committee in June, 1923, a report was given to the NEA at its Oakland convention in July, 1923, and to the Hays Office. The Judd report [20] contained many recommendations, among them the recommendation from McClusky's administrative survey report that a clearinghouse of visual instruction information be formed. The direct result was the establishment of the Department of Visual Education in the National Education Association.

The Judd report also revealed that visual instruction was receiving inadequate financial support, that educators were forced to rely almost entirely on national advertisers for their films because these could be obtained free and because they had no means of knowing what was done elsewhere, and that educators had no exchange of information on current methods or how their own work could be organized and administered effectively.

The prevailing theme was the lack of uniform practices in the administration of visual instruction. In some cities, slides and films were prepared in lesson sets and sent to a school circuit. In other cities, the school administrator requested whatever material he wanted. Some school systems provided delivery service; in others, the teachers had to pick up their own materials and equipment. In most city systems, only part of the schools secured their films direct from the visual instruction administrative agency. The others preferred to make their own arrangements with film exchanges and industrial firms and to purchase and operate their own equipment. In some cities and

[18] The Crandall subcommittee was the first to investigate the possibility of excerpting theatrical films for educational use. This was first made possible on a large scale when the Progressive Education Association established the Commission on Human Relations in 1936. Hugh Hartshorne and Mark A. May, in 1928, also did some excerpting of theatrical films for educational use in connection with their *Studies in Deceit.* See Chap. 6 of this history for further details.

[19] F. Dean McClusky was assisted by A. Loretta Clark of the Los Angeles public schools and Charles Roach of the Extension Division of the University of Iowa.

[20] See Charles H. Judd, *Report of the Committee on Visual Education and Cooperation with the Motion Picture Producers and Distributors, Inc., to the National Education Association,* Washington, D.C., NEA, 1923.

in some university and college extension divisions, films were sent without expense to the users; in others, they were rented. In some cases, the school children themselves contributed to help defray film costs. Similar diversities also appeared in the matter of projectors. Some schools used trained projectionists; others instructed their teachers in projector operation; and still others had older boys operate their projectors.

The Judd report also pointed up the fire hazards in connection with the projection of films [21] and recommended that "the use of inflammable films should be restricted to licensed persons and exhibition places fully equipped with fire protective devices." [22]

The report goes on to say that there were:

> . . . few films in existence which were created with the definite purpose of using them as adjuncts in the teaching of specific lessons in the conventional subjects. . . . Also, the schools showed a considerable number of recreational and amusement films, and in a good many cases, these were pretty frankly employed as a sort of sugar-coating to make the diet of advertising films somewhat more palatable.[23]

The Judd Committee reached the conclusion that

> Much work needs to be done in educational experimentation and research having for its purpose the discovery and development of the best methods for using motion pictures in teaching. . . . Second, . . . a clearing-house for information is greatly needed.[24]

The Judd Committee and Commercialism. Charles H. Judd asked that the NEA Committee on Cooperation with the Motion Picture Producers and Distributors of America (the Judd Committee) be discontinued and a new committee appointed. Because of the experience of the past year with commercial organizations, Judd recommended:

> . . . that this new committee be specifically instructed not to attempt to organize any plan of picture censorship and that the Committee be instructed not to give its approval directly or indirectly to any projecting apparatus or any film or any plan for the preparation of scenarios or films. The experience of the year has shown the unqualified wisdom of the restrictions here recommended. The present committee has been literally besieged by promoters of all kinds of plans for the production of projectors and particular films.[25]

---

[21] The Scarborough School, Scarborough-on-Hudson, New York, was the first school to provide a permanent fireproof projection booth and to establish permanently equipped facilities for projecting silent and sound films.
[22] Judd, *op. cit.*, pp. 3–4.
[23] *Ibid.*, p. 8.
[24] *Loc. cit.*
[25] *Ibid.*, p. 5.

Despite this recommendation, the committee was continued and Thomas E. Finegan, superintendent of public instruction in Pennsylvania, became chairman of the committee when Judd withdrew in 1923. Beginning in the fall of 1926, Frank Cody, superintendent of schools in Detroit, served as chairman until the committee was dissolved in 1927.

During the period from 1923 to 1927, the Committee on Cooperation with the MPPDA (which was often referred to as the Visual Education Committee after Judd left it) was financed by the Hays Office and literally "built its own empire" by paralleling or dominating the work of the Department of Visual Instruction in the National Education Association. In a 1924 committee report made by Chairman Finegan, it was announced that five subcommittees had been appointed: "(1) on legislation; (2) on designation of communities doing excellent work in visual education; (3) on courses of study; (4) on gathering materials relative to administrative methods in current use, etc.; (5) on cooperation and research." [26] The roster of these committees listed thirteen names, of which nine were leaders in the Department of Visual Instruction of the NEA, the National Academy of Visual Instruction, and the Visual Instruction Association of America. What is more, the committee had begun to work very closely with the Eastman Kodak Company in planning the Eastman experiments with 16-mm instructional films and the chairman became director of the Eastman Teaching Films Division in September, 1926!

Developments leading to merger of national visual instruction organizations

Probably the most significant early event in the history of the visual instruction movement took place in February, 1932, when the three existing national visual education organizations were merged.[27] Nelson Greene, editor of *Educational Screen,* called it "the greatest step forward to date in the advance of the visual movement." [28] Since 1923, these organizations had been working parallel to each other with much duplication and overlap of activities. In this confusion, many wondered why three organizations existed and why some people were members of all three.

Early Barriers to Merger.   Although the three surviving national visual instruction organizations had the same general motivation for organizing, there were fundamental differences separating them. One basic policy con-

[26] F. Dean McClusky, "The Coalition of 1932," *Audiovisual Instruction,* vol. 7 (September, 1962), pp. 502–506.
[27] The three national visual instruction organizations in existence in 1932 were the Department of Visual Instruction of the National Education Association, the National Academy of Visual Instruction, and the Visual Instruction Association of America.
[28] "Editorial," *Educational Screen,* vol. 11 (March, 1932), p. 66.

flict centered in commercial versus professional interests. In the National Academy of Visual Instruction, individuals with commercial affiliation were not permitted to vote or hold office. In the Visual Instruction Association of America, on the other hand, active membership was open to educators and commercial persons alike. This basic controversy was camouflaged by the argument that the academy was dominated by representatives of college and university extension divisions from the Midwestern region of the United States. Although it was true that the academy leadership was centered in the Midwest and that all of its officers were associated with extension divisions, three of the seven members of the academy's executive committee were from the Chicago, Cleveland, and Newark city school systems.

When the Visual Instruction Association of America was first proposed in March, 1922, its effect on the academy was instantaneous. At the Third Annual Convention held at Lexington, Kentucky, from April 18 to 20, the academy took five significant steps to meet the competition of a new organization backed by commercial interests. First, it became an affiliate of the NEA Department of Superintendence and beginning in February, 1923, held all subsequent annual meetings concurrently with those of the Department of Superintendence. Second, it elected a new slate of officers representing the East, Midwest, large cities, universities, and even museums. Third, the academy's newly elected president, Dudley Grant Hayes, director of visual education in the Chicago schools, and Alfred Abrams, head of the Division of Visual Education of the New York State Department of Education, began negotiations with the National Education Association for the establishment of a Department of Visual Instruction.[29] Fourth, the academy reinforced its policy of excluding individuals with commercial connections from voting membership. Fifth, it recommended that a full-time secretariat be established. Meanwhile, J. W. Shepherd of the University of Oklahoma called for unity in the following words:

> The National Academy is already in the field. It has the definite backing of a large share of those most active. . . . It stands pledged by its constitution to high ideals and lofty purposes. Its policies are still in the making and can be readily shaped to reach worthy ends. The organization, therefore, should be not only given an opportunity to prove its merit but it should also be given the definite support of all interests.[30]

The Merger Movement. It is difficult to document the precise time when a decision was made to set aside the differences separating the three national

[29] McClusky observes that "it must seem strange that the Academy having tried unsuccessfully to bring about unity in the profession would now deliberately take steps to create another rival professional organization." This was due, as McClusky says, to the strong desire for official professional status and recognition. McClusky, *op. cit.,* p. 505.

[30] See J. W. Shepherd, "Are More Organizations Needed?" *Educational Screen,* vol. 1 (April, 1922), pp. 107–108.

visual instruction organizations and to work for their merger. The merger idea first took definitive form when F. Dean McClusky was president of the academy in 1930–1931. McClusky was particularly qualified to provide the national leadership in bringing about a merger because of his long experience in the visual instruction movement and because of his rather unique professional role at that time. In addition to being president of the academy, he was also first vice-president of the Department of Visual Instruction of the NEA, a member of the executive committee of the Visual Instruction Association of America, and director of the Scarborough School, New York, where he had the backing of Frank A. Vanderlip, an ardent supporter of visual instruction.

McClusky's efforts in achieving a merger were aided by Charles Roach in Los Angeles; William H. Dudley of the University of Wisconsin, founder of the academy; William Gregory of Cleveland; John Hollinger of Pittsburgh; Abraham Krasker of Boston; and Ellsworth Dent of the University of Kansas, secretary of the academy. Nelson Greene, editor of *Educational Screen*, also supported the proposed merger with enthusiasm. The first step taken by McClusky was to determine the status of the Visual Instruction Association of America. This was easily done when the Association voted to change its name to the Metropolitan New York Branch of the National Academy of Visual Instruction and to make the necessary changes in its constitution and bylaws. With this accomplished, Abraham Krasker with McClusky's help formed a Massachusetts branch of the academy.

With the academy's position thus strengthened, a committee consisting of McClusky and Grace Fisher Ramsey went to the National Education Association for the purpose of negotiating a merger of the academy and the Department of Visual Instruction. These negotiations were successful, and the department voted at its Los Angeles 1931 summer convention to merge with the academy. All that remained was the approval of the membership of the academy. This final step was taken by the membership at its twelfth and final convention held on February 23–24, 1932, in the National Press Club, Washington, D.C. There it voted to merge with the department. Simultaneously, a vote was cast for the merger of the publications of the two organizations—the *Visual Instruction News* and the *Educational Screen*.

First Officers of New Association.   The first president of the Department of Visual Instruction of the NEA, following the merger of the three national organizations, was Charles F. Hoban, Sr., director of the Pennsylvania State Library and Museum and director of visual education for Pennsylvania. F. Dean McClusky was elected first vice-president; W. W. Whittinghill, second vice-president; and Ellsworth Dent, secretary-treasurer. Those selected for the first executive committee included Grace Fisher Ramsey,

William Dudley, John A. Hollinger, Abraham Krasker, A. G. Balcom, and Daniel Knowlton.[31]

Teacher education in visual instruction

The expansion of the visual instruction movement brought with it the demand for formal teacher education in visual instruction. F. Dean Mc-Clusky, Joseph J. Weber, W. M. Gregory, and A. G. Balcom were particularly vocal in stressing this aspect. McClusky aptly stated in 1923 that "the movement for visual education will progress in direct ratio to the number of teachers who are trained in the technique of visual instruction." [32] He said further that ". . . textbooks and syllabi must be prepared . . . courses of study must be introduced into normal schools . . . teachers must be given an opportunity to learn the advantages and disadvantages of visual instruction through formal and informal instruction." [33]

Weber observed that the visual instruction movement rested upon a number of facts. He said:

> The sense of vision plays an important role in the educative process; the exclusive use of language in education dulls interest and tends to verbalism; the perfection of photography has extended the material environment of the learners; experimental education has revealed evidence that visual aids vitalize the curriculum and thus effect marked economies in the learning process.
>
> *These considerations justify the formulation of visual aids courses in normal schools, colleges, and universities,* at least temporarily until the transition from the old to the new methodology is complete.[34]

In the meantime, a beginning was made in offering courses in visual instruction in scattered areas of the country.

First Teacher Education Courses in Visual Instruction. Probably the first course in visual instruction offered for official credit was given at the University of Minnesota in 1918 by Albert M. Field.[35] Other early visual

---

[31] The author of this history is deeply indebted to F. Dean McClusky for supplying unpublished data concerning the merger of the national visual instruction organizations.

[32] F. Dean McClusky, "The Administration of Visual Education: A National Survey." Unpublished report made to the NEA, 1923, p. 193.

[33] *Loc. cit.*

[34] Joseph J. Weber, "Picture Values in Education," *Educational Screen*, vol. 7 (1928), p. 131.

[35] The University of Minnesota visual instruction course description reads as follows: "Designed to prepare persons for presenting materials by means of slides, films, charts, etc. Students assisted in assembling materials for their own use and in acquiring skill and technique in preparation and operation of various mediums."

instruction courses were offered at the University of Kansas and North Carolina State Teachers College in the fall of 1921. It is not known who taught the course at North Carolina, but Joseph J. Weber probably developed one of the first comprehensive courses in visual instruction at the University of Kansas. This same course was given at the University of Texas and the University of Arkansas during the summers of 1923 and 1925, respectively.

The Dorris Survey.   Anna V. Dorris of San Francisco State College made a survey in 1922 to determine the provisions that were being made for teacher education in visual instruction. A questionnaire was sent to 171 normal schools, of which 30 replied, and to 114 colleges and universities, of which 37 replied. Among the normal schools, four offered regular courses in visual education and two offered summer session courses. The Michigan Normal School offered one noncredit course. One university taught "graphs"; [36] another gave a course on photography and slide making. Seventeen of the thirty-seven colleges and universities reported that they operated film distribution centers. Only four normal schools reported such service.[37]

The McClusky National Survey of 1923.   As we have seen, F. Dean McClusky conducted a nationwide survey of visual instruction administrative practices as part of the investigations made by the Judd Committee of the National Education Association. In the process of making this survey, McClusky and his assistants uncovered much valuable data concerning teacher education. In general, two types of instruction prevailed. One is characterized as "training in service" and the other as "training in preparation for service." [38] It was observed in the survey that much training in service has been concerned with the technique of handling visual equipment rather than the technique of instruction.[39]

---

[36] Beginning with the summer quarter of 1918, the first course in "Graphic Methods" was offered at Stanford University by J. Harold Williams. The description of the course in the university announcement read as follows: "188. *Graphic Methods of Presenting Facts.* This course is designed to give practice in the methods of graphics which are serviceable in the popular portrayal of statistical data. In addition to graphic presentation, some attention will be given to a consideration of the merits of various tabular publicity. There are no prerequisites for the course, but a knowledge of lettering is desirable. Intended primarily to show prospective school officers how best to display statistical facts." J. Harold Williams, *Graphic Methods in Education.* Boston, Houghton Mifflin Company, 1924, pp. v–vi.

[37] Anna V. Dorris, interview, Aug. 10, 1951.

[38] In Newark, McClusky found that the director of visual instruction "spent several weeks during the spring of 1923 instructing teachers in the use of stereopticons." At Kansas City, "the director of visual instruction held a number of informal teacher conferences dealing with the use of visual aids." He found that Los Angeles had begun to give "training in the use of motion picture projectors at the bureau." *Op. cit.,* p. 153.

[39] McClusky found that five city normal schools located in Chicago, Cleveland, Detroit, San Francisco, and St. Louis, offered courses in visual education. The instructors of these courses were usually the city visual education directors or coordinators. *Loc. cit.*

In 1922–1923, some twenty-one educational institutions offered courses in visual instruction, usually in the summer session. Also, conferences of teachers of visual instruction were held at the Universities of Missouri and Utah. In addition, the State Department of Education in Michigan gave a series of short, informal courses in the normal schools of the state the objectives of which were to familiarize teachers with the theory and techniques of using films in teaching, the sources and care of films, and instruction in the operation and care of a motion picture projector. Individual instruction in the operation of projectors was given on request, and all teachers in the immediate area of the school were invited to attend discussions and conferences on the weekends.

It is interesting to note the problems which confronted the visual instruction administrator in 1923. In this same survey, McClusky stated these problems in the form of the following recommendations:

a.   A clearing house for information needs to be established. Every department and bureau has acquired much experience of value which should become the common knowledge of all.

b.   Educational institutions and city school systems should materially increase the financial support of bureaus of visual education, thus placing them on a sound and respectable economic basis.

c.   Departments of visual instruction should secure funds and time for carrying forward experiments and surveys in the field.

d.   The training of teachers in the use and value of visual instruction should be promoted by leaders of the movement.

e.   The administrative status of directors of visual instruction needs to be clearly defined. Their work should be so organized that the utmost co-operation is made possible between them and other school officials.

f.   Directors of visual instruction should draw up a uniform set of record and report forms, thus enabling each one to interpret intelligently the statistics gathered by another.

g.   Educational experts should assist in the creation of all visual aids, and not postpone co-operation until the materials are ready for distribution.

h.   All activities of visual instruction should look toward the mental development of the individual child in the school or classroom.

i.   Bureaus of visual instruction should avoid dependence on free film and other donations to build up their collections.

j.   Departments of visual instruction in city school systems need to take stock at regular intervals of their own equipment and that of individual schools within their jurisdiction.

k.   Methods of selecting visual materials for school use need to be systematically analyzed, and a more scientific procedure evolved.

l.   Catalogues need to be carefully graded and systematically arranged to correlate with the course of study.

m. Rules and regulations covering service should not be too involved or numerous. Periodic changes should be avoided.

n. Lesson aids and descriptive notes accompanying visual materials should stimulate the teacher to make self active preparation for the lesson.

o. In cities where visual instruction is organized, an attempt should be made by school authorities to direct the work along systematically planned lines. Much needless expense will thus be saved.

p. City and state bureaus should make systematic studies of the materials in circulation in terms of their use by patrons.

q. Adequate housing, storage and transportation facilities should be furnished to every bureau.

r. Bureaus of visual instruction should be encouraged to study and to provide good wholesome entertainment films for school use.

s. Those state institutions and city school systems which contemplate the organization of visual instruction in a separate department should build institutions based on pioneers in the field.[40]

The National Academy of Visual Instruction Survey.   In 1924, the National Academy of Visual Instruction made a survey indicating that twenty-three educational institutions were offering courses in visual instruction as electives. In three institutions, they were given by correspondence; the majority were offered in summer sessions. The survey also found that a type of teacher education in visual instruction was offered in teacher institutes in Berkeley, Detroit, Newark, and Kansas City.[41]

The Balcom Survey.   In 1924, A. G. Balcom made a survey of normal schools and colleges of the country. When he analyzed the results, he found that about half of the eighty-two institutions which responded to his questionnaire gave any training in the teaching value of the slide and less than half gave training in the operation of a stereopticon. Less than half reported that films were used, a still smaller percentage (twelve) gave instruction on the classroom use of the film, and only five reported giving any instruction in the operation of a motion picture projector.[42]

Later Surveys.   A survey of college courses in February, 1925, showed that emphasis was put upon the technical aspects of photography and the mechanics of projection. Visual instruction courses were generally elective rather than required in teacher education institutions.[43]

[40] *Ibid.*, pp. 181–184.
[41] F. Dean McClusky, "Finding the Facts of Visual Education, II: Growth through Teacher Training," *Educational Screen*, vol. 4 (April–May, 1925), pp. 203–205, 272–276.
[42] *Addresses and Proceedings of the 62nd Annual Meeting of the National Education Association*, Washington, D.C., June 29–July 4, 1924, vol. 62, pp. 971–974.
[43] William H. Gregory, "A Teachers' Training Course in Visual Aids," *Educational Screen*, vol. 4 (February, 1925), pp. 88–90.

In 1926, a committee on teacher education recommended to the Department of Visual Instruction of the National Education Association that a definite laboratory course be established for student teachers and teachers in service. The committee's report also pointed to the fact that several teacher institutions were offering courses in visual instruction and that the University of Wisconsin had created a professorship in visual instruction.[44]

In 1936, W. Gayle Starnes's comprehensive study showed a significant increase in visual instruction courses since Anna V. Dorris made the first teacher education survey of visual instruction courses in 1922. A striking aspect of his study detailed the extreme differences in course content, materials used, and credit offered.[45] A survey made in 1940 by the Office of Education showed that 114 colleges and universities, comprising 12 percent of the 933 education institutions whose catalogs were examined, offered a total of 140 courses, usually in the department of education.[46] A National Education Association questionnaire was sent out this same year to 150 educational institutions offering courses for prospective secondary school teachers. Of the seventy-six returns, forty-two colleges reported that they offered ninety-two courses. All these surveys revealed a need for teacher education in the use of audiovisual materials.[47]

Classification of Visual Instruction Courses.   Visual instruction courses varying from two to three hours of credit have been given during the academic year, in summer sessions, or by extension. Their growth has been continuing since 1921. In 1937, a significant increase occurred when thirty-seven new courses were initiated. A variety of courses in visual instruction have included short courses, workshops, correspondence courses, and off-campus courses. Short courses or workshops have been held for those teachers unable to attend a regular course. Correspondence courses, first offered in 1924, have not been given to any great extent. Off-campus courses have generally been conducted in large cities as a regular semester.[48]

Organization of Visual Instruction Courses.   An unresolved problem has been centered in the organization of visual instruction courses as to the comparable merits of a core or basic course as against an integrated approach

[44] J. V. Ankeney, "Report of Committee on Teacher Training in Visual Instruction," *Educational Screen*, vol. 5 (October, 1926), pp. 489–491.
[45] W. Gayle Starnes, *The Present Status of Teacher Training in the Use of Visual Aids.* Lexington, Ky., University of Kentucky, 1936, 40 pp.
[46] Katherine M. Cook and Florence E. Reynolds, *Opportunities for the Preparation of Teachers in the Use of Visual Aids in Instruction.* U.S. Office of Education, Federal Security Agency, Pamphlet no. 89, 1940, 13 pp.
[47] E. Winifred Crawford, "A Study of the Status of Visual Education Courses in Teacher-training Institutions," *Journal of Secondary Education*, vol. 9 (May, 1940), pp. 161–170.
[48] Robert Eulette de Kieffer, "The Status of Teacher-training in Audio-Visual Education in the Forty-eight States." Unpublished doctoral dissertation submitted to the College of Education, State University of Iowa, 1948.

through the exploitation of visual materials in other courses. Dunn and Schneider list the three most common points of view in regard to visual instruction as follows:

> (1) It is an essential part of practically every field of education, and the best possible preparation of teachers to make use of visual materials is to observe and use them in their functional relationships in each course. (2) Special courses are necessary in order to effect the necessary learnings involved in the full scope of visual education. (3) A combination or compromise between the two positions is the best solution.[49]

Some early visual instruction programs illustrating these various types of organization have been those of Fresno State College, New Jersey's four-year teachers' colleges, Bucknell University, San Francisco State College, and the Winnetka (Illinois) public schools. At Fresno State College where in 1937 an integrated plan was in effect, W. F. Tidyman stated: "In defense of the integrated plan, it may be said that it squares with our currently accepted philosophy of learning in integrated, lifelike situations, and that the tendency in the administration of teachers' colleges is to reduce the number of highly specialized professional courses, rather than to increase them." [50]

An illustration of the compromise position which utilizes every department of the colleges and also offers a basic course is to be found in New Jersey's curriculum. This plan, developed in 1937, offered a course in visual instruction in the third year for the purpose of organizing, supplementing, and systematizing the more incidental factual material of audiovisual education that was supposed to be obtained in other courses. For example, courses in geography supposedly used maps, excursions, slides, still pictures, and models; courses in English utilized motion picture appreciation in the study of literature and developed discrimination and appreciation of the art of the motion picture; courses in the physical sciences included the study of the mechanics of projection or photography; courses in psychology dealt with perception and learning.[51]

The San Francisco State College plan offered a full-credit course to teachers in 1923 with the idea of encouraging the wider use of audiovisual materials. By the time they had completed these courses, the teachers had assembled their own collections of mounted pictures, exhibits, charts, and graphs.[52] Another aspect of visual instruction was apparent in the Winnetka

---

[49] Edgar Dale, Fannie W. Dunn, Charles F. Hoban, Jr., and Etta Schneider, *Motion Pictures in Education*. New York, The H. W. Wilson Company, 1937, p. 371.

[50] Quoted in John S. Carroll, *Teacher Education and Visual Education for the Modern School*. San Diego, Calif., Office of Superintendent of Schools, 1948, p. 23.

[51] Dale et al., *op. cit.* Introduction to "Part Six, Teacher Preparation in Visual Education," by Fannie W. Dunn and Etta Schneider, p. 372.

[52] Anna V. Dorris, *Visual Instruction in the Public Schools*. Boston, Ginn and Company, 1928, pp. 377–379.

TABLE 7.1   Outline of San Francisco State Teachers College Early Visual Instruction Course

I.   The scope of visual education
  1.   Why the need of improving our methods?
    a.   Post-war situation
    b.   Need of conserving time
    c.   Need of greater efficiency
    d.   Provide for individual differences
    e.   Make learning a living experience
II.   The use of visual instruction outside the schools
  1.   Commercial and industrial institutions
  2.   Government
  3.   Natural and medical sciences
  4.   Missionaries
  5.   Athletes
III.   Reasons underlying the success of visual education
  1.   History of object and visual learning
  2.   Psychological reasons
  3.   Experimental tests
  4.   Relation of visual instruction to progress and retardation
IV.   What other states and education institutions are accomplishing in visual education
  1.   State boards
  2.   Universities
  3.   Normal schools
  4.   City schools
V.   Practical pedagogical methods of procedure for the use of visual aids in classroom teaching
  1.   Concrete demonstrations of uses of materials
    a.   The preview to introduce a topic to be studied
    b.   For concrete information during the study period, to enrich the text, solve problems or explain some difficulty (the project lesson made a living experience)
    c.   The review
VI.   The larger use of visual aids in teaching
  1.   Flat pictures; demonstration of materials
    a.   Where they may or may not be used to the best advantage in teaching
    b.   Sources of materials and how to get collections
  2.   Exhibits and excursions
    a.   Demonstration of their uses to enrich all subjects of the curriculum
    b.   Laboratory work
  3.   Charts, maps, globes, and graphs
    a.   Special uses of the graphs as a means of teaching

      4. The use of the stereograph to enrich all subjects
      5. How to operate a stereoptican lantern and the use of slides in classroom instruction
        a. Demonstrations of different materials
        b. The making of slides—laboratory work
      6. The moving picture as a means of teaching
        a. Best methods for its use
        b. Materials available for classroom teachers
        c. Classification of materials according to subjects
        d. How to operate a portable moving picture machine
VII. The place of the museum in visual education
    1. How to start a distributing center
VIII. How to equip a school for visual education
    1. Ways and means of earning money for individual schools
  IX. After-school entertainments
    1. How to manage entertainments
    2. How to secure materials
    3. Suggestions for programs

SOURCE: F. Dean McClusky, "The Administration of Visual Education: A National Survey." Unpublished report made to the NEA, 1923, pp. 202–203. Course described was given by Anna V. Dorris.

TABLE 7.2   **Outline of Kansas University Early Visual Instruction Course**

  I. The psychology of visual aids
    1. Primary sources of knowledge
    2. Visual sensation, perception, and imagery
    3. Comprehension, retention, etc.
    4. Standards for evaluating visual aids
    5. The word-picture balance
    6. Emotional effects
    7. Moral value, etc.
 II. Types and their sources
    1. Diagrams
    2. Sketches
    3. Photographs
    4. Stereographs
    5. Lantern slides
    6. Moving pictures
    7. Models
    8. Museum exhibits; and where to get these
III. Administrative problems
    1. Booking
    2. Renting
    3. Purchasing
    4. Circulating visual aids

IV. General and special methods
    1. General methods, and
    2. Methods in the various school subjects
 V. Picture projection technique
    1. Learning to operate projectors, and so on.

SOURCE: F. Dean McClusky, "The Administration of Visual Education: A National Survey." Unpublished report made to the NEA, 1923, p. 199. Course given in 1922 summer session by Joseph J. Weber.

TABLE 7.3   **Outline of Cleveland School of Education and Western Reserve University Early Visual Instruction Course**

  I. Fundamental principles of visual education
 II. Visual aids
    1. Types:
        a. Diagrams and charts
        b. Pictures
        c. Stereographs
        d. Lantern slides
        e. Motion pictures
        f. Museum exhibits
            (1) Natural history museum
            (2) Art museum
            (3) Historical museum
    2. Sources of visual aids:
        a. Museums
        b. Commercial firms
        c. Industrial concerns
        d. United States Government departments
        e. State extension divisions
 III. Types of exhibits and classroom methods
 IV. Simple and complete exhibits for illustrative uses
  V. Pictures, photographs, and stereographs
 VI. Charts, graphs, and diagrams
 VII. Lantern slides for classroom use and lesson plans
VIII. Moving pictures: Selection, methods of use, sources
 IX. School lectures and regular classroom instruction
  X. Museums and special instruction
 XI. Museum loan exhibits
 XII. Field lessons: Studies of industrial plants and civic institutions; field lessons in geography and nature study
XIII. Measuring the results of visual education
XIV. Program of visual instruction by subjects and grades

SOURCE: F. Dean McClusky, "The Administration of Visual Education: A National Survey." Unpublished report made to the NEA, 1923, p. 198. Course was taught in 1922 summer session by William M. Gregory and William E. Krieger. Two semester hours of credit were granted for completion of the course.

TABLE 7.4   Core Course Offered by State of Pennsylvania in 1935

I.   Name of course: *Visual-sensory aids in education* (Core Course) 3 hours per week, 3 semester hours credit

II. General description of the course

This course is based upon the philosophy that sensory experiences and mental activities parallel each other in the learning process. Visual and other sensory aids, therefore, should hold a major place in the teaching of practically all subjects and on all levels of learning. To be a well balanced course, and of the greatest value to prospective teachers and the teachers in service, it should give training in and an effective technic for the use of all types of visual-sensory aids. This core course should be mandatory on the part of every person preparing to teach in the public schools. The course is designed for the preparation of teachers of the various subjects, and should contain those elements common to practically every subject.

III. Objectives

1. To learn the meaning of the common terms used in visual-sensory education (Give the student a concrete and meaningful vocabulary)

2. The development of skill in selecting the suitable teaching aids from those available for the teaching of a specific subject

3. The development of a projection technic which will assure an efficient use of all the essential projectors in classroom work

4. To provide the prospective teacher with a body of knowledge as well as a direct acquaintance with the useful sources of information which will be helpful in the teaching of the various subjects of the curriculum

5. To give training in the organization of the visual-sensory aids for the various subjects so that the aids may be on hand, available, and usable in the classroom

6. The development of a proper technic for the efficient use of all the teaching aids

7. To acquaint the prospective teacher with the value of research in determining educational materials and methods

8. To acquaint the prospective teacher with the psychological aspects underlying visual-sensory aids

9. To acquaint the prospective teacher, or the teacher in service, with minimum standards for visual-sensory equipment and standards for evaluating the various visual-sensory aids

IV. Method

The lecture-demonstration, discussion, and laboratory method will be used throughout the course. Certain phases of the work can be best presented by the instructor in lecture-demonstration form. Other phases of the work lend themselves to other methods of instruction. Projects suitable for the various grades will be worked out by the group. Emphasis will be placed upon suitable methods of presentation and ways of further stimulating the interest of the student. The student will be taught how and when to use visual and other sensory aids. Maps, specimens, objects, models, the blackboard, projectors, slides, films, field trips, etc., will constitute the materials of the course.

V. Outline of the course
   1. Research—summary of research investigation in visual instruction
   2. Historical background
   3. Psychological aspects and verbalism
   4. Projectors and projection technics
       Still and motion picture projectors; housing, care, technics
   5. The school journey
       Organizing, conducting, checking results
   6. Museum procedure
   7. Pictorial materials
       Standards for evaluating, mounting, and filing of flats
       Housing and care of stereographs
       Making lantern slides
       Mending films and film-strips
       Housing and care of slides and films
       Technics for all
   8. Object-specimen-model
       Assembling, housing, care, sources
   9. Photography
       Still and motion picture technics
       Developing films and making prints
       Standards and sources
   10. Blackboard and bulletin board technics
   11. Administrating and budgeting visual materials
   12. Radio-vision
       Apparatus, procedure, and programs
   13. Bibliography
VI. Brief bibliography
   1. Cameron, J. R. "Motion Picture Projection"
   2. Dorris, Anna V. "Visual Instruction in the Public Schools"
   3. "Educational Screen" (a magazine)
   4. Freeman, Frank N. "Visual Education"
   5. Johnson, William H. "Fundamentals in Visual Instruction"
   6. Merton, Elds. "Visual Instruction"
   7. Routzahn, E. G. "A.B.C. of Exhibit Planning"
   8. Pa. Dept. Public Instruction: "The School Journey Bulletin"; "The Object-Specimen-Model Bulletin"
   9. Weber, J. J. "Picture Values in Education"
   10. Wood and Freeman. "Motion Pictures in the Classroom"

SOURCE: *A Summary of the Techniques of Visual-Sensory Aids for Teachers in Service and Teachers in Training.* Harrisburg, Pa., Commonwealth of Pennsylvania, 1935.

public schools which, through their department of education, took part in the film service offered by the state university. Students enrolled in the Graduate Teachers College of Winnetka did most of their work in the Winnetka schools using visual materials furnished by the visual instruction department.[53]

Scope and Content of Visual Instruction Courses. The scope of visual instructional courses has theoretically been quite broad. Dunn and Schneider consider it to include:

> . . . orientation both historically and philosophically; acquaintance with all types of visual aids, from the excursion to the sound motion picture, both as to their writing, slide making and the like; knowledge of sources of both free and commercial materials; criteria for selection; technical and mechanical problems in the use, care, and repair of apparatus and equipment; methods of use in various school fields and on the several educational levels, including psychology and techniques; application of the theatrical motion picture to education; and problems of supervision and administration.[54]

Probably the first outline of a course in visual instruction was prepared by Albert Field of the University of Minnesota in 1918.[55] Other early visual instruction course outlines were prepared by B. A. Aughinbaugh,[56] Anna V. Dorris, William M. Gregory,[57] H. A. Henderson,[58] J. Raymond Hutchinson,[59] F. Dean McClusky, et al.,[60] C. J. Primm, and J. J. Weber. Many other suggested courses of study have appeared in various educational journals. The core course offered by the state of Pennsylvania was issued in mimeographed form in 1935 for the use of instructors in the normal schools of the state.[61] Some of the course reports dealt with specific aspects of visual instruction. For example, a course at the American Museum of Natural History in New York City in 1930 concerned itself only with the mechanics of visual instruction.[62]

[53] Carroll, *op. cit.*, pp. 25–26.
[54] Dale et al., *op. cit.*, pp. 371–372.
[55] 1918 *University of Minnesota Course Catalog.*
[56] B. A. Aughinbaugh, "Outline for Course in Visual Instruction," *Educational Screen,* vol. 8 (December, 1929), pp. 307–308.
[57] Gregory, *op. cit.*
[58] H. A. Henderson, "What Should a Course in Visual Instruction Include?" *Educational Screen,* vol. 2 (June, 1923), p. 186.
[59] J. Raymond Hutchinson, "Fundamentals of Visual Education," *School Executive,* vol. 55 (January, 1936), pp. 186–188.
[60] F. Dean McClusky, John J. Jenkins, Daniel C. Knowlton, and Elda Merton, *Visual Instruction: Syllabus of a Proposed Textbook for Use in Teacher-Training Schools.* Meadville, Pa., Keystone View Company, 1932. (Mimeographed.)
[61] *A Summary of the Techniques of Visual-Sensory Aids for Teachers in Service and Teachers in Training.* Harrisburg, Pa., Commonwealth of Pennsylvania, 1935.
[62] Dale et al., *op. cit.*, p. 456.

In 1932, a committee appointed by the Department of Visual Instruction made a report on a "Proposed Core Course in Visual Instruction." This report stated that:

> Visual instruction has become an integral part of the school curriculum. Visual instruction teachers and school administrators no longer need argue for a visual–sensory aids program. It is an accepted reality. The problem now is to determine those common elements of the course and perfect suitable techniques for carrying out the program. . . . The merged organizations of visual education contemplate carrying out the far-reaching resolution set forth at the Los Angeles Meeting of the Department of Visual Instruction.[63]

The resolution at the Los Angeles Meeting of the Department of Visual Instruction read:

> Resolved, That the Department of Visual Instruction of the National Education Association earnestly recommend that a course in visual and other sensory aids in teaching be established and that teacher-training institutions in every state be required to organize and offer such courses beginning with the scholastic year of 1931–1932.[64]

State Departments of Education.　　Almost since the beginning of the visual instruction movement, state agencies have established separate visual instruction divisions which have provided leadership and financial support by serving as lending libraries, by publishing visual instruction materials, by providing preservice and in-service training, and in obtaining certification laws for visual instruction.

On October 10, 1934, the Pennsylvania State Council of Education passed the following resolution: "Resolved that all applicants for permanent teaching certificates on and after September 1, 1935, shall be required to present evidence of having completed an approved course in visual and sensory techniques." [65] Thus, Pennsylvania was the first state to require a course in visual instruction for a teacher's credential. Later, in 1937, the state of New Jersey required that a course in visual instruction be added to the curriculum of the four-year teachers' colleges. A syllabus, *Visual Aids in Education,* was written by the New Jersey State Committee for the Improvement of Visual Instruction for use in New Jersey colleges of education.[66]

[63] *Proceedings of the 70th Annual Meeting of the National Education Association,* Atlantic City, N.J., June 25–July 1, 1932, vol. 70, p. 790.

[64] *Proceedings of the 69th Annual Meeing of the National Education Association,* Los Angeles, Calif., June 27–July 3, 1931, vol. 69, p. 963.

[65] "Certification of Secondary School Teachers of Academic Subjects," section 4, *Permanent College Certificate,* Department of Public Instruction, Harrisburg, Pa.

[66] C. W. Leman, *Visual Aids in Education.* Ann Arbor, Mich., State Teachers College, Edwards Brothers, Inc., 1941, p. 75.

A number of state departments of education have offered in-service training to teachers and administrators. One of the most frequent types of in-service training has been carried out by means of conferences and institutes. During such programs, teachers are provided with an opportunity to examine various types of audiovisual equipment, observe classroom audiovisual demonstrations, and listen to lectures and panel discussions on various aspects of audiovisual education.

In-service training by state departments of education has also manifested itself in the form of many helpful published audiovisual materials. Such publications have included audiovisual bulletins, catalogs of available audiovisual materials, and lists of audiovisual materials supplementing units of state courses of study.

State departments of education have further contributed to in-service teacher education by assisting individual schools in organizing their own in-service education programs in visual instruction. In addition, some state divisions have carried on a school visitation service by sending visual instruction consultants to those schools which encountered special problems.

University Extension Divisions.   University extension divisions have distributed audiovisual materials for educational purposes for a number of years. Traditionally, they have also assisted their own institutions in the preservice education of teachers in visual instruction by supplying materials and equipment and making their staff members available for the teaching of visual instruction courses. These divisions have offered short courses, correspondence courses, and off-campus courses; sponsored and conducted conferences and institutes; and published various materials for the in-service education of teachers in audiovisual instruction.

Four-year Institutions.   The primary agency for teacher education in visual instruction has been the four-year institutions. Their practices have varied extremely and many have been handicaped by a lack of suitable equipment. Many, however, have expanded their activities, offering short courses and correspondence courses, conducting conferences and institutes, assisting schools in organizing in-service education of teachers, offering a school visitation service, and establishing film rental libraries.

Early Teacher Education Conferences.   State departments of education, university extension divisions, and four-year institutions have conducted a number of conferences and institutes on teacher education in visual instruction. Two of the early significant conferences on teacher education were initiated by the American Council on Education through its Committee on Motion Pictures in Education.

A Conference on Teacher Training in Visual Instruction convened on

November 5, 1936, at the University of Wisconsin in Milwaukee, Wisconsin, with a number of prominent visual instruction leaders present.[67] The leading questions discussed included the following:

1. Should there be a general course in visual instruction required for every teacher in training, as in the state of Pennsylvania?
2. Should this be given as a separate course, or should a series of units be taught in such fields as science, school administration, etc.?
3. If such courses are to be required, do we have now the personnel to teach them? If not, how can this situation be remedied?
4. What should be the content of a general course in visual instruction?
5. How much credit should be given or required for a teacher-training course?
6. To what extent can the material of such a course be individualized to let teachers work out their material in the fields in which they expect to teach?
7. Should teachers of special subjects, such as science, mathematics, art, etc., also be required to give units of instruction on visual aids? How should this be set up?
8. What degree of skill do we wish in operating the various types of equipment?
9. How can we most expeditiously develop these skills? . . .
10. What shall be the nature and extent of the in-service training of teachers in the use of visual aids?
11. Is one of the most important problems in the entire field that of getting the college instructors of teachers in training to use visual aids in their work?
12. To what extent are national, state, regional, and local film libraries a factor in the establishment of adequate teacher training courses?
13. What can groups such as this one do to promote the introduction of courses in visual instruction in the teacher training institutions?
14. What reference materials, especially for reading, are desirable for a course in visual instruction?
15. What is the minimum equipment that should be available for giving such a course? [68]

An interesting outcome of these discussions was a statement of minimum equipment for a course in visual instruction.

On January 18, 1937, a second conference was sponsored by the American Council on Education at Columbia University in New York City. At this meeting, as at the preceding one, all the problems of teacher preparation in

[67] *A Conference on Teacher Training in Visual Instruction.* Washington, D.C., American Council on Education, 1936.
[68] *Ibid.*, pp. 2–3.

visual instruction were discussed by those concerned with teacher education in this field. These discussions served to clarify many points and gave additional impetus to the organization of other conferences and institutes by various educational agencies.[69]

TABLE 7.5   Early Visual Education Bureaus in City Schools

City	Date bureau established	Name of director	Title of person in charge
St. Louis	1905	Amelia Meissner	Curator, Educational Museum
Reading	1908	Levi W. Mengel	Director, Reading Public Museum and Art Gallery
Cleveland	1909	W. M. Gregory	Director, Educational Museum
Philadelphia	1915(?)	Ada F. Liveright	Librarian, Pedagogical Library
Chicago	1917	Dudley C. Hays	Director, Bureau of Visual Instruction
Newark	1918	A. S. Balcom	Ass't Supt. of Schools in Charge of Visual Instruction
Detroit	1919	B. A. Barnes[*]	Supervisor of Visual Instruction
Detroit	1919[†]	Julia Gilmore	Curator, Children's Museum
Kansas City	1919	Rupert Peters	Director, Division of Visual Instruction
Los Angeles	1920[‡]	A. Loretta Clark	Acting Director, Visual Education Dept.
New York	1920	E. L. Crandall	Director of Public Lectures and Visual Instruction
Atlanta	1922	E. R. Enlow	Supervisor of Visual Instruction
Pittsburgh	1922	John Hollinger	Director of Dept. of Visual Instruction and Nature Study
Berkeley	1922	Anna V. Dorris	Director of Visual Instruction
Sacramento	1922	O. G. Cummings	Director of Visual Instruction
Buffalo	1920[§]	Carlos Cummings	Director of Visual Instruction
Buffalo	1923	Orrin L. Pease	Supervisor of Visual Instruction
Oakland	1923	H. O. Welty[¶]	Department of Visual Instruction

[*] Appointed for 1923–24.
[†] Children's Museum under general direction of the supervisor of visual instruction.
[‡] Organized as a separate department, 1923; formerly division of the City School Library.
[§] Buffalo Society of Natural Sciences, Department of Visual Instruction, subsidized in part by city for service to public schools.
[¶] Chairman of committee which organized department, started operations September, 1923.
SOURCE: F. Dean McClusky, "The Administration of Visual Education: A National Survey." Unpublished report made to the NEA, 1923, p. 11.

[69] *Teacher Training in Modern Teaching Aids.* Report of conference sponsored jointly by Teachers College, Columbia University, and the American Council on Education, held at Teachers College, Columbia University, New York City, Jan. 18, 1937.

Early visual instruction journals

One of the most important landmarks in the visual instruction movement can be seen in the founding of journals devoted exclusively to visual instruction. By April, 1921, four such publications had been established: *Moving Picture Age, Educational Film Magazine, Visual Education,* and *The Screen.*

Reel and Slide **and** *Moving Picture Age.*   *Reel and Slide* was the first journal devoted to visual instruction. This pioneer periodical which first appeared in March, 1918, was "a monthly magazine to make the screen a greater power in education and business." [70] It was first edited by Lynne S. Metcalfe and published by the Reel Publishing Company of New York. In October, 1919, the title was changed to *Moving Picture Age* when a group of educators were persuaded to join the governing board.

Moving Picture Age achieved a reputation for genuine service to the visual instruction movement. It became the official organ of the National Academy of Visual Instruction and published the first annual annotated catalog of instructional or nontheatrical films. Entitled *1001 Films,* this catalog was a forerunner of *The Bluebook of 16 mm Films* (later *The Bluebook of Audio-Visual Materials*) subsequently published by *Educational Screen.*

Moving Picture Age began its existence with policies that were flexible enough to meet the conditions existing in the second decade of this century. The early issues of "The Only Independent Magazine in the Field of Visual Instruction" indicate that subscribers were expected to accept as authoritative the editorial contributions of men who inserted a commercial bias. However, it is also clear that these same issues contained contributions from financially disinterested persons.

In accordance with the publishers' wishes, the editorial policies of the magazine were revamped in 1921 when Milton Ford Baldwin became editor and a distinguished group of contributing editors, most of them educators, was added to the editorial staff.[71] The magazine drew considerable criticism

[70] *Reel and Slide* (March, 1918).
[71] Contributing editors of *Moving Picture Age* were J. V. Ankeney, associate professor of visual education, College of Agriculture, Experiment Station, University of Missouri; A. G. Balcom, assistant superintendent of schools, Newark, New Jersey; Mrs. Woodallen Chapman, chairman, Motion Picture Committee, General Federation of Women's Clubs, New York City; A. Loretto Clark, Visual Education Division, Los Angeles city schools; William H. Dudley, chief of Bureau of Visual Instruction, University of Wisconsin; James N. Emery, supervising principal, Pawtucket, Rhode Island; W. M. Gregory, curator, Educational Museum, Cleveland, Ohio; Samuel Guard, director of information, American Farm Bureau Federation, Chicago; Austin C. Lescarboura, managing editor, *Scientific American,* New York City; F. Dean McClusky, instructor in education, University of

when it ruled against using any contributions written by persons with a financial interest in any commercial enterprise in visual instruction. This, of course, was a complete reversal of the policy previously in force.

Finally, in December, 1922, *Moving Picture Age* merged with the newly established *Educational Screen* when it became clear that it was "in no sense a perfect servant of the field of visual instruction." [72] Nostalgic in mood, the final editorial of *Moving Picture Age* reads as follows:

> From time to time we have recognized flaws in the magazine's attempts to serve; and just before the amalgamation of publications was broached we had laid plans for the strengthening and broadening of the assistance rendered by the *Moving Picture Age*. And yet, although not setting itself up as a model in any sense, this publication has at least aspired to be dependable, honest, and practical: the subscriber has seen it appear without fail twelve times a year, while other publications have withered and died; he has seen it take issue editorially upon matters that needed frank treatment, when the more comfortable method would have been to overlook the subject; he has seen it emphasize the practical needs of the man in the field and pay but secondary attention to the theory of visual instruction, on the basis that both were valuable but the first always imperative. [73]

The Screen. "A Journal of Motion Pictures for Business, School and Church," *The Screen* was established in January, 1920, by the Aldan Publishing Company of New York. The first editor was Albert H. Gross; the associate editor was Ruth Madlon. [74] In the spring of 1922, *The Screen* went out of existence.

Educational Film Magazine. This journal was also established in the early twenties in New York City. Its first editor was Dolph Eastman. After a brief career, it ceased publication in the spring of 1922.

Visual Education. In January, 1920, the Society for Visual Education, a new organization for producing and distributing visual aids, began the publication of *Visual Education*. This monthly house organ, "A Magazine Devoted to the Cause of American Education," brought together an extraordinary amount of useful information concerning educational films. The

---

Illinois; Charles Roach, Visual Instruction Service, Iowa State College of Agriculture; Rowland Rogers, chairman, Curriculum Committee, Visual Instruction Association of New York; Roy L. Smith, Simpson Methodist Church, Minneapolis, Minnesota; and J. J. Weber, associate professor of education, University of Kansas. *Moving Picture Age*, vol. 4 (January, 1921), p. 3.

[72] *Moving Picture Age*, vol. 5 (December, 1922), p. 4.

[73] *Loc. cit.*

[74] *The Screen*, vol. 1, no. 1 (January, 1920).

executive viewpoint of Harley Clarke, and the educational one of Forest Ray Moulton set the policy and tone. Nelson L. Greene was the first editor. The journal was later edited by W. C. Bagley and F. R. Moulton.[75]

With the broad policy of utilizing all avenues to expand and develop visual instruction, the columns publicized many competing enterprises. Also, authoritative articles about new developments were featured, uses of non-theatrical films illustrated and described, and discussions of new instructional films included. Subscribers were encouraged to make the magazine a medium for the exchange of pertinent ideas in the visual instruction field. Although *Visual Education* was a commercial house organ, it rarely fell below its high educational standards.

The December, 1924, issue of *Visual Education* announced its merger with the *Educational Screen*. The editors made the following comment in the last issue:

> The Society for Visual Education, from its foundation more than five years ago, has served education by the dissemination of information regarding all visual aids and practices throughout the early stages of the development of the visual field, in addition to the pursuit of its other essential activities—the production and distribution of visual aids. The sale of the magazine has been arranged in order that the time and energy of the Society for Visual Education can be devoted more specifically to the activities of production and distribution.[76]

Visual Review.   In 1926, the Society for Visual Education reentered the publishing field with *Visual Review*. This periodical, first edited by Marie Witham, has since discontinued publication.[77]

Educational Screen.   Late in 1921, *Educational Screen* was established in Chicago under the leadership of Herbert E. Slaught of the University of Chicago. The directorate was composed of educators "from university professors to grade school principals—and of business executives and experts in the publishing field who have been connected with established publications." [78]

A short time later, Nelson L. Greene, former professor of languages and literature and the first editor of *Visual Education,* was selected to serve as first editor of *Educational Screen.*

The first issue of the magazine appeared in January, 1922, with the

[75] *Visual Education*, vol. 1, no. 1 (January, 1920). Moulton was the cofounder and secretary of the Society for Visual Education, Inc., and was also connected with the University of Chicago. Bagley was professor of education, Teachers College, Columbia University.
[76] *Visual Education*, vol. 5 (1924), p. 419.
[77] *Visual Review* (1926).
[78] *Educational Screen*, vol. 1 (January, 1922), p. 8.

slogan "The Independent Magazine Devoted to the New Influence in National Education." [79] The editorial of the first issue proclaimed that:

> The Educational Screen is not the official organ of anything or anybody. It is published to give American education, and every American who believes education important, the thing that they have needed ever since the so-called "visual movement" started—namely, a magazine devoted to the educational cause and to no other; a magazine distinctly intellectual and critical, rather than commercial and propagandist; a magazine written and produced exclusively by those whose scholarly training, experience, and reputation qualify them to discuss educational matters. [80]

The purpose of *Educational Screen* was stated as follows:

> This magazine intends to get at the truth about visual education— in all its phases and its broadest aspects—and serve it up in a form palatable to thinking Americans.
> We shall endeavor to supply for you the best in theory, opinion, and experience that the country affords. . . .
> We shall wade through the welter of "literature" provoked by the movies . . . and offer a digest of all that is worth your attention.
> We shall present a monthly survey of really significant visual activities along educational lines which will keep you constantly in touch with everything that points toward progress in this undeveloped and more or less unknown field.
> We shall develop at the earliest possible moment a technical department. . . .
> We shall become the one impartial and authoritative source of information on the new field. . . .
> We shall aim at something unique in regard to the theatrical "movie." [81]

The *Educational Screen,* which became the first official organ of the Department of Visual Instruction of the National Education Association, made many notable contributions to the visual instruction movement. [82] Be-

---

[79] In 1925, the first slogan of the *Educational Screen* was changed to "The Only Magazine Devoted to the New Influence in National Education," when it became the only magazine devoted exclusively to visual education. *Educational Screen,* vol. 4, no. 1 (January, 1925).

[80] *Educational Screen,* vol. 1 (January, 1922), p. 8.

[81] *Ibid.,* pp. 5–6.

[82] *Educational Screen* made a notable contribution to the visual instruction movement by opening its pages to professional organizations which could not then afford the luxury of a publication. The Visual Instruction Association of America, the National Academy of Visual Instruction, the Better Films Committee of the National Congress of Mothers and Parent-Teachers Associations, and the Film Council of America are examples of those organizations which enjoyed this privilege. Following the merger of the Visual Instruction Association of America and the Department of Visual Instruction of the National Education Association in 1932, DVI arranged for space in the magazine to be devoted

ginning with the November, 1922, issue, it devoted a portion of its space to the Visual Instruction Association of America. At the end of 1922, *Educational Screen* absorbed *Moving Picture Age;* in its second year, several other visual education magazines were discontinued; at the close of the third, it announced the purchase of *Visual Education.* This left *Educational Screen* as the only visual instruction magazine in 1925. The last acquisition also made it possible for the *Educational Screen* to expand its pages and add to its departments. Simultaneously, it began the separate publication of important books and pamphlets in visual instruction. An example of this activity was the continued publication of *1001 Films* which was begun by *Moving Picture Age* in 1920. In 1932, the *Educational Screen* acquired the *Visual Instruction News.* The name of the *Educational Screen* was changed in 1956 to *Educational Screen and Audiovisual Guide* as a result of another merger.

Educational Screen has the distinction of publishing one of the first comprehensive catalogs of films available for school use,[83] and of being the first to print a systematic summary of research as a guide to the utilization of visual materials, as well as the first to give critical appraisals of the theatrical film.

Visual Instruction News.   In January, 1927, the Bureau of Visual Instruction at the University of Kansas began to publish the *Visual Instruction News* under the sponsorship of the National Academy of Visual Instruction. Ellsworth C. Dent was its first and only editor; Dorothea Bowen was his assistant. This periodical was issued four times annually until the National Academy of Visual Instruction merged with the Department of Visual Instruction of the National Education Association in 1932. The April, 1932, issue was the first combined publication of the *Visual Instruction News* and the *Educational Screen.*

Film and Radio Guide.   In 1935, William Lewin founded and became editor of *Film and Radio Guide.* A few years previously he had begun to implement a 1923 Judd Committee recommendation by publishing illustrated guides to theatrical motion picture appreciation because he believed that outstanding theatrical films could be utilized in the classroom. The *Film and Radio Guide* (later changed to the *Audio-Visual Guide*) extended the guide idea further.

---

to official news, notes, and proceedings of the organization. DVI's first "News and Notes" appeared in the May, 1932, issue. This arrangement continued until June, 1955, when the Department (now called the Department of Audiovisual Instruction) decided to publish its own journal. No cost to DVI was ever involved. For a comprehensive history of the *Educational Screen,* see F. Dean McClusky, "What Was AV Journalism in 1922," *Educational Screen and Audiovisual Guide* (January, 1962), pp. 18–20.

[83] *The Bluebook of Non-Theatrical Films* was first published in 1925.

On the twentieth anniversary of the founding of this periodical, Mc-Cluskey listed these contributions to the audiovisual instruction movement.

> First, it fostered closer cooperation between the theatrical motion picture industry and schools by publishing its guides. . . .
>
> Second, it has published bibliographies and unit outlines which have been both practical and helpful to teachers and professionals in the audio-visual field.
>
> Third, *Audio-Visual Guide*, following World War II, originated and promoted the establishment of pilot programs and audio-visual demonstration centers in secondary schools throughout the United States.[84]

In 1956, the *Audio-Visual Guide* merged with the *Educational Screen.*

Early visual instruction textbooks and guides

The first modern visual instruction monograph or guide was *Visual Education,* published in 1906 by the Keystone View Company. With the exception of two important bulletins printed by the U.S. Bureau of Education, no significant visual instruction publications appeared between 1906 and 1919. In 1915, the Bureau published Carl G. Rathmann's account, *The Educational Museum of the St. Louis Public Schools;* and in 1919, it distributed F. W. Reynolds and Carl Anderson's *Motion Pictures and Motion Picture Equipment.*

During the twenties, a number of significant visual instruction books were published. The first handbook which concerned itself with the purely mechanical aspects of visual instruction was Austin C. Lescarboura's *The Cinema Handbook* (1921). Gladys and Henry Bollman wrote the first full-size book devoted to visual instruction and included information about visual materials for educational, religious, and social work in their *Motion Pictures for Community Needs* (1922). Don Carlos Ellis and Laura Thornborough's *Motion Pictures in Education* (1923) covered the history, principles, use, and source of visual materials, with an emphasis upon motion pictures. In 1924, *Visual Education* was published. Although this book was primarily a research report of the University of Chicago's experimental studies of the motion picture, it does contain some helpful material on the use of the film for the classroom in the introductory section. Other important visual instruction books published in the twenties include: A. P. Hollis's *Motion Pictures for Instruction* (1926), William H. Johnson's *Fundamentals in*

[84] F. Dean McClusky, "On the Occasion of Audio-Visual Guide's Twentieth Anniversary," *Audio-Visual Guide* (April, 1955), p. 5.

Visual Education (1927), and Anna V. Dorris's *Visual Instruction in the Public Schools* (1928).[85]

Visual instruction books began to be published at an increased rate in the thirties. F. Dean McClusky's *Visual Instruction—Its Value and Its Needs* (1932) presented an analysis of the status of visual instruction; W. W. Charters's *Motion Pictures and Youth* (1933) contained a summary of the twelve Payne Fund studies; and F. L. Devereux et al. discussed the many aspects of the sound film in the classroom in *The Educational Talking Picture* (1933). In 1934, the Department of Elementary School Principals of the National Education Association published *Aids to Teaching in the Elementary School*. Moreover, Ellsworth Dent's *Audio-Visual Handbook* (1934) appeared for the first time and Cline M. Koon's report on *Motion Pictures in Education in the United States* (1934) was issued. In 1937, three notable visual instruction books were published. They were M. R. Brunstetter's *How to Use the Educational Sound Film;* Edgar Dale, F. W. Dunn, C. F. Hoban, Jr., and E. Schneider's *Motion Pictures in Education;* [86] and C. F. Hoban, C. F. Hoban, Jr., and S. B. Zisman's *Visualizing the Curriculum.*[87] Three other important visual instruction books published during the thirties were Elizabeth Laine's *Motion Pictures and Radio* (1938), Grace F. Ramsey's *Educational Work in Museums of the United States* (1938), and H. C. Atyeo's *The Excursion as a Teaching Technique* (1939).[88] In 1936, the H. W. Wilson Company published the first comprehensive catalog of educational films—the *Educational Film Catalog* (changed to *Educational Film Guide* in 1945).

In the early forties, Harry C. McKown and Alvin B. Roberts wrote *Audio-Visual Aids to Instruction* (1940) and Charles F. Hoban, Jr., prepared *Focus on Learning* (1942) for the Committee on Motion Pictures in Education of the American Council on Education.

[85] This was the first comprehensive textbook in visual instruction and the first to be concerned with integration of visual materials with the school curriculum.

[86] *Motion Pictures in Education* was the first comprehensive summary of the literature of motion pictures and related aspects of visual instruction.

[87] *Visualizing the Curriculum* was probably the most important visual education textbook written during the thirties because of its systematic treatment of the relation between the concrete materials of teaching and the learning process.

[88] Atyeo's *The Excursion as a Teaching Technique* gives one of the most complete historical accounts of the excursion, or field trip. He notes that the adaptation of the excursion idea in the United States was stimulated by scholars who had received their training in German universities in the late nineties and early twenties. Van Liew is credited as being the first important influence in stimulating interest in the field trip in the United States. C. F. Hoban was mainly responsible for the endorsement of the excursion method by the Pennsylvania Department of Education in 1927. National recognition was first given to the field trip at a conference of the Association of Childhood Education in 1931. With the emergence of the "new education," field trips were widely adopted in many experimental schools throughout the United States. The development of the European youth hostel plan, school surveys, school camping, and other community service projects stemmed from the early school excursion movement.

Early administrative history of visual instruction

The most comprehensive source of data concerned with the early administrative history of visual instruction is the unpublished administrative survey made by F. Dean McClusky in 1923 for the National Education Association Judd Committee.[89] In this survey, McClusky reported on such subjects as salaries of visual instruction personnel,[90] value of equipment and materials, types and amounts of materials and equipment, visual instruction department budgets, distribution methods, and film and utilization procedures employed.

Cost of Visual Instruction.   The cost of visual instruction in fourteen city school systems in 1923 was summarized by McClusky as follows:

1. The total sum expended for visual education was $373,218.80. This is approximately .15 of one percent of all school expenditures.
2. The value of equipment and materials in the possession of the departments is estimated at $371,872.00.
3. The largest total expenditure reported by a city is $91,004.24 (Los Angeles). The smallest is $2190.00 (Sacramento). The average is $24,881.25. The city with the largest budget for visual instruction is Chicago. The budget is given at $30,400.00.
4. One finds by analyzing the visual education budgets; that 37.30 percent was spent for salaries; that 15.40 percent was spent for equipment such as projectors, stereopticons, etc.; that 14.70 percent went for film rentals; that 7.69 percent went to slides added to the library; that 6.76 percent was spent for the purpose of films; and so on down to the .39 percent spent for the purchase of miscellaneous materials.
5. The sum spent for the rental and purchase of moving pictures is surprisingly small, being about $48,660.49.[91]

Types and Amount of Visual Materials and Equipment.   McClusky reports the following types and amounts of visual material and equipment used in city departments of visual instruction in 1923:

1. There were 686 projectors of all types in the sixteen cities most active in visual instruction in 1922–23. Portable or semi-portable projectors were also common.
2. Eleven city departments have established libraries consisting of 1755 reels of film of which 36.18 percent were loaned to the de-

[89] F. Dean McClusky, "The Administration of Visual Education: A National Survey." Unpublished report made to the NEA, 1924.
[90] Personnel of city departments of visual instruction ranged from "one to twelve with a median of five" in 1923. *Ibid.*, p. 43.
[91] *Ibid.*, pp. 43–44.

partments by industrial firms, government bureaus, and state bureaus. Many of the remaining 63.82 percent classified as "owned" were donated to the departments.

3. Fifteen city departments either rent or borrow film for distribution. In 1922–23, 3852 reels were rented and 317 were borrowed on the short loan basis.

4. There were 1642 stereopticons in the cities surveyed, of which 7.67 percent are owned by the departments of visual instruction. The number of stereopticons is 2.4 times the number of projectors.

5. Fourteen city departments are building libraries of slides totaling 236,884. These range in size from Chicago which boasts 85,000 to Buffalo with 337 slides. Many thousands of slides are also the property of individual schools within the cities.

6. The total number of stereographs owned by departments is 63,601 and by individual schools is 268,072. Three departments, Los Angeles, Buffalo, and St. Louis, are circulating a large number of stereographs.

7. Seven departments have collections of exhibits for circulatory purposes. The size of these collections ranges from 1500 "groups" (St. Louis) to 14 "cases" (Kansas City).

8. The chief stock in trade of the city departments is the slide which is followed in order by the moving picture projector, stereopticon, stereograph, film, picture exhibit, graphic booklet, chart, costume doll, set of apparatus, and model.

9. In many cities, exhibits, pictures, charts and models are circulated by public museums and libraries.[92]

It is interesting to note that the McClusky survey showed that a larger percentage of the schools in 1923 were using slides, stereographs, pictures, and exhibits, rather than films. Slides were the most widely used visual media.

Distribution Methods. One of the principal problems of bureaus of visual instruction concerned the most efficient method of distribution of materials. Two methods were commonly used: the "circuit" and the "special-order" methods, both differing in purpose and operation. Both were often used by the same department of visual instruction.

The circuit method can best be described as a film which is passed from school to school until it reaches each school on an established circuit. This type of service was so maintained that each school on the circuit could depend on the reception of specific films or visual materials at regular intervals throughout the school year. The principal advocates of the circuit method were Iowa State College and the University of Wisconsin. For example, in 1922–1923, Iowa State College served sixty-six schools. Churches, farm

---

[92] *Ibid.*, pp. 44–46.

bureaus, and others received slide service on eleven circuits during this academic year. W. H. Dudley, director of the University of Wisconsin Bureau of Visual Instruction, expressed the opinion that the circuit plan of distribution can be carried on quite successfully if there is a "systematic and constructive effort to have a yearly program worked out in advance and if the users are instructed and educated in the proper use of slides and films before they are received." [93] In the year 1919–1920, with thirteen circuits in operation, the visual instruction service of the University of Wisconsin was extended to some 275 Wisconsin communities and more than twenty thousand slides and one thousand reels of film were distributed.

The cities of Atlanta, Detroit, Kansas City, Newark, New York, and Sacramento used the circuit method of distribution in 1923. New York, Atlanta, and Sacramento depended on rented films for their circuit service while the cities of Detroit, Kansas City, and Newark purchased their own films in addition to renting and borrowing them. Films for these circuits were selected by the director of the visual instruction department in each city, but in New York, a committee of teachers and commercial producers previewed the films to be used. Generally, films were booked for the circuit at the beginning of each school semester, but Atlanta booked its films a month in advance and Detroit booked its films for the circuit at the first of each week. Some cities adopted the practice of sending printed or mimeographed outlines and lecture notes with films or other visual material to the school a few days in advance or along with the materials.

The second, or special-order, method of distribution is relatively simple in contrast to the circuit method. In order to secure a film, a teacher or principal in any school in a given school system contacted the visual instruction department and made his request known for a specific day and hour. Usually, the visual instruction department transported the film to and from the school. Four distinct practices were established in the special ordering of visual materials. First, ". . . the film may be purchased outright by the department and placed at the disposal of the schools"; second, ". . . the film may be borrowed by the department for a year or longer from government bureaus and national manufacturing concerns and distributed to the schools which desire to make use of such materials"; third, ". . . the departments may rent or lease for a period of time reels which are listed along with those already available at the department"; and fourth, ". . . the departments may act as a broker by ordering films for schools from exchanges, university bureaus, and other distribution agencies." [94]

Some cities, such as Kansas City and Los Angeles, followed all four practices.

---

[93] W. H. Dudley, *Organization for Visual Instruction.* U.S. Bureau of Education Bulletin 7, 1921, p. 11.
[94] *Ibid.*, pp. 54–55.

Nondepartmentalized Visual Instruction. The systematization of visual instruction also took place in city school systems which did not formally organize departments. In a 1923 survey made for the National Education Association, McClusky found three types of organization that had evolved in the city schools.[95] The first approximated a visual department, consisting of a visual education committee composed of teachers and administrators which concerned itself with the problems and administration of visual instruction in the school system. Typical examples of this type of organization were the city systems of Dayton, Indianapolis, Providence, and San Francisco. As an illustration, the Dayton (Ohio) Board of Education authorized the superintendent to appoint a committee of three elementary school principals and two supervisors to administer the visual instruction program.

A second type of organization was identical with the first in that a committee was placed in control of visual instruction. However, the constituent members were representatives of a group of teachers and principals interested in visual education, rather than official representatives of the superintendent or board of education. Examples of this type were in the city school systems of Portland, Seattle, and Tacoma.

The third type of organization was confined to the individual school where responsibility for visual instruction rested entirely with the principal or teacher of each school within a district, independent of the city visual instruction department.[95]

End of an era: 1918–1942

We have seen that the early years of the visual (audiovisual) instruction movement were principally characterized by the organization of bureaus or departments of visual instruction which concentrated on the collection and distribution of a wide array of instructional media. This early period of emergence came to a close with the advent of World War II. Since the visual instruction movement and instructional technology are closely related, we turn to the next chapter for a case study of instructional technology within the industrial and military sectors during World War II.

[95] *Ibid.*, pp. 80–85.

chapter 8

**a case study:
instructional technology
in industry and the military
during world war II**

The development of instructional technology in American schools slowed down during the war years due to lack of equipment, materials, and instructional specialists. Conversely, a period of expansion began in the industrial and military sectors. This was brought about by four important developments: (1) the establishment of training programs in industry and in the military which produced unprecedented demands for an effective technology of instruction; (2) the application of a technology of instruction based on prewar scientific research; (3) the emergence of an official military policy which encouraged the production of a wide variety of instructional materials and a broad use of instructional media; and (4) the allocation of almost unlimited financial resources (at least $100 million) for the implementation of this technology of instruction. In a vast industrial and military proving ground, old concepts of learning were tested and new concepts emerged which held significant implications for the development of instructional technology in American education.

Industrial training

World War II brought an unprecedented need to train millions of industrial workers as rapidly and as effectively as possible. The U.S. Office of Education, under the leadership of the United States Commissioner John W. Studebaker, assumed the major burden of meeting this challenge.

Division of Visual Aids for War Training.   The U.S. Office of Education, which had a traditional interest in training films, requested funds for the production of training films in the fiscal budget of 1940–1941. This was at first refused, but when the international situation worsened, President Franklin D. Roosevelt supported this request.

In January, 1941, the U.S. Office of Education formed the Division of Visual Aids for War Training with Floyde E. Brooker as director. This choice was appropriate because Brooker had served for many years as associate director of the American Council on Education's research studies in the area of instructional technology prior to the war and had gained valuable experience in instructional film production. Brooker's first problems were to promote training films and to inform congressmen, government officials, vocational instructors, and laymen concerning their function and use. Arguments for and against the various types of instructional media were heard. Brooker observed that "men who started out by asking what motion picture stars would be used ended with a new appreciation of an entirely different kind of motion picture." [1]

Between January and June, 1941, the staff of the Division of Visual Aids for War Training increased from one to three, working space was secured, preliminary plans were made, and synopses of the first twenty proposed films were written. By October, 1942, the staff had increased to nine and production contracts were being awarded to producers throughout the country. In the spring of 1943, the Division received an appropriation of $2 million for further expansion of the staff and for the production of new materials. Regional offices were established in Los Angeles, Chicago, and New York City to handle productions in their respective sections of the country. By January, 1944, the new productions were beginning to appear in schools and in training centers. By June 1, 1945, most of the contemplated productions had been completed.

[1] Floyde E. Brooker, *Training Films for Industry*. Federal Security Agency, U.S. Office of Education Bulletin 13, 1946, p. 2.

First U.S. Office of Education Training Films.   By June 5, 1941, the first film of the production program was completed and delivered to the U.S. Office of Education, where a hopeful, tense group of persons sat down to find out whether or not films could speed training. Brooker recorded this experience as follows:

> The projection was in a huge auditorium with a projector in the last stages of usefulness. The curtains at the windows, billowing open with every puff of air, admitted beams of bright sunlight. The sound drizzled through a sound system that provided its own static. The room was far too light—when the curtains billowed, the dim picture disappeared. No audience ever sat more tensely than the four individuals who were almost lost in the middle of the auditorium. The picture ended . . . and almost at once the argument started. It's confusing . . . it goes too fast . . . the job is too technical . . . it's not confusing to shop students . . . it's a step by step explanation . . . the picture would be clear if the curtains would not billow open . . . the film is made for trainees who have already seen the machine.
>
> The suggestion was made that the film be shown again. There was no rewind equipment so two of the individuals improvised by putting the 35 mm reels on pencils to do the job of rewinding. The second showing was started. Brief splashes of light continued to wash the picture off the screen . . . and usually at key points of explanation. This time it became clear that the individuals experienced in shop work viewed the picture in one way, and those inexperienced in shop work viewed it another. Some thought it too elementary while the others thought it too technical; some thought it went too slowly, the others were certain it went too fast. Finally, it was decided to await the coming of the second and third pictures before arriving at any decision. It was also decided that vocational shop instructors were really the ones to make the decision.[2]

By July 2, 1941, more training films were completed. These were viewed at the White House by President Roosevelt, at the Bureau of the Budget, by officials of the Federal Security Agency, the Navy Department, and a number of war agencies then being formed. They were also shown to a committee of congressmen. The reactions were mixed. Some were unexpected. Some thought the skills being taught were so simple that they could not understand why training programs were even necessary. Others thought the jobs were so difficult that no training films could solve the problem. The use of films as a training medium, however, gradually began to gain the favor of key government officials, including President Roosevelt himself, when selected groups of these films began to be used in vocational and industrial training centers in Hartford, Boston, Worcester, Springfield, New York City, Buffalo, Detroit, Cleveland, Chicago, Cincinnati, Philadelphia, Baltimore,

[2] *Ibid.,* pp. 2–3.

Camden, Paterson, Newark, and Washington, D.C. The unanimous judgment of all who used these films was that they were an effective aid in their training programs.

Film Production.   Two basic film production plans were considered. The first was to set up a complete producing unit. The alternative was to use existing facilities and the experienced personnel of commercial producers. It was decided that the Division of Visual Aids for War Training would become an administering and supervising unit rather than a producing organization. This would involve planning, research, policy making, administration of fiscal and contractual obligations, and supervision of all aspects of production and distribution.

The Division first undertook to determine the subject areas where the training need was most critical. Once the area was approved, subject-matter specialists conducted preliminary research to decide on the specific aspects to be filmed. Then a visual aids specialist and a technical specialist cooperatively worked out a content outline or synopsis for the proposed film. When the synopsis was approved by the Division, the film was undertaken.

In order to make the film most useful to both experienced and inexperienced teachers, a visual aids unit was created, consisting of the motion picture, a silent filmstrip correlated with it, and an instructors' manual. The filmstrip was designed as a planned review of the motion picture; the manual gave instructions to the teacher in the use of the film and the filmstrip. The basic purpose of the training film was considered to be that of presenting pictorially those aspects of a subject which could be shown most effectively by use of the film. Each film in a series was considered to be the equivalent of a lesson, based on a specific task to be learned.

In the initial production of these training film series, a number of problems arose. First, the educators had to fight the entire motion picture industry because of a conflict between the educational and theatrical cutting of a film. Second, the verbal tradition which emphasizes words rather than pictures handicapped the making of training films. It was finally concluded that "the film maker must first commit himself to a specific picture," and "the training film maker cannot exercise complete control of his content." [3] In other words, training film production is a cooperative process.

A number of production principles evolved as a result of this experience in relation to film audience, content, and form. Three basic assumptions were made regarding the film audience. It was assumed that the trainee would want to learn how to do the job, that the trainee would see each film several times, and that each motion picture, as part of a visual aids unit, would be accompanied by a silent filmstrip and an instructors' manual. It was also assumed that the films would be based on conveying information,

[3] *Ibid.*, p. 24.

principles, and attitudes in terms of the performance of specific jobs. The object was to develop films for self-identification whereby the learner would be invited, as it were, to live the experience shown in the film.

A basic decision pertaining to form was that the films would be organized around visual content. This signified the automatic limiting of the content to be covered in a single film. This decision to limit the scope of the content made it easier to develop an instructional sequence. Since film length was thus determined by content or concepts rather than by the mechanical size of reels, the U.S. Office of Education's 16-mm productions ran from 275 to 1,150 feet, averaging close to 650 feet per title.

Probably the most important contributions made to instructional technology by the experience of this Division were the development of the "operator's viewpoint" and the "first-person commentary" approaches in film production. The first requirement was that the viewpoint of the camera should always be that of the operator's own eyes. Quite often, this logic ran contrary to accepted production techniques and caused some difficulty. Adherence to this principle, however, meant that everyone in the audience saw the operation from the viewpoint from which he was most likely to learn and as if he were actually doing the job. This reversed the usual procedure which shows a demonstration from the side of the machine opposite the demonstrator. Another result of this technique was the introduction of more camera movement and the elimination of camera angles presenting familiar material in an unfamiliar way.

The "first-person commentary" was designed to keep the commentary closely related to the content of every scene. It was decided that the particular role of the commentary would be to name the objects shown, to indicate the degree of generalization applied to the content of the picture, and to overcome the failure of having the camera tell the entire story. Also, verbalism was avoided as much as possible in the writing of the commentary. Sound effects were used when they were needed to develop a complete sense of familiarity with the job. With a few minor exceptions musical backgrounds were not used. Color films were not produced because of the difficulty of obtaining color during the war and because it was thought that color would not add to the reality of the presentation.

Brooker describes some of the many problems associated with wartime film production as follows:

> Training film production required machine tools, jigs, cutters, blueprints, castings, work pieces, and skilled operators at the very time in our history when these were the most scarce. Arbors were made by the operator working all night to turn one the right size; dividing heads were secured by rushing with a motorcycle to borrow one from a shop where the operator on the night shift was ill, and his part of the picture was shot between midnight and dawn. Raw stock was on priority, and

when for instance, a horse kicked over a can of unexposed film, difficulties arose that were hard to explain. Telegrams requesting the loan of machine tools went unanswered, and shipbuilding jobs, partially photographed on the day shift, were completed by the night shift and when the camera crews returned—the work was gone.[4]

Despite the difficulties, between January, 1941, and June, 1945, the Division of Visual Aids for War Training produced 457 visual aids units— 457 sound motion pictures, 432 silent filmstrips, and 457 instructors' manuals.

Developing Patterns of Distribution.   In order to achieve the widest possible use of the U.S. Office of Education films, a plan had to be developed which would meet the following basic objectives:

1. Distribution had to be based on sales. The films were to be available at a nominal cost to every individual, school, or agency who could use them.
2. Distribution system had to pay for itself—no funds had been appropriated for this purpose. Later Congress specified that sales of the films should also bring return to Government which would amortize the production cost of the films.
3. It was necessary to have facilities for previewing the pictures before purchases.
4. It was desirable to work out a plan which would use existing facilities for distribution rather than to create a large organization within the Government.[5]

These requirements were stated in a bid invitation sent to all commercial distributors. Ultimately, the success of this plan proved its efficiency.

Evaluation and Conclusions.   The characteristics of the training films of the Division of Visual Aids for War Training were given as follows:

1. The films were produced in the instructional tradition. In this sense of the term they are instructional films furthering instructional objectives in terms of generally accepted educational philosophy and psychology.
2. The films produced were planned to further many different objectives by using a wide variety of methods. Films were produced to provide orientation, introduce ideal work patterns, present the factors of judgment, develop the acquisition of facts and information, and to serve as a basis and a source of motivation for discussion, as well as to develop physical, mental, and social skills.
3. These films, according to current terminology, are referred to as training films, but it would be a mistake to consider them as being

[4] *Ibid.,* p. 5.
[5] *Ibid.,* p. 19.

alike, as serving only skill objectives, and as being limited in usefulness to only training programs. It might be more accurate if the
collective term used in speaking of the entire body of productions
was "instructional films."

4. The production program was a pioneering one. The development
   of the visual aids unit, the production of films in an integrated
   series, the production of films to further physical skills acquisition,
   and others . . . were activities never before undertaken to the
   same extent tried by this program.
5. The program was also experimental. The use of stream-of-conscious-
   ness commentary in the problems of pattern making, the intimate
   type of commentary in the films on aircraft maintenance, the pattern of organization followed in the nursing films, the introductions
   used in the elementary wood working series . . . all these factors,
   and others, are experimental. To provide experimental ideas with
   concrete form is to make available the raw material requisite for
   further research and study.[6]

The evaluation of the training films was made primarily by collecting
the judgments of directors in the training program, by conducting informal
spot surveys, and by the records of the film used by training groups. A summary of the observations of training directors was stated as follows:

1. The use of the films speeded up training without any loss of effectiveness. The estimates on this point ranged from 10 percent
   to "a film doing in 20 minutes what it would take two weeks under
   the usual system to do." There was general agreement, however,
   that the acceleration of the training with films did not lead to any
   loss in effectiveness.
2. The use of films made the class work more interesting and resulted
   in less absenteeism. All the training directors were asked to report
   on this point and they agreed that this was true.
3. Films made for the university and college level were at times useful on lower grade levels. Reports have come in of films such as
   the "Slide Rule" being used effectively and successfully on the
   lower high school levels.[7]

The general conclusions reached by the staff of the Division follow:

1. Training films will work. They can be used effectively to train more
   people, more quickly, and in more subject matter. As training films,
   they have not as yet really been tried. Their present success is
   based on only a partial use. Films were designed to expedite the
   development of a physical skill; most of them were actually used
   to provide orientation, to provide facts and information, and to
   explain principles of operation.

[6] *Ibid.,* p. 84.
[7] *Loc. cit.*

2. It can be said that we know much about the production of an effective training film—or that we know little about the production of an effective training film. Both can be said with equal validity. In comparison with what we would like to know, the second half of the statement seems the more true and the more important. The use of pictorial forms of communication is so new that we do not yet have the facts needed to produce the most effective possible training film. Stated another way—we do not as yet know or fully comprehend the logic, grammar, or rhetoric of this form of communication. The fact that it has proven so effective, with partial use and with the present imperfect state of our understanding, should serve to indicate undeveloped possibilities and to stimulate more research and study.

3. The field of visual aids is new, the tools it uses are powerful, but the general lack of understanding of the field is so pervasive that there are inherent dangers requiring the most serious consideration. Films are not general panaceas, they will not solve all instructional problems; they are not "good" per se, they are "good" only as the producers make them so and as the instructors use them. There is danger that over-optimism may cause an over-expansion that is as dangerous as it is unnecessary.

4. New patterns of production will have to be developed before the true and unhampered production of instructional films can take place. It is quite likely that today's accepted division of labor may have to be reconsidered and that new divisions of labor may have to be developed. It also is more than likely that production more fully integrated will develop producers specializing in the production of a single type of instructional film. This specialization cannot come, however, until the market can support it.

5. There is, at the present time, a serious need for professional training courses in the field of visual education. The production of an effective training film requires thorough knowledge and competency in the broad field of education, film production, and the technical aspects of the film content. It is probably impossible to secure all three of these in the same individual. It is desirable, however, to keep the smallest possible number of individuals who must work closely together in order to produce an effective film. It follows that it is most desirable that a broad understanding of education and of film techniques be combined in the person responsible for instructional film production. The need for the development of such individuals is a growing one. It becomes increasingly doubtful that a background of skill and competency in film production alone is enough to insure the production of an effective instructional film.

6. Instructional films can be produced in great numbers, but this should not be confused with mass production or with assembly line production. They will turn out to be good or bad according

to whether some individual becomes definitely and personally interested in them. They are artistic forms, and, as such, must result from the "loving care" of some one individual.

7. Along with the need for better and more complete knowledge of the production of films and the film media of communication, there goes the need for a better understanding of the manner in which students learn from films. There is some indication that a kind of almost unconscious learning takes place when students view a film. This leads the students to believe that they know more than they do, and paradoxically leads them to actually know in practice more than they think they know or can verbally express. These are only first guesses, but certainly there is serious need for additional and more definite information on this point.[8]

Development of military training programs

There had been recognition in the armed services prior to World War II that instructional technology held important implications for military training. During World War I, the Army and the Navy had introduced training films and had begun to establish procedures for the instructional use of such media as slides, filmstrips, and models. The urgent and rapid expansion of military training due to World War II created a new demand for training materials.

The dominant influence in the character of military training programs was exerted by civilian educators. For a number of years previously, educators had conducted experimental research on instructional media and had developed a technology of instruction. In the armed services these same educators came into contact with artists, communications specialists, advertising people, and theatrical and motion picture personnel. These specialized groups combined to develop a technology of instruction for military application. At the same time, military direction provided stability and continuity in the training program.

The entire war experience was summed up by Hoban as follows:

> In developing films for these important educational purposes, the Army applied to educational films the dramatic techniques hitherto used only in entertainment films. These techniques resulted in films which were emotionally possessive as well as intellectually stimulating, and, as a consequence, Army films penetrated deeper into the recesses of the human mind than do school films which coldly present a series of related facts without relating these facts to the backgrounds, interests, motives, and actions of the people to whom they are shown. Behind

[8] *Ibid.*, pp. 86–87.

the developments in Army films was a broad concept of the dynamics of human behavior, an empirical understanding of the reasons why people behave as they do, and a positive approach to the direction and control of human behavior. In the past, schools and colleges have been primarily concerned with what people know, assuming that what they know will influence what they do. The Army, on the other hand, was responsible for what men do as well as what they know, and to make this responsibility even greater, for what men do under conditions which frequently call for supreme sacrifice of life or body. Its films, therefore, dealt not only with *what men must know* but also *what men must do*, and *why they must do it*.[9]

Early Surveys of Training Needs.   Surveys by both the Navy and Army at the beginning of the war revealed that the utilization of instructional media was unsatisfactory. What is more, instructional equipment was generally lacking or was obsolete. Instructors were often inexperienced and frequently failed to use what visual media they possessed at the appropriate times or in effective ways. A survey conducted in 1941 by Lt. Colonel Darryl Zanuck for the Army disclosed a widespread lack of understanding of the proper function of instructional films. One result of this survey was the establishment of a visual aids section in the Office of the Chief Signal Officer to develop an effective utilization program for films, filmstrips, and other instructional media.[10]

A similar problem was experienced in early Navy training. A survey conducted in 1942 revealed that about one-fourth of the Navy instructors did not use films at all and about one-half used them inadequately. About 97 percent of the officers interviewed in the survey expressed a need for training in the use of instructional media. The Navy survey itself covered seven points: (1) present film utilization, (2) film needs, (3) film distribution, (4) cataloguing, (5) continuing services, (6) film production, and (7) special problems, such as administrative location within the Navy. The recommendations called for:

1. A greatly expanded program of training film production.
2. Increased funds and personnel for Training Film Unit.
3. The establishment of Bureau film liaison officers.
4. Development of additional film distribution centers.
5. The development of a production manual.
6. Study by appropriate bureaus of the subjects suggested during the survey for new films.
7. The production of morale films.
8. A study of the use of training films in the Fleet.

[9] Charles F. Hoban, Jr., *Movies That Teach*. New York, The Dryden Press, Inc., 1946, pp. 21–22.
[10] U.S. Army, "Training Films in the Second World War," 1941, pp. 106–108.

9. Procurement and distribution of several thousand 16 mm. motion picture projectors and an equal number of 35 mm. film strip projectors.[11]

The results of these recommendations can be seen from the following actions:

1. Request from the Bureau of Naval Personnel to all Training Activities to study their curricula in order to devise ways to employ visual media to the maximum extent.[12]

2. Request from the Chief of Naval Personnel to the Chiefs of the various bureaus for similar action, and for the appointment of training film liaison officers.[13]

3. Request from the Chief of Naval Personnel to Chief of Bureau of Ships for procurement of fifty-five hundred 16 mm. motion picture projectors for delivery to Naval Training Activities.[14]

4. Request from the Chief of Naval Personnel to Commandants of the First, Fifth, Ninth, Eleventh, Twelfth, and Thirteenth Naval Districts for the establishment of Training Aids Libraries for service to the forces afloat and to the training activities of the districts concerned.[15]

5. Initiation of a program of audio-visual aids utilization to forces afloat.[16]

6. Organization by the Bureau of Naval Personnel of a Navy-wide program of audio-visual aids utilization, and assignment of a staff of officers to carry on the program.[17]

It created considerable interest in training films throughout Navy training establishments and provided many officers with information on the proper method of requesting the production of new films. It gave a solid foundation of fact on which to base the expanded film production program. Without question, the Survey was one of the most important events in the Training Film Branch.[18]

Both the Army and Navy surveys led to the decentralization of film libraries and the establishment of central and sub-libraries at camps and bases. As a result, the creation of libraries highlighted the need for training

[11] See U.S. Navy Bureau of Aeronautics, *Audio-Visual Instruction Survey Report*, section 2, 1942, pp. 10–12.
[12] BuPers ltr. P-243-EK, S85-1/PII-1 (2350), dated Dec. 2, 1942, to All Training Activities.
[13] BuPers ltr. P-243-EK, S85-1/PII-1 (992), dated Dec. 1, 1942, to BuAer.
[14] BuPers ltr. P-243-JLG, S85-1/PII-1 (2372), prep. Dec. 3, 1942, dated Dec. 4, 1942, to BuShips.
[15] BuPers ltr. P-243-ED, P/II-2/ND5 (24), dated Dec. 3, 1942, to Commandant, Fifth N.D.
[16] BuPers ltr. P-243-EK, prep. Dec. 2, 1942, to Cominch.
[17] *Loc. cit.*
[18] U.S. Navy Bureau of Aeronautics, *Audio-Visual Instruction Survey Report, Basic History, Training Film and Motion Picture Branch*, section 2, 1942, p. 8.

aids officers. As training programs developed in both the Army and the Navy, training aids officers were secured to serve as coordinators of audiovisual materials. In special schools, the training aids officer cooperated with other staff administrators in developing specific statements of objectives in each course of the curriculum.

Instructional Media Used in the Armed Services.   The instructional media used in the armed services training programs during World War II included projected, graphic, sound, three-dimensional and "realistic" aids, supplemented by manuals, guides, handbooks, bulletins, and other training literature. Much of this printed material was produced for the preparation of the instructor. It was not to be used in the classroom itself nor was the textbook to be a substitute for lesson planning.

Graphics used in the armed services included charts, graphs, posters, maps, cartoons, and schematic drawings. Graphic portfolios or "transvision" booklets illustrated a sequence of related equipment or processes. The United States Armed Forces Institute (USAFI) used a graphic chart kit—a set of colored charts used as instructional media in twenty-three basic courses. Photography was used effectively by the Navy to develop such graphic presentation sets as "Heaving a Line" (showing the actual heaving of a line in various stages), and its Self-Teaching Recognition Tests (juxtaposition of similar but distinguishable silhouettes for identification training).

Devices and demonstrations of various kinds were also used in the armed services. Synthetic trainers helped develop specific skills and discrimination. Some of these trainers achieved almost perfect simulation of the real situation. One type of Link trainer, for example, provided a cadet pilot with a moving view of the earth over which he was passing, accompanied by the realistic sound of aircraft engines on recordings. Mockups simulated many types of equipment operation. Also, various types of models and "breadboards" showed the operation and layout of equipment. A miniature model, for example, was functionally complete in showing a port installation. Other areas of combat operations were also realistically simulated. The Army Engineering Corps at Fort Belvoir, Virginia, trained in a "tropic" building where men working in high temperature in a high-humidity room were taught installation and maintenance of air-conditioning equipment. Many schools in various branches had exhibit rooms where displays of all types of equipment and some of the conditions of their use were shown by the use of sand tables. Models, mockups, breadboards,[19] and other such devices became standard instructional equipment in military classrooms.

[19] Breadboards clarified mechanical operations and theories. Instruction on electrical equipment frequently made use of breadboards. The circuits of a particular service radio might be laid out, part by part, on one large board. Circuits could be traced, the function of each part discussed, and the results of failure of parts demonstrated. The combined use of graphics, models, mockups, breadboards, and films was common in mobile training units in the Army and the Navy.

Projected visual media of all types were used in military training programs during this period. Films and filmstrips were shown extensively. The *Catalog of Training Films for the Navy, Marine Corps, and Coast Guard* listed approximately nine thousand films available in 1945. The Army Air Force's *Training Film and Film Strip Catalog* listed several thousand films. The Army film *Military Training* (TF7-295) was probably the best filmic expression of why, how, and what was taught in the Army. Produced in 1941, it was widely used in disseminating the Army's philosophy and methods of teaching. The Navy later produced *Film Tactics* and *Methods of Teaching* for purposes of instructor training. In all these instructor training films, emphasis was upon teaching methods rather than content. Films varied from simple animations to highly technical expositions.

In some cases, slides were used for instruction. An unusual still projection device was the Navy's visual aid projector. The visual aid projector, with transparencies and accessories, projected charts, drawings, photographs, and miniature models, with animation of the projected image by means of pointing, writing, or marking on the transparent plates of the device. "Vectograph" equipment provided three-dimensional presentations of photographs and drawings through the use of polaroid viewers. Stereoscopic illustration was also introduced through the use of stereographs in lantern slide projectors.

Many self-instructional devices and materials were also developed. Graphic aids and posters were displayed everywhere for educational purposes. Systematic programs created poster series on fire prevention, security, first aid, venereal disease, and other vital subjects. Also, large-scale war maps were printed weekly by the thousands as a joint Army-Navy service for all troops at home and abroad. Cartoon series—simple lessons illustrating the right and wrong ways of doing things—were often employed. A cartoon character called Little Dilbert was "engaged" by the Navy to teach simple lessons. In the training of illiterates, cartoon characters such as Superman helped in reading and writing programs. By 1944, the Navy had developed a series of training aids through which a sailor might practice code, test himself on his knowledge of Navy flags or his ability to recognize ships and aircraft, check his prowess in free gunnery, or practice other skills. Some of these devices were types of teaching machines whereby the individual could test himself as he developed a particular skill.

Auditory devices were used widely in several aspects of service training. Learning the Morse Code was facilitated by the use of disc, wire, and tape recordings, and recorders. Disc recordings were used to teach air-traffic or communications procedures, to provide "cockpit checkouts" for pilots, to test pilot or crew reactions in a variety of emergencies, etc. Recordings were also effectively employed to simulate sounds of equipment, actual combat noises, and other sounds of military life.

Undoubtedly, the most important use of recordings during World War

II was in the teaching of foreign languages. This was, in effect, the beginning of the modern language laboratory. The procedure in this language instruction program was to record the language lessons on a series of records, provide playback equipment, and supply supplementary printed or typewritten materials. The Army Specialized Training Program known as "area studies" covered several foreign countries and offered an integrated study of the language, customs, geography, and culture of each, for the enlightenment of prospective Army officers. Primary stress was put on modern European languages, but oriental languages were also taught at oriental language school centers. For example, Chinese was offered to Army officers and enlisted men at the Chinese Language School of Yale University with the use of dictation machines (sound scribers). The Navy's oriental language program provided for the recording of the entire first book of the course in Japanese on approximately sixty-two recordings. Students were provided with playback equipment and tape recordings so that they could play the records in their rooms and hear their own speech. The oriental language school at Boulder, Colorado, had its own radio station which broadcast a half-hour program of news each evening, which students were required to hear and report on the following morning. Sound recordings were produced in forty languages in the Navy language laboratories, together with accompanying texts containing the romanized transcriptions, and translations. These intensive language training programs developed in the armed services during World War II provided the principal impetus for the development of language laboratories in the postwar years.[20]

Instructional Materials Produced in the Armed Services. Since there was a scarcity of adequate equipment and instructional materials in the early days of World War II, military schools and instructors improvised a number of instructional devices for use in their training programs. As a result, there was little uniformity in Army instructional materials until the Training Aids Division was established in the Army Ground Forces in September, 1943. In each branch of the Army, a training aids officer was placed in charge of training devices, graphics, film library, and publications. Specialized training organizations included the Infantry School at Fort Benning, the Engineers School at Fort Belvoir, and the Ordnance School at the Aberdeen Proving Ground. Such key schools, including those at Fort Lee, Fort Sill, and Fort Monmouth, developed specialized facilities and methods for their particular arm of the service and provided leadership in special demonstrations of training devices, graphics, films, and filmstrips. Hundreds of Army Air Force schools made their own contributions.

[20] Recordings were also used to cover the full scope of a teaching unit, in the selection and testing of personnel, for practice drills, for explanations and demonstrations, and for creating vicarious experiences in dramatic form.

The Navy had similar schools, among which the Great Lakes School at Great Lakes, Illinois, and the ordnance and fire control school at Anacostia, D.C., were especially important. The destroyer base at San Diego, California, under the command of Captain Byron McCandless, made the first extensive use of military instructional technology in the Navy.

Out of the training aids centers emerged some production units. The Training Aids Division, located at various times in Washington, D.C.; Orlando, Florida; and New York City, was the Army Air Force's main producing agency. However, the actual production of standard training devices and films was accomplished by various Army Air Force agencies and commercial firms. Training equipment considered necessary was designed by the Training Equipment Branch of the Engineering Division. Air Force training films were first produced by the Signal Corps, but in 1942 a separate training film production unit was established at Wright Field. Simultaneously, commercial film studios in Hollywood began to produce orientation, morale, and enlistment films for the Army Air Force. The Hollywood unit later took over the function of the Training Film Unit at Wright Field, and thereafter the Hollywood Eighteenth Base Unit and a New York Fifth Base Unit operated under the Army Air Force Headquarters Office of Motion Pictures. The central agency for the production of training materials in the Navy was the Bureau of Aeronautics.

The Training Aids Development Center was established in New York City in 1942 by the Bureau of Naval Personnel. Three major departments were developed in this agency: an engineering department to produce mockups, models, and other three-dimensional aids; an engineering illustration department to produce technical charts and cross-sectional illustrations; and a graphics department to develop charts and posters.[21]

The production of complex training materials for Navy training was the chief function of the Bureau of Aeronautics. A Division of Special Devices developed a number of synthetic devices for training in the estimation of ranges, in airborne gunnery (both fixed and flexible), in the recognition of friendly and enemy planes, and in a variety of other phases of aviation training. For example, a Pursuit Trainer was designed, "with the fleeing enemy plane projected on a screen ahead, on which is also projected a background

---

[21] The War Services Program of the Works Progress Administration, a development of the WPA Federal Art Project, had offered its help to the armed services. However, the training materials produced were not given wide application. It became obvious that the design and development of training aids by this organization could make an important contribution effected by a wider distribution of materials. In order to implement this concept, the Navy requested the WPA to extend cooperation on a national scale to the Navy, by making known all training aids previously developed and by undertaking the development of specific training aids for the Bureau of Naval Personnel. See William Exton, Jr., *Audiovisual Aids to Instruction*. New York, McGraw-Hill Book Company, 1947, pp. 18–19.

of clouds. As the pilot manipulates his controls, the objects on the screen rotate and move as they may be seen to do if he carried out the same maneuvers in actual flight." [22]

In another type of trainer produced by the Bell Laboratories for the Navy Special Devices Division, a fuselage with all standard equipment was provided, except that no one could "see out." The controls and indicators were all connected electronically to a control panel operated by an instructor. The general effect was that the bomber crew manned their plane, took off, maneuvered, cruised, patroled, navigated, and eventually returned and landed; and in so doing they operated all their equipment just as they would in actual flight.

The Army's expanding program of photographic functions and operations within the Signal Corps brought about the establishment of the Army Pictorial Service in mid-1942. By late 1942, the Army Pictorial Service had formed the Photographic Equipment Branch to review requirements for various projection devices and other pictorial equipment. Signal Corps specifications for projectors were practically nonexistent at that time, but with the establishment of the Pictorial Engineering and Research Laboratory (PEARL) in early 1943, the Army standardization of projectors and other pictorial materials was begun. It was also the responsibility of the Laboratory to investigate, design, and develop new types of photographic equipment. This was the nucleus of the Photographic Branch of Squier Signal Laboratory (SCEL), Fort Monmouth, New Jersey.

At the beginning of the war, the Chief Signal Officer was assigned the responsibility for providing visual training aids, which included: the production and distribution of training films, combat photography for both military and historical purposes; morale of troops in presentation of theatrical motion pictures; and photographic laboratory development and research, as well as all aspects of ground and aerial photography. These responsibilities were discharged through three widely separated and inadequately housed facilities. They consisted of the photographic laboratories at the Army War College in Washington and two training film production laboratories, one at Fort Monmouth and the other at Wright Field. Each had a specialized function. The Signal Corps Photographic Laboratory at the Army War College was the still picture center; the Training Film Production Laboratory at Fort Monmouth specialized in producing training films for the various branches of the ground forces; and the Training Film Production Laboratory at Wright Field produced training films exclusively for the Army Air Forces. Photographic training was conducted formally at Fort Monmouth.

There had been a long debate over whether the Signal Corps should purchase the Paramount Studio at Astoria, Long Island, which was on the

[22] *Ibid.,* p. 321.

market. For months, Colonel Melvin E. Gillette, commander of the Signal Corps Training Film Production Laboratory at Fort Monmouth, had urged the purchase of this studio because it would provide an up-to-date plant where all training film production, processing, and distribution could be centered, leaving the Signal Corps Photographic Laboratory at Washington free to concentrate on still picture production. In February, 1942, the purchase of the Paramount studio was finally authorized and in May, 1942, the modest Fort Monmouth Training Film Production Laboratory moved to Long Island. The courses in still photography were also transferred there and consolidated with the motion picture courses of the laboratory to form the Training Division of the new Signal Corps Photographic Center. Once established, the Photographic Center outgrew its quarters several times before the war ended.

The Photographic Center made a significant contribution to instructional technology by way of establishing new techniques and uses for training films. Motion picture training at Astoria began with an eight-week course which was later lengthened to twelve, and finally to seventeen, weeks. Training was highly practical. A student was given a short period of instruction in the mechanical details of photographic equipment and then directly ushered into the process of producing a film. After learning story coverage, he made a series of phantom shots out of doors on a controlled problem, under close supervision. Then he was given a live film to shoot. The next phase of his training included the coverage of simple daily assignments around New York City, instruction on 16-mm film and color film, and more complicated assignments in editing and working on press arrangements. Little theory or training literature was involved until late in the war. Throughout the learning period, particular attention was given to actual field conditions that might be encountered. Hasty fortifications were built after long marches over difficult terrain, overnight bivouacs were designed to train students how to use and protect their equipment under adverse weather conditions, and practice shooting of films was done from moving vehicles.

The Signal Corps Photographic Center at Astoria, together with its Washington, D.C., Culver City, and Burbank, California, units made an impressive record in wartime training film production. By July, 1942, it had ten training film units in the field, four teams making film bulletins, one team filming scenes for the Special Services Branch, and one making propaganda pictures for the Bureau of Public Relations. Selective Service provided first-class professional photographers, actors, scriptwriters, and laboratory technicians. As a result, training films produced by the Signal Corps Photographic Center became increasingly more professional and effective.

The Chief of Staff, General George C. Marshall, was so enthusiastic about the use of films that he was eager to extend their use to include orientation for troops. Early in 1942, Colonel Schlosberg of the Army Pictorial

Service was directed to find a qualified person in the motion picture industry to direct a series of orientation films. Frank Capra agreed to undertake the work, and was commissioned as a major in the Signal Corps. By the end of April, 1942, Hollywood writers under Capra's guidance had completed a series of scripts based on the Signal Corps Bureau of Public Relations lectures. In June, 1942, a special unit consisting of men drawn from the various technical fields was activated for the purpose of producing a series of orientation films entitled *Why We Fight*. Altogether, Capra produced seventeen excellent, highly successful feature films, at the rate of one about every two months, during the approximately three years he was assigned to this work.

Most of the difficulties that beset the Army's training film program occurred during the first eighteen months of the war. The demand for material was too great and too sudden. Also, recruits from the commercial field were new to Army procedures and to the production of films as training aids. Instructors and educational advisors, on the other hand, knew the effectiveness of visual aids but were not familiar with the techniques needed to produce them effectively. Regular Army men knew what they wanted their men to know and to do, but they were not aware of the limitations and the capabilities of films. Nevertheless, a substantial production record was achieved. During the fiscal year 1943, approximately 135,000 16-mm prints and 24,000 35-mm prints were made available to film libraries in the United States and overseas. There were 200,000 bookings of forty-four subjects filmed for the Corps of Engineers alone. Some 655,600 still picture prints were distributed for technical and publicity use. More than 16,000 16-mm projectors were procured from several commercial manufacturers.[23]

During the war years, the United States Army Air Force produced more than four hundred training films and over six hundred filmstrips. Films were produced by the Army Air Force First Motion Picture Unit, Culver City, California. Filmstrips were developed in five Filmstrip Preparation Units located in different sections of the country. In addition to films and filmstrips, a number of training devices were designed for training in perceptual motor skills—flying an aircraft, operating a radar set and interpreting scope presentations, firing at a rapidly moving target, recognizing friendly and enemy aircraft, and the like. Also, some special applications of films and filmstrips were made to solve many new operational problems. For example, stereovision was used to interpret aerial photographs; high-speed photography was employed to slow down explosive action for study; and operational events were recorded on film.

[23] For a complete history of the United States Signal Corps Photographic Center training film activities during World War II, see George R. Thompson, D. R. Harris, Pauline M. Oakes, and Dulany Terrett, *The Signal Corps: The Test.* Office of the Chief of Military History, Department of the Army, 1957. See also George R. Thompson and D. R. Harris, *The Signal Corps: The Outcome.*

The United States Coast Guard also produced a number of training films and filmstrips, as well as many other types of materials. Early in its training program, the Coast Guard discovered that the process could be considerably accelerated by (1) using integrated kits of motion pictures and discussional slide films; (2) correlating "show-how" filmstrips with "practice-how" training aids; (3) including class examinations with discussional filmstrips; and (4) packaging related films together.[24]

Distribution of Instructional Materials. At the beginning of the war, instructional materials were distributed direct from agencies in the War and Navy Departments. However, it soon became obvious that central distribution was too inefficient to meet increasing demands. A survey made by the Navy in September, 1942, revealed that the distribution of films had increased from two thousand prints in January, 1942, to approximately fifty thousand in August, 1942. As a consequence, distribution was decentralized in both the Navy and the Army.

In the Army, the old Visual Aids Section of the Signal Corps was abolished and a new section formed, the Film Distribution and Utilization Branch. Distribution agencies were established in the Navy in both the Bureau of Aeronautics (later under the Chief of Naval Operations) and the Bureau of Naval Personnel, each of which submitted lists to the Training Film Unit for initial distribution of films. The Coast Guard and the Marine Corps also made use of the Training Film Unit for their films. The Army, Navy, and their aviation forces established film library systems in selected areas nearest to the classrooms which needed them.[25]

A description of the distribution system of the armed services by Hoban follows:

> It was characteristic of the film distribution systems of the various branches of the armed services that each was organized in a *network* which covered the entire country, and that this network was duplicated in each overseas theater where American troops or naval units were deployed. In the military and naval distribution systems there was for each, one central agency charged with supply of all films, equipment, and projectors. In each theater of operation, service command, or naval

---

[24] Exton, *op. cit.*, pp. 82–88.

[25] The Educational Film Library Association was formed in Chicago, March 17–18, 1943, for the purpose of reviewing the arrangements established by government agencies for the free distribution of their films. It was recognized by all present that unless educational institutions and agencies were given an opportunity to qualify as depositories, they would not be able to meet requests for government war films from school and adult groups. The first officers of EFLA were: L. C. Larson, chairman; Bruce A. Findlay, vice-chairman; and R. Russell Munn, secretary. Donald Slesinger, then director of the American Film Center, served as acting administrative director. EFLA provided the impetus for the organization of the Sixteen Millimeter Advisory Committee, formed in November, 1943, for protection of the interests of educators.

district, a similar agency gave direct service to installations within the command area, and on all large posts there was a local agency which supplied all military or naval units with film service. Thus, one central film supply agency served a Central Film Library in each theater, service command, or naval district, and these, in turn, served the film libraries of local posts, camps, or stations. The film library or training-aids section on the post served the local consumer—the instructor and the troops. Under this system, any training officer could obtain any film he needed through the service chain stemming out of one central agency of supply. In the case of the Army, this central supply agency was the Signal Corps Photographic Center, Long Island City, New York.[26]

Utilization of Instructional Materials.   Cumulative data show that during some of the most intensive thirty-day training periods, more than 200,000 prints of 16-mm training films—almost a quarter of a million projections—were shown to military personnel.

The success of the various training aids programs was largely due to the standardization of the curricula and the publicizing of the training materials available. The extent of use of instructional media was tremendous. It has been estimated that over four million film showings were made before Army Ground and Service Force audiences in the continental United States from July 1, 1943, to June 30, 1945. Four surveys by the Utilization and Evaluation Section of the Training Aids Division, Bureau of Naval Personnel, indicated that graphics, devices, and films were widely used in training. However, these reports also emphasized the need for better planning of training so that preparation for films and follow-up discussions could take place. The last two surveys reported personal evaluations of films and filmstrips by instructors in schools ashore. These reports showed that Navy schools made wide use of all types of instructional media although not always with great effectiveness.

The four educational objectives of the United States Army in the use of motion pictures were summarized by Hoban as follows:

1. Orientation in the moral purposes for which the war was fought, the nature of our allies and our enemies, and the importance of the part played by various components of the Army.
2. Understanding of and habituation in self-control and proper conduct of the individual soldier.
3. Information on current material development and military progress on all fronts.
4. Instruction in basic technical subjects and skills.[27]

[26] Charles F. Hoban, Jr., *Movies That Teach.* New York, The Dryden Press, Inc., 1946, pp. 111–112.
[27] *Ibid.,* pp. 22–23.

Among the many attempts to test the effectiveness of instructional technology was a study by the United States Army Air Force of the filmstrip as an instructional medium. This revealed that:

1. A large percentage of training aids officers and instructors indicated confidence in filmstrips as a major aid in teaching.
2. Practically all instructors and training aids officers indicated a real desire to use filmstrips more extensively in training.
3. Instructors were making only a partial use of available strips, primarily because of improper practices in selection and integration of filmstrips into courses of instruction.
4. Instructors and training aids officers lacked training and experience in the use of visual aids and in teaching.
5. Techniques and practices in selection and integration of filmstrips into the curriculum fell short as judged by generally accepted practices and criteria.
6. The nonuse and/or disuse of filmstrips was caused primarily by shortcomings and defects in application of filmstrips to training problems.[28]

Other research demonstrated that a film may have definite effects on attitudes. One test group of soldiers saw the film *Battle for Britain,* while a second group did not. Among those who had not seen the film, only 46 percent believed that Britain would have been conquered had it not been for determined resistance, whereas 70 percent of those who had seen the film expressed such a belief. Still another study made by the Psychological Test Film Unit of the Army Air Force compared learnings derived from (a) a training film, (b) studying a well-illustrated manual, and (c) an organized lecture using nineteen lantern slides. It was found that both the superior and inferior portions of the film group did significantly better than did the other two groups.

In 1945, the Training Aids Division of the Bureau of Naval Personnel conducted a survey of instructor opinions of 159 motion pictures and forty-five filmstrips. The opinions of these instructors were summarized as follows:

1. Navy instructors think training films constitute an effective part of the training program.
2. Motion pictures are considered more valuable in training than filmstrips in the specific instructional units under consideration.
3. Training films are reasonably well adapted to the curriculum in which they are being used.
4. Films can be successfully used to present highly technical subjects in a clear and understandable manner.

[28] John R. Miles and Charles R. Spain, *Audio-Visual Aids in the Armed Services.* Washington, D.C., American Council on Education, 1947, p. 63.

5. Navy instructors believe that men learn more, remember longer, and show more interest in learning when training films are used than when more traditional methods are employed.
6. Films tend to standardize training, shorten training time, and make instruction more practical.
7. Instructors generally think the present length of training films is satisfactory, but more think they should be longer than think they should be shorter.
8. Instructors think that slightly more humor, drama, and combat scenes should be included in both films and filmstrips.[29]

Instructional technology came of age during World War II. As Brooker says, "In the long run the period of World War II will mark the crossover from regarding films as an educational luxury to regarding them as a necessity."[30] Printed materials often became secondary in importance while training devices became the major medium of instruction. When questioned about the lack of research concerning the effectiveness of training aids, officers usually gave lack of time and personnel as the reasons. They often stated that utilization techniques known in instructional technology prior to the war served as a valuable guide to their efforts. For example, many officers reported that the Motion Picture Project of the American Council on Education, completed just before the war, profoundly affected the Navy program, both in terms of broad concepts of use and in providing experienced key personnel.[31]

Wartime Problems. A look at the armed services' war experiences, in retrospect, reveals a series of problems in bold relief. As film production increased, a point was reached at which the services' production facilities across the country were being used to capacity with the result that serious bottlenecks developed. The consequent delays evoked criticism that "it takes too long!" Another wartime problem that impeded production was the lack of trained personnel. There was a constant shortage of artists, writers, cutters, editors, photographers, and other specialists. The most serious consequence of inadequately trained personnel was the effect on the technical and educational quality of the films.

The Army produced its own films in its own studios; the Navy, on the other hand, had most of its work done on contract. However, both found that they had to resort to the two methods for certain films.

Although there is a great deal of material available in the files of the various armed services concerning their wartime training activities in rela-

---

[29] *Ibid.*, pp. 73–74.
[30] Floyde E. Brooker, "Communication in the Modern World," in *Audio-Visual Materials of Instruction*, The Forty-eighth Yearbook of the National Society for the Study of Education, part I. Chicago, The University of Chicago Press, 1949, p. 17.
[31] See Chap. 15 of this history for a discussion of the Motion Picture Project.

tion to production, distribution, and utilization, no detailed study has yet been made of this data. Regardless of this gap in our knowledge, we can wholeheartedly say with Goldner:

> The armed services—Army, Army Air Force, Navy, Marine Corps, Coast Guard—all, made records that will stand. Their patterns of operation, their standards and criteria, and their personnel and facilities had to be developed rapidly to meet highly specialized needs of a pressing and varied nature and under conditions never before experienced. The training needs out of which the training film programs emerged, and which they were organized to meet, were greater in number, more complex, and more urgent than any that had been encountered in the history of the country.[32]

Implications of war experience for instructional technology

The war effort brought the first significant convergence of the audio-visual tributary with the mainstream of instructional technology. Also, as a result of the war experience, both audiovisualists and educators generally developed an increased sensitivity to the applicability of scientific theories of learning to practical problems of instruction. Moreover, there evolved an increased sophistication concerning the function and role of the media and/or communications specialist within the total context of instructional technology.

[32] Orville Goldner, "Films in the Armed Services," in Godfrey M. Elliott (ed.), *Film and Education*. New York, Philosophical Library, Inc., 1948, p. 395.

chapter 9

the audiovisual instruction
movement: development

Following World War II, a period of expansion began in the audiovisual instruction movement. During the decade 1945–1955, the growth curve of the movement continued at a steady pace with a brief leveling-out period between 1950 and 1955. Beginning with 1955, a transition period began which is still in progress. During the first decade of this period, from 1955 to 1965, language laboratories, television, teaching machines, classroom communication devices, multimedia presentations, and the beginning use of computers as teaching machines and as controls of more complex instructional systems made their appearance.

Simultaneously, there arose an uneasiness among many audiovisualists concerning the adequacy of the audiovisual label with reference to these new media, as well as dissatisfaction with the traditional rationale supporting their practices. As a result, there was a movement in the early sixties toward a redefinition of audiovisual instruction in terms of learning and communication theory.[1] Moreover, it was becoming apparent that the audiovisual movement was tending toward convergence with the broad stream of instructional technology. Thus the history of the transitional period, short as it is, contrasts dramatically with the earlier history of the audiovisual instruction movement, primarily because of a greater dependence on psychological theory and research.

State audiovisual programs

State leadership in advancing the use of audiovisual media increased steadily after World War II with the growth of teacher education requirements and the budgeting of considerable sums for the purchase of audiovisual materials. In Virginia, for example, a $1.25 million legislative appropriation was used to supply every school in the state with a motion picture projector, films, filmstrips, maps, slides, and other audiovisual materials.[2]

The States Audiovisual Education Study (SAVES), concluded in 1963 by Noel and staff, pointed out that:

> In the nation as a whole, a total of 75 positions were reported in State departments of education which carry a designated audiovisual title: these occurred in 32 states (64%). Twenty-three states (46%) reported one or more fulltime SDE staff occupied designated audiovisual positions on a part-time basis in 15 states (30%). These states included 7 states (14%) which had already reported fulltime positions, so that in 8 states the full responsibility is carried by a part-time designated person. In the remaining 18 states (36%) which reported no designated audiovisual position, this responsibility is carried by a staff member whose major assignment lies outside the new educational media field. . . . Thus, in 27 states major responsibility for new educational media is carried by personnel with other departmental duties.[3]

Examples of the many types of activities performed by personnel in state audiovisual programs, as reported in the SAVES study, are the following:

> Assisting local schools in new media matters pertaining to curriculum revision.

[1] See "The Changing Role of the Audiovisual Process in Education: A Definition and a Glossary of Related Terms," *AV Communication Review*, supplement 6 (January–February, 1963).
[2] James W. Brown, *The Virginia Plan for Audio-Visual Education*. Chicago, The University of Chicago Press, 1947.
[3] Francis W. Noel et al., *Practices of State Departments of Education in New Educational Media/Audiovisual Education during 1960–61*, Los Angeles, University of Southern California Press, 1963, II-3 to II-4.

Preparing utilization guides, study resource units, bibliographic materials, and similar publications.

Holding conferences and workshops for professional and lay personnel to provide information, stimulation, and guidelines for the use of new media.

Developing standards for new media availabilities and utilization (equipment, materials, services) as part of over-all accreditation procedures (forty-four of the states engaged in this activity, although there was great variation in types of services performed).

Developing and enforcing teacher certification standards involving knowledges and skills in utilizing new media and equipment (in six states for classroom teachers; in ten states for supervisory and administrative certificates; five states for librarians; seven states for new media supervisors).

Developing and publishing building and facilities standards (usually in cooperation with the state department of education's department of plant planning) as related to new media installations.

Conducting research studies and surveys regarding uses and contributions of new media to the school instructional program.

Producing various instructional materials (twenty-one states) for use by schools and staff members of state departments of education.

Distributing new media on short-term loan bases to schools (fifteen states) or within the state department of education only (twenty-seven states).

Supervising state-wide programs of educational television (twenty state departments had some legal responsibilities for this).[4]

County audiovisual programs

Although postwar growth in county audiovisual programs was not as impressive as that in state audiovisual programs, substantial progress was made generally. The rise of such programs in the 1950s and 1960s enabled increasing numbers of smaller school districts and county school units to enjoy the advantages of centralized audiovisual services. Spokane and King Counties in the state of Washington, Dade County in Florida, and Hanover County in North Carolina are examples of counties which developed outstanding audiovisual programs. Notable county programs were also developed in Indiana, Kentucky, Michigan, New Jersey, and California. In California, for example, every county had a full-time or part-time audiovisual director or coordinator, and many developed large libraries of audiovisual materials. Los Angeles and San Diego are models for county audiovisual programs.

[4] *Ibid.*

City audiovisual programs

Another impressive index of the postwar growth of the audiovisual instruction movement can be seen in the expenditure for audiovisual materials by city school systems. In 1953–1954, the NEA conducted a national survey which revealed that the median amount of money for audiovisual materials had increased from a 1946 total of 35 cents to 65 cents per pupil for all districts reporting. This study also showed that 86 percent of the cities over 100,000 in population had organized audiovisual programs and that more than two-thirds of the urban school districts included in the study had established audiovisual centers.[5]

College and university audiovisual programs

The postwar trend has been for the college or university audiovisual center to become a resource center or a centralized administrative organization for educational media services, as well as a research-oriented center for the study of media in the teaching-learning process. One of the more recent developments in higher education is an emphasis on research that relates to innovations in instructional practices. Much experimentation has been stimulated by appropriations resulting from the National Defense Education Act (NDEA) and by support from private foundations such as the Ford Foundation.[6]

Teacher education in audiovisual instruction

A 1959 report by de Kieffer [7] revealed that there were 560 colleges and universities offering audiovisual courses for teachers. In addition, many in-service courses were offered by city schools, county audiovisual departments, and state departments of education. Connelly's study [8] of state requirements relating to audiovisual instruction showed that, as of 1962, only twelve states made no legal provision for audiovisual instruction.

[5] See "Audio-Visual Education in Urban School Districts, 1953–54," *NEA Research Bulletin,* vol. 33, no. 3, Washington, D.C. (October, 1955).
[6] See James W. Brown and James W. Thornton, Jr. (eds.), *New Media in Higher Education.* Washington, D.C., Association for Higher Education and Department of Audiovisual Instruction, NEA, 1963.
[7] Robert E. de Kieffer, "AV Activities of Colleges and Universities in Teacher Education," *AV Communication Review,* vol. 7, no. 2 (Spring, 1959), pp. 122–137.
[8] John W. Connelly, Jr., *Report of State Laws on Audio-Visual Media of Instruction in Public Schools and on Establishment of Educational Television Stations.* U.S. Office of Education, 1962.

Evaluation of Audiovisual Instruction. Several evaluative criteria have been developed for audiovisual courses. One of the first comprehensive evaluation instruments was devised by Schwartz in 1950.[9] In the spring of 1954, the Department of Audiovisual Instruction of the NEA released a set of standards against which the work of a teacher education institution might measure itself on a self-appraisal basis.[10]

Stimulated by the 1958 Lake Okoboji (Iowa) Audiovisual Leadership Conference, the Department of Audiovisual Instruction, National Education Association, devoted the January, 1959, issue of *Audiovisual Instruction* to the subject of teacher education. Up to 1959, according to Allen, "the research in the area of teacher education to utilize new educational media with maximum effectiveness is characterized by status studies and questionnaire surveys. Practically no experimental research has been conducted on ways to train teachers, either in colleges and universities or in-service training situations." The major conclusions from the evaluation-type surveys, Allen says, were that "(a) teacher inertia is an outstanding deterrent to the use of media, (2) a small percentage of the teachers use the greatest percentage of materials, and (c) teachers with preparation used more media and with greater effectiveness." [11]

In 1965, William R. Fulton of the University of Oklahoma developed a self-evaluation instrument for appraising educational media programs in elementary and secondary schools of all sizes and in colleges and universities. He identified six elements as being essential to an adequate educational media program. They are: (1) administrative commitment to a system-wide or institution-wide educational media program; (2) educational media as an integral part of curriculum and instruction; (3) an educational media center; (4) adequate physical facilities for the use of educational media; (5) an adequate budget for the educational media program; and (6) an adequate educational media staff. Each section is preceded by a brief statement of pertinent criteria which accompanies the instrument.

Another recent effort to examine the implications of the use of the newer media for teacher education is represented by W. C. Meierhenry's study, *Media Competencies for Teachers.*[12]

Professional Preparation of Audiovisual Personnel. The demand for professional positions for audiovisual specialists was not very great until the fifties. Advanced graduate programs were limited to a few institutions. Doc-

[9] John C. Schwartz, *Evaluative Criteria for an Audio-Visual Instructional Program.* Dubuque, Iowa, William C. Brown Company, 1950.
[10] Department of Audiovisual Instruction, Committee on Teacher Education, *Evaluation Schedules in Audio-Visual Instruction.* Washington, D.C., NEA, 1954.
[11] William Allen (ed.), *A Summary of the Lake Okoboji Audiovisual Leadership Conference Held at the Iowa Lakeside Laboratory, Milford, Iowa, during the Years 1955–1959.* Washington, D.C., Department of Audiovisual Instruction, NEA, 1960, p. 88.
[12] W. C. Meierhenry, *Media Competencies for Teachers.* Contract No. 5-0730-2-12-6, NDEA Title VII, Part B, U.S. Office of Education, Apr. 1, 1965, to Mar. 31, 1966.

toral dissertations completed in the audiovisual field between 1951 and 1956 almost doubled the number of studies previously completed.[13]

With the growth of graduate programs in audiovisual education, there came to be greater concern with professional certification for audiovisual personnel. Two proposals were made for credential programs, but there was a marked difference of opinion among audiovisual educators on the desirability of establishing special certification requirements for audiovisual specialists. The first proposal for certification came at a California audiovisual administration workshop in 1947. This workshop group recommended that an audiovisual director should be required to complete either a supervisory or administrative credential on the elementary or secondary level, plus one course in the administration of audiovisual programs and another in supervision of instruction and curriculum in audiovisual education. Later, in 1951, a more detailed credential program was suggested by the Audio-Visual Instructional Directors in Indiana. The Indiana Teacher Training and Licensing Commission approved these requirements, and in 1952 a special credential was offered by the Indiana State Department of Education. The Indiana credential program was presented to the Committee on Professional Education of the NEA Department of Audiovisual Instruction (DAVI) and was approved at the February, 1952, meeting. The following recommendations were made:

1. That DAVI go on record urging appropriate state groups to take steps in their individual states to bring about suitable action to establish certification requirements for audiovisual directors.
2. That DAVI assist appropriate state groups by supplying them with a suggested pattern of requirements for certification of audiovisual directors.
3. That DAVI recommend that experience as an audiovisual director prior to the effective date of certification be counted toward professional course requirements in audiovisual education.
4. That DAVI recommend that such state certification requirements become effective within three to five years.[14]

In calling for "a technological leap forward in education," a DAVI task force ten years later realized that:

> A new kind of professional will be required to provide leadership in design, implementation, and evaluation of programs in education which make the fullest use of new media. The functions performed by this leader and the resources he brings will be among the essential determinants of success or failure in tomorrow's schools.[15]

[13] John Moldstad, "Doctoral Dissertations in Audio-Visual Education," *AV Communication Review*, vol. 4, no. 3 (Fall, 1956), pp. 291–333. Supplements are issued periodically.

[14] *Boston Conference Proceedings*, NEA, Department of Audiovisual Instruction. Washington, D.C., 1952, pp. 15–16.

[15] Barry Morris (ed.), "The Function of Media in the Public Schools," *Audiovisual Instruction*, vol. 8 (January, 1963), p. 11.

In the meantime, the Department of Audiovisual Instruction, National Education Association, has manifested an official concern with regard to the new professional preparation required by the audiovisual or media specialist, through its sponsorship of seminars, its commission (known as the Professional Education of Media Specialists, or PEMS, Commission), and its publications. Moreover, four major recent studies sponsored by the U.S. Office of Education have dealt with the problem of educating audiovisual specialists. The report of the first of these, published in 1964, is *The Content and Pattern for the Professional Training of Audiovisual Communication Specialists* (popularly known as the STEMS Project-Seminars on Training of Education Media Specialists).[16] In the same year, the report of a project directed by Morris L. Cogan and Harold Lancour of the University of Pittsburgh was published. C. Walter Stone edited this report, entitled *The Professional Education of Media Service Personnel.*[17] The third of these studies is that conducted by Paul D. Holtzman and A. W. VanderMeer of Pennsylvania State University, *Interdisciplinary Graduate Programs in Communication: A Descriptive Study.*[18] Finally, in the fall of 1965, another report appeared under the title *A Study of Regional Instructional Media Resources: Phase I–Manpower.* Ann M. Martin of the University of Pittsburgh was the director of this project.[19]

Today more than sixty institutions and thirty states are offering a minimum of one graduate course in each of three areas: utilization, production, and administration. Moreover, one may find programs leading to the doctorate degree in audiovisual education in a number of leading universities. For example, one may earn a doctorate with audiovisual specialization at Columbia University, Indiana University, Michigan State University, New York University, Ohio State University, University of Southern California, and Syracuse University.[20]

Audiovisual Instruction and Library Education.   For many years, audiovisualists and library educators have made an effort to combine the collection and distribution of audiovisual materials and books. In June, 1947, a grant to support a Film Advisory Service at the American Library Associa-

---

[16] Robert O. Hall (ed.), *The Content and Pattern for the Professional Training of Audiovisual Communication Specialists.* NDEA Title VII Project no. B-208, U.S. Office of Education, 1964.

[17] C. W. Stone (ed.), *The Professional Education of Media Service Personnel.* Pittsburgh, Pa., Graduate Library School, University of Pittsburgh, 1964.

[18] P. D. Holtzman and A. W. VanderMeer, *Interdisciplinary Graduate Programs in Communication: A Descriptive Study.* University Park, Pa., Pennsylvania State University, 1965.

[19] Ann M. Martin, *A Study of Regional Instructional Media Resources: Phase I—Manpower.* Pittsburgh, Pa., Center for Library and Educational Media Studies, University of Pittsburgh, 1965.

[20] See F. F. Harcleroad (ed.), "The Education of the AV Communications Specialist," *AV Communication Review,* vol. 8 (September–October, 1960), pp. 3–96.

tion was made by the Carnegie Corporation for the purpose of demonstrating that public libraries could serve as centers for the distribution of audiovisual materials as well as books. As early as 1949, the American Association of School Librarians sponsored publication of Margaret Rufsvold's *Audio-Visual School Library Service.*[21] In this book detailed information was given to guide the traditionally book-oriented librarian in establishing an instructional materials center. With the report of the Lieberman study in 1955,[22] it became apparent that there was a need for a graduate program for curriculum materials specialists. To meet this need, San Jose State College in California inaugurated the first integrated program of its kind during the 1954–1955 academic year.

Audiovisual Textbooks.   A number of new audiovisual textbooks designed for use in audiovisual courses have appeared in recent years. For example, some of the more notable are: James W. Brown, Richard B. Lewis, and Fred F. Harcleroad's *A-V Instruction* (McGraw-Hill, 1964); James W. Brown and Kenneth D. Norberg's *Administering Educational Media* (McGraw-Hill, 1965); A. J. Foy Cross and Irene F. Cypher's *Audio-Visual Education* (Crowell, 1961); Edgar Dale's *Audio-Visual Methods in Teaching* (Dryden, 1954); Carlton W. H. Erickson's *Fundamentals of Teaching with Audiovisual Technology* (Macmillan, 1965); Robert de Kieffer and Lee W. Cochran's *Manual of Audio-Visual Techniques* (Prentice-Hall, 1962); James S. Kinder's *Audio-Visual Materials and Techniques* (American Book Company, 1959); R. M. Thomas and S. G. Swartout's *Integrated Teaching Materials* (Longmans, Green & Co., 1960); and W. A. Wittich and Charles F. Schuller's *Audio-Visual Materials: Their Nature and Use* (Harper and Row, 1967). Meanwhile, the first comprehensive bibliography of audiovisual publications, *The A-V Bibliography* (William C. Brown Company, 1950), compiled by F. Dean McClusky, and the first comprehensive audiovisual equipment manual, *The Audio-Visual Equipment Manual* (Dryden, 1957), developed by James D. Finn, appeared.

Professional sponsor of audiovisual instruction movement: National Education Association

Since the early twenties, the National Education Association has been an active supporter of the audiovisual instruction movement. In 1945, the growth and importance of the audiovisual movement was duly recognized

---

[21] Margaret Rufsvold, *Audio-Visual School Library Service.* Chicago, American Association of School Librarians, ALA, 1949.
[22] Irving Lieberman, *Audio-Visual Instruction in Library Education.* New York, School of Library Service, Columbia University, 1955.

when the National Education Association established a Division of Audiovisual Instructional Services for the purpose of providing "leadership for better education through the use of audiovisual media and concepts in instruction and in professional communication." [23]

Department of Audiovisual Instruction.   We have seen that the National Education Association first sponsored the audiovisual instruction movement in 1923 when it founded the Department of Visual Instruction (changed to Department of Audiovisual Instruction in 1947). After World War II, the NEA provided DAVI with an executive secretary and a full-time staff. Between 1948 and 1950, DAVI was reorganized with a new committee structure and increased professional activity. For example, in 1948, DAVI began the first systematic collection and distribution of audiovisual information to schools and to the various educational agencies of the nation. This program also involved cooperation with state departments of education and state legislatures so that audiovisual facilities and instructional programs might be improved in teacher education institutions.

The acceleration of the postwar activities of DAVI became evident in the fifties when cooperative "idea" and "audiovisual" course material exchange projects were established, fourteen national committees were formed to consider problems in fourteen areas of audiovisual education, the staff of the DAVI national office was increased, a packet of utilization materials were developed, significant conferences were sponsored, and the first group of notable DAVI publications began to appear. The first DAVI audiovisual administration yearbook, *The School Administrator and His Audiovisual Program,* and the first edition of the annual *National Tape Recording Catalog* were published in 1954. The establishment of two journals, *AV Communication Review* (1953) and *Audiovisual Instruction* (1956), were historic DAVI landmarks. In 1960, DAVI took the lead in the programed instruction movement by publication of the definitive work *Teaching Machines and Programmed Learning* by Arthur A. Lumsdaine and Robert Glaser. A second volume, *Teaching Machines and Programed Learning, II,* was published in 1965 under the editorship of Robert Glaser. These are only examples of some of the more important DAVI publications in recent years. Many other valuable publications have appeared throughout the years of its activity.

Beginning in 1954, DAVI became engaged in the actual production of audiovisual materials. Examples of some of these productions include *The NEA in Action—1954,* a color filmstrip covering the highlights of the NEA's annual report; *The DAVI School Service Plan*—a seven-minute film describing membership services; *Television Kits*—film clips for interpreting audio-

[23] From *Outline of the Purpose and Functions of the Division of Audiovisual Instructional Services,* NEA and DAVI, n.d., p. 1. (Mimeographed report.)

visual education to television audiences; a series of 2 × 2 slides to accompany brochures on planning of schools; and a sound filmstrip and guide, *Take-home Learning Through Controlled Ventilation.*

In addition to its significant publications and production projects, DAVI contributed in many other ways to the development of the audiovisual instruction movement. Two important achievements were accomplished in 1954: the DAVI Archives Committee established the first Archives Library for the audiovisual field at the State University of Iowa; and the DAVI Radio and Recordings Committee founded the first National Tape Depository at Kent (Ohio) University, later moved to the University of Colorado at Boulder. Also in 1954, the DAVI College and University Committee compiled eleven loose-leaf volumes on aspects of audiovisual instruction in institutions of higher learning and sponsored the first full-scale classroom exhibit featuring facilities for the effective use of instructional materials, in New York City. DAVI also actively participated in various research activities and provided consultants in the areas of accreditation, school buildings, public information, audiovisual administration, and educational television. One of its most important activities in the late fifties and the early sixties was focused on the implementation of the National Defense Education Act (NDEA) and the improvement of methods to develop audiovisual competencies during the preservice teacher education period. It has exerted a particular effort in attempting to professionalize the audiovisual specialist and to provide answers concerning the management and organization of the media field. In connection with these last two activities, DAVI sponsored a Seminar on Professional Education at the 1960 DAVI National Convention in Cincinnati. It has made redefinition of the role of the audiovisual specialist the focus of work done in recent years.

AV Communication Review.   We have already indicated that the *AV Communication Review* was a landmark in DAVI publishing history. However, it is also important that we understand the historical circumstances which brought this significant publication into being.

It seems clear that James D. Finn deserves the major credit for the founding and success of *AV Communication Review.* He became concerned as a graduate student with the lack of easily accessible audiovisual research data. When Finn became chairman of the DAVI Committee on Professional Education in 1951, he began to work actively to establish a new journal of audiovisual theory and research. The first step was to initiate a meeting with C. J. VerHalen, Jr., and Harry Simonson, publisher and editor, respectively, of *Film World,* to discuss the possibilities of subsidizing a new quarterly publication. VerHalen agreed to subsidize such a publication without influencing its content but expressed the desire that it assume a broad communications perspective. When Finn transmitted this generous offer to DAVI, it was received rather coldly, undoubtedly because of certain power struggles then going on within the organization. Also, some members wished to avoid another commercial tie because their experience with *Educational Screen* had not been entirely satisfactory. William H. Allen, chairman of the DAVI Research Committee, had, for example, been unable to get adequate research coverage in *Educational Screen*, which was then the official outlet for DAVI.[24]

Thus the VerHalen offer was turned down by DAVI and a decision was made to proceed instead with the publication of a new quarterly journal of its own. Finn and Allen were appointed coeditors. Shortly after, Finn withdrew and became editor of *Teaching Tools*, a VerHalen publication.[25]

After the first issue of the *AV Communication Review* had been published in 1953, Editor Allen and Finn, as a member of the editorial board, wrote the first charter for the journal. This charter was adopted by the DAVI board of directors without substantial changes and remains in effect.

Audiovisual Instruction.   In 1956, DAVI established its second journal, *Instructional Materials*, as a step forward to a broader approach to instruction. In the very next issue, however, there appeared heated discussions concerning the implications of the title, and within six months, the title was changed to *Audiovisual Instruction*. It had seemed to some that the loss of the term "audiovisual" indicated a premature redefinition of the field.

NEA Technological Development Project.   In the fall of 1960, the Educational Media Branch of the U.S. Office of Education entered into contract with the National Education Association for an overall assessment of the problems created by the impact of technology on education. The project was known as the Technological Development Project (TDP); headquarters were located in the School of Education, University of Southern California; and the director was James D. Finn, professor of education. A second office for the project was maintained in the National Education Association in Washington. The project lasted from October, 1960, to February, 1963.

Information was gathered and synthesized from existing studies, observations, surveys, interviews, and experiments, as well as through original studies. Project findings were disseminated by a series of ten occasional

---

[24] William H. Allen has stated that he is certain that the *AV Communication Review* would never have started—at least at that time—if the *Educational Screen* had been willing to devote even one page per issue to research. Because of this situation, Allen, as chairman of the DAVI Research Committee, recommended the establishment of a research journal by DAVI about the same time that Finn began to work for a similar goal. William H. Allen, letter, July 1, 1961.

[25] *Teaching Tools* was discontinued in 1960.

papers, three monographs, a series of articles in various professional journals, and several audiovisual presentations.[26]

Growth in audiovisual theory

Historically, the use of audiovisual media has been little influenced by theory-oriented research. Following World War II, increasing attention has been devoted to the implications of learning theory for the design of audiovisual materials. Thus Smith and Van Ormer [27] attempted to formulate relationships between learning theory and instructional film research in 1949; T. S. Kendler et al.,[28] studied the relationships of learning theory and the design of audiovisual materials in 1951; James J. Gibson [29] developed "A Theory of Pictorial Perception" for the use of audiovisual media in 1954; Neal E. Miller [30] prepared a paper, "Scientific Principles for Maximum Learning from Motion Pictures and Research Implications," in 1957; and a special supplement of *AV Communication Review*, "Learning Theory and AV Utilization," was published in 1961.[31]

With the emergence of the communications interest in recent years, some atempts have been made to relate the audiovisual field to communication theory.[32] However, most audiovisualists continued to define their field by referring "to such special kinds of communication devices and procedures as motion pictures, filmstrips, television, radio, recordings, graphic illustra-

[26] Studies made include Charnel Anderson, *History of Instructional Technology, I: Technology in American Education, 1650–1900;* Paul Saettler, *History of Instructional Technology, II: The Technical Development of the New Media;* James D. Finn and Donald G. Perrin, *Teaching Machines and Programed Learning, 1962: A Survey of the Industry;* George Gerbner, *Instructional Technology and the Press;* Forrest M. Townsend, *Automation in Educational Administration, I: Vending Machines in Education;* James D. Finn, Donald G. Perrin, and Lee E. Campion, *Studies in the Growth of Instructional Technology, I: Audio-Visual Instrumentation for Instruction in the Public Schools, 1930–1960: A Basis for Take-off;* Donald Bushnell, *The Computer in Education;* H. W. Leverenz and Malcolm Townsley, *The Design of Instructional Equipment: Two Views;* A. Frank Redding, *The Revolution in the Textbook Publishing Industry;* and Lee E. Campion and Clarice Y. Kelley, *Studies in the Growth of Instructional Technology, II: A Directory of Closed-circuit Television Installations in American Education with a Pattern of Growth.*

[27] K. R. Smith and E. B. Van Ormer, *Learning Theories and Instructional Film Research,* Technical Report SDC 269-7-6, Port Washington, N.Y., Special Devices Center, 1949.

[28] T. S. Kendler et al., "Implications of Learning Theory for the Design of Audio-Visual Aids," HRRL Mimeo Report 12(a), U.S.A.F. HRRL, Bolling AFB; November, 1951.

[29] James J. Gibson, "A Theory of Pictorial Perception," *AV Communication Review,* vol. 2 (Winter, 1954), pp. 3–23.

[30] Neal E. Miller et al., "Graphic Communication and the Crisis in Education," *AV Communication Review,* vol. 5, Special supplement (Summer, 1957), p. 3.

[31] "Learning Theory and AV Utilization," *AV Communication Review,* supplement 4 (September–October, 1961).

[32] See George Gerbner, "Towards a General Model of Communication," *AV Communication Review,* vol. 3 (Summer, 1956), pp. 171–199.

tions, school journeys, models, and demonstrations." [33] Thus, rather than defining communication, or audiovisual communication, the field has usually been defined by listing devices and procedures or by inventorying machines. Meanwhile, developments in learning and communication theory, as well as the impact of new technological developments, produced a series of theoretical, definitional, and terminological problems for the audiovisual field which have yet to be resolved.[34]

Relationship of the audiovisual instruction movement to instructional technology

We have completed our examination of the audiovisual instruction movement first begun in Chapter 7 of this book. But before we conclude this section, it seems important to point out the relationship of the audiovisual complex to the concept of instructional technology.

First of all, a rarely made historical distinction needs to be drawn between the audiovisual movement, whose traditional primary concern has been with the use of specific media, and a technology of instruction which is primarily oriented toward psychological principles and empirical data based on the total teaching-learning process. Part 1 of this book reflects much of this history of instructional technology which reaches, as we have seen, back to the era of the Elder Sophists. On the other hand, the audiovisual instruction movement was a relatively late development of this century and emerged as a small, specialized movement almost completely separated from the mainstream of instructional technology. References to the audiovisual instruction movement rarely appear in histories of educational practice or in books devoted to the psychology of learning. For example, in Cremin's recent definitive history [35] of the Progressive Education Movement in American education, the term "audiovisual" or "audiovisual instruction" does not appear at all.

Although the audiovisual movement has been little affected by learning theory, communication theory, or by theories of group process, social change, innovation, and diffusion, it does have a research tradition. As we shall see in Part 3 of this book, this tradition has been confined largely to studies of the comparative effectiveness of conventional procedures and selected types of so-called visual or audiovisual media in attaining the same objectives.

---

[33] William H. Allen, *Audio-Visual Communication Research.* Santa Monica, Calif., System Development Corporation, 1958, p. 5.

[34] DAVI established a Commission on Definition and Terminology in 1961 for the purpose of solving problems of definition and terminology. Although a monograph was the result of the commission's effort in 1963, there remains a need to explore new areas of instructional technology.

[35] Lawrence A. Cremin, *The Transformation of the Schools: Progressivism in American Education, 1876–1957.* New York, Alfred A. Knopf, Inc., 1961.

Despite the absence or paucity of significant differences produced by this pattern of audiovisual research, it has been the one area where the audiovisual movement and instructional technology never became separated.

The discontinuity of the audiovisual movement with the discipline of instructional technology can probably best be illustrated by developments in programed instruction. For example, Montessori began developing programed instructional devices during the first decade of this century just about the same time that the visual instruction movement was beginning to germinate. About a decade later, Pressey and others began their experiments in programed instruction. Yet, for four decades or more, there was no connection between these two developments! Also, it is clear from the historical development of the audiovisual movement that it has generally ignored psychological theory, stressing group presentation of materials without explicit regard for individual differences in learning ability. Instructional technology, on the contrary, as reflected in the programed approach, is increasingly dependent on theory and empirical data. We have seen further examples of this progressive, systematic teaching-learning conceptual development of instructional technology in Chapter 4 of this book.

Without question, the audiovisual instruction movement has been an important, viable force in American educational practices. However, the writer believes that the future will bring an increasing convergence between the audiovisual movement and instructional technology and that the audiovisual field will eventually become assimilated with the developing mainstream of instructional technology.

chapter 10

evolution of instructional radio

We turn now to another tradition of instructional technology, the use of radio as an educational technique. Although experiments in aural instructional broadcasting began in the middle twenties of this century, there is still little dependable knowledge pertaining to the effective instructional use of radio.

The growth of instructional radio occurred primarily during the decade 1925–1935. It was during this period that the first formal courses in radio education were established at colleges and universities; the first professional conferences, institutes, and organizations concerned with radio education were formed; the first systematic radio research projects were launched; and the U.S. Office of Education first organized a Radio Section designed to meet the growing professional needs of radio education.

By the late thirties, the growth period of radio education had already reached its decline. With the advent of World War II, professional activity in instructional radio came to a standstill and has failed to appreciably revive. Today it is easier to find a television set than a radio receiver in most schools. Very few authentic "schools of the air" still exist, and even school systems which operate their own radio station often fail to utilize it properly or integrate its programing with the school curriculum.

Early schools of the air

A number of public school systems have pioneered in the extensive use of radio as an instructional medium. This has been especially true in the cities of Cleveland, Chicago, Detroit, Portland, Des Moines, Buffalo, and Rochester. For example, in Rochester, a rather unique arrangement was created by coordinating the educational work of the public schools with that of the Rochester Civic Music Association, the Rochester Public Library, and the Rochester Museum of Arts and Sciences.

In the early years of radio many institutions of higher learning set up their own stations and established schools of the air. Notable schools of the air were founded at the Universities of Wisconsin, Kansas, Michigan, Minnesota, and at Oregon State College. These first years in university broadcasting were generally ineffective because many a professor repeated his classroom lecture before the microphone without realizing that a good lecturer was not necessarily an effective broadcaster. Moreover, they did not realize that radio technique was not easy to master and that much research and experimentation would be needed before radio could be used as an effective medium of instruction.

The Ohio School of the Air: A Case Study.   The Ohio School of the Air was organized under what appeared to be the most favorable conditions. Financial support was provided by the state, and cooperation and aid were received from the Payne Fund, Ohio State University, Station WLW of Cincinnati, as well as from numerous civic-minded persons. Despite this auspicious beginning, however, the Ohio School of the Air was disbanded less than one decade after it had been established.

The story of the origin of the Ohio School of the Air can best be told in the words of Ben H. Darrow, its founder:

> After varied and interesting experiences in country life institute work, and with the agricultural extension of Maryland State College, I found myself in 1924 in charge of children's programs at Station WLS, Chicago. I became intensely interested in educational broadcasting then, but left WLS to promote a patent. . . .
>
> More and more there grew upon me the idea of a National School of the Air. I was convinced that the radio might become a tremendous

agency for public-school education. The idea presupposed three big "ifs." IF educators could be induced officially to sponsor the project. IF a radio station might be persuaded to broadcast educational programs free of charge, and IF financial support could be secured to pay the cost of administration, a school of the air could be established.

From one end of the country to the other I traveled, speaking to enlist the aid of organizations and individuals to help me put my idea across. Finally, late in 1927, the Payne Study and Experiment Fund of New York became sufficiently interested to put me on its staff to investigate and develop the possibilities of broadcasting for schools on a national scale, under the guidance of organized educational authorities.[1]

In October, 1928, the Payne Fund offered Darrow financial assistance for the establishment of a school of the air if he could obtain official educational sponsorship. As a consequence, Darrow approached J. L. Clifton, superintendent of public instruction for the state of Ohio, and received his support. Prior to this time, Darrow had secured radio facilities on WAIU, Columbus, Ohio. However, when the time for broadcasting came, a crisis arose because the WAIU transmitter was destroyed by fire. WTAM, Cleveland, agreed to provide broadcast time but would not pay the telephone line charges from Columbus to Cleveland. Darrow's problem of finding broadcast facilities was finally solved when the free use of WLW, Cincinnati, was offered. This acquisition not only assured satisfactory reception for the school broadcasts but also extended the broadcast range from Canada to the Gulf states and from the Atlantic Ocean to the Western plains.

Darrow now began to consider the program content of his school broadcasts. He relates:

> During November and December (1928) many feverish days and nights were spent in determining the curriculum, listing and enlisting radio teachers, determining the number of broadcasts and the length of each feature, providing for shifting of classes, the time of day, the formation of the first draft of the program, the choice of theme and signature for the hour, the issuance of lesson leaflets, the writing of press releases, the gathering of lesson materials, preparation of manuscripts, and finally, the rehearsals for the first broadcast.[2]

The Ohio School of the Air finally made its debut on January 7, 1929, with a weekly broadcast schedule as follows:

Weekly Schedule

Monday: Story plays and rhythmics and health talks, alternating.
Current events.
History dramalogs.

[1] Ben H. Darrow, "The Origin and Growth of the Ohio School of the Air." Unpublished manuscript, p. 3.
[2] *Ibid.*, pp. 7–8.

Tuesday: Special features, question and answer periods.
               Art appreciation.
               Civil government, by those who govern.
Wednesday: Stories for younger pupils.
               Stories for intermediate grades.
               Stories for upper grades.
Thursday: Dramatization of literature for high schools.
               Geography.
Friday: No program in deference to the Damrosch lessons in
               music.[3]

This schedule possessed sufficient flexibility to include outstanding public events. On January 14, 1929, for instance, the gubernatorial inauguration ceremonies of Ohio were broadcast, followed on March 4, 1929, by a broadcast of the presidential inauguration. This first year of the Ohio School of the Air also featured broadcasts of the Ohio Senate and House sessions on March 12 and 17, respectively.

In spite of these achievements, Darrow did not carry out one part of the experiment he had wanted to initiate: there was no adequate provision made for lesson leaflets during the first months. However, some advance programs and lesson materials in mimeographed form, entitled *Guide Book to the Radio Journeys of the School of the Air,* were sent to schools.

The first year of this school of the air proved to Darrow "that schools, colleges, libraries, magazines, schools of drama, theaters, and radio stations could furnish broadcasting teachers of worth—that schools could and would equip to hear the broadcasts—that teachers and pupils received added benefits from the introduction of radio." [4]

The second year allowed more time to prepare lessons with an expanded staff. Cline M. Koon was made assistant director. Gwendolyn Jenkins became the dramatic coach, and Ruth Carter made contacts with listeners. A teachers' manual called the *Ohio School of the Air Courier* was prepared and issued monthly to teachers using the broadcasts.

One of the many notable events in the history of the Ohio School of the Air occurred on January 19, 1931, when a temporary studio was established in the headquarters of the National Education Association in Washington, D.C. As a result, a whole series of outstanding educational programs were produced.

Other accomplishments during the 1929–1931 period were as follows:

> The staff had become more nearly adequate. The lesson materials had reached schools on time—nearly ten thousand copies of a 266-page *Courier.*

[3] *Ibid.,* pp. 8–11.
[4] *Ibid.,* p. 30.

The audience had grown several fold and was still growing . . . research had functioned.

The first broadcasts ever made from the NEA Headquarters had presented, for the first time by radio, a President's Cabinet as speakers. A series of Living Writers and Adventurers had set a new high in classroom appeal. The first Radio Institute (statewide) and the first National Radio Institute had been held. The first Parent-Teachers meetings had been held by radio. It had been a golden age—but what was to come? [5]

What was to come soon became evident. In January, 1931, the Ohio legislature reduced the appropriation for the Ohio School of the Air to such an extent that it seemed impossible for it to continue. But by selling radio lesson plans, renting scripts, discontinuing the rental of telephone lines, and with the aid of a small grant from the National Committee on Education by Radio, the Ohio School of the Air managed to survive until 1937 when all appropriations were curtailed by the legislature. [6]

Despite its own failure, the Ohio School of the Air made three significant contributions to instructional technology: it provided a model and impetus for the establishment of similar schools of the air; it demonstrated that radio could be used as an effective instructional technique; and it produced a wealth of important research data concerning radio instruction.

RCA Educational Hour.   One of the first national schools of the air began on October 26, 1928, under the sponsorship of the National Broadcasting Company. [7]

Forty-eight half-hour lessons in music appreciation were arranged for four grade groups ranging from the third to the twelfth, inclusive. Walter Damrosch, conductor of the New York Symphony Orchestra, organized these lessons, assisted by eminent music educators. A seventy-page *Teacher's Manual*, containing a schedule of broadcasts for the school year, was sent free of charge to all teachers using the broadcasts. The *Manual* also contained a list of guide questions for each lesson as well as lists of available phonograph records of musical selections to be played. A symphony orchestra demonstrated the lessons as they were taught, with the purpose of supplementing rather than supplanting local instruction in music appreciation.

This first national school of the air was the most ambitious music education program ever undertaken. Widespread publicity, the finest broadcasting

---

[5] *Ibid.*, p. 54.

[6] When the Ohio School of the Air was disbanded, WLW, Cincinnati, continued much of its work in the Nation's School of the Air.

[7] The first experimental broadcast of this program series was held on Jan. 21, 1928, in the New York studios of the National Broadcasting Company. Two more experimental programs were broadcast on Feb. 11 and 17, 1928. These tests proved so satisfactory that it was decided that a regular series should be instituted.

facilities then available, and one of the country's greatest musical organizations combined to make the effort unsurpassed in educational broadcasting. As a result, the program produced an overwhelming response from listeners. More than fifty thousand letters were received the first year, and polls indicated an audience of more than three million listeners.

This school of the air continued until the retirement of Damrosch in 1942. As nothing before, these broadcasts had shown the value of a national school of the air and had awakened many educators to the educational potential of radio.

The American School of the Air.   The second national school of the air was launched over the Columbia Broadcasting System on February 4, 1930. A year previously, the Columbia Broadcasting System had announced that it would proceed with educational broadcasts as soon as it had received the report of the Advisory Committee on Education by Radio. In the meantime, the Griggsby-Grunow Company of Chicago decided to sponsor such a series and employed Ray Erlandson, a former school principal and a member of the staff of the National Education Association, as their educational director. Erlandson, with program men of the Columbia network, planned a series to be broadcast every Tuesday and Thursday afternoon to the intermediate and junior high school grades. Alice Keith, formerly of the Cleveland schools, was appointed the broadcasting director. Furthermore, Miss Keith organized an advisory faculty headed by William C. Bagley of Teachers College, Columbia University, and an advisory committee consisting of such people as Secretary of the Interior Ray Lyman Wilbur, Commissioner of Education William J. Cooper, Frank Cody, Willis Sutton, Angelo Patri, and twenty-nine others.

The American School of the Air continued under commercial sponsorship until May, 1930. In the fall of 1930, the Columbia Broadcasting System took over the program until it was terminated in 1940.[8]

The World Radio University.   The idea for an international school of the air was first conceived by Walter Lemmon, a young radio engineer, when he

[8] The curriculum of the American School of the Air was changed many times during the course of its existence. In general, the focus was upon such subjects as literature, science, nature study, music, and the social studies. The Columbia Broadcasting System enlarged the scope of the American School of the Air in 1940 by changing its name to School of the Air of the Americas and beaming its programs to twenty-two nations in the Western Hemisphere. The American School of the Air was discontinued in 1940. Gilbert Seldes astutely observed: "*The American School of the Air* was for years a morning program, available in classrooms, highly praised by educators and offered as an example of public service by the company. The fatality was that a half-hour of education broke the mood of the daytime serial; sponsors who wanted to buy a block of quarter-hours, letting the audience flow from one to the other, could not tolerate this dam in the stream; and no one wanted to start from scratch after the educational program was over, knowing that the home audience was committed elsewhere." Gilbert Seldes, *The Great Audience.* New York, The Viking Press, Inc., 1950, p. 123.

was assigned to Woodrow Wilson's peace ship, the George Washington. It was here that he had been impressed with the lack of communication between delegates during their tedious peace conversations. He realized that something revolutionary would have to be done if people of contrasting cultures were to be brought together in mutual understanding.

In 1935, Lemmon built an experimental 20,000-watt shortwave transmitter on the South Shore near Boston, Massachusetts. This station, known as W1XAL, began to broadcast a series of radio courses in literature, music, economics, languages, aviation, astronomy, and electronics, in 1937, in cooperation with the Massachusetts Institute of Technology, Mount Holyoke College, Boston University, Harvard University, Brown University, Tufts College, and Wellesley College. In 1938, a Basic English course was beamed to the Latin American countries, and by the following year the World Radio University was speaking directly to thirty-one countries in twenty-four languages.[9]

Educational stations

Educational stations were the real pioneers of radio education. Ohio State University began to broadcast weather reports and other information as early as 1912; the University of Wisconsin station began broadcasting in 1916; and the State University of Iowa began operating its station in 1919. These early stations were not "educational stations" in the true sense but were actually experimental stations built by electrical engineering or physics departments.

First Educational Stations. The Radio Division of the ·U.S. Department of Commerce began licensing both commercial and educational stations in 1921. The first license issued to an educational institution was to the Latter Day Saints' University of Salt Lake City, Utah, on an unlisted day and month in 1921.[10] On January 13, 1922, two more broadcast licenses were issued for educational stations—to the University of Wisconsin and the University of Minnesota.[11] Shortly after the issuance of these licenses, a number of other educational institutions applied for and received licenses.

Programing of these early educational stations reflected the pedantry of the typical classroom. White says, "To a student of educational radio, prowling through yellowed scripts, it seems almost incredible that teachers

[9] W1XAL (changed to WRUL in 1939) was probably the first noncommercial station operated on a listener-subscription basis. Supporting subscribers were organized as the World Wide Broadcasting Foundation.
[10] S. E. Frost, Jr., *Education's Own Stations*. Chicago, The University of Chicago Press, 1937, p. 178.
[11] *Ibid.*, p. 464.

who presumably hoped to reach men's minds elected to attempt it with anaesthetics. Surely, secrets of audience psychology readily mastered by semi-literate movie stars and dance-band leaders are not hidden from the academicians." [12]

Microphones were set up in classrooms in order to pick up a lecture as a professor gave it. Extension divisions of educational institutions conducted radio courses, but these too often lacked the appeal for a mass audience. Aside from the dull educational programs, there undoubtedly were many that possessed a more widespread interest. Campus bands, orchestras, and dramatic productions were also presented on the college or university stations.

Administrators of some institutions believed that individuals listening to educational programs from the campus station would be motivated to enroll in courses at their institution. Other administrators saw the educational station as an excellent medium for publicity purposes. Generally, very few saw any great potential in radio education. Most of the administrators, as well as many faculty members, were not overly enthusiastic about radio; many others were indifferent and even antagonistic. A vivid example of this attitude is given by Levering Tyson. While doing extension work at Columbia University, Tyson read one morning the story of the KDKA broadcast of the Harding-Cox election returns. So overwhelmed was he with the idea that this new medium would be ideal for his work in extension education that he immediately wanted to utilize it. Tyson tells his story as follows:

> I did not even finish my bacon and eggs that morning but hurried over to the University. At five minutes after nine I walked into President Butler's anteroom. Of course he was not there, but I waited and at a quarter to eleven he walked in. I told him what I had read, and my enthusiasm had not been dimmed at all by my long wait. In effect he said, "Tyson, don't bother about that. There are gadgets turning up every week in this country, and this won't amount to anything." I argued but did not get to first base, and I finally left his office downcast. [13]

Tyson's story illustrates the indifference and even condescension on the part of many educators toward radio in its early days. Conceptions of radio as a plaything which had little or no relevance to instruction were commonplace. Despite these prevailing attitudes, a few persuasive educators believed that radio could serve as an effective instructional tool. If these educators had not insisted on their point of view, instructional technology might have lost the educational radio station.

[12] Llewellyn White, *The American Radio.* Chicago, The University of Chicago Press, 1947, p. 101.
[13] Levering Tyson, "Looking Ahead," in *Education on the Air.* Columbus, Ohio, Ohio State University Press, 1936, p. 58.

Federal Regulation and Educational Broadcasting. In response to the expansion of the uses of radio, Herbert Hoover—then Secretary of Commerce —called four historic Hoover Conferences for the purpose of discussing problems of the control and support of American radio. In the fourth and last of these conferences, held in Washington in November, 1925, Hoover voiced a decision which would determine the future course of radio broadcasting in the United States, when he said:

> The decision that we should not imitate some of our foreign colleagues with governmentally controlled broadcasting supported by a tax upon the listener has secured for us a far greater variety of programs and excellence in service free of cost to the listener. This decision has avoided the pitfalls of political, religious, and social conflicts in the use of free speech in this medium.[14]

Educator Levering Tyson, who attended this conference, made the statement that "we in America decided then that we were going to have a commercialized radio." [15] If Secretary Hoover and the members of the four national conferences were generally convinced that the surest way to retain freedom of the air was through the maintenance of commercial radio, their stand directly affected the development of educational broadcasting. Educational stations simply could not compete financially or maintain the same production standards as commercial stations. This may have been the time when the United States sold her cultural birthright.

A large measure of blame for the existing system of American broadcasting can undoubtedly be attributed to the Federal Radio Commission. This regulatory agency (first created in 1927), by repeatedly ostracizing educational stations, made it technically possible for an increase in the number and power of commercial stations. Frequently, the Commission rationalized its preference by contending that educational stations produced inferior programs. Ironically, this same criterion was never applied to commercial stations. There soon became apparent a clear need for a sweeping reorganization within the Commission itself or for a new regulatory agency which would do an efficient and just job.

In July, 1934, acting on the recommendation of President Roosevelt, Congress passed the Communications Act which assigned the following specific task to the re-created Commission:

> The Commission shall study the proposal that Congress by statute allocate fixed percentages of radio broadcasting facilities to particular types or kinds of nonprofit radio programs, or to persons identified with particular types or kinds of nonprofit activities, and shall report to Con-

[14] Fourth National Radio Conference, *Proceedings and Recommendations for Regulation of Radio* (Nov. 9–11, 1925), p. 3.
[15] Tyson, *op. cit.*, p. 61.

gress, not later than February 1, 1935, its recommendations altogether with its reasons for the same.[16]

As the hearings got under way, it became apparent that the battle between commercial broadcasters and educators was about to be restaged. It also became obvious that those educators advocating a definite allocation of frequencies for education as well as some government control had not succeeded in convincing the Federal Communications Commission of their case. Part of this was because the educators were divided among themselves. The more moderate group, represented by the National Advisory Council on Radio in Education, urged that efforts be made to work with existing commercial facilities because they felt that education was not yet prepared to use additional facilities. This view was also taken by the U.S. Office of Education. At the other end of the spectrum was an extreme fringe of educators who advocated a tax on commercial stations to be used for the construction of a chain of government- and state-owned stations and for the control of commercial program content.

The commercial broadcasters, on the other hand, were united in their own interest. They countered the accusations of the educators by indicating a complete willingness to cooperate with educators at all times. The networks maintained that an allocation of frequencies for educational broadcasting would only disrupt a successful system of broadcasting that had just begun to function. One pointed argument was that the educators themselves could not agree as to what type of broadcasting system was desirable. Finally, the commercial broadcasters pleaded for cooperation rather than for competition and conflict.

It was clear that the educators had failed to make a united case before the Commission. As a result, the Commission recommended to Congress that the present system be continued. It also proposed a national conference to make plans for cooperative efforts by educators and commercial broadcasters.

White has made an excellent analysis of the government's role in educational broadcasting as follows:

> The Federal Communications Commission found itself caught in the spiral of precedent: in the beginning the commercial people had got the best frequencies, the most power; ever since, when a noncommercial station had applied for a share of favors thus pre-empted, the pre-emptors could cite not only the law of possession but also the inevitable fact that they "served a wider area." Having for so long tolerated the situation, the educators discovered belatedly that the Federal Communications Commission was bound to accept them at their own estimate. . . .
>
> The Commission sought to cover its sins of omission by reporting

[16] White, *op. cit.*, p. 157.

to the Congress that "it would appear that the interests of the nonprofit organizations may be better served by the use of existing facilities." Pontius Pilate could not have done better.

As a palliative to the death sentence they thus passed on the educators, the Federal Communications Commission added that "it is our firm intention to assist the nonprofit organizations to obtain the fullest opportunities for expression." Not until 1945, when it set aside twenty FM channels for educational broadcasting, did the Federal Communications Commission lift more than an occasional hesitant finger to implement that pledge.[17]

Decline of Educational Stations. Educational stations had hardly completed their first burst of growth before their decline could be observed. The advent of stringent federal regulation, the rise of national commercial networks, and their use of inexperienced faculty were the chief factors promoting their failure.

It is true that some educational stations made an attempt to develop creative instructional programing, but these efforts were rare. Some educators tried to get their institutions to finance formal courses of instruction by radio; some even went so far as to suggest college credits for courses; but these men were labeled by many of their colleagues as "radicals" or "fanatics." [18]

The cause or causes of the decline of educational stations is a subject of considerable controversy. An extensive analysis by Frost [19] revealed some thirty-nine causes underlying the loss of educational licenses. The majority were ostensibly lost because of financial reasons. Some educators complained that the licensing authority was antagonistic to their efforts or that commercial interests attempted to eliminate them, but Frost's study gives little credence to this accusation. However, there is another consideration commonly overlooked in studies of causal factors. Financial failure may have been only a partial cause. Since the licensing authority had accepted the philosophy of commercial radio, no place was left for educational stations which had to withdraw when costly commercial standards were applied to their operation. Regardless of the explanations offered, it is clear that educators were generally apathetic toward educational broadcasting.

FM Channels for Educational Broadcasting. For the first time, the Federal Communications Commission allocated a portion of the FM band for educational stations in 1938. In 1941, the Commission again reserved educa-

---

[17] *Ibid.*, pp. 109–110.
[18] *Radio in Education, op. cit.*, p. 4.
[19] See S. E. Frost, Jr., *Is American Radio Democratic?* Chicago, The University of Chicago Press, 1937.

tional channels, this time on the FM band between 42 and 43 megacycles. The third allocation of educational channels came in 1945 when the Commission changed the FM band. Throughout this period when the Commission was making these educational reservations, commercial radio was complacent: the off-the-band AM frequencies were commercially worthless; the short-lived FM change could not be stopped; and finally the opening of 100 FM channels created more space than commercial interests could occupy.

The first educational FM station (WBOE) was established by the Cleveland public schools in 1938, but World War II forced a freeze on FM before significant educational FM broadcasting could develop. The assignment of channels for educational broadcasting in 1945 stimulated the interest of educators, and by December of that year more than forty educational institutions had filed application for an educational FM station. In order to encourage educators to take advantage of educational channels, the FCC made it possible (in 1948) to build low-power 10-watt stations.

A number of states developed plans for educational FM networks, but most of these plans did not materialize. The states of Indiana, Minnesota, Texas, Wisconsin, and New York have succeeded in developing comprehensive educational FM networks. At this writing, the Empire State FM School of the Air (formed in 1949), with twenty FM stations, comprises the world's largest educational FM network. However, the "usual result has been a spark of interest, a meeting of a few interested schoolmen, a map showing possible station locations, and then general apathy." [20]

Preliminary Committee on Educational Broadcasting

The Preliminary Committee on Educational Broadcasting was among the first of many organizations that were established to meet the need of (a) clarifying objectives; (b) exchanging relevant information; and (c) fortifying and ensuring the progress of instructional radio. B. H. Darrow was largely responsible for its organization through his effort to convince educators of the need for a national school of the air.

The Preliminary Committee on Educational Broadcasting was first formed to investigate the feasibility of a national school of the air at the NEA Department of Superintendence meeting in Boston in 1927. The results of a survey made by the committee were announced in the spring of 1928. The majority of those educators who responded indicated that they wanted a national school of the air.[21]

[20] William B. Levenson and Edward Stasheff, *Teaching through Radio and Television*. New York, Rinehart & Company, Inc., 1952, p. 523.
[21] *National Survey by the Preliminary Committee on Educational Broadcasting*. Payne Fund, December, 1927.

Advisory Committee on Education by Radio

In May, 1929, the members of the Preliminary Committee on Educational Broadcasting requested Secretary of the Interior Ray Lyman Wilbur to appoint a committee to investigate the possibilities of instructional radio. Accordingly, he convened the so-called Wilbur conference on May 24, 1929, in Washington, D.C. The first meeting was an emotionally charged discussion reflecting the fear of commercial domination of educational broadcasting. There was a consensus that educators should control educational broadcasting, but they also conceded that little was known about instructional radio. It was decided that a survey should be taken and that Secretary Wilbur should appoint a committee composed of educators and commercial broadcasters, as well as other interested persons.[22] On June 6, 1929, Wilbur appointed the Advisory Committee on Education by Radio. Meanwhile, the Payne Fund and the Carnegie Corporation made grants to support the work of this committee.

The Advisory Committee completed its work in four meetings. The first meeting was held in Chicago, June 13, 1929, under the chairmanship of United States Commissioner of Education William J. Cooper. The second meeting was held October 18, 1929, at Pittsburgh, Pennsylvania; and the third and fourth meetings, on November 6 and December 30, 1929, in Washington, D.C.

Progress reports were received from all the subcommittees at the November meeting and the first complete report of the results of the survey was submitted at the last meeting. H. R. Shipherd of the fact-finding subcommittee made a forty-seven-page report which immediately drew the ire of the commercial broadcasters present. His most controversial recommendation was that a National University for National Radio Education be established. Shipherd's report was followed by that of Armstrong Perry, also of the fact-finding subcommittee. Perry stressed three points:

> (1) That educators interested in educational broadcasting have come to a realization that the key to the situation lies with those who have facilities to broadcast; (2) That this makes the control of radio channels the most important problem of the many which this new institution brings to the front; (3) That educators, as a result, generally feel that some air channels should be reserved exclusively for educational purposes.[23]

[22] The Advisory Committee on Education by Radio consisted of sixteen members: W. W. Charters, J. L. Clifton, Frank Cody, J. H. Finley, H. J. Stonier, G. B. Zehmer, H. R. Shipherd, W. G. Chambers, M. H. Aylesworth, W. S. Paley, J. A. Moyer, Mrs. H. H. Moorhead, Alice Keith, Katherine Ludington, W. J. Cooper, and Ira E. Robinson.

[23] *Report of the Advisory Committee on Education by Radio, Appointed by the Secretary of the Interior.* Columbus, Ohio, The F. J. Heer Publishing Company, 1930, 246 pp.

Both Shipherd and Perry plainly indicated in their reports that the activity of commercial stations and the Federal Radio Commission did not provide sufficiently for educational broadcasting. Perry was of the following opinion:

> . . . that the educators of the country must either arrive at a consensus of opinion, formulate a plan of action and secure the assistance of the Federal Government, or see the broadcasting facilities of the country come so firmly under the control of commercial groups that education by radio would be directed by business men instead of by professional educators.[24]

Shipherd summarized the lack of cooperation between educators and commercial broadcasters as follows:

> General lack of co-operation between the two groups appears: as in (a) widespread distrust among educators of commercial motives and "propaganda"; (b) the belief among educational stations that they are given the inferior positions on the broadcasting spectrum and in the allocation of hours; (c) the tendency among commercial stations to reduce educational programs to shorter and poorer periods as their time becomes more salable; (d) the practice among the commercial stations of offering educational programs to cultivate general good will and create publicity, rather than to build up a sound educational method and research with the help and guidance of educational experts.[25]

The representatives of the commercial networks obviously did not share these views, although they expressed an eager willingness to accord education a more distinguished role in the broadcasting structure. Warren H. Pierce, then educational director of the Columbia Broadcasting System, stated that the broadcasting companies were "willing to give ample time for educational programs and would attempt to exercise no censorship whatever." John Elwood, then vice-president of the National Broadcasting Company, concurred in this point of view by saying that "both companies had been giving much time to educational subjects and that one of the companies estimated that approximately 22 percent of its time on the air is now given over to programs of an educational nature."

The most significant result of the Advisory Committee's work was the series of recommendations which came out of the fact-finding subcommittee survey. These recommendations, in part, were as follows:

1. That there be established in the Office of Education, Department of the Interior, a section devoted to education by radio. . . .
2. That the funds necessary for financing such a section in the Office of Education be provided in the regular budget for the Department of the Interior.

[24] *Ibid.*, p. 51.
[25] *Ibid.*, p. 36.

3. That there be set up in connection with this unit an Advisory Committee representing educational institutions, commercial broadcasters, and the general public.

4. That an effort be made to secure from interested persons or foundations an amount of money sufficient to bring to the microphone, for a period of two to three years, a high grade program in certain formal school subjects and to check carefully the results obtained.

5. That the Secretary bring to the attention of the Federal Radio Commission the importance of the educational interests in broadcasting.[26]

When foundation funds were exhausted in 1930, the Advisory Committee was discontinued. Meanwhile, an atmosphere of distrust still existed among many educators and commercial broadcasters. This conflict was clearly discernible when the two major commercial networks (NBC and CBS) openly opposed the recommendations made by the fact-finding committee.

Actually, there was a growing split among the educators themselves. One group had worked quite satisfactorily with the networks in developing educational programs and believed that the needs of education could continue to be best served without disturbing the *status quo* of radio broadcasting. Another group felt that, unless remedial legislation was secured, the educators would be driven from the field by commercial broadcasters. Some commercial stations had requested and been granted the use of wavelengths previously assigned to educational stations. It appeared to many educators that it would only be a short time before a gradual encroachment would eliminate the educator from radio. These two points of view, unfortunately, had the adverse effect of diminishing the strength of a unified front in instructional radio. The schism led ultimately to the establishment of the National Advisory Council on Radio in Education, representing the first group, and to the National Committee on Education by Radio, representing the latter group.

National Advisory Council on Radio in Education

This council grew out of an idea advanced by the American Association for Adult Education soon after the passage of the Radio Act of 1927. Nothing formal was done to promote it until the presidential campaign of 1928 was concluded. It then appeared that Herbert Hoover, the new President, and Ray Lyman Wilbur, his Secretary of the Interior, were both favorably disposed toward the proposals for radio education being advanced by the American Association for Adult Education. William J. Cooper, United States Commissioner of Education, also joined in the early discussions.

[26] *Ibid.*, pp. 75–76.

While Wilbur appointed a committee to investigate the radio situation as it affected education, the Carnegie Corporation of New York gave a grant to the American Association for Adult Education for a survey of instructional broadcasting. In its effort to bring together top people, the Carnegie staff succeeded in enlisting the interest and support of the Rockefeller Foundation, as well as such leaders in commercial radio as Owen D. Young, the acting chief of the General Electric Company and a member of the board of the National Broadcasting Company. The government was then approached through General Saltzman, chairman of the Federal Radio Commission (now the Federal Communications Commission).

These diverse groups united in an agreement to create an experimental organization that would combine the interests of the government, the commercial broadcasters, educational and semi-educational agencies, and outstanding citizens interested in instructional broadcasting. This organization, the National Advisory Council on Radio in Education, was composed of forty members and began to function actively on July 1, 1930. Funds for its support for a three-year period were granted by the Rockefeller Foundation and the Carnegie Foundation Corporation.

The goals of the council were to further the "development of the art of radio broadcasting in American education" and to make an "analysis of the problems faced by those in the educational world, or in the broadcasting industry, or elsewhere, who are engaged in or are sympathetic to educational broadcasting." The council also undertook "to assemble and interpret the content of broadcast programs and information concerning the practices and experience of broadcasting stations in conducting or developing educational features as part of such programs" and "to stimulate and suggest problems and projects for research or experiment with a view to increasing the effectiveness of broadcasting in education." Other objectives voiced by the council included those of publishing "the opportunities for education in the utilization of broadcasting as such opportunities are discovered." In summary, the council stated that every effort would be made "to mobilize the best educational thought of the country to devise, develop and present suitable programs, to be brought into fruitful contact with the most appropriate facilities." [27]

Commercialism and Radio Education. The council had hardly gotten under way before a major split occurred in radio educator ranks. Commissioner Cooper now became the sponsor of a new organization with an entirely different policy, the National Committee on Education by Radio, which is discussed more fully in the next section of this chapter. Briefly, the

[27] Levering Tyson, *National Advisory Council on Radio in Education, Inc.* Information ser. no. 1, Bulletin, New York, National Advisory Council on Radio in Education, Inc., 1936, p. 4.

National Committee, intent on changing the American system of broadcasting to more closely resemble the British system, proposed that 15 percent of the total broadcasting frequencies be set aside for educational service. This antagonized commercial broadcasters who hastened to fight the proposal. Industry reaction to these attacks was described by Tyson as follows:

> The upshot was that industry people as a whole were forced to take the attitude, "well if these people are asking for a fight, we will give it to them." Of course, the result was foreordained. The allocation of channels was never made and from that point on, the commercial boys rode high, wide, and handsome. We have now reaped the result, what with singing commercials and all the other obnoxious features which detract from the real job that, in my opinion, radio broadcasting might have accomplished.[28]

In the booklet *Four Years of Network Broadcasting*, there appears a most thorough indictment of commercial broadcasters in regard to their treatment of educational broadcasters. This minority report by the members of the Advisory Council's Committee on Civic Education by Radio is the most completely documented source of an actual case history of the conflict between educational and commercial broadcasting. The experience of this committee demonstrated:

> . . . a conflict between the commercial interests of the National Broadcasting Company and the educational uses of the radio which threatens to become almost fatal to the latter. Educational broadcasting has become the poor relation of commercial broadcasting, and the pauperization of the latter has increased in direct proportion to the growing affluence of the former.
>
> It is well to remember at this time that the Federal Radio Act of 1927 required that broadcasting be conducted in the public interest, convenience, and necessity. Also, it might be recalled that the NBC was formed originally without any idea that its operations were to show a profit, but to present a well-rounded program service to the American public.[29]

Although the council's objective of establishing a cooperative working relationship with commercial broadcasters was thus shattered by the activities of the National Committee on Education by Radio, the council turned to other activities such as experimentation, demonstration, research, and conferences.

An extensive library was created and monographs were published cover-

[28] Levering Tyson, letter dated Oct. 26, 1951.
[29] *Four Years of Network Broadcasting*, A Report by the Committee on Civic Education by Radio of the National Advisory Council on Radio in Education and the American Political Science Association. Reprinted from *Radio and Education*, Chicago, The University of Chicago Press, 1936, pp. 49–50.

ing every aspect of radio instruction. Annual assemblies were held for the purpose of providing a meeting ground for all those interested in educational broadcasting.[30]

The most notable work of the council was its series of educational broadcasts on the radio networks of the National Broadcasting Company. These broadcasts, which established a pattern for many outstanding educational broadcasts, were made in conjunction with some sixty cooperating American agencies. Programs were broadcast in the subject fields of history, government, law, art, medicine, economics, and labor. These programs were mainly straight talks or lectures and, as a result, often did not compete favorably with commercial programs. Probably the *You and Your Government* series which was broadcast during 1935–1936 enjoyed the most favorable reception.

The council discontinued its operations in 1938 when the Rockefeller Foundation withdrew its funds.

National Committee on Education by Radio

The organization of the National Advisory Council for Radio in Education did not satisfy the demands of many educators who felt that such a move was not an adequate answer or solution to the situation that existed. Among this dissenting group were the presidents of many state universities, representatives of state departments of education, the heads of important national educational associations, and the directors of educational stations. Although these educational leaders realized that cooperation with commercial interests was desirable, they were apprehensive of the steady decline of educational stations and disturbed by the aggressive nature of radio advertising. Furthermore, they held little or no hope for the eventual cooperation and goodwill of commercial broadcasters.

Some educators from land-grant colleges reasoned that radio grants should be made in the public interest just as land grants were made to colleges by the various states. These educators felt that the only remedy would be to organize on their own to achieve their real objectives. This conviction became so strong that educational broadcasters asked the United States Commissioner of Education to call a national conference for the purpose of determining ways and means for self-preservation.

The Commissioner of Education called a conference on radio and edu-

[30] The first annual assembly was held at the New School for Social Research at New York City, May, 1931; the second at Buffalo, New York, May, 1932; the third at New York City, May, 1933; the fourth at Chicago, October, 1934; and the fifth and final assembly at Columbus, Ohio, May, 1935, in joint session with the Institute (Sixth) for Education by Radio (now Institute for Education by Radio-Television). Reports of all these meetings are published in a series of volumes entitled *Radio and Education, op. cit.*

cation at Chicago on October 13, 1930. After much discussion, the conference was adjourned with the following resolutions:

1. The appointment of a committee to represent "the Association of College and University Broadcasting Stations, the Land-Grant College Association, the National University Extension Association, the National Association of State University Presidents, the National Education Association, the National Catholic Educational Association, the Jesuit Education Association, the National Advisory Council on Radio in Education, the Payne Fund, and other similar groups." Commissioner Cooper was to appoint this committee.
2. The protecting and promoting of broadcasting originating in educational institutions.
3. The promotion of broadcasting by educational institutions.
4. Legislation by Congress "which will permanently and exclusively assign to educational institutions and government educational agencies a minimum of fifteen (15) per cent of all radio broadcasting channels which are or may become available to the United States."
5. The calling of "an organization meeting of this committee at the earliest possible moment." [31]

Commissioner William J. Cooper immediately appointed the requested committee and asked Joy Elmer Morgan of the National Education Association to act as temporary chairman. Shortly after, the Payne Fund supplied a small grant for the work of organization. On December 30, 1930, the committee held its first meeting at Washington, D.C., and designated itself the National Committee on Education by Radio. The committee was made up of the accredited representatives of nine educational organizations.[32]

Before the second meeting on February 28, 1931, Joy Elmer Morgan had been elected permanent chairman for the ensuing year; headquarters for the committee had been temporarily established at the Hotel Martinique in Washington, later to be moved to the National Education Association; and

[31] Frank Ernest Hill, *Tune in for Education.* New York, National Committee on Education by Radio, 1942, pp. 16–17.

[32] The first members of the National Committee were as follows: The National Education Association, represented by Joy Elmer Morgan, editor of the *Journal* and first chairman of the committee; The American Council on Education: John Henry MacCracken, Washington, D.C.; The Association of Land-grant Colleges and Universities: H. Umberger, Kansas State College, Manhattan, Kansas; The Jesuit Education Association: Rev. Charles A. Robinson, S. J., St. Louis University, St. Louis, Missouri; The National Association of College and University Broadcasting Stations: Robert C. Higgy, director, Station WEAO, Ohio State University, Columbus, Ohio; The National Association of State University Presidents: Arthur G. Crane, president, University of Wyoming, Laramie, Wyoming; The National Catholic Educational Association: Charles N. Lischka, Washington, D.C.; The National Council of State Superintendents: J. L. Clifton, director of education, Columbus, Ohio; and The National University Extension Association: J. O. Keller, head of engineering extension, Pennsylvania State College, State College, Pennsylvania. The National Committee on Education by Radio, *Education by Radio,* vol. 1, no. 1 (Feb. 12, 1931), p. 1.

a bulletin, *Education by Radio*, was published. Also in early February, a Service Bureau, housed in the National Press Building and directed by Armstrong Perry and Horace L. Lohnes, was created by the committee. By April, the committee had chosen Tracy F. Tyler to be its research director and secretary.

The objectives of the National Committee were:

> . . . to foster research and experimentation in the field of education by radio; to safeguard and serve the interests of broadcasting stations associated with educational institutions, to encourage their further development, and to promote the coordination of the existing facilities for educational broadcasting; to inform the members of the organizations represented on the Committee, educational journals, the general public, and the state and national governments as to the growing possibilities of radio as an instrument for improving the individual and national life; to develop plans and create agencies for the broadcasting of nationwide educational programs; to bring about legislation which would permanently and exclusively assign to educational institutions and to government educational agencies a minimum of fifteen per cent of all radio broadcasting channels available to the United States.[33]

The Committee and Commercial Broadcasters.   The National Committee immediately launched a vituperative assault against the growing domination of the commercial broadcasters in radio broadcasting. Through its bulletin, *Education by Radio*, an endless cannonade was hurled at the "monopolistic" commercial broadcasters.

This rebellion began with a reaffirmation of Herbert Hoover's words on monopoly: "The question of monopoly in radio communication must be squarely met. It is not conceivable that the American people will allow this new-born system of communication to fall into the power of any individual, group, or combination." [34]

Since radio education had already lost considerable ground, the first task of the National Committee was that of conservation of the radio channels remaining. An immediate attempt was made to save or recover a fair share of broadcasting frequencies for education. The first decisive step was taken in the form of legislation.

On January 8, 1931, Senator Simeon D. Fess of Ohio, with the support of the National Committee, introduced in Congress a bill which would provide a 15 percent educational reservation of radio broadcasting channels. Although little was done to push the bill (which remained buried in committee from January, 1931, until Congress began to consider the Communications Act of 1934), its introduction had two immediate results: it produced a vociferous defense and stimulated new aggression from commercial broad-

[33] *Loc. cit.*
[34] *Education by Radio*, vol. 1, no. 7 (Mar. 26, 1931), p. 25.

casters, and it drove a decisive wedge between the two disputing groups of educators by interrupting a planned program of cooperation between the National Advisory Council on Education by Radio and the commercial networks (NBC and CBS).

Congress finally passed the new Communications Act in 1934; this was also the crucial year in the attempt to secure educational reservations. The organizers and chief protagonists in support of the Fess bill were Catholic organizations and some of the groups associated with the National Committee on Education by Radio.[35]

It was almost inevitable that the Fess bill would be defeated. Not even all the groups who were members of the National Committee on Education by Radio gave the Fess bill their active support; the National Advisory Council on Education in Radio took no position whatsoever on the Fess bill. As a consequence, the Fess bill did not report out of committee and lost whatever consideration it may have had in Congress.[36]

Special Services for Educational Broadcasters. The original objective of the National Committee included specific service functions that would aid, protect, and give counsel to educational broadcasters. The first formal undertaking in this direction was made with the establishment of a Service Bureau on February 2, 1931. Its function was to provide "a representative on the ground in Washington for stations which are not able to spend large sums for travel." [37] It also provided legal aid and attempted to help educators preserve what they already possessed.

Another helpful routine task begun by the bureau was the meticulous examination of all the Federal Radio Commission reports in order to determine potential threats to educational stations by commercial interests.

[35] Catholic interest in educational reservations dated back to the Federal Radio Commission spectrum reallocations decisions which favored general-interest stations over special-point-of-view stations. Religious stations had been hard hit by this policy and one of the hardest hit had been WLWL, owned by the Paulist Fathers in New York City.

[36] New York Congressman Rudd drafted a bill incorporating the suggestion of the Paulist Fathers of New York that 25 percent of the radio channels should be reserved for educational, religious, agricultural, labor, and similar organizations. The congressional committee voted against the bill, but its rejected proposals were embodied in an amendment to the Communications Act of 1934 by Senators Wagner of New York and Hatfield of West Virginia. The Wagner-Hatfield amendment was eventually defeated 42 to 23. With the defeat of the Wagner-Hatfield amendment, any real prospect for legislative reservations disappeared. However, Sec. 307(c) of the new Communications Act (1934) ordered Federal Communications Commission hearings on the desirability of reservations. During October and November, 1934, the Commission heard 135 witnesses. The educators lacked unity, but the industry mobilized all its forces and overcame any threat of reservations. On January 22, 1935, the FCC reported to Congress recommending that: "At this time no fixed percentages of radio broadcast facilities be allocated by statute to particular types or kinds of nonprofit radio programs or to persons identified with particular types or kinds of nonprofit activities." *FCC Monograph*, no. 11861, Jan. 22, 1935, pp. 5–6.

[37] Hill, *op. cit.*, p. 23.

A significant activity begun by the National Committee was its script service for educational or instructional purposes—the first of its kind, which set a historical precedent for the script service later inaugurated by the U.S. Office of Education.

Probably the most important single activity of the National Committee was its dissemination of information through its bulletin *Education by Radio.* Early in 1931, the National Committee published the program schedules of educational stations, reported on the use of radio for instructional purposes in school systems throughout the country, and provided the results of important surveys in radio education.

Research in radio instruction was also an important function of the National Committee. Probably the most extensive sponsored research was Tracy Tyler's *An Appraisal of Radio Broadcasting in the Land-grant Colleges and State Universities* (1933).[38]

Committee Sponsors National Educational Radio Conference.   By the spring of 1934, the National Committee had been in existence for three years, during which time radio, together with other agencies and institutions of American life, was being subjected to scrutiny regarding its cultural contribution to society.

It was therefore apropos that the National Committee sponsored on May 7–8, 1934, in Washington, D.C., "The First National Conference on the Use of Radio as a Cultural Agency." The general trends of the addresses, discussions, and committee reports reflected views antagonistic to commercial broadcasters. Also, there was a prevailing attitude which favored some measure of government control of radio broadcasting. Probably the single most important result of this conference was a report of a committee on "Fundamental Principles Which Should Underlie American Radio Policy," advocating government control.[39]

A Plan for a System of Educational Broadcasting.   After an extensive survey of the civic and cultural possibilities of radio, Arthur G. Crane developed "A Plan for an American System of Radio Broadcasting to Serve the

---

[38] Tracy F. Tyler, *An Appraisal of Radio Broadcasting in the Land-grant Colleges and State Universities.* Prepared under the direction of the Joint Radio Survey Committee on Education, Washington, D.C., The National Committee on Education by Radio, 1933.

[39] This committee consisted of the following ten members: Arthur G. Crane of the University of Wyoming; W. G. Chambers, dean of the school of education, Pennsylvania State College; W. W. Charters, director of the Bureau of Educational Research, Ohio State University; Jerome Davis, Yale Divinity School; Harold B. McCarthy, manager, Station WHA, Madison, Wisconsin; Walter E. Myer, Civic Education Service, Washington, D.C.; Reverend Charles A. Robinson, S.J., St. Louis University; James Rorty, author, New York City; and Armstrong Perry and Tracy F. Tyler, both of the National Committee.

Welfare of the American People." [40] The plan, presented to the Federal Communications Commission on May 15, 1935, proposed a system of public councils or boards—state, regional, and national—to develop public-service broadcasting. The Federal government would construct and operate stations to broadcast the programs developed by the various councils. The objectives of such councils would be:

(1) to aid educational and civic organizations in the region in mobilizing and coordinating their broadcasting resources and to raise the quality and number of their presentations;

(2) to demonstrate and emphasize the value of radio as an instrument of democracy;

(3) to give the listening audience in the region a wider range of choice in serious broadcasts, including programs distinctive to the area.[41]

Crane was primarily responsible for developing this concept of radio councils although the National Committee had germinated the idea. It had always been the committee's belief that: ". . . the American states should play an organized part in cultural broadcasting and . . . the federal government should make some positive contribution to education on the air." [42]

Early Radio Councils.   The first development of a radio council based on the Crane plan began in New Mexico in the fall of 1935, but it never materialized because of lack of funds. Early in 1936, there was considerable enthusiasm for a similar council, but, here again, there were no positive results for a variety of elusive reasons.

The first council plan which developed according to the National Committee conception was the Rocky Mountain Radio Council. The council itself grew out of ". . . the recognition of need on the part of three distinct groups: the owners of commercial radio stations in the area; the educational and civic organizations of the two states of Colorado and Wyoming; and radio listeners." [43]

The first organization meeting of the council was held on January 29, 1938. The executive committee selected Robert B. Hudson, formerly director of the Adult Education Council of Denver, and Charles Anderson of the staff of Station KOA, Denver, as staff members. A short time later, these men received Rockefeller Foundation fellowships for radio training in New York City.

[40] Crane organized a subcommittee consisting of J. O. Keller and Father Charles A. Robinson.

[41] *Education by Radio,* vol. 11, no. 4 (Fourth Quarter, 1941), p. 38.

[42] Hill, *op. cit.,* p. 76.

[43] S. Howard Evans, "The Rocky Mountain Radio Council," *Education by Radio,* vol. 10, no. 7 (Second Quarter, 1940).

Although financial, technical, and personnel problems hampered the early development of the Rocky Mountain Council, it began active broadcasting on December 23, 1939.[44] During its first test period from December 23, 1939, to July 31, 1940, the council produced 222 educational radio programs. The members of the council produced their own scriptwriters, actors, and production directors. In addition, a Transcription Library Service was established in the University of Colorado, and transcriptions of these broadcasts were made available to schools and civic groups in the Rocky Mountain region. With the advent of World War II, the Rocky Mountain Radio Council was discontinued because of lack of funds.[45]

Contributions of National Committee.   Many changes occurred from the time the National Committee was founded in 1930 to the time it went out of existence in 1941. The most significant were in the attitudes of commercial broadcasters, the Federal Communications Commission, and the educators, themselves, toward instructional radio.

The shift in attitude of the commercial broadcasters could be seen in the networks' temporary installation of education departments (now all disbanded), their adoption of a broadcasters' code, and their spending of large sums of money on cultural and educational programs. On the other hand, the Federal Communications Commission began to assume a more vigilant and aggressive policy in relation to questionable programing and

[44] Robert Hudson, the chosen director of the Rocky Mountain Council, became ill shortly after he completed his radio training in New York City. While the board was debating his replacement, he recovered in time to begin his work in the fall of 1939. Another obstacle appeared with the rise of war in Europe. When this occurred, the General Education Board was willing to supply only $5,000 instead of providing sufficient support for a five-year experiment. Along with these problems were numerous technical problems.

[45] The pioneer radio council was the University Broadcasting Council—composed of the University of Chicago, Northwestern University, De Paul University, the three existing commercial networks (Mutual, NBC, and CBS), and any independent stations that wished to join. Allen Miller conceived the council and obtained the support of the Rockefeller Foundation and the Carnegie Corporation for four years beginning in July, 1935, at an annual budget of $55,000. The administrative control of the council was vested in a board of trustees, with each university represented by two members. The broadcasts of the council were unusually successful. Programs developed by the council included *The Northwestern Stand* and *Of Men and Books,* as well as other outstanding educational programs. Miller realized that the high performance standards of the council could not be maintained when the yearly contributions were reduced by the withdrawal of the University of Chicago in 1939. By the fall of 1940, the council was disbanded.

In the late 1930s, so-called consulting councils were organized in several cities. These councils have made audience studies, established production committees, developed study courses in radio, promoted better programs, and established educational programs in program discrimination. One of the earliest consulting councils was the Ohio Civic Broadcasting Committee (1938). The Radio Council on Children's Programs was organized in New York City in 1940. Other notable councils include the Radio Council of Greater Cleveland, the Cedar Rapids Council, the Des Moines Radio Council, the Portland Radio Council, the Radio Council of New Jersey, and the Pioneer Radio Council of Western Massachusetts.

monopolistic practices. Also, it eventually succeeded in setting aside definite channels for educational broadcasting.

Educators likewise altered their approach to educational radio. Radio research became an established activity. Colleges and universities began incorporating radio courses as part of their regular program so that the industry could be assured of properly trained personnel in order that teachers might utilize radio more effectively in their instructional procedures. Moreover, public and private schools began to make wider use of radio and many began to apply for their own frequency modulation licenses. Another important outgrowth was the organization of the Association for Education by Radio, a group composed of educators who were actually doing educational broadcasting or who were actively using radio in their classrooms.

These developments ran parallel with many of the accomplishments of the National Committee on Education by Radio itself. An evaluation by the committee of its own achievements has been stated in its final report as follows:

> Glancing back to 1930 and the objectives of the National Committee as outlined by its organizers, one sees that the Committee has completed the cycle of its activities. It is gratifying to have had the opportunity to play a part in the development of this great medium and to have contributed to the advancement of the American way of life. It is now ready to turn its activities over to the newer groups, groups which did not exist at the time of its founding in 1930.
>
> The National Committee on Education by Radio can look back on the eleven years of its history with both pride and humility. It has made mistakes; in some cases it has created animosities; it has at time lost hard-fought battles for the rights of education. But the story of the Committee—from a total point of view—is one of progress and accomplishment.[46]

Instructional radio activities of the U.S. Office of Education

The U.S. Office of Education was one of the first national organizations to promote the use of radio instruction. John J. Tigert, United States Commissioner of Education, clearly indicated his interest in the use of radio for instructional purposes as early as 1924.

Establishment of Radio Section. In accordance with a recommendation of the Advisory Committee established in 1929 under the chairmanship of United States Commissioner of Education William J. Cooper, Congressional approval established a Radio Section and staff in the Office of Education on

[46] *Education by Radio*, vol. 11, no. 4 (Fourth Quarter, 1941), p. 40.

July 1, 1931. Cline M. Koon, assistant director of the Ohio School of the Air, was made the first senior radio specialist on the payroll of the Office of Education.

The purposes of the Radio Section were stated as follows:

1. Organize and maintain an informational service for all who are interested in the field of education by radio.
2. Keep the educational and governmental interests of the country posted and alive to the importance of this new educational device.
3. Initiate and assist with research studies of radio as an educational agency in regularly organized schools and for adult students.
4. Attempt to prevent conflicts and duplication of effort between various educational broadcasting interests.
5. On invitation of state departments of education, institutions of learning and national broadcasting chains, assist in setting up and evaluating broadcast programs of educational material.[47]

Through the years, the U.S. Office of Education Radio Section has issued a radio manual, bibliographies, glossaries, a newsletter, extensive catalogs of scripts and transcriptions, and numerous pamphlets on radio instruction.

Radio Education Project.   A major instructional radio research project of the U.S. Office of Education began in 1935 when Commissioner John W. Studebaker proposed to the Department of the Interior that an educational radio project be established by a grant from emergency relief funds. After a conference with President Franklin D. Roosevelt, an allocation of $75,000 was made to the Office of Education on December 20, 1935, to create a Radio Education Project. The purpose as stated by the President was:

> To present high-grade radio programs over radio facilities offered free to the Office of Education by commercial radio corporations for public service programs in accordance with the provisions of the basic law governing radio wave-lengths, using talent—actors, singers, directors and playwrights in the ranks of those on relief.[48]

William D. Boutwell, of the regular Office of Education staff, was named director of the project by Commissioner Studebaker. The project formally began when a small group met at the National Press Club in Washington, D.C., on December 16, 1935. Among them were Major Silas M. Ransopher, assistant educational director of the Civilian Conservation Corps; Guy McKinney, director of information for the CCC; Ray Hoyt, editor of *Happy Days;* Shannon Allen, production director of WRC and

[47] U.S. Department of the Interior, Office of Education, *The Purpose of the Office of Education in Regard to Education by Radio,* Bulletin 57031, September, 1931.
[48] Quoted in an address by William Boutwell at the 2d National Conference on Educational Broadcasting, Chicago, Ill., Nov. 29, 1937.

WMAL; and Philip Cohen, educational advisor of a CCC camp in Pennsylvania.

The original staff was composed of CCC advisers and commercial broadcasters who set up an organization comprising the following units: a Script Division for writing programs; a Production Division in charge of programs; an Audience Preparation Division; a Business Division for the work of answering listeners' mail, keeping accounts of time, and ordering supplies; a Personnel Division; and an Educational Radio Script Exchange Division.

When Commissioner Studebaker proposed the formation of an Advisory Committee to include representatives of both of the major radio networks, the National Broadcasting Company named Franklin Dunham and the Columbia Broadcasting System chose Edward R. Murrow. Studebaker selected Ned Dearborn, dean of the General Education Division, New York University, and Mrs. Sidonie Gruenberg of the Child Study Association of America as additional members of this committee.

In February, 1936, sixteen program ideas were presented to the Advisory Committee. Dunham and Murrow each selected three proposals and the Office of Education Script Division then began to prepare scripts on these ideas. For the National Broadcasting Company, the Office of Education created *Answer Me This*, a social science question-and-answer program, and *Have You Heard*, a natural science program on the "wise-person-and-stooge" pattern. For the Columbia Broadcasting System, the Script Division prepared a safety education program called *Safety Musketeers*. Early in March, the committee heard and approved samples of these programs. *Answer Me This* went on the air on March 16, 1936, over the NBC network, followed three days later by *Have You Heard*. *Safety Musketeers* made its debut on CBS early in May, 1936. Other programs presented were: *Treasures Next Door, The World Is Yours, Let Freedom Ring,* and *Brave New World.*

The public response to these programs was impressive. During the first year, more than 366,000 letters were received. When offers of supplementary material were made, the volume of mail almost doubled. The Office of Education, by experimentation with various approaches to the problem of adapting education to radio, found some limitations in the medium and learned many effective broadcasting techniques. One important fact that became obvious was that radio had greater possibilities for the stimulation of learning than it had for systematic teaching. Indeed, the Radio Project made such an important contribution to the understanding and use of radio for education that it was allocated an additional $130,000 in October, 1936, so that it could be continued for another school year. In spite of a splendid record of achievement, the Radio Project was cut off from further funds by Congress in 1940, and all active radio production by the Office of Education ceased. It has since concentrated on the development of a script, transcription, and information exchange.

Early in 1936, Commissioner of Education John Studebaker, on the recommendation of William D. Boutwell, director of the Radio Project, had decided that training in the educational use of radio might be provided by the establishment of a center where teachers and students could obtain experience in the writing and producing of programs. New York University had planned for radio instruction as early as May, 1934, when the Division of Adult Education was established. By 1936, deliberations were under way for the creation of a radio workshop at New York University. Eventually, this proposed radio workshop was made possible by a cooperative arrangement between the U.S. Office of Education and the Division of General Education of New York University. Boutwell and the Division of General Education joined forces in setting it up. The first session of the workshop was conducted during the summer of 1936; the second, in January and February, 1937; the third, during April and May, 1937; and the fourth, in July and August, 1937.

This radio workshop, which also received the cooperation of the Educational Director of the National Broadcasting Company, the Director of Talks of the Columbia Broadcasting System, and of many other New York City stations, was different in many respects from all other similar attempts in training. First of all, "it afforded opportunity for a study not of one or two stations but of a dozen, and these included the central plants of the three national networks." [49] Also, the instructors, the visiting lecturers, and the opportunities for practice were outstanding. Workshop students were offered the opportunity to attend rehearsals and broadcasts of the five programs of the Office of Education then on the air. The composition of the classes was unique in that only teachers or students who expected to be teachers and who intended to make broadcasting a part of their educational activities were admitted to the workshop.

The success of this workshop set the pattern for the establishment of many others in all parts of the country. An alumni association and a Radio Laboratory Club were formed, and the term "workshop" came into common usage.

Institute for Education by Radio-Television

The Institute for Education by Radio-Television (formerly the Institute for Education by Radio) was organized at Ohio State University in 1930 as a direct consequence of an earlier institute held in the House of Representatives at Columbus, Ohio, on November 22–23, 1929. This early radio institute, sponsored by the Ohio Department of Education, was attended

[49] Frank Ernest Hill, *Listen and Learn.* New York, American Association for Adult Education, 1937, p. 125.

by the superintendents and teachers who were participating in the Ohio School of the Air.

Such radio instruction pioneers as J. L. Clifton, Ben H. Darrow, W. W. Charters, and Edgar Dale were among those taking part. Clifton stated that its purpose was to discuss freely the ramifications of the many problems in educational broadcasting. Darrow presented a brief history of educational broadcasting and Charters analyzed the work of the Federal Radio Commission as it pertained to the use of radio for instruction. Dale led a discussion on the use and effectiveness of radio instruction.

During this first radio institute, Cline M. Koon, assistant director of the Ohio School of the Air, proposed that similar institutes be organized on a national basis. Out of this suggestion came the idea for establishing an annual national institute for educational broadcasting. Charters received a grant from the Payne Fund and thus the Institute for Education by Radio held its first annual meeting at Ohio State University from June 23 to July 3, 1930.

More than one hundred representatives of both commercial and educational broadcasters attended the first meeting of the institute. Every section of the United States and three foreign countries were represented. The sessions themselves consisted of forty-six well-prepared addresses on various phases of educational broadcasting. These proceedings and those of succeeding institutes have been published in annual volumes titled *Education on the Air.*

The objectives of the first Institute for Education by Radio and of succeeding institutes have been: (a) to enable teachers in educational broadcasting to become acquainted with each other, (b) to pool existing information, (c) to make the information available for general use by publishing the proceedings of the institute, and (d) to develop a plan for cooperative fact finding and research.[50]

The objectives that were first stated by the founding members of the institute have been realized in many ways. The institute has grown from a group comprising a few more than one hundred persons to one with over a thousand. The institute has always been a place where workshops and discussions dealing with every problem of educational broadcasting have had free rein. Above all, the institute has been a sounding board in the continual controversy between commercial and educational broadcasters. Simmering resentments and misunderstandings have at times violently erupted at these meetings. Even when all surface appearances seemed to reflect a spirit of cooperation and goodwill between educators and commercial broadcasters, the endless discord between these two groups can clearly be seen in the papers published in the *Education on the Air* yearbooks.

[50] First program of Institute for Education by Radio.

The institute has survived because it is one of the few places where the problems of educational broadcasting can be thoroughly thought through by all groups interested in either instructional radio or television.

Federal Radio Education Committee

In 1935, the Federal Radio Education Committee was established, consisting of forty leading educators and commercial radio representatives. John W. Studebaker, then United States Commissioner of Education, served as chairman. Funds were secured from the broadcasting industry and from various foundations. National conferences were held, studies made, reports and newsletters published. However, by the early forties, FREC had become only a relic of an idealistic compromise between educators and the radio industry, and it has long since faded away.

National Association of Educational Broadcasters

On November 12, 1925, broadcasters attending the Fourth National Radio Conference in Washington, D.C., adopted a resolution calling for full recognition by the Department of Commerce of the needs of educational broadcasting stations and recommending that "adequate, definite and specific provision should be made for these services within the broadcast band of frequencies." [51]

As a consequence, a group of educational broadcasters attending this conference formed the Association of College and University Broadcasting Stations.

The purpose of the organization was stated as follows:

> Believing that radio is in its very nature one of the most important factors in our national and international welfare, we, the representatives of institutions of higher learning, engaged in educational broadcasting, do associate ourselves together to promote, by mutual cooperation and united effort, the dissemination of knowledge to the end that both the technical and educational features of broadcasting may be extended to all. [52]

The first annual convention of the ACUBS was held in Columbus, Ohio, on July 1 and 2, 1930, in conjunction with the Institute for Education by Radio. At this convention, plans for better coordination and a more unified

---

[51] Copy of resolution included in report of conference by W. I. Griffith.
[52] From original constitution of Association of College and University Broadcasting Stations.

organization were made. President Robert Higgy, director of WOSU, Ohio State University, became the first executive secretary and the first regular mimeographed *Bulletin* was sent to ACUBS members.

During the years from 1930 to 1936, the National Association of Educational Broadcasters (name of organization changed at the 1934 convention in Columbus, Ohio) was handicapped by the decline of educational stations, limited membership (there were only twenty active dues-paying members in 1933), and lack of finances. In the spring of 1936, the first effort was made to develop a permanent headquarters and some type of program exchange. Also, during this year the *Newsletter* was started as the official publication and was issued more or less regularly by the executive secretary, Harold Engel.

The late 1930s failed to produce many important changes in educational broadcasting or in the NAEB. Some exchange of programs was made by some of the educational stations and there was some experimentation in rebroadcasting direct pickups from nearby stations. Early in 1938, the Federal Communications Commission reserved twenty-five channels in the ultrahigh (later FM) frequency band for noncommercial educational broadcasting, but the NAEB *Newsletters* of this period fail to reflect any great interest in FM on the part of most educational broadcasters.

During World War II, there was little change in the NAEB. Membership still failed to increase (there were only twenty-three member stations in 1944), but its financial condition improved somewhat. Plans for a permanent headquarters were again considered in 1945 but not realized until 1951. Largely through the efforts of Wilbur Schramm of the University of Illinois, the NAEB received a grant in 1951 from the Kellogg Foundation for the establishment of a permanent NAEB headquarters at the University of Illinois and an NAEB tape network.[53] The grant also provided funds to allow the NAEB to hold annual seminars for the training of educational broadcasters and to conduct radio instruction research.[54]

As a result of a merger with the Association for Education by Radio-Television in 1956, the NAEB became the major national radio education organization. NAEB continues to provide the basic leadership in instructional radio.[55]

[53] The development of the NAEB Tape Network in 1951 was the outgrowth of the noninterconnected tape network developed by Seymour N. Siegel of Station WNYC, New York City, in 1949.

[54] Much of the postwar development of NAEB can be attributed to the stimulus afforded by the Allerton House Conferences of 1949 and 1950 at the University of Illinois. See Robert B. Hudson, "Allerton House 1949, 1950," *Hollywood Quarterly*, vol. 5 (Spring, 1951), p. 239.

[55] For a complete history of the NAEB, see Harold E. Hill, *The National Association of Educational Broadcasters: A History*. Urbana, Ill., The National Association of Educational Broadcasters, 1954.

University Association for Professional Radio Education

This organization, organized as the University Association for Professional Radio Education in 1947, is composed primarily of educational broadcasters in colleges and universities. It has emphasized the exchange of radio instruction information, the establishment of professional standards for courses in radio instruction, and the development of a curriculum for radio courses. Beginning in 1956, the Association began publishing a quarterly, titled *Journal of Broadcasting*.

Trends in instructional radio

By the middle sixties, publications and research relating to instructional radio had virtually ceased; course offerings in radio instruction were considerably reduced; commercial radio networks had closed their radio education departments and discontinued their school broadcasts; and the once-vigorous leadership of the Radio Section of the U.S. Office of Education had disappeared. It was evident that educational broadcasting was shifting its focus from radio to television. Whether intentional or not, radio instruction by the sixties had become the stepchild of instructional technology.

**development of
instructional television**

While radio instruction declined, instructional television
brought about a general expansion of instructional technology. We have seen that education had long struggled
for recognition in its effort to secure reserved channels
for educational broadcasting. A historic victory was won
on April 14, 1952, when the Federal Communications
Commission set aside 242 (the number is now 274) channels for the exclusive use of education, with each state
receiving one or more assignments.

Since this eventful date, instructional television has
been under test. Credit and noncredit courses have been
given on open and closed-circuit television, programs of
a wide educational and cultural interest have been offered
on educational television stations, and many experimental
studies have been completed.[1] Many educators consider

[1] Instructional television has probably been subjected to more research than any other instructional innovation.

educational television an outstanding success;[2] others talk of the "disenchantments of educational television."[3]

A historic opportunity for educational television

At the close of World War II, it was clear that television as a new medium of communication would expand rapidly. Thus the Federal Communications Commission issued a *Notice of Proposed Rule Making* in May, 1948, which raised questions about technical standards and channel assignments. Hearings were subsequently held on this proposal and on September 10, 1948, the FCC issued a *Report and Order*, known as the "freeze order," suspending all new television station construction until further notice.

The next development occurred in July, 1949, with a *Notice of Further Proposed Rule Making*. Among its appendixes this *Notice* included a revised plan for television channel assignments—none of which was reserved for education. Frieda Hennock, alone among the seven Commissioners, proposed in a dissenting opinion that part of the UHF band should be reserved for educational use.

On August 26, 1949, United States Commissioner of Education Earl J. McGrath filed a *Notice of Appearance and Comments* which proposed that witnesses representing the United States Office of Education should present evidence to show the need for setting aside educational television channels. Although the FCC had scheduled hearings on educational television channels for November, 1950, as late as October, educators had done little in preparation for them. As in years past in the case of radio education, opinions were divided. The U.S. Office of Education, the NEA, and Miss Hennock were demanding educational reservations in VHF. The NAEB had asked for UHF channels only. There was also an issue between "nonprofit" stations for education and "noncommercial" ones.

Commissioner Hennock started the ball rolling for education by inviting a group to her home on October 16, 1950. This meeting proved to be a landmark in educational broadcasting because it marked the beginning of the Joint Committee (later Council) on Educational Television. In its initial ad hoc stage, it included I. Keith Tyler, who was elected chairman; Belmont Farley of the NEA as secretary-treasurer; and a strategy committee of Robert Hudson, Edgar Fuller, and Stuart Haydon. Richard Hull, as NAEB President, presided at the meeting. The results of this meeting authorized the

[2] Alexander J. Stoddard has expressed the point of view that "no new elementary school should be built today without a television studio and closed-circuit apparatus and connections for telecasting to all parts of the building and play spaces." See Alexander J. Stoddard, *Schools for Tomorrow: An Educator's Blueprint.* New York, The Fund for the Advancement of Education, 1957.
[3] See John Mercer and Sam Becker, "The Disenchantment of Educational Television," *AV Communication Review,* vol. 3 (Spring, 1955), pp. 173–182.

Joint Committee on Educational Television to make a presentation on behalf of the seven national organizations whose members were represented at the meeting (the Association of Land-grant Colleges, the Association of State University Presidents, the National Association of State Universities, the National Council of Chief State School Officers, and the National Education Association).

The immediate problem was to find outstanding educators willing to come to Washington to testify at the FCC hearings in November. Money would be needed to defray the cost of the trip. Seymour Siegel, the new president of the NAEB, and George Probst managed this fund raising. Meanwhile, I. Keith Tyler sought help from the American Council on Education and the NEA. Early in November, as a result of a suggestion from Miss Hennock, Tyler and Belmont Farley went to New York and retained as committee counsel General Telford Taylor, former general counsel to the FCC and former United States Prosecutor at the Nuremburg trials. Subsequently, it was decided that the JCET would ask for at least one VHF channel in every metropolitan area and every major educational center as well as 20 percent of the UHF channels (following the FM precedent).

First FCC Hearings on Educational Television. United States Commissioner of Education Earl J. McGrath opened the first of a series of FCC hearings on educational television on November 27, 1950, with the following words:

> In its January 16, 1945 report, the Commission guaranteed that the applications of educational institutions for television licenses would be treated "on an equal basis with applications from non-educational applicants." At that time, the Commission felt unready to reserve a television band for educational use because there seemed to be insufficient evidence of an effective interest in the use of television by educational institutions and systems. My purpose in appearing today is to suggest that that conclusion should be re-examined.
>
> The responsibility of government to protect the public interest in all times is a clearly recognized principle, particularly so when a new frontier is being opened. The shameless exploitation of natural resources in the opening of the great west has demonstrated the result of government failure to protect the public interest—likewise the concern of the National Government in protecting and furthering the cause of education goes back to our national beginnings . . . in adopting an ordinance which reserved part of the public lands for educational purposes, thereby establishing a precedent.[4]

Testimony was heard from sixty-one persons: educators, public officials, prominent members of Congress, university presidents, deans and professors,

---

[4] Testimony of Commissioner of Education Earl J. McGrath before the Federal Communications Commission on Nov. 27, 1950. Docket nos. 8736, 8975, and 8976.

state and city superintendents of schools, and others interested in educational television. All these witnesses favored the request for educational reservations. Aside from the Columbia Broadcasting System, adverse testimony by commercial interests was restrained.

Monitoring Study of Commercial Television. Concerned by the resistance offered by CBS as well as by the National Association of Broadcasters, Telford Taylor suggested that a log of current commercial programs be presented to the FCC to improve the presentation of the JCET case. I. Keith Tyler, George Probst, and Richard Hull endorsed this suggestion and enlisted sociologist Donald Horton of the University of Chicago and Dallas Smythe, a research specialist from the University of Illinois, in the project. Horton and Smythe monitored seven New York City television stations for more than twelve hours a day, with the help of women volunteers, from January 4–19, 1951.[5]

The results of this ordeal were eyestrain, recurrent headaches, a very low opinion of commercial television, and some very incriminating findings. Among the mass of findings was the significant fact that no time was given to educational programs as such. Most of the so-called children's programs bore little or no relation to the tastes and needs of children. The monitoring study proved to be a milestone in television research. Similar studies were made in Chicago, Los Angeles, and New York City in subsequent years.

Second FCC Hearings on Educational Television. When the second hearings on educational television were resumed in Washington, D.C., on January 22, 1951, the findings of the monitoring study by the JCET were presented together with the results of a survey of television in the Northeastern region of the United States.

Of a total of seventy-six witnesses testifying at the second hearing, seventy-one supported the educators' request. Five witnesses representing the commercial television interests opposed the allocation of television channels, although admitting that television could be a potentially effective means of instruction.

Assignment of Educational Television Channels. In April, 1952, the FCC issued its *Sixth Report and Order* which reserved 242 television channels (80 VHF and 162 UHF) for educational use. Following this action, a series of important events took place in educational television. A number of states held statewide conferences to arouse interest in the activation of these reserved channels. Committees were organized throughout the country to study the financial, programing, and engineering aspects of constructing television stations. Governors and legislatures took steps to investigate the

[5] Dallas W. Smythe and Donald Horton, *New York Television, Jan. 4–19, 1951.* Monitoring Study 1, NAEB, 1951.

instructional potential of television. Many national foundations became supporters of the educational television movement. Altogether, it marked the beginning of a new era in instructional technology.

Development of educational television broadcasting

At this writing, more than one hundred educational television stations are in operation. Only one (KTHE, Los Angeles, UHF) has failed. Others are under construction or under active consideration. In addition, more than three hundred closed-circuit educational television systems have been established throughout the country.

First Educational Television Stations. In February, 1950, WOI-TV at Iowa State College began regular program operation as a commercial station and became the first nonexperimental, educationally owned television station in the United States. KUHT, jointly licensed to the University of Houston and the Houston Board of Education, became the first educational, noncommercial station on May 12, 1953.[6]

Organizational Patterns of Educational Stations. Educational television stations have usually followed three basic organizational patterns. Following is a brief description of each plan, accompanied by a partial list of operating stations in the three categories:

1. *Single-agency station* provides that one educational institution is the licensee. The school board, college, or university that holds the license may be responsible for the financial aspects of the operation, but other educational and cultural groups may be members of an advisory board dealing with station management and policy and also contribute financial support. Stations organized in this manner include:

Station	Channel	Agency	Location
KUAT	6	University of Arizona	Tucson, Ariz.
KRMA	6	Denver Public Schools, Licensee; Council for Educational Television	Denver, Colo.
WILL	12	University of Illinois	Champaign–Urbana, Ill.
KUON	12	University of Nebraska	Lincoln, Nebr.
WOSU	34	Ohio State University	Columbus, Ohio
WMVS	10	Milwaukee Board of Vocational and Adult Education	Milwaukee, Wis.

[6] For a detailed history of some of the pioneer educational television stations, see John Walker Powell, *Channels of Learning.* Washington, D.C., Public Affairs Press, 1962.

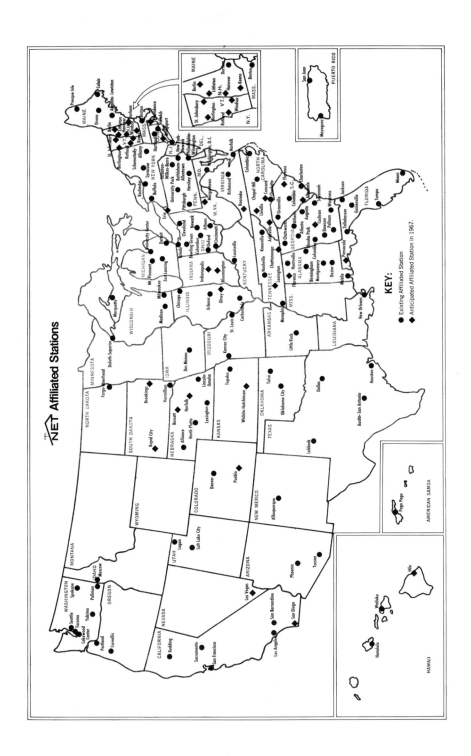

NET Affiliated Stations

KEY:
● Existing Affiliated Station
◆ Anticipated Affiliated Station in 1967.

N.E.T. Affiliated Stations — January, 1967

Alabama
Birmingham........ WBIQ 10
Cheaha State Park... WCIQ 7
Dozier........... WDIQ 2
*Florence.......... WFIQ 36
Huntsville......... WHIQ 25
Mobile........... WEIQ 42
Montgomery........ WAIQ 26

American Samoa
Pago Pago .... KVZK 2

Arkansas
Little Rock......... KETS-TV........ 2

Arizona
Phoenix .... KAET 8
Tucson .... KUAT 6

California
Los Angeles........ KCET 28
Redding.......... KIXE 9
Sacramento........ KVIE 6
San Bernardino...... KVCR-TV........ 24
*San Diego .... KEBS-TV......... 15
San Francisco ...... KQED 9

Colorado
Denver .... KRMA-TV........ 6
*Pueblo 8

Connecticut
*Bridgeport 49
Hartford .... WEDH-TV....... 24
Norwich .... WEDN-TV....... 53

District of Columbia
Washington .... WETA 26

Florida
Gainesville......... WUFT 5
Jacksonville........ WJCT 7
Miami........... WTHS-TV 2
*Pensacola .... WSRE 23
Tallahassee .... WFSU-TV 11
Tampa........... WEDU.......... 3

Georgia
Augusta .... WCES-TV 20
Athens .... WGTV 8
Atlanta .... WETV 30
Chatsworth......... WCLP-TV 18
*Cochran .... WDCO-TV 15
Columbus.......... WJSP-TV 28
Dawson .... WACS-TV 25
Pelham........... WABW-TV 14
Savannah .... WVAN-TV 9
Waycross .... WXGA-TV 8

Hawaii
*Hilo............ 4
Honolulu .... KHET 11
Wailuku.......... KMEB.......... 10

Idaho
Moscow .... KUID-TV 12

Illinois
Carbondale .... WSIU-TV........ 8
Chicago .... WTTW.......... 11
*Olney .... WUSI-TV......... 45
Urbana........... WILL-TV......... 12

Indiana
*Bloomington .... WTIU 30
*Indianapolis........ 20

Iowa
Des Moines........ KDPS-TV........ 11

Kansas
Topeka .... KTWU-TV 11
*Wichita-Hutchinson 8

Kentucky
Louisville .... WFPK-TV....... 15

Louisiana
New Orleans .... WYES-TV 8

Maine
Augusta .... WCBB.......... 10
Calais .... WMED-TV 13
Orono .... WMEB-TV 12
Presque Isle ...... WMEM-TV 10

Massachusetts
Boston .... WGBH-TV........ 2

Michigan
Detroit .... WTVS 56
East Lansing ...... WMSB 10
Marquette .... WNMR-TV....... 3
Mt. Pleasant....... WCMU-TV....... 14
University Center ... WUCM-TV....... 19

Minnesota
Duluth-
Superior, Wis...... WDSE-TV 8

Missouri
Kansas City .... KCSD-TV........ 19
St. Louis .... KETC-TV........ 9

Nebraska
*Norfolk 16
Alliance .... KTNE-TV........ 13
*Bassett.......... 7
Lexington.......... KLNE-TV........ 3
Lincoln........... KUON-TV 12
North Platte........ KPNE-TV........ 9

Nevada
*Las Vegas 10

New Hampshire
*Berlin .... WEDB-TV....... 40
Durham .... WENH-TV 11
*Hanover .... WHED-TV 15
*Keene........... WKEW-TV 52
*Littleton.......... WLED-TV 49

New Mexico
Albuquerque .... KNME-TV 5

New York
Buffalo .... WNED-TV 17
New York-
Newark, N.J. ...... WNDT........... 13
Rochester .... WXXI........... 21
Schenectady....... WMHT.......... 17
Syracuse .... WCNY-TV 24

North Carolina
*Asheville .... WVLE 33
Chapel Hill........ WUNC-TV 4
Charlotte .... WTVI........... 42
Columbia.......... WUNB-TV 2
*Concord 58
*Linville 18

North Dakota
Fargo-
Moorhead, Minn.... KFME 13

Ohio
Athens .... WOUB-TV 20
Bowling Green ..... WBGU-TV 70
Cincinnati.......... WCET 48
Columbus.......... WOSU-TV 34
Cleveland.......... WVIZ-TV 25
Newark........... WGSF........... 28
Oxford .... WMUB-TV 14
Toledo........... WGTE-TV 30

Oklahoma
Oklahoma City...... KETA-TV........ 13
Tulsa............ KOED-TV 11

Oregon
Corvallis.......... KOAC-TV 7
Portland .... KOAP-TV........ 10

Pennsylvania
Bethlehem-
Allentown .... WLVT-TV 39
*Erie............ WQLN 46
Hershey .... WITF-TV........ 33
Philadelphia-
Wilmington, Del.... WHYY-TV 12
Pittsburgh .... WQED 13
Scranton/
Wilkes-Barre ..... WVIA-TV 44
University Park ..... WPSX-TV........ 3

Puerto Rico
Mayaguez .... WIPM-TV 3
San Juan .... WIPR-TV........ 6

Rhode Island
*Providence 36

South Carolina
*Allendale 14
Charleston .... WITV 7
Columbia .... WRLK-TV 35
*Florence.......... 30
Greenville .... WNTV 29

South Dakota
*Brookings 8
*Rapid City .... KBHE-TV 9
Vermillion.......... KUSD-TV 2

Tennessee
*Chattanooga ...... WTCI 45
*Lexington.......... 11
Memphis .... WKNO-TV 10
Nashville .... WDCN-TV....... 2
Knoxville .... WSJK-TV........ 2

Texas
Austin-
San Antonio...... KLRN 9
Dallas .... KERA-TV......... 13
Houston .... KUHT 8
Lubbock .... KTXT-TV......... 5

Utah
Logan .... KUSU-TV 12
Salt Lake City ..... KUED 7

Vermont
*Burlington .... WETK 33
*Rutland.......... WVER 28
*St. Johnsbury ..... WVTB.......... 20
*Windsor .... WVTA 41

Virginia
Norfolk .... WHRO-TV....... 15
Richmond .... WCVE-TV 23
*Roanoke.......... WBRA-TV 15

Washington
Lakewood Center ... KPEC-TV........ 56
Pullman .... KWSC-TV 10
Seattle .... KCTS-TV........ 9
Spokane.......... KSPS-TV........ 7
Tacoma.......... KTPS 62
Yakima .... KYVE-TV 47

West Virginia
*Morgantown ...... WWVU-TV 35

Wisconsin
Madison .... WHA-TV 21
Milwaukee......... WMVS-TV 10

*Planned for activation in 1967

National Educational Television, 10 Columbus Circle, New York, N.Y. 10019

Fig. 11.1   *Map showing NET affiliated educational television stations.*

2. *Community stations* are usually licensed to a single organization such as a nonprofit association organized for this purpose by educational, civic, and cultural interests. The following are stations representative of this organizational setup:

Station	Channel	Agency	Location
WQED	13	Metropolitan Pittsburgh Educational Television Station, Licensee	Pittsburgh, Pa.
WTTW	11	Chicago Educational Television Association, Licensee; Chicago public schools, area colleges and universities, and other cultural organizations	Chicago, Ill.
KCTS	9	University of Washington, Licensee; Advisory Board includes members from University, Seattle Pacific College, public schools, public library, King County School Directors Association	Seattle, Wash.
KETC	9	St. Louis Educational Television Commission, Licensee	St. Louis, Mo.
KQED	9	Bay Area Educational Television Association, Licensee	San Francisco, Calif.

3. *State network stations* are activated under a statewide plan in which a state educational agency or a duly constituted TV authority is the licensee. ETV stations are generally planned as members of a network to be interconnected by microwave relay so that programing originating in one location can be supplied to other station outlets. Some of the stations in operation under this plan are:

Station	Channel	Commission or Authority	Location
WAIZ	2	Alabama Educational Television Commission	Andalusia, Ala.
WBIQ	10	Alabama Educational Television Commission	Birmingham, Ala.

Station	Channel	Commission or Authority	Location
WCIQ	7	Alabama Educational Television Commission	Munford, Ala.
KETA	13	Oklahoma Educational Television Authority	Oklahoma City, Okla.
KOED	11	Not licensed to OETA	Tulsa, Okla.
WUFT	5	Florida Educational Television Commission	Gainesville, Fla.
WJCT	7	Florida Educational Television Commission	Jacksonville, Fla.
WTHS	2	Florida Educational Television Commission	Miami, Fla.
WEDU	3	Florida Educational Television Commission	Tampa–St. Petersburg, Fla.[7]

Programing. Educational television programing has not generally kept pace with commercial television in gaining public acceptance. Many citizens are still unaware that a local educational television station exists. One major reason for the slow public acceptance of educational television may be the limited number of hours that educational television stations are on the air. What is more, educational television stations are usually off the air on weekends. Weekday schedules of many of the stations have often been irregular. Some stations operate on split schedules, some offer daytime programs rotated with evening programs on alternate days, while others broadcast only in the mornings. Most stations offer regular program schedules during the 7 to 9 P.M. period, exclusive of weekends.

Programing for educational stations has developed on a trial-and-error basis. Many stations began broadcasting without plans for programs. In the early years of educational television, it was not unusual for some stations to carry programs which had been put together a few hours before broadcast time. Limitations in staff and budget have often restricted the development of creative programing.

Sydney Head has suggested that many of the a priori assumptions concerning the limitations of commercial programing as compared to noncommercial programing may be fallacious. For example, he believes that "commercial television does as good a job in handling controversy as noncommercial television—possibly a better job." [8] He says further "that ETV

[7] Philip Lewis, *Educational Television Guidebook*. New York, McGraw-Hill Book Company, 1961, pp. 28–29.
[8] Sydney W. Head, "A Friendly Critic on ETV Programs," in *Educational Television the Next Ten Years*. Stanford, Calif., The Institute for Communication Research, Stanford University, 1962, p. 126.

has created precious little that is genuinely new and exciting while commercial television has done a good deal in this direction." [9] Irving Gitlin, a commercial television producer, says that "unless educational television stations can find some way to produce on a regular basis, dramatic, artistic programs and series which will become a habit for most of the television set owners in their communities, they will not get either the money or the loyalty they need." [10]

Hudson pointed up the needed breakthrough in programing for educational television stations as involving:

> (1) trained staff personnel in adequate supply; (2) a faculty and performing artists assigned on a rotating basis and observers of the contemporary cultural and political scene; (3) studio and transmission and reception facilities and money with which to operate them in all major localities; (4) a nation-wide interconnected educational television network; and (5) a commitment by educators to use the television instrument as a tool of education. [11]

Personnel.   The number of full-time personnel on educational television stations ranges from four to forty-seven with an average of about sixteen. Faced with this constant shortage of trained personnel, station managers have depended on universities and colleges for free assistance or have assigned students to specific station responsibilities. One of the primary problems has to do with obtaining sufficient trained broadcast engineers. Trained production personnel have been drawn principally from the radio, theater, and motion picture fields. Some have been graduates of colleges offering work in radio, television, and films; others have come with no particular experience and have learned on the job. Television instructors on the faculties of colleges and universities have, for the most part, failed to provide effective instruction in television because they, themselves, have not developed the skills necessary for this new medium of instruction. Furthermore, they have not always been sufficiently familiar with the theory and research available on aspects of the communication and learning processes which are pertinent to their teaching situation.

Financing.   One of the most difficult problems of educational television stations has been that of obtaining adequate financial support. The majority of the stations have been controlled by universities, colleges, public school systems, state legislatures, or other tax-supported bodies.

The greatest single source of revenue has been the foundation grant.

[9] *Ibid.*, p. 129.
[10] Irving Gitlin, "A Commercial Broadcaster on ETV Programs," in *ibid.*, p. 138.
[11] Robert B. Hudson, "How the National Program Center Sees the Outlook," in *ibid.*, p. 153.

For example, during the decade 1955–1965, the Ford Foundation invested about $70 million in educational television. Another source of money, apart from public tax money, has been contracts for programs produced locally for national distribution. A source of revenue which needs further development is voluntary contributions from the public in the form of member subscribers.

Although the educational television movement was aided by funds made available by the National Defense Education Act (NDEA) of 1958, the first direct allocation of federal funds was made in 1962 when President John F. Kennedy signed into law the Communications Act which provided $32 million for the construction of educational television stations. (ETV stations also became eligible to receive donations of United States surplus property.) Today many of the grants made to educational television in earlier days are terminating with little prospect of being renewed. Thus there still remains the perennial problem of adequate financing.

The UHF Problem.   Of the 274 channels reserved for education, 182 are UHF and only 92 are in the VHF band. The FCC decision to use UHF was originally based on a conviction that it was usable, but unexpected problems occurred. As frequencies go higher, broadcasting and reception become more critical because the UHF wave is more easily interrupted by hills, trees, or buildings. It is therefore not presently practical to duplicate on UHF the coverage provided by VHF stations. However, UHF (and VHF) service can be extended by supplementary low-power stations.

Meanwhile the problem of UHF is still one which needs to be solved. It appears likely that educational television stations might eventually have to shift entirely to UHF channels. With the ever-growing demand for VHF channels by commercial broadcasters, educational television might face the picking-off of valuable reservations, one by one. For example, several VHF educational reservations have already been lost to commercial interests. Thus, the only security of educational television stations would seem to lie in Congressional action making it mandatory for the FCC to preserve channels for educational television, regardless of whether they are activated or not.

Educational Television Networks.   Educators have consistently expressed the view that regional and national arrangements are essential for the production and sharing of programs. The first formal proposal for a national educational television network was made in 1952 at the Educational Television Programs Institute.[12]

The first statewide educational television network was developed in

[12] *Television in Education.* A summary report, reprinted from the complete proceedings of the Educational Television Programs Institute held at Pennsylvania State College, Apr. 20–24, 1952. Washington, D.C., American Council on Education, 1952.

Alabama in 1952. The purpose of the network was to raise the standard of instruction throughout the state, a goal most observers seem to agree has been successfully achieved. Alabama's instructional television network utilizes five television stations, offering television classes on the elementary and secondary level to some 158,000 students. Taken all together, at least six hundred schools are making use of instructional telecasts in Alabama.

Statewide interconnection is now in process or under construction in several states, and planning for such interconnection is under way in others. Regional networking is a reality in the Northeast and will undoubtedly expand to other areas. Some educational television linkage has already occurred in California, Florida, Oregon, and Oklahoma.

National interconnection is unquestionably the next goal of educational television. It is likely that educational television stations in the United States will, within the next decade, be connected by coaxial cable and microwave relay to form a true "fourth network." However, many problems will have to be solved before this network becomes possible. Meanwhile, educational television programs continue to be exchanged and distributed by the National Educational Television and Radio Center and by other agencies as well.

After national interconnection has been achieved, an even more interesting prospect is the possibility of a worldwide educational television by means of communication satellites.

National organizations

More than any single organization, the Fund for Adult Education of the Ford Foundation provided the unifying impetus in the national educational television movement. Although enthusiasts of educational television were scattered throughout the country, most educators and the general public were not awaiting its advent. What had been the dream of a few was thus caught by the Fund and transformed into an organized reality within a social climate ripe for some breakthrough in education. Other agencies, such as the National Association of Educational Broadcasters, must be given due credit for their important efforts in developing national educational television. But the Fund alone among organized groups uniquely mobilized latent forces at the precise historical moment of greatest opportunity.

The Fund for Adult Education.   The Fund was established in April, 1951, with Ford Foundation financing, for the following purposes: (1) to create awareness of the major elements and issues of modern culture, (2) to develop concern with them, (3) to develop materials for their study, (4) to instigate activity in learning about them, and (5) to encourage association of adults in such activity. These purposes also became the guiding principle in its vision of how television could serve an educational function.

The Fund for Adult Education was the first to recognize the needs of educational television, secure money for its support, and sustain it until the Fund for the Advancement of Education, in 1954, and the Ford Foundation itself, in 1955–1956, also became involved in educational television.

Early in 1951, Paul G. Hoffman, Robert Hutchins, and Chester Davis, the directorial triumvirate of the Ford Foundation, invited Cyril Scott Fletcher, president of Encyclopedia Britannica Films, to serve as president of the new Fund for Adult Education. He assumed this position at the founding meeting on April 5, 1951.

The Fund established its first headquarters in Pasadena, California, with other offices in Chicago and New York City. Robert J. Blakely, an Iowa editorial writer, was in charge of the Midwest office; Delbert Clark (followed by John Osman) was in charge of East Coast activities. In mid-1951, Ann Campbell Spinney, an educational radio writer and educational administrator, joined the New York office, and a little later in the year the post of Director for the Mass Media was given to G. H. Griffiths, an educational film producer. Fletcher, Griffiths, and Spinney, along with Robert Hudson, an early consultant, deserve most of the credit for developing national educational television during its formative years.

The Fund's policies on educational television did not develop immediately, although the question of educational broadcasting had been considered from the outset. There had been a request from the Ford Foundation that the Fund take over the problem of developing liberal adult education programs for the mass media. The first approach was a series of experimental programs known as *Omnibus*, produced by a television-radio workshop under the direction of Robert Saudek over a commercial television network. The *Omnibus* idea came from James Young, who had come to the Foundation from the J. Walter Thompson advertising agency as a consultant in the mass media. Young's concept was to develop a higher cultural level in commercial television by obtaining multiple sponsors who would have no control over program content. To Robert Hudson, a pioneer radio educator and also a consultant to the Fund, *Omnibus* was another example of the industry's misunderstanding of the nature of educational broadcasting. Meanwhile, Saudek assiduously avoided associating the word "education" with the *Omnibus* programs, holding it would be "the kiss of death." After a few months of these telecasts, the Fund's board decided that the approach taken by *Omnibus* was television for cultural entertainment rather than educational television and gave the workshop back to the Foundation.

The next question which had to be resolved was how far the Ford Foundation was willing to go in providing the Fund with the necessary finances to support educational television. Its founding grant for the mass media had been $3 million, supplemented periodically by such items as the $1.2 million for the television-radio workshop. Finally in 1956 the Fund received a five-year terminal grant of $17.5 million which did not, however, include the promotion of educational television. When the Fund finally grasped the full scope and meaning of educational television, it became clear that special grants would have to be made.

C. S. Fletcher originally asked the Ford Foundation for $5 million so that the Fund might assist in the construction and maintenance of educational television stations and develop a national program and distribution center. When Fletcher outlined his plans to the Foundation trustees, they pointed out that Henry Ford preferred one elaborate model educational television station which would provide an outstanding example to others throughout the country. However, Fletcher, himself, convinced Ford that the Fund's plans were feasible and won his assent. The Fund then received $4.75 million (later supplemented by another $4 million) to develop its own policies for educational television.

From the beginning the Fund was insistent that it should not hold a monopoly but that other foundations should be involved in the development of national educational television. Another policy was that the Fund would provide financial assistance until a qualified group could be organized to administer a grant.

The Fund's first action in regard to educational television was to provide an emergency grant of $90,000 to the Joint Committee on Educational Television through the American Council on Education. The Fund also gave early support to educational film production and to the development of new types of educational television programs by assisting such organizations as the National Association of Educational Broadcasters and pioneer educational television stations. It created a national program center and a national organization to advance educational television. Finally, the Fund provided financial assistance for the development of educational television stations. Before the *Sixth Report and Order* of April, 1952, these steps had all been taken and the basic decisions made regarding the future development of educational television. The later development of the Fund's policies is clearly reflected in the following history of the key national agencies associated with the growth of educational television in the United States.[13]

Joint Council on Educational Broadcasting.   The Joint Council (originally established as the Joint Committee on Educational Television) was organized on October 16, 1950, in Washington, D.C.[14] Its original purpose

[13] The Fund for Adult Education was discontinued in 1961. For a complete report of its activities, see *A Ten Year Report of the Fund for Adult Education, 1951–1961.*
[14] The Joint Council is an amalgamation of seven or so educational organizations. It began with a grant of $90,000 from the Fund for Adult Education.

was to coordinate the testimony of educators before the Federal Communications Commission hearings in 1950 and 1951.

Since its formation, the Joint Council has:

> Served as a source of information on television channel allocations and government regulations and actions relating to educational television.
>
> Provided speakers and field workers for groups planning to establish stations.
>
> Supplied information on legal, technical, and engineering matters while stations were still in planning stages.
>
> Maintained legal representation for educational television in Washington, D.C.
>
> Sponsored the First National Conference on Educational Television (May 4, 1953).
>
> Published a factsheet, *JCET Reports* (a reference service which included information about the status of national educational television), and a periodic *Educational Television Newsletter*.

The Joint Council, which at one time existed under a grant from the Ford Foundation, is now literally at the bottom of its till. The grants of the industrial foundations that have supported it in recent years are terminating. Regardless of its fate, there is no doubt that the Joint Council deserves major credit for its important role in disseminating information and stimulating educators to take advantage of educational television.

American Council on Education.   The American Council on Education has contributed to educational television through sponsorship of significant national conferences and seminars and by its publication of important books and bulletins.

National Association of Educational Broadcasters.   We have seen that the National Association of Educational Broadcasters was established in the middle twenties by a group of radio educators. With the advent of television, the NAEB has become one of the principal organizations concerned with national educational television policy.

National Educational Television and Radio Center.   Today the focal point of national educational television is centered in the National Educational Television and Radio Center (NET), created in 1952 by the Fund for Adult Education. The center was and is an indispensable producer and clearinghouse for educational programs of all kinds. The center's functions have been threefold: (1) to contract for the production of new programs; (2) to acquire completed films from other sources; and (3) to exchange programs among educational television stations.

Although the center was first developed in 1952, its chief heritage came from the experiences and concepts of instructional radio of the twenties and thirties. It was recognized then that a central program center for multiple stations not bound by an interconnected network was indispensable.

A few months after the FCC had made reservations for educational television, the Fund for Adult Education assigned Robert Hudson, professor of the communications division at the University of Illinois, to explore the problems of establishing a production and exchange center for the development of educational television and radio programs. In October, 1952, the Fund made a grant of $1.35 million for the establishment of an Educational Television and Radio Center.

Shortly after the founding of the center, an organizing committee was formed which consisted of George Stoddard, president of the University of Illinois; Robert Calkins, president of the Brookings Institution of Washington; Harold Lasswell, professor of law at Yale University; and Ralph Lowell, of the Lowell Institute of Boston; with C. Scott Fletcher serving as president.

Early in 1953 the center was physically located in Ann Arbor, Michigan, with Grant Leenhouts, an educational film producer, as consultant and acting executive. Harry K. Newburn, president of the University of Oregon, was selected as president of the center in June, 1953.

Because it was believed at first that theatrical, industrial, or educational film footage would provide needed resources for educational television, a project was established with the Film Council of America for the purpose of evaluating hundreds of films for possible use on educational stations. It was soon discovered, however, that few films prepared for group viewing could be successfully adapted to the intimate demands of the television medium. Moreover, there were almost insurmountable legal barriers in the clearance of most film material.[15]

The center began its national educational (NET) program service in May, 1954, by supplying five hours of programs per week to the four affiliated stations then operating. A large proportion of these early kinescopes was furnished by WOI-TV, Iowa State College. The Extended Services Plan developed in 1954 made NET programs available, after the affiliated stations

---

[15] An NAEB advisory committee (Burton Paulu, Graydon Ausmus, Harold McCarty, George Probst, and Richard Hull) to the center, along with Harry Skornia, Robert Hudson, Ralph Steetle, James Miles, and Frank Schooley, met at the second Gunflint Lodge Conference in August, 1953, and expressed their concern that stations were getting on the air faster than the center was ready to supply them with programs. They also recommended that the center establish network charges for programs provided to affiliated stations and that it make grants or pay commissions to stations that produced programs for the center.

had shown them, for broadcast by educational institutions in cities where no educational television stations existed. In 1955, the NET Film Service, co-operatively planned with Indiana University, inaugurated a service whereby NET films became available for nonbroadcast viewing in educational institutions. Meanwhile, regular and larger grants from the Ford Foundation have made it possible for the center to implement its activities more effectively. For example, the center moved its administrative offices to New York City in 1959, added the word "national" to its title, and increased its programing to ten hours per week. In addition, John F. White, manager of WQED, Pittsburgh, succeeded Newburn as president and found new sources of income.

In 1959–1960, Westinghouse gave the center the means to produce the series *Reading Out Loud;* the Humble Refining Company underwrote the distribution of the BBC Shakespeare cycle, *An Age of Kings,* in 1962; and Pyramid Books published study guides to accompany the series. In May, 1960, White announced that the center had received from the Ford Foundation a supplemental grant of about $2.7 million for videotape recorders, $350,000 from the Ampex Corporation for the same purpose, and $750,000 from the Minnesota Mining Corporation in videotape. Meanwhile, the Ford Foundation allotted another half million for support of the Broadcasting Foundation of America when it was taken over by the center. Another supporting grant of $350,000 came from the U.S. Office of Education. Affiliation fees ($9,600 per station) constituted an additional important source of income.

An international division was established in the center in 1960 to bring about the exchange of programs with other countries. Production contracts have been made with Canada, Great Britain, Australia, Yugoslavia, the U.S.S.R., France, Italy, and Germany.

The suggestion of a "university of the air" is embodied in the center's departmental divisions of programing into humanities, fine arts, science, social science, public affairs, and children's programs. This is supplemented by a television faculty concept. For example, Mme. Anne Slavk spent three years in Boston preparing and recording *Parlons français* for use in elementary schools; Professor Harvey White of the University of California spent a year in Pittsburgh broadcasting and recording a high school physics course, another year in New York City developing a graduate, physics television course for teachers; John Dodds of Stanford University took a year off to work on *American Memoir;* Huston Smith and Ralph Patrick of Washington University spent a semester preparing *Search for America;* and Professor Zechariah Chafee, Jr. of Harvard spent the last year of his life broadcasting and recording his course on constitutional law.

In the humanities and the arts, aside from the productions of Shakespeare, Tolstoy, Ibsen, and Gorky, programs in recent years have included a series on photography as a fine art, ballet programs, and symphonic concerts with distinguished American and European orchestras and soloists. In the social sciences and public affairs, there were such programs as *History of the Negro People, Metropolis,* and *Capitol Hill.* Also, science programs are being enriched by collaboration with the National Science Foundation, Westinghouse Laboratories, the American Medical Association, the Public Health Service, and pharmaceutical companies.

As the center enters its second decade, there is the promise of a national network that may be capable of reaching a large majority of the American people. There is no question that the accomplishments of the center have far exceeded the hopes of its founders and that it has become a potent force in American educational television.

Emergence of instructional television

It is first necessary that we make an important historical distinction between the terms *educational television* and *instructional television.* Educational television usually has referred to any type of educational video program presented for any serious purpose, whether to teach something to someone or to develop a broad cultural understanding. Instructional television has referred to open or closed-circuit video programs primarily designed to teach a specific body of subject matter as part of a formal course of study to particular groups of students in school or at home.

The first instructional applications of television occurred between 1932 and 1939 at the State University of Iowa. Following World War II, instructional television was initiated on commercial stations because educational stations were concerned at first with problems of financing, staffing, and developing programs for general adult use. By the middle fifties, however, instructional television began to receive serious attention from educational broadcasters. By the sixties almost every course in the public school, college, or university curriculum was being taught somewhere by either open or closed-circuit television, on educational or commercial stations, or in educational institutions.

Instructional Television on Commercial Stations. Some of the pioneer instructional telecasts begun in 1948 on commercial stations include those to the Philadelphia public schools by Martha Gable and her associates, the dynamic lectures on Shakespeare by Dr. Frank Baxter in Los Angeles, and the Johns Hopkins *Science Review.*

Probably the most ambitious instructional series broadcast on commercial stations has been the National Broadcasting Company's *Continental Classroom,* begun in 1958. These televised courses have been offered for credit by various institutions of higher learning throughout the country and have attracted large audiences in spite of early morning broadcasts.[16] Also, the programs have been taped, kinescoped, and distributed by NBC in cooperation with educational institutions and foundations.

It has been estimated by Lewis [17] that 560 school districts and 117 colleges and universities are using commercial channels for regular instructional purposes. Thus the use of commercial stations for instructional television constitutes a significant part of instructional broadcasting in the United States.

Instructional Television on Educational Stations.   Much of the impetus to instructional television on educational stations can be traced to the pioneer instructional broadcasting experiments in the cities of St. Louis, Pittsburgh, and Chicago, and in the state of Alabama.

The St. Louis Educational Commission and the St. Louis public schools made a joint proposal to the Fund for the Advancement of Education in the early fifties to offer several courses exclusively over television without supplementary classroom instruction. The pupils were to receive this instruction in groups of up to 150. Accordingly, in the fall of 1955, the St. Louis public schools began providing televised instruction over educational station KETC. Courses were offered in ninth-grade grammar and English composition for thirty minutes, five days a week. Lessons in second-grade spelling were telecast for two semesters in the spring and fall of 1956. The results of the St. Louis experiment showed that televised instruction could not be expected to carry the complete instructional burden and that a combination of televised instruction and some follow-up instruction by classroom teachers was necessary.[18]

Another pioneer experimental television program series began in Pittsburgh, Pennsylvania, at the time the St. Louis experiment was undertaken. The purpose of the Pittsburgh experiment was to raise the quality of teaching by selecting outstanding teachers and freeing them from other duties so that they might concentrate on the preparation of instructional television programs. Grade school and high school students viewed the resulting telecasts over educational station WQED. Their classes were of conventional size with their regular teachers in attendance. Follow-up instruction was provided at the end of the telecasts. Pittsburgh not only attempted to present superior teachers on television but also tried to offer courses which

[16] A similar college course credit series has been *Sunrise Semester*, presented by New York University and produced and distributed by the Columbia Broadcasting System.
[17] Philip Lewis, *Educational Television Guidebook.* New York, McGraw-Hill Book Company, 1961, p. 26.
[18] Early G. Herringhaus, *An Investigation of Television Teaching.* St. Louis Public Schools, 1957.

could not be given under conventional arrangements. For example, conversational French and Russian courses were telecast. In 1956, Harvey E. White of the University of California developed a new high school physics course and presented it over WQED.[19] Televised instruction was given in fifth-grade arithmetic, reading, and social studies.

From the Pittsburgh experiment it was impossible to conclude which was superior—regular classroom teaching or televised teaching supplemented by classroom activity. The results showed, however, that the effectiveness of televised lessons depended to an important degree on the quality of the follow-up by classroom teachers.[20]

An impressive experiment was undertaken by the Chicago City Junior College in 1956. A final report on its first three years of experimental activity indicates that nine courses were taught each year on WTTW. The courses were purposely varied and constituted offerings in social science, physical science, literature, biology, English composition, mathematics, modern languages, business, and other typical college courses. Students were screened and admitted in the usual way, but instead of attending classes, they viewed telecasts at home and kept up with a prepared study guide. Written assignments were submitted and returned by mail. During the experimentation period, about five thousand students per semester registered for the combined courses, and about 65 percent of the students who enrolled for the television courses completed them. According to evaluations made, it was concluded that junior college courses can be taught as effectively by television as in the classroom.[21]

A reference has been made in this chapter to the Alabama statewide instructional television network, which began in 1952. The utilization of television has already solved many problems peculiar to Alabama's educational system. Taken all together, at least six hundred schools are making use of these instructional telecasts.

Closed-circuit Instructional Television. The best known and one of the most elaborate closed-circuit facilities in the United States was built as a result of a grant from the Ford Foundation in Washington County, Maryland, and started operations in 1956. Even before that time, the country board of education had planned the installation of television receivers in new schools to overcome some of the problems confronting them. The chief prob-

---

[19] EBF, Inc., filmed White's entire physics course of 162 half-hour lessons in both color and black-and-white. This series is now offered to any school or school system for use as a film or television presentation. It had an important influence on the initiation of the *Continental Classroom* national television series.

[20] *Teaching by Television.* A report from the Ford Foundation and the Fund for the Advancement of Education. New York, Ford Foundation, 1959, pp. 37–39.

[21] Clifford G. Erickson and Hyman M. Chausow, *Chicago's TV College.* Chicago, Chicago City Junior College, August, 1960.

lem was the lack of adequately trained teachers. Of 352 teachers in elementary schools, 97 had no bachelor's degree, and 75 had only emergency teaching certificates.

With the assistance of equipment manufacturers, six studios were provided with vidicon cameras, film projection facilities, and a videotape recorder. This made it possible to produce twenty-five instructional telecasts each day during a school week on such subjects as remedial reading, art, social studies, music, arithmetic, advanced mathematics, general science, United States history, English, French, biology, chemistry, and guidance. As this closed-circuit system expanded, new courses were added until more than fifty courses were included in the television program.[22]

The telecasts were transmitted to the schools in Washington County from a television center adjacent to the Board of Education offices in Hagerstown, Maryland. By 1963, every public school in the county was linked to the television circuit.[23]

Another pioneer closed-circuit instructional television experiment began in 1954, with the aid of Ford Foundation funds, at Pennsylvania State University. Cameras were mounted in ordinary classrooms and connected by coaxial cable to other classrooms where matched groups of students viewed the lessons. Other courses were offered to classes by television only, and extensive experimentation was done with talk-back systems whereby the student could ask the instructor a question and get an immediate response. The original experiments indicated that the use of television did not seem to reduce the quality of instruction or to lower student accomplishment. This experiment also demonstrated that once a closed-circuit system has been installed, a decreased cost of instruction per student can be realized if the system is used effectively.

The growth of closed-circuit instructional television in recent years has been impressive. Evidence is accumulating which indicates that closed-circuit transmission is limited in its instructional applications only by the creativity of those who use it. For example, the combination of closed-circuit television with other instructional media—tape recordings, films, filmstrips, and teaching machines—may provide the basis for some fruitful instructional innovations.

Midwest Program of Airborne Television Instruction.   A novel approach to instructional television is offered by the example of the Midwest Program of Airborne Television Instruction, Inc. (MPATI), which was formed in

---

[22] During the 1956–1961 period, a study known as the Washington County Closed-circuit Educational Television Project was conducted. Details of this study are discussed in Chap. 15 of this book.

[23] See Washington County Board of Education, *Washington County Closed-circuit Television Report.* Hagerstown, Md., 1963.

1959 by a group of Midwestern educators. Much of this project was carried out in conjunction with the Purdue Research Foundation at Purdue University.

First of all, MPATI recorded, with Ford Foundation funds, a comprehensive series of videotape lessons covering a variety of subject-matter areas on the elementary and secondary school levels. Then, through the resources of fifteen educational television stations in a six-state area, thirty-four courses were televised to approximately 2,000 schools and an estimated 400,000 students. In order to reach schools not served by these stations, MPATI developed a plan to transmit these programs from an airplane circling about 23,000 feet over the north central part of Indiana. Technical problems thus far have limited this phase of MPATI's operations, but the feasibility of such a method of signal distribution over wide areas has been clearly demonstrated.[24]

The first demonstration telecasts began in April, 1961; complete programing started in September, 1961. The system has provided seventy-two half-hour television lessons in a five-hour day by broadcasting five separate programs simultaneously, four days a week, during the school year.

The cost of establishing MPATI exceeded $8 million. It has been estimated that maximum use of this system would demand about $10 million annually. Since the Ford Foundation grant was terminated in 1966, it is expected to be sustained largely by member schools in the years ahead. However, it is likely that airborne television may be obsolete within a decade, with communications satellites accomplishing the same kind of coverage that airborne pioneered.

The future of instructional television

The history of instructional technology clearly reveals that many of the bright promises being made for instructional television were essentially the same held out for instructional films and instructional radio. In fact, in many of the suggested instructional uses of television, there is discussion of taped versions, which reduces the television screen to the status of a projector for filmed content. However, there can be little doubt that a wider use of television in teaching may be expected, especially in some subject areas and for such instructional approaches as demonstrations, laboratory procedures, and formal or scientific observations. It also seems likely that as much as 50 percent of the college degree program will be available for credit via television and that school buildings will be more frequently designed for the use of instructional television. Part of the school day may be devoted to the

[24] The technique of rebroadcasting television signals from aircraft was first developed by Charles E. Nobles, an engineer in the Westinghouse Baltimore laboratory, in 1944.

large television class and the rest to small-group discussions and independent study or laboratory sessions.

It is difficult to predict the future development of open-circuit instructional television, although undoubtedly all educational stations in the United States will be shifted eventually to UHF bands. It is likely that open-circuit television will be used less frequently for direct, in-school instruction on the elementary and secondary school levels. This prediction is made despite the present increase of telecourses offered on open-circuit television. As closed-circuit television becomes progressively cheaper and easier to use, school administrators will undoubtedly prefer it for its adaptability to the problems of individual schools and to different instructional arrangements.

Instructional television may, perhaps, reach a plateau within the next decade due to competition from new technological developments just as television itself challenged the use of instructional radio and films. For example, an 8-mm magnetic sound projector has been developed which handles a preloaded film cartridge and produces a sound color film clearer and sharper than television to be shown by rear projection in daylight. Moreover, there are likely to be technical developments involving new combinations of television with other media or devices. A case in point is an electronic wire blackboard system which transmits audio and handwriting over regular telephone lines to television receivers and provides for questioning from students. In this system, a one-hour class can be conducted in New York for classrooms in Los Angeles for about $700 an hour, as compared to about $3,500 an hour for closed-circuit television. Obviously then, television, or any other instructional medium, may be partially or totally replaced by a cheaper or more efficient device which accomplishes the same objectives.

There is no question that instructional television can make a contribution to learning. One of television's greatest contributions lies in the fact that it can free the teacher for more individual work with learners and can provide the impetus for reevaluating instructional approaches or for introducing new ones. From a learning viewpoint, television is unquestionably superior in providing closeup views which live demonstrations cannot always supply. Similarly, it provides a more intimate, personal contact with the teacher than the live classroom situation where sixty or more students are involved. Also, television, by sharing the good teacher, makes it possible to have a good teacher in every subject in every school. Moreover, it can be distributed and used in schools and areas where facilities and skills are frequently lacking. Thus instructional television may eventually provide some valuable guidelines for the development of a technology of instruction, with the emphasis not on the gadget but on the problem of facilitating learning.[25]

[25] See the *Report of the Carnegie Commission on Educational Television* (January, 1967) for far-reaching changes in noncommercial television.

chapter 12

**the rise of
programed instruction**

We have seen that much of the historical development of instructional technology has been focused on the use of media for presenting stimulus materials rather than on psychological learning theory as a basis for a technology of instruction. The recent rise of programed instruction offers a distinct contrast to this historical motif. In the case of programed instruction, psychological theory actually spawned media for the purpose of incorporating principles of learning, instead of merely introducing a post hoc theoretical rationale for instructional media.

Beginnings of programed instruction

The concept of programed instruction can probably be traced to the Elder Sophists of ancient Greece (see Chapter 2). We know that Comenius anticipated programed instruction five hundred years ago. Also, we know that early devices for automating particular teaching functions were invented in the first decade of the nineteenth century.

Montessori: Pioneer of Modern Programed Instruction.   Probably the first systematic attempt to implement a psychological theory of learning with a mechanism was made by Maria Montessori soon after she initiated her first Casa dei Bambini in Rome in 1907 (see Chapter 4). The Montessori didactic apparatus anticipated modern concepts of programed instruction. One of her devices, for example, consisted of a block of wood with ten holes of different diameters and ten wooden cylinders to fit the holes. This device was dependent on the activity of the young learner for its use. It was necessarily self-corrective with immediate feedback since (1) a learner could not put a cylinder into too small a hole, and (2) if he put one into too large a hole, he would have, at the end of the sequence, a cylinder left over that would not go into the only remaining hole.

In another type of device, the child was presented with a series of wooden forms and insets. After learning to place the pieces in position quickly and accurately, he was given a set of cards bearing blue silhouettes of the same forms, followed by another card series in which only the contours were shown in heavy blue lines, and finally a set showing the contours in a fine blue line. The learner's task was to place the wooden insets first over the corresponding silhouettes, then over the heavily drawn outlines, and finally over the line drawings. Since each wooden inset covered the corresponding silhouette or outline exactly, if any portion of blue showed, the learner knew he had made a mistake.[1]

Early Contributions of Pressey.   Sidney L. Pressey, a psychologist at Ohio State University, exhibited a device anticipating the contemporary teaching machine at the 1925 meetings of the American Psychological Association. This device had four multiple-choice questions and answers in a window, and four keys. If the student thought the second answer was correct, he pressed the second key; if he was right, the next question was turned up. If the second was not the right answer, the initial question remained in the window, and the learner persisted until he found the right one. Meanwhile, a record of all tries was kept automatically.

There were two unique features of this early device that are still unrealized. First, a simple mechanical arrangement made it possible to lift a lever which reversed the action and transformed the machine into a self-scoring, record-keeping, testing device. Secondly, a simple attachment made possible the placing of a reward dial set for any desired goal-score which,

[1] Maria Montessori, *The Montessori Method*, tr. by A. E. George. Philadelphia, J. B. Lippincott Company, 1912, p. 190.

if attained, automatically gave the learner a candy lozenge.[2] Thus Pressey's device both taught and tested by providing immediate feedback to the learner as to whether or not he was learning what he was supposed to learn.

Meanwhile, Pressey's former student, J. C. Peterson, devised "chemo-sheets" in which the learner checked his choice of answers to multiple-choice questions with a swab, finding that wrong answers instantaneously turned red and correct ones blue.[3] Later Pressey devised a punchboard device and a selective-review apparatus using cards.[4] In more recent years, he has urged what he calls adjunct autoinstruction, which calls for a whole array of in-structional media—textbooks, films, television, etc.—to be used in conjunction with programed instruction.

Pressey developed a number of other devices and conducted many ex-periments with autoinstruction during the 1920s and the early 1930s, but their impact on instructional technology was almost inconsequential. Al-though he discontinued this first phase of his work in 1932 because of lack of funds (Pressey financed most of his device construction out of his own pocket), he remained confident that automated instruction would eventually generate an "industrial revolution" in education.[5] Except for sporadic de-velopments (mainly during World War II), Pressey's work was virtually for-gotten until B. F. Skinner of Harvard University stimulated a new surge of interest in programed instruction in the middle 1950s.

Programed Instruction during World War II.   Several military training devices constructed in the 1940s and 1950s were developed to teach skills by individualized self-instructional methods. These devices, called *phase checks,* both taught and tested. Each step of a skill, such as the disassembly-assembly of a piece of equipment, was organized on the assumption that constructed responses with immediate automatic feedback had a special value in learning. This was a linear program in which the learner's problem was to complete the steps involved in learning a manual skill or to accomplish certain ter-minal behaviors.[6] Thus the basic concepts of contemporary programed instruction were anticipated.

[2] Sidney L. Pressey, "Autoinstruction: Perspectives, Problems, Potentials," in E. R. Hilgard (ed.), *Theories of Learning and Instruction,* Sixty-third Yearbook of the National So-ciety for the Study of Education, part I. Chicago, The University of Chicago Press, 1964, pp. 355–356.
[3] *Ibid.,* p. 356.
[4] When using Pressey's punchboard device, the student punched with his pencil through a cover paper. His pencil went deepest when he found the right answer.
[5] Sidney L. Pressey, "A Third and Fourth Contribution toward the Coming 'Industrial Revolution' in Education," *School and Society,* vol. 36 (1932), pp. 1–5.
[6] H. B. English invented a device used in 1918 to help train soldiers to squeeze a rifle trigger. It provided visual feedback through the use of a manometer which revealed to the soldier a change in the height of a liquid column. If he squeezed the trigger smoothly or spasmodically, the mercury column would rise correspondingly and provide visual feed-back. See H. B. English, "How Psychology Can Facilitate Military Training: A Concrete Example," *Journal of Applied Psychology,* vol. 26 (February, 1942), pp. 3–7.

Crowder's Intrinsic Programing.   Norman A. Crowder developed a programed instruction approach somewhat similar to Pressey's in the 1950s when he was associated with the United States Air Force and engaged in training troubleshooters to find malfunctions in electronic equipment. Crowder's intrinsic or branching style of programing, as represented in Tutortexts or "scrambled textbooks," consists of steps which contain a limited amount of information, usually less than a page, and a multiple-choice question presented at the same time. After reading the text, the learner chooses whichever answer he thinks is correct and then proceeds to the step indicated by his choice. If an incorrect answer is given, the learner is directed to information designed to overcome the cause of his error and is then returned to the step where the error occurred. Thus the Crowder program simulates a tutor by performing the functions of presenting material, examining the learner, and providing corrective instruction or advancement to new information, based on the learner's performance.[7]

Skinner: Father of the Contemporary Programed Instruction Movement. In a 1954 paper entitled "The Science of Learning and the Art of Teaching,"[8] B. F. Skinner of Harvard University supplied the first significant impetus to the contemporary programed instruction movement. Although Skinner's techniques of programed instruction were not wholly new, he was the first to call the attention of the academic community to the educational possibilities inherent in programed instruction and the first to demonstrate a simple, practical learning device based on the principles of operant conditioning.

Skinner, like Pressey before him, focused attention on the device and christened it a "teaching machine." Since the machine rather than the instructional program within drew primary attention, more machines than programs were produced during the first years of the movement, and many commercial companies competed in their development.

The programing approach designed by Skinner was based almost exclusively on work which he and his colleagues had done in animal laboratory research. As to the applicability of this research, he pointed out that "the advances which have recently been made in our control of the learning process suggest a thorough revision of classroom practices, and fortunately, they tell us how revision can be brought about. This is not, of course, the first time that the results of an experimental science have been brought to bear upon the practical problems of education. The modern classroom does

[7] N. A. Crowder, "Automatic Tutoring by Intrinsic Programming," in Arthur A. Lumsdaine and Robert Glaser (eds.), *Teaching Machines and Programmed Learning: A Source Book.* Washington, D.C., Department of Audiovisual Instruction, NEA, 1960, pp. 286–298.

[8] This paper was presented at a conference on current trends in psychology at the University of Pittsburgh in March, 1954, and it also appeared in *Current Trends in Psychology and the Behavioral Sciences,* published by The University of Pittsburgh Press, 1955.

not, however, offer much evidence that research in the field of learning has been respected or used." [9]

The basic Skinner approach to programed instruction is based on the notion of operant conditioning in which the learner's responses are "shaped" to pronounce and to write responses correctly and whereby his behavior is brought under various types of stimulus control. Thus a relatively small unit of information, called a *frame*, is presented to the learner as a *stimulus*. The learner is then required to make a *response* to this information by completing a statement or answering a statement about it. By a *feedback* system, he is informed as to the correctness of his response. If he has been wrong, he may even be told why; if he is correct, his response is *reinforced*. The learner is next presented with a second frame and the stimulus-response-reinforcement cycle is repeated until a series of hundreds or thousands of frames present a complete *program* in a logical sequence of information.

Effective Skinnerian programing requires instructional sequences simplified to such a degree that the learner hardly ever makes an error. If the learner makes too many errors—more than 5 to 10 percent—the program is considered to be in need of revision.

During the decade following the introduction of Skinnerian programs, a majority of those produced were Skinnerian or variations. Yet research had already raised doubts concerning the theoretical validity of Skinnerian programs, despite extravagant claims for the method (see last section in this chapter on Programed Instruction and Theories of Learning). It is possible that within another decade Skinnerian programs may become obsolete, to be replaced by new methods of programed instruction with a sounder theoretical underpinning. Whether or not this is so, Skinner must be credited with reviving the concept of programed instruction and with setting the stage for a closer relationship between the behavioral sciences and instructional technology.

Early school use of programed instruction

American schools have been generally slow to adopt programed instruction. As yet, there has been no widespread movement of school systems to train their teachers in the use of programs nor any general movement, even in colleges and universities, to introduce programed instruction. In 1962 and again in 1963, the Center for Programed Instruction, at the request of the U.S. Office of Education, conducted a survey to determine patterns of use of programed instruction in schools throughout the country.[10] In each year, the

---

[9] B. F. Skinner, "The Science of Learning and the Art of Teaching," in *Teaching Machines and Programmed Learning, op. cit.*, p. 107.

[10] Center for Programed Instruction, *The Use of Programed Instruction in U.S. Schools.* Washington, D.C., 1965.

largest single category of responses was obtained from school administrators who considered themselves nonusers of programed materials. It was reported, however, that nonusers were usually familiar with some of the terminology of programed instruction and indicated that they had seen programed instructional materials of some kind or had read some of the basic literature.[11] Within those schools using programs in 1962, teachers and curriculum coordinators played the dominant role in initiating programed instruction; by the 1960's, the principal had replaced the curriculum coordinator as àn innovator.

Although the most common use of programed materials indicated by the 1962 and 1963 surveys was within large school systems, the programs were tried in most cases with individuals or small groups of students, rather than with entire classes. There also appeared to be more frequent use of programed materials in junior high schools than in either senior high or elementary schools. Most programs used were in the areas of mathematics (60 percent), followed by English (21 percent), foreign language (4 percent), spelling (4 percent), science (3 percent), and social science (3 percent). Teacher evaluations of programs (four out of five came from commercial sources) were generally favorable with only about 5 percent opposed.[12]

First School Use of Programed Instruction. We have seen that the first sustained use of programed instruction occurred in Montessori's Case dei Bambini and in later Montessori schools which implemented her methods. Aside from the early experiments of Pressey and others [13] in the 1920s and 1930s, programed instruction was first employed in higher education, on a regular basis, as part of courses in behavioral psychology taught by B. F. Skinner and James G. Holland [14] at Harvard University in 1957. The second pioneering use of programed instruction in higher education occurred in 1958 when Evans, Glaser, and Homme [15] of the University of Pittsburgh

---

[11] Two journals devoted exclusively to programed instruction are the *Journal of Programed Instruction* and *Programed Instruction,* published by the Center for Programed Instruction of the Institute of Educational Technology, Teachers College, Columbia University, New York City. The Center for Programed Instruction, under contract from the U.S. Office of Education, publishes an annual catalog of programs available.

[12] *The Use of Programed Instruction in U.S. Schools, op. cit.*

[13] James K. Little used Pressey's devices as part of the regular class procedure throughout a course in educational psychology in 1934. See James K. Little, "Results of Use of Machines for Testing and for Drill upon Learning in Educational Psychology," *Journal of Experimental Education,* vol. 3 (September, 1934), pp. 59–65.

[14] James G. Holland, "A Teaching Machine Program in Psychology," in E. Galanter (ed.), *Automatic Teaching: The State of the Art.* New York, John Wiley & Sons, Inc., 1959, pp. 69–84.

[15] J. L. Evans, R. Glaser, and L. E. Homme, "An Investigation of 'Teaching Machine' Variables Using Learning Programs in Symbolic Logic," *Journal of Educational Research,* vol. 55 (June–July 1962), pp. 433–450.

printed programs in a unique book format designed to simulate certain characteristics of a teaching machine.

The first sustained use of programed instruction in a public elementary school began in 1957 at the Mystic School in Winchester, Massachusetts, when Douglas Porter [16] conducted, under the sponsorship of the U.S. Office of Education, a year-long experiment in teaching spelling to second and third graders. The first use of programed instruction in a secondary school was started in 1959 when Eigen and Komoski [17] conducted an experiment in teaching modern mathematics.

A Case Study: Denver, Colorado.   The public school system of Denver, Colorado, was among the first large city systems to investigate the possibilities of programed instruction. It was through superintendent Kenneth Oberholtzer's personal interest that, in 1960, Denver became the first school system to free teachers from classroom duties to be trained as programers.

The pioneer in the Denver development was Jerry E. Reed,[18] a supervising teacher of English who, in the spring of 1960, was sent to Collegiate School in New York City to learn about programed instruction. Reed spent three weeks at the Collegiate School and then returned to Denver to begin preparing programed materials on English correctness. Meanwhile, six other English teachers were relieved of classroom duties and assigned to work with Reed. Together they produced 2,800 frames, covering sixteen units of work, during the summer of 1960. When the teachers went back to their classes in the fall, their programs still needed testing and editing. However, just about this time a decision was made to try English 2600, a new commercial program which covered almost the same ground and was aimed at the same tenth-grade level as the Denver teacher-made units.

In trying out English 2600, Denver was assisted by a research team from the Stanford University Institute for Communication Research that was engaged jointly with the Denver schools on an educational television project. A research design was made and the English 2600 program was tested during the school year of 1960–1961.

The results of this experiment showed that there was substantial learning in all ability groups. It was also discovered that the program proved to be more effective with accelerated classes but that the accelerated students were also the ones who complained most because they were bored with the

[16] Douglas Porter, *An Application of Reinforcement Principles to Classroom Teaching.* Cambridge, Mass., Graduate School of Education, Harvard University, May, 1961.
[17] L. D. Eigen and P. K. Komoski, *Research Summary No. 1 of the Collegiate School Automated Teaching Project.* New York, Center for Programed Instruction, 1960.
[18] The decision to send Reed to New York City was made on the basis that he was *not* attracted to programed instruction. The rationale of this decision was that if Reed became enthusiastic about the method, then other English teachers also might be expected to accept it.

repetition. The regular classes did about as well with the program as with class practice. On the other hand, the low achievers who did not use the program scored higher in achievement than those who did.

It was obvious from this experiment that the English 2600 program did not meet Denver's needs for low-ability students. As a result, attention was shifted again to the 2,800 frames prepared by the Denver teachers, and in the summer of 1961 Reed recruited the best writers from the previous year for additional work on the English programs. They revised portions and developed short booklets to implement the "lay reader system" of teaching English composition. Under this system, developed by Paul Diederich of the Educational Testing Service and pioneered in the Denver schools, the student's written work was first checked by a lay reader for the purpose of identifying specific key errors. Each type of error was recorded on an error grid (an ingenious device which provides the English instructor with a profile of his students and the kinds of errors they make). With the error grid serving as a basis for diagnosis, the student was assigned to a series of programed units to remedy the types of errors revealed by his written work.

In another major experiment with programed instruction—its second—Denver assigned Del Barcus, a young teacher of Spanish, to a full-time task of constructing a sixth-grade Spanish program. This was to be part of the Denver-Stanford research project designed to test the use of programed materials in combination with instructional television in the teaching of Spanish. One aspect of this experiement was to use television to facilitate the transition from the wholly audiolingual method of language teaching, which the students had experienced up to the sixth grade, to a combination of speaking-listening and reading-writing. Since there was no program in existence to meet these needs, Barcus began developing a program designed to teach word recognition, reading, and writing. Barcus worked through 1960–1961 and much of 1961–1962 before he had developed and thoroughly tested his program.

When it came time to implement the program, Denver had already learned from its experience with the English programs something about the effective introduction of programed instruction. Thus, teachers who were to use the Spanish program were paid to come to a series of Saturday morning workshops where they had an opportunity to try parts of the program and discuss its use. The value of these workshops cannot be underestimated because they contributed in large part to the ultimate success of the Spanish program.

The results of the Spanish program experiment, which involved more than six thousand students, provided the general finding that when the new program was used for part of the classroom time, the amount of learning was substantially increased. In other words, the program plus classroom teaching was more effective than either alone. Another significant finding of the experiment was that the more enthusiastic the teacher was about programed instruction, the better work the students did on the program, even though they worked privately or on an independent basis. Another significant finding was that there appears to be an optimum time to introduce certain types of programs to particular learners. For example, many of the sixth-grade students who used the Spanish program in the first semester could not take full advantage of the program because they had not acquired sufficiently the necessary skills of listening and speaking. When the program was first introduced in the second semester, it proved to be more effective.

The success of the Spanish program created a new climate for programed instruction in the Denver schools and generated great enthusiasm among the teachers as well as the administration. As a consequence, teachers began to ask for programs, and some of them took steps toward preparing their own. Another development occurred in 1963, when Barcus was appointed as a supervising teacher with primary responsibility for programed instruction in Denver.

In reviewing the early programed instruction experiences of Denver, it is clear that no dramatic instructional innovations were produced. Perhaps the one exception to this generalization might be found in the instance of the creation of a teaching team, consisting of a master television teacher, a classroom teacher, and cooperative parents, whereby Spanish was taught to elementary children. Teachers usually thought of programs as part of teaching teams, headed by the classroom teacher. For example, a mathematics teacher used a program to teach his students to use the slide rule, or a third-grade teacher used a programed tape to drill his students on the multiplication tables.

As we look back on the Denver experience, it is apparent that the most significant lesson learned is that it is a difficult, time-consuming task to introduce programed instruction as an instructional innovation. This appears to be true whether the school system prepares its own programs or whether it selects commercial programs. Despite its early difficulties, however, Denver has made a growing commitment to programed instruction.[19]

A Case Study: Manhasset, Long Island, New York.   Early in 1960, the Manhasset Junior High School administration enthusiastically supported the use of programed instruction and began to make plans for an experimental study. After three months of preliminary study, the experiment began in January, 1961, with the same English 2600 program used in Denver. The experimental design was such that one seventh-grade class and two eighth-grade classes would be taught solely by the English 2600 program, while all other classes in these grades would continue to be taught by the usual

[19] See Wilbur Schramm (ed.), *Four Cases of Programed Instruction.* New York, Fund for the Advancement of Education, 1964, pp. 30–40.

methods. Grammar was taught to the experimental group in three half-hour class periods per week and the students were given minimum assistance by monitoring teachers. Teachers in the other classes taught grammer, as before, as part of a ninety-minute English–social studies block period.

The results of this experiment revealed that the experimental groups in grades seven and eight made significantly higher grades. However, Herbart and Foshay found it difficult to interpret the findings and observed that "the test used was the one designed to test the material of the English 2600 program, and no clear evidence exists that the content taught in the other classes was comparable." [20] Although the experimental design was far from adequate, the conclusions drawn from observations convinced the administration and the eighth-grade teachers that it would be worthwhile to continue the program. The seventh-grade teachers, on the other hand, decided against using the program during the subsequent year because they felt the English 2600 program was far beyond the scope and depth of what was customarily taught in grade seven.

The eighth-grade teachers used the English 2600 program the following year to teach all eighth-grade classes, with some changes to meet those needs of students which had become apparent during the previous year's observation. It had been noted, for example, that students worked better when they were encouraged to call on a teacher for help with a difficult frame. What was needed was a less formal classroom climate in which there could be more teacher-learner interaction. Thus the plan for the use of the English 2600 program during the second year called for a large room equipped with enough desks to seat over one hundred students, where different class groups could simultaneously complete their programs. As each student finished his program, he joined a teacher in another room where he could write compositions and receive individual assistance in conferences with the teacher.

The second-year results led teachers to examine a number of assumptions [21] they had held about teaching and to organize new instructional patterns. For example, the teachers began to develop an informal, team teaching structure which enabled them to become involved in joint planning, teaching, and evaluation of the program. In addition, they began to hold individual conferences once or twice a week for each student, they established a class in remedial grammar, and they developed a system of grouping homogeneously in relation to speed and accuracy in English grammar.[22]

The Manhasset experience with programed instruction did not provide

[20] *Ibid.*, p. 20.
[21] It had been anticipated that the brighter students would be the first to finish the program, but in practice, it was the students of low ability who were first to leave the large program group since they found the program beyond their capacity and desired individual help.
[22] Schramm, *op. cit.*, pp. 18–27.

the model that Denver did for introducing programed instruction. In this respect, it was somewhat disappointing. Also, the use of only one regular program and the lack of precise experimental data deprived the project of the scope and depth one might have otherwise expected from an administration which had so strongly supported the concept of programed instruction. Although some worthwhile instructional innovations were introduced, they were by no means foreseen by the Manhasset administration when programed instruction was first initiated in 1960.

Comparative Analysis of the Denver and Manhasset Case Histories. The case histories of Denver and Manhasset are only two illustrations of the early American school use of programed instruction. Other early experiments in the school use of programed instruction were conducted in such diverse places as Roanoke, Virginia (1960),[23] Provo, Utah (1961),[24] and Pittsburgh, Pennsylvania (1962); [25] but it is apparent from a study of the case histories of these early uses that certain themes run through the Denver and Manhasset cases which tend to be representative of many of the early school histories of programed instruction.

The Denver and Manhasset cases indicate that while programed instruction may introduce a more flexible instructional pattern, it can also generate new problems. Since programs are more difficult to adapt to curriculum changes than textbooks, a change in the curriculum could easily make a program obsolete, or a program could hamper or obstruct a desirable curriculum change. In the case of the Manhasset district, for example, when it discontinued the Encyclopedia Britannica Films elementary algebra program TEMAC to change to new mathematics, the TEMAC teaching became obsolete since the machines could not be adapted to the new subject matter.

Both the Denver and Manhasset cases illustrate different attitudes toward individualized instruction. In Denver, the teacher-made programs were designed, from the first, to be teacher aids; the goal was to keep the students together rather than to encourage divergent rates of progress. In Manhasset, some efforts were made to individualize the study of English grammar in the eighth grade. On the other hand, Denver chose to discard the English 2600 program in favor of individualizing instruction, while Manhasset considered the same program an ideal way to free the teacher for individualized instruction.

In both the Denver and Manhasset cases, it is clear that teacher attitudes toward programed instruction proved to be a critical factor in the success of programed instruction. For example, in Denver it was found that students did better with a program when the teacher's attitude was favorable toward

[23] E. Rushton, *The Roanoke Story*. Chicago, Encyclopedia Britannica, Inc., 1963.
[24] Schramm, *op. cit.*, pp. 66–94.
[25] R. Glaser, J. H. Reynolds, and Margaret C. Fullick, *Programed Instruction in the Intact Classroom*. Pittsburgh, Learning Research and Development Center, University of Pittsburgh, 1963.

programed instruction. This was quite obvious in the cases of the Denver teachers of Spanish and the eighth-grade teachers in Manhasset. It even held true when all the teacher did was keep order!

Finally, the Denver and Manhasset cases support the need for structuring the learning environment to bring about optimal learning conditions. The Manhasset teachers, for example, who initially attempted to use the grammar program for individual instruction soon found that they would have to make extensive modifications in existing classroom structure and organization and that they would need to adopt new teacher roles before individualized instruction could be accomplished. Thus it seems clear that the use of programed instruction may eventually serve as a vital agent of educational change.

Programed instruction and computer-based systems

In recent years a number of computer-based systems have been developed and used experimentally in programed instruction, but the tendency has been to use computers to simulate a Skinner-type program or a Crowder-type programed text rather than to achieve instructional goals which would be impossible or impractical to accomplish by other means. What is more, the instructional potential of computer-based systems has thus far been largely unrealized because the concepts of cybernetics have been generally unknown in the field of instructional technology.[26]

Pask: Pioneer of Adaptive Teaching Systems. Gordon Pask of the Systems Research Laboratory in London, England, developed the first so-called instructional adaptive machines in 1953. These devices are not well known to educators because they have thus far been concerned primarily with the teaching of skills needed by the industrial and military sectors. Perhaps the best known adaptive teaching machine is one devised by Pask for the training of card punch operators. This device, known as SAKI (Self-organizing Automatic Keyboard Instructor), consists of (a) a near-vertical display panel which exhibits exercise materials; (b) a real-size keyboard which the trainee must learn to operate without actually looking at the keys; (c) a "cue information" display of lights which helps the trainee to locate particular keys without his having to look for them directly; and (d) an adaptive computer which senses the characteristics of the trainee and adjusts the training routine to suit his requirements.[27]

---

[26] See Karl U. Smith and Margaret F. Smith, *Cybernetic Principles of Learning and Educational Design.* New York, Holt, Rinehart and Winston, Inc., 1966.
[27] Brian N. Lewis and Gordon Pask, "The Theory and Practice of Adaptive Teaching Systems," in Robert Glaser (ed.), *Teaching Machines and Programed Learning, II, Data and Directions.* Washington, D.C., Department of Audiovisual Instruction, NEA, 1965, p. 242.

Lewis and Pask [28] constructed and experimented with an adaptive teaching system whereby a centralized computer induced students to teach each other or placed them in tutorial relationship to one another. To implement the general principles involved in this system a group of three students was used. Whereas typical programed materials are designed to handle the task of instructing and testing students, this particular system "provides an adaptively controlled environment in which the students are invited and encouraged to develop interaction patterns that enable them to become their own best instructors." [29] In order to implement this system, the computer system "computes objective measures of the progress made by any particular students (and combinations of students), and, on the basis of these computations, it adjusts their working conditions in ways that seem most likely to insure that progress will continue." [30] Pask's work, provocative as it now appears, is but the first of many steps toward a computer-based programed instructional system which will adapt itself to the responses and needs of individual students.

Autotelic Responsive Environments. A direct influence of Pask can be seen in the example of handling individual differences offered by the work of O. K. Moore at Hamden Hall Country Day School near New Haven, Connecticut. Moore's instructional approach, first begun in 1960, is designed to develop an instructional situation which he calls an autotelic responsive environment. To date, Moore's work has focused on the teaching of nursery-school children (starting as young as two years old) to read and type.

In teaching children to read, Moore has them strike the keys of a computer-based electric typewriter so engineered that the typewriter becomes actively responsive to the keys pressed by the child. Thus, as the child sees the letter struck, he simultaneously hears the name of the letter from an auditory response within the system. After a period of free exploration on the keyboard, further programed instructions tell the child what letter to strike. By keeping all keys except the named one fixed, the electronic teacher gradually teaches the child the entire keyboard. By means of additional programing, the child is able to take dictation from the computer, pressing keys and forming words and sentences with little error.

The results of this experiment provided the impressive evidence that children who had experienced this approach during its first two years in use had entered the first grade with a fourth-grade, or higher, level of reading

[28] Pask, "Interaction Between a Group of Subjects and an Adaptive Automaton to Produce a Self-organizing System for Decision-making," in M. C. Yovits, G. T. Jacobi, and G. D. Goldstein (eds.), *Self-organizing Systems—1962*. Washington, D.C., Spartan Books, 1962.
[29] Lewis and Pask, *op. cit.*, p. 259.
[30] *Loc. cit.*

ability. Moreover, the motor dexterity and control of these children, as reflected in their writing, was like that typical of seven- and eight-year-olds.[31]

Moore's programed instruction approach holds challenging implications for the future directions of computer-based programed instruction. It seems likely that all students will get individualized programs which they may determine themselves and complete at their own pace. The most apparent implication of computer-based programed instruction is that we must develop our knowledge about the more complex instructional strategies which cannot be implemented in any way yet known other than by the use of the computer-based system.

The machine-program conceptual dichotomy

Two opposed schools of thought arose in the programed instruction movement, which might be characterized as the machine-program conceptual dichotomy. The early machine viewpoint emphasized the use of machines and the problems of developing highly sophisticated instrumentation for automating the instructional process. The concern of this view focused on discovering decisive machine functions and specifying the manner in which each is to be accomplished, rather than on methods of programing or implementation of learning theory.

The program (and current) school of thought places emphasis instead on the development of programs based on an analysis of learning and the goals of instruction. The predominant concept inherent in this orientation is that programed instruction should be based on learning theory. What is more, this view holds that programed instruction should provide a means for studying more complex experimental designs to determine teacher-learner interactions so that more effective instructional strategies may be developed.

This conceptual dichotomy has cut deeper than might be assumed and has been further exacerbated by competing commercial interests in the development of machines and programs. For example, the Finn-Perrin survey [32] revealed that an almost equal number of companies were occupied either with producing machines or developing programed instruction and were prone to make exaggerated advertising claims without adequate program testing. In most cases, commercial producers have supported almost no research on programing nor have they made any serious attempt to stray from familiar formats or introduce programing innovations. As a result, programs

---

[31] O. K. Moore, "Autotelic Response Environments and Exceptional Children," *Special Children in Century 21*. Seattle, Wash., Special Child Publications, 1964.
[32] James D. Finn and Donald G. Perrin, *Teaching Machines and Programed Learning, 1962: A Survey of the Industry*. Washington, D.C., NEA Technological Development Project, 1962.

have tended to congeal into stereotyped forms just at a time when more flexible approaches to programed instruction might have been expected.

Another facet of the machine-program dichotomy is the prevailing conception that programs (software) are more important than machines (hardware). Also, machines and programs are now perceived as having separate, distinct functions. It is obvious that the simple nature of most current teaching machines makes it appear as if the program is the essential item and the device in which it is placed is merely a dispensing mechanism. This arbitrary division of functions appears questionable in the light of the recent development of more sophisticated computer-based instructional systems. Thus, with specially constructed man-machine computer-based teaching systems operating in accordance with cybernetic principles of learning, it will be difficult to separate machine from program functions. They both will be accomplished by a complex combination of display, switching, and computer operations. Therefore, in considering the relationship of a machine and a program, it is important to understand that the prevailing concept of a teaching machine is indeed quite primitive and in need of reformulation.

Programed instruction and theories of learning

Although a whole range of learning theory positions have been reflected in programed instruction to date, there is little question that the movement has thus far been dominated by the Skinnerian operant conditioning theory of learning, as previously stated. It is still too early to assess the final effects of this theoretical envelopment on the future evolvement of programed instruction, but it is apparent that there is increasing opposition to the Skinnerian view and that a countermovement has already begun. It is hardly surprising to find that the traditionally antagonistic theoretical positions of S-R (stimulus-response) associationists and gestalt-field psychologists have each become a rallying point in programed instruction.

Programed Instruction and Learning Theory Crisis.   According to a recent view of Pressey, "there is disturbing evidence that current autoinstruction is not up to the claims made for it, that the current 'boom' might be followed by a 'bust.' " [33] Further, he declares:

> The archvillain leading so many people astray is declared to be learning theory! No less a charge is made than that the whole trend of American research and theory as regards learning has been based on a false premise—that the important features of human learning are to be found in animals. Instead, the all-important fact is that human has

[33] Sidney L. Pressey, "Teaching Machine (and Learning Theory) Crisis," *Journal of Applied Psychology*, vol. 47 (February, 1963), pp. 1–6.

transcended animal learning. Language, number, such skills as silent reading, make possible facilitations of learning, and kinds of learning, impossible even for the apes. Autoinstruction should enhance such potentials. Instead, current animal derived procedures in autoinstruction destroy meaningful structure to present fragments serially in programs, and replace processes of cognitive clarification with largely rote reinforcings of bit learnings.[34]

Thelen's provocative critique of Skinnerian concepts of teaching machines and programed instruction voices the following doubts and criticisms:

First, the notion that the learner must be rewarded at each step is by no means proved. Experiments similar to Skinner's studies on rats have shown that latent learning unguided and unrewarded does take place.

Second, if we assume that reward is necessary at each step, the question becomes one of deciding how to give the reward. The present answer is to have steps so easy that the student makes very few errors. . . . The doubt is that continuous success is in fact rewarding. . . . Reports that boredom sets in after the first few hours of programed instruction seem to be practical evidence.

Third, the criterion of a good linear program so far used is that it be error free; but the relationship between this criterion and any educational criterion remains completely unestablished.

Fourth, while the art of programing is very much concerned with developing an effective sequence of items, two experiments have already revealed that the students learned just as much when the items were presented in random order as when they were presented in the sequence designed by the programers. This finding suggests that if the purpose of the program is to give information, then sequence does not matter. If the purpose is to teach principles that must be developed over a set of items, then it appears unlikely that principles will be learned through present types of sequences.

Fifth, the role of the teacher is unspecified.

Sixth, the talk of individual differences is misleading. The same program is used with all the students, the mental skills required of all the students are the same, and the content is covered in the same way.

Seventh, the notion that learning is better when it is active and that the machine requires activity is uncertain in its application to present programs. A number of experiments show no differences in learning when the student actually makes the responses as compared with when he merely reads the items.

Eighth, there is no control over student purposes or motives. His posture is to be extraordinarily docile, and he is not expected to participate in goal-setting.

---

[34] *Loc. cit.*

Finally present programs are designed to be teacher-proof and self-contained . . . they cannot deal with unanticipated or emergent purposes, feelings, or ideas.[35]

The above objections to the Skinnerian assumptions underlying programed instruction are reflected in many of the controversial issues which have arisen in recent years. An S-R-theory-centered programer considers learning a change of behavior which occurs as the result of practice or doing. To a gestalt-field programer, learning is a cognitive process of developing new insights or modifying old ones. In preparing programed materials, the gestalt-field programer is concerned with helping the learner to pursue his purposes, see new ways of utilizing elements of his environment, and get a sense of, or feeling for, pattern or relationships. Learning, according to this view, is essentially a purposive, explorative, imaginative, creative enterprise. This conception breaks completely with the Skinnerian concept that programed instruction is mainly a process of shaping complex forms of behavior in passive learners by bringing it under many sorts of external stimulus control.

The theoretical issues which have arisen in programed instruction are not only pertinent to programing approaches but are likely to be basic in any theory of instructional technology.

Toward a Field-centered Approach to Programed Instruction. Since it is obvious that a countertendency away from Skinnerian programed instruction neoorthodoxy has already begun, it is of historical importance that we examine the less familiar field-centered approach to programed instruction. Thelen has summarized the following specifications as a starting set for programed materials:

1. The student would be able to define his purpose in using the materials in terms of a question to be answered, a relationship to be sought, a skill to be learned, and he would have solid reasons which, for him, justify his learning of these things.
2. The materials would present reasonably large or molar "situations" containing many elements, and the student would devise his own path through these elements, taking them in any order he chooses, going back and forth among them. . . .
3. Each of these molar situations would involve at least two phases: discovery of the pattern followed by immediate application, summarizing, prediction, or raising of further questions. . . .
4. During the "search" phase, the student would get immediate feedback when he had classified each element appropriately.
5. During the application or assimilation phase, feedback could not be built into the program because any of a large number of specu-

---

[35] Herbert A. Thelen, "Programed Materials Today: Critique and Proposal," *The Elementary School Journal*, vol. 64 (1963), pp. 189–196.

lations or answers might be right—at least from the point of view of the student. The feedback for this phase would have to be reserved for a non-material third phase: class discussion which begins with the testimony of several students.

6. The programed materials thus would lead into class discussion; the reported speculations and difficulties of the students during the second phase would be testimony from which the agenda for discussion is generated.

7. The discussion would be concerned both with the students' speculations and conclusions and with the way in which the students arrived at these answers.

8. Diagnosis of the discussion would lead into the formulation of what the students need to study next, and a variety of activities as appropriate, including further work with programed materials, would then be initiated.[36]

It is of interest to note that current work in adaptive teaching systems and computer simulation of learner-machine interactions has already begun to incorporate some of the foregoing specifications. There are also many indications that programed instruction is shifting toward explorations of the significant interactions in integrated instructional systems composed of teachers, learners, media, and subject matter. Instructional systems research and development are not likely therefore to be confined to specific machines or techniques but will extend to a cybernetic analysis of the learner as a feedback system in the context of his interactions with his total environment. In the next chapter, we will explore some of the historical and conceptual developments which have led to a systems approach to instruction and, simultaneously, toward a science and technology of instruction.

[36] Herbert A. Thelen, "Programed Instruction: Insight vs. Conditioning," *Education*, vol. 83 (March, 1963), pp. 416–420.

chapter *13*

**the systems approach
to instruction:
a prospective view**

In the present book, we have been serving primarily as
reporters, but also as interpreters (no human report can
be absolutely objective) and critics. With the possible exception of programed instruction, all of the historical
instructional approaches presented so far in Part 2 fall
short of a truly scientific technology of instruction. In
contrast, the systems approach to instruction offers a conceptual framework which, hopefully, can provide a model
for the achievement of this ideal. Since we are merely on
the frontier of this development, much of this chapter
will necessarily depart from the retrospective treatment
of previous chapters and will be focused instead on prospective developments.

Origin of the systems concept

Systems engineering—the invention, design, and integration of an entire assembly of equipment (as distinct from the invention and design of the components) geared to the accomplishment of a broad objective—is a concept which has been fundamental to practical engineering since the beginning of the industrial revolution. One of the most successful applications of the systems concept in the military sphere was the development of the atomic bomb.

In the early 1950s, two events of great significance took place in the history of systems development. First, the Air Force formalized the systems concept. Second, it drew together within the Air Research and Development Command those research and development agencies concerned with systems, their hardware components, and their human components. These developments came about as the result of a need to improve the predominantly manual air defense control and warning system established over large areas of the United States, Canada, and the peripheral oceans. A radically better air defense control system was needed, and in 1953, the intensive development of the first automated electronic system was undertaken by the Air Force and the Massachusetts Institute of Technology's Lincoln Laboratory. About five years later, the first elements of the Semi-Automatic Ground Environment system began operations on the East Coast, and several years later, the system had been completely deployed throughout the United States.

During the 1953–1960 period, the systems analyst, programmer, and systems designer emerged, and the term "systems approach" was introduced to combat the prevailing engineers' concept that hardware was the key to a successful system. About 1960, the phrase "total systems approach" came to be used to describe the interaction of men and machines within the context of an organization in terms of specific tasks and outcomes. As a result of the pioneer military applications, there is an accelerating development of systems technology in many industrial, scientific, business, and governmental sectors as well, involving a complex, integrated organization of men and machines, ideas, procedures, and management.

Recent developments in automation suggest self-contained systems with inputs, outputs, and a mechanism of control. With the introduction of large-scale electronic data processing equipment, computerized information systems have been developed for many applications. Physical distribution systems have received increasing attention from manufacturers and shippers. Concepts of logistics have embraced systems concepts which place emphasis on the total system of material flow rather than on functions, departments, or institutions which may be involved in the processing. Attention has been focused increasingly on massive engineering projects involving weapons systems and space technology systems. For example, the functioning of the Nike-Zeus antimissile missile must be coordinated with the early warning system, ground facilities, and operating personnel into one operating, integrated weapons system. These examples could be augmented with many more to illustrate the pervasiveness of systems concepts today in many sectors of American endeavor.

A systems approach to instructional communication

In the education sector, it is becoming increasingly apparent to scientifically oriented educators that education must discard its folklore approach to instruction and move forward to new frontiers; this includes the development of instructional systems based on behavioral science theory, research, and development. As we have shown in the fourth chapter of this book, American education is operating on a primitive level of technological sophistication compared with other sectors of society. A sophisticated technological culture integrates research and development with application; a primitive culture sees little or no connection. In education today, we have a situation that produces a low level of expectation and aspiration for further technological growth. Professional organizations of teachers tend, for example, to be concerned with working conditions not much beyond the level of hand labor.

Within the educational context, the methods and media of communications, patterns of planning and utilization, and a modern logistics of instruction must be organized into instructional systems in order to secure more effective and efficient learning. If we are to cope adequately with the urgent needs and problems of education in a swiftly changing technological culture, a more systematic approach to communication and learning is vital. Because the approach to instruction hitherto has been piecemeal, the result has been a disconnected, fragmented series of innovations. What is needed are integrated, organized systems of instruction, perhaps computer-controlled, in which all components (including teachers) of the instructional process are fitted together into a system that is capable of providing individualized instruction for each learner-communicant.

The characteristics of an instructional system

The concept of an instructional system implies both a *goal*, or purpose, and interaction and/or communication between components or parts. In the case of instructional man-machine systems, the components are individual humans (teachers, learners, administrators, specialists, etc.) and the machines they control. Machines are not necessarily part of an instructional system, but when men and machines do cooperate, the result is a man-machine system. Kennedy has defined a man-machine system as an organization whose components are men and machines working together to achieve a common goal and tied together by a communications network.[1]

A systems approach to instruction implies a scientific study of the kind of instruction required by each learner, the time when it is needed, and the appropriate design, organization, and operation of a system which can achieve behavioral goals. In its broadest sense, an instructional system is a set of interrelated components (not aids or adjuncts) in mutual interaction. According to Allport it is:

> . . . any recognizably delimited aggregate of dynamic elements that are in some way interconnected and interdependent and that continue to operate together according to certain laws and in such a way as to produce some characteristic total effect. A system, in other words, is something that is concerned with some kind of activity and preserves a kind of integration and unity; and a particular system can be recognized as distinct from other systems to which, however, it may be dynamically related. Systems may be complex; they may be made up of interdependent sub-systems, each of which, though less autonomous than the entire aggregate, is nevertheless fairly distinguishable in operation.[2]

The Organismic Concept of Systems. Although much theoretical work has been done on biological systems (the living organism), no conceptual framework has been developed for describing how to combine human capabilities with machine capabilities to achieve system goals. The organismic open-system concept of the biologist Ludwig von Bertalanffy,[3] however, offers a fruitful biological analogy for systems theory. The basis of his concept is that a living organism is not a collection of separate elements but a definite system possessing organization and wholeness. An organism is an open system which maintains a constant state while matter and energy which enter it keep changing (so-called dynamic equilibrium). A central feature of the organismic outlook is its emphasis on the dynamic mutual interaction of subsystems operating as functional processes. That is, in biological terms, a total organism is a system whose behavior is influenced by a still larger

[1] John L. Kennedy, "Psychology and Systems Development," in Robert M. Gagne (ed.), *Psychological Principles in System Development.* New York, Holt, Rinehart and Winston, Inc., 1962, p. 16.
[2] F. H. Allport, *Theories of Perception and the Concept of Structure.* New York, John Wiley & Sons, Inc., 1955, p. 469.
[3] Ludwig von Bertalanffy, *Problems of Life: An Evaluation of Modern Biological Thought.* New York, John Wiley & Sons, Inc., 1952.

system—the organism-in-its-environment. Life is purposive in the sense that it maintains itself in steady states, is self-regulating, and actively explores and manipulates its environment. Life is interactive rather than reactive, and organisms exchange energy and information with their environment.

Such a description of an organismic system adequately fits the instructional setting. The instructional system is a man-made system which has a dynamic interaction with its environment—teachers, learners, instructional resources, procedures, administrators, school board, parents, local community, government, and many other agencies. Furthermore, the instructional system is a system of interrelated parts working in conjunction with each other in order to accomplish a number of goals.

Instructional System Prototypes. Modern instructional technology is moving toward the application of man-machine systems to the instructional communication process. Although a fully integrated total instructional system does not exist as yet in American education, several prototypes have been developed. One such is the Heath de Rochemont system for teaching French, *Parlons français*. Another, the Zacharias program in physics, developed earlier under the sponsorship of the Physical Science Study Committee, has some of the characteristics of a system. Currently, one can also find packaged courses of instruction built around new content and concepts, containing correlated paperback books, films, filmstrips, laboratory manuals, programed materials (in both text and machine form), tapes, and selected apparatus. Technically, however, none of these constitutes a true instructional system because all have been developed mechanistically rather than in accordance with scientific principles of instructional system design derived from behavioral science theory, research, and development.

Computer-based Information Retrieval Systems. An information retrieval system is a man-machine system that can gather, classify, and store selected data, then retrieving and disseminating this information on demand. Extrapolating from the present developments in electronic data processing, it is obvious that information retrieval systems can become important subsystems in an integrated instructional system. For example, various schools may be linked by data transmission lines to central information centers where items of information can be automatically indexed, abstracted, and coded into magnetic tape files for subsequent use. Such information centers, using machine language translators, will make it possible for individual teachers to utilize key data from the major libraries of the world. What is more, optical scanners linked to digital computers will examine, analyze, and code documentary and factual material so that it can be retrieved instantaneously and automatically disseminated.

The use of the information retrieval system in instructional systems will make it possible to individualize instruction to an extent never before thought possible. For example, computer-based independent study cubicles can provide individual assistance for the learner in reading text material, supplying research data, or arranging content in graded levels of difficulty. This system will also have the potential to provide for individual learner differences in learning rate, background, understanding, or perception. Sequences of material can be retrieved, organized, and diagnosed in terms of each individual's learning problems.

Rapid changes and the vast accumulation of knowledge in specialized areas make it difficult for the teacher to keep fully informed in his own field. The computer-based information retrieval system can assist him to bridge gaps in the information in his resource materials and to expand his own reservoir of knowledge.

The basic principles of instructional systems development

The purpose of this section is to provide a broad overview of the basic principles and considerations involved in instructional systems development. It is beyond the scope of this book to develop strategies of innovation or to do more than merely suggest the financial, administrative, or organizational requirements of instructional systems. We shall indicate the implications of the systems concept for educational change in the next section of this chapter.

There is no doubt that the movement toward the development of total instructional systems will be evolutionary rather than revolutionary. The need to develop new organizational and staffing arrangements in order to implement different types of instructional systems will pose tremendous problems for educational administration. The continuing trend toward fewer and larger school district units will undoubtedly affect the character and developmental patterns of instructional systems in the years ahead. Also, there is no doubt that instructional systems will increase the complexity and cost of instruction. Parallel trends in all kinds of governmental and municipal services place education in an increasingly competitive position for revenues. It must be recognized, however, that quality education does cost money and that it will cost even more as education moves progressively out of a nontechnological folk culture into a technological society. Despite the significance of the fiscal factor in instructional system development, agencies of the federal government and private agencies, national in scope, have been committed to exploring the implications of instructional technology and have sponsored many programs for the application of new instructional media on a large scale.

A basic assumption of the instructional system development concept in this book is that the teacher-communicator and the learner-communicants are the major components and are mutually interacting in a total communication situation. This is opposed to the theoretical notion that an instructional system is deterministic in the sense that the system is designed to change learner behavior in the desired direction by providing the right stimuli at the proper time. In this latter view, learning is nonpurposive habit formation, and habits are formed through conditioning which attaches desired responses to specific stimuli. Teachers who adopt this mechanistic approach to learning decide specifically what behavior they want learners to manifest and then proceed in a systematic manner to stimulate them in such a way as to evoke and fix those behaviors.

Any reasonably complex system, however, requires a true interaction between teachers and learners so that new understandings can be developed or old ones modified. Understandings occur when the learner pursues his purposes and sees new ways of utilizing elements of his environment, including his own bodily structure. Some way must be found, therefore, for thinking about an instructional system as a mutual interaction process in terms of system goals. The design of an instructional system which is to achieve some defined purpose requires thorough and continuous consideration of the interacting functions of all components of the system.

What we propose to do in this section is to describe in broad outline the three major stages of instructional system development. These are design, development, and evaluation (testing and operation). It must be noted that all these may be occurring simultaneously or may overlap throughout every stage of the instructional system developmental process. As the design of instructional messages becomes progressively refined for specific learner-communicants, changes may be required in either iconic or noniconic modes of communication; this in turn may create a need for different combinations of instructional media, which may call for a new instructional approach by a teacher or instructional team. Such interactions can also reveal faulty assumptions concerning the messages to be communicated, the nature of the learner, the instructional media selected, the method or procedure used, and even the goals established for the instructional system.

The Design Stage.   Davis summarizes the entire task of instructional system design in what she calls the "elemental sentence of systems design." The design sentence is "Where, when, with what, and with whom you must accomplish what, for whom, and where." [4] Instructional system design begins, therefore, with a specification of goals or purposes for the system. These goals constitute the instructional objectives to be achieved and provide the frame of reference for decisions about the functions of subsystems,

[4] Don D. Bushnell (ed.), *The Automation of School Information Systems.* Monograph 1, Washington, D.C., Department of Audiovisual Instruction, NEA, 1964, p. 126.

the major parts of the total system, and the ways in which they may be connected to fulfill system goals. From our viewpoint, learner goals and purposes stem from felt needs or tensions. In terms of the teacher-communicator, all instructional system design should be structured by a need situation. This does not imply that the whole instructional system should be based on the immediate interests and problems of learners. Although the felt needs, interests, and problems of learners need attention in any learning situation, the primary tasks of the teacher-communicator are to aid learners in formulating goals which meet their needs and to help them develop socially necessary goals.

A systematic technology of instruction cannot evolve until the important problem of instructional goal specification is satisfactorily solved. One current solution has resulted in the revival of the old division of behavior into cognitive, affective, and psychomotor. (See Benjamin S. Bloom (ed.), *Taxonomy of Educational Objectives, Handbook I, Cognitive Domain,* 1956; D. R. Krathwohl et al., *Handbook II, Affective Domain,* 1964.) This approach is unsatisfactory because it mechanistically fragments the learner and his behavior, instead of viewing him as interacting within a total communication-learning situation.

Once the purpose and function of the instructional system has been stated, the teacher-designer can proceed to describe in specific terms the nature of learners, the kind of teacher or teaching team required, the nature of instructional problem areas, nonteaching staff requirements, instructional resources, and instructional system staff functions. In essence, instructional system task descriptions will include statements describing specific teacher, learner, and environment variables constituting an instructional system. For example, some classroom environment variables might be (1) class size, (2) physical characteristics of the classroom, (3) psychological climate (permissive, authoritarian, or democratic), (4) methods or procedures and ways in which instructional media are used, (5) degree and level of participation by learners.

Teacher-communicator variables might include (1) symbolic strategies employed, (2) relationship of instructional objectives to learners, (3) amount and quality of personal contact between teacher and learner, (4) amount and quality of learner participation in classroom activities. (In an intellectually divergent climate, the learner tends to state ideas and make intellectual discoveries.)

Learner variables relevant to instructional system design may be (1) intelligence, (2) level of motivation, (3) previous experience or knowledge of subject matter being presented, (4) perceptual sets or structure of the learner.

These variables, and many more, illustrate what may be part of the content of instructional task description. Beyond these variables, there are the practical considerations of facilities, equipment, media, maximum time allowances, etc., which any instructional system design must take into account. These specifications must be described in detail so that the instructional systems designer or the group designing team can know what has to be done, what resources it has available, and the nature of the limitations involved.

Instructional task analysis, another aspect of the design stage, differs from task description in that inferences are based on a knowledge of human behavior in terms of what concepts, abilities, skills, attitudes, and understandings are required for a learner to achieve a specific instructional goal. The results of task analysis provide the means for decisions about those learner qualities that can be developed, the kind of behavior that can be facilitated by particular procedures, methods, or media, and furnish a reliable basis for the design of instructional systems.

According to Gagne, the principles of task analysis imply the following activities: (1) A task to be learned should be analyzed into component tasks which may be learned in different ways and which require different instructional practices. (2) The successful achievement of the component tasks is required for performance of a final task. (3) The component tasks have a hierarchical relationship to each other so that successful achievement of one component task is required for successful achievement of the subsequent component task. (4) This suggests that, in designing a training program, the following steps must be taken: "(a) identifying the component tasks of final performance; (b) insuring that each of these component tasks is fully achieved; and (c) arranging the total learning situation in a sequence which will insure optimal mediational effects from one component to another." [5]

The Development Stage.   Once the requirements of the instructional system have been established, the development stage can be undertaken. This includes such processes as the implementation of research on learning; the strategy of development of methods, materials, and procedures; the structuring of instructional messages (iconic and noniconic signs) within the total instructional communication system situation; and the planning, production, selection, management, and utilization of various human and machine components of the instructional system. In this stage, there may also be a concern with the selection, training, and/or development of an instructional team to bring about the most effective interaction between man-man and man-machine components in terms of achieving instructional system objectives.

The Operation and Evaluation Stage.   Once the various developmental activities have been completed, it is time to assemble the instructional system

[5] Gagne, *op. cit.*, p. 88.

as a whole and put it into operation. This process should not be done all at once but should be carried out in a series of stages. The final stages of system testing will probably take several years before it may be said to be in operational use.

Instructional system evaluation involves the systematic scientific observation and measurement of its capabilities in terms of its goals and purposes. Before an instructional system can be evaluated in a controlled environment, there must be some means of manipulating the instrumental context within which the system operates. Simulation is an important tool for this purpose. In the following pages, therefore, we shall focus our attention on the use of simulation techniques for instructional system evaluation.

In the simulation approach to evaluation, the emphasis is placed on a close resemblance to the real-life instructional communication situation. Some recent classroom simulation experiments show, for example, that a teacher can practice instruction under simulated conditions and obtain an immediate feedback concerning his teaching behavior.

Kersh (at the Center for Teaching Research in the Oregon State System of Higher Education) has reported on a classroom simulation project for student teachers.[6] A single sixth-grade classroom was simulated through the use of films and printed materials. The simulated materials included a complete set of cumulative records on each member of the class, a short description of the hypothetical school and community, and orientation films showing Mr. Land, a fictitious supervising teacher, working with his class in typical fashion. The main body of materials used in the instructional phase included a total of sixty problem sequences on film, each with alternative feedback sequences designed to show the student teacher the possible consequences of his handling of a problem. These sixty programed sequences were divided into three sets of twenty sequences (each set equaled one day) and roughly paralleled the types of problems encountered.

In the simulated classroom, the student teacher is able to practice teaching behavior with only a few observers present. Any type of practical problem in classroom management and in group or individual methods may be created. What is more, it is possible to provide the learner with immediate knowledge of the results of his actions simply by shifting from one film to another directly after he tries a certain kind of behavior. The purpose of this technique is not intended to be rigid nor is it designed to teach the learner precisely how to react to each classroom situation. Instead, the objective is to develop a learning set or perception toward a specific class of teaching problems.

Simulation studies for the education and evaluation of school administrators have been carried out under the sponsorship of the University Council

[6] Bert Y. Kersh, *Classroom Simulation: A New Dimension in Teacher Education.* Final report, NDEA Title VII Project, no. 886, U.S. Office of Education, 1963.

for Educational Administration. In a recent study, for example, an entire school setting was simulated through the use of films, tape recordings, and printed materials. The most realistic experience for the principal in this study was sitting behind a desk and dealing with problems, one at a time. The principal was required to respond to each problem and to record in great detail the type of action he would typically take. Although this study was primarily designed for the evaluation of administrators, the same materials have been used for instructional purposes.

The Systems Development Corporation (Santa Monica, California) has developed CLASS, an experimental Computer-based Laboratory for Automated School Systems, as a part of a Systems Simulation Research Laboratory. CLASS permits simultaneous automated instruction of twenty students, each of whom receives an individualized sequence of instructional materials adapted to his particular needs. Each has a manually operated film viewer containing 2,000 frames of instructional material. In addition, he has a response device, linked to the computer, which indicates the sequence of slides to be seen, enables him to respond to questions, and presents immediate knowledge of results. Provision is made for two teachers in CLASS to activate computer-generated displays showing the performance records and current progress of any learner or group of learners.

Simulation has the advantage of demonstrating to the teacher-designer what instructional system goals have been realized, as well as giving him some understanding of improvements which need to be made. Furthermore, when educational innovations are introduced in instructional systems, it can be determined in advance what the effects of changes will be and whether or not they might prove too costly or inadequate from a learning viewpoint.

The implications of the systems concept for educational change

School systems have long been relatively resistant to needed reform and change. The role of the teacher has changed little in the last century. The typical teacher with thirty learners (a few more or less) in a series of equal-sized boxes (conventional classrooms) spread out on the ground or stacked on top of each other persists as the basic unit of formal instruction. The textbook is still at the center of classroom activity and is the major determinant of curricular content.

A survey of change in New York State schools following the launching of Sputnik I is a case in point.

> The study revealed that despite the number of new programs introduced, most of the accompanying changes took place within the existing structural framework of the schools. Schools had tended to adopt new textbooks, alter the content of some traditional courses, add honors sections in some subjects, change the way they selected students for instructional groups, and accelerate the pace at which bright students

moved through a standard sequence of courses. Few innovations embodied changes in the kind of people employed, in the way they were organized to work together, in the types of instructional materials they used, or in the times and places at which they taught. In short, schools as structured institutions had remained stable.[7]

Instructional Change.   We cannot expect the systems concept to have a significant impact on instructional practices or procedures until there is less resistance to change or until new approaches to instructional method are explored. For example, solutions to learning problems cannot be found by investigating class size or grouping learners by ability. Such approaches are usually devices of administrative convenience and are often based on the assumption that there should be a stable classroom consisting of *one* teacher with *N* number of learners.

According to Hilgard, a strategy of innovation should be developed including the following steps:

> Provide (a) a sound research-based program, validated in tryout, (b) the program packaged in such a way as to be available, as in good textbooks, supplementary readings in the form of pamphlets, films, programs for teaching machines, and guides for the teacher, (c) testing materials by which it can be ascertained if the objectives of the program have indeed been realized, with appropriate normative data on these evaluative instruments, (d) in-service training of the teacher to overcome the teacher's resistance to something new and to gain his enthusiastic acceptance of the program as something valuable as well as to train him in its use, and (e) support for the program from the community, school boards, parents, and others concerned with the schools.[8]

It is obvious that we need to know more about the process of instructional change. A valuable source of guidance for instructional innovation can be found in a recent publication, *Innovation in Education,* ed. by Matthew Miles. (New York, Teachers College Press, Columbia University, 1964.)

Change in Educational Organization.   Systems concepts have a number of implications for educational organization change. Using system theory as a model, for example, Griffiths formulated the following propositions for educational organization change:

1.   The major impetus for change in organizations is from the outside.

[7] Henry M. Brickell, *Organizing New York State for Educational Change.* Albany, N.Y., State Education Department, 1961, pp. 18–19.
[8] Ernest R. Hilgard, "A Perspective on the Relationship between Learning Theory and Educational Practices," in E. R. Hilgard (ed.), *Theories of Learning and Instruction,* The Sixty-third Yearbook of the National Society for the Study of Education, part I. Chicago, The University of Chicago Press, 1964, p. 414.

2. The degree and duration of change in organizations is directly proportional to the intensity of the stimulus from the suprasystem.
3. Change in an organization is more probable if the successor to the chief administrator is from the outside of the organization than if he is from inside the organization.
4. When change in an organization does occur, it will tend to occur from the top down, not the bottom up.
5. Living systems respond to continuously increasing stress first by a lag in response, then by an over-compensatory response, and finally by catastrophic collapse of the system.
6. The number of innovations expected is inversely proportional to the tenure of the chief administrator.
7. The more hierarchical the structure of an organization, the less the possibility of change.
8. The more functional the dynamic interplay of subsystems, the less the change in an organization.[9]

In a practical operating systems approach to instruction, an educational organization in support of a system should establish the following functional arrangements: (1) a problem-posing function in which prototype, model instructional systems would be developed for experimental purposes; (2) a research and development function underlying model instructional systems, and a continuous research and development activity that would be designed to bring about innovations in instructional practice; (3) a logistical function which can support the R & D function with funds, materials, and manpower; (4) a coordinating function which can implement the problem-posing, R & D, and logistical functions. Involved in this process is the development of a technology of instruction, the modification of educational programs by research and development, and the evaluation of instruction.

In order to implement such important functions in instructional systems development, educational research and development centers will need to be established from which a technologically oriented science of instruction can emerge. The Human Resources Research Office (Hum RRO) of the Army is a practical example of such an organization.

Change in Educational Staffing. It seems imperative that the administrative or managerial functions required in instructional systems development and operation be given to a technical staff rather than to the teaching members of the system. What is more, it is important to realize that the *majority* of the instructional system staff should be nonteaching members. The nonteaching instructional system staff will assist the teaching members in specialized functions: graphic art, film and television production, photography, sec-

[9] Daniel E. Griffiths, "The Nature and Meaning of Theory," The Sixty-third Yearbook of the National Society for the Study of Education, part II, *Behavioral Science and Educational Administration.* Chicago, The University of Chicago Press, 1964, pp. 117–118.

retarial, engineering, programing, etc. Other personnel who may not be directly attached to the instructional system staff but who may render a number of valuable services to various instructional systems might include counselors, psychologists, curriculum consultants, research workers, librarians, audiovisual or communications specialists, and instructional technologists.

We have obviously implied a teacher team concept in instructional systems operation. According to Shaplin, team teaching is a type of instructional organization involving teaching personnel and the students assigned to them, in which two or more teachers, working together, are given responsibility for all, or a significant part, of the instruction of one group of students.[10]

The team concept in instructional systems development may necessitate the introduction of a personnel hierarchy into education. Although such a reorganization would change education in a revolutionary way, there is some evidence available from pilot hierarchical team teaching arrangements to suggest certain generalizations. On the whole, the evidence indicates (1) the existing corps of teachers finds it difficult to accept hierarchy before having direct experience with it; (2) veteran teachers who join hierarchical teams usually develop positive attitudes toward hierarchy, though some do not; (3) young teachers who begin their careers in hierarchical teams find hierarchy to be both helpful and desirable; (4) there is a strong relationship between the competence of the leader and the team members' feelings about the hierarchy; (5) learners, especially at the elementary level, tend to value and approve of all the members of the team regardless of their roles; and (6) competition for leadership roles does become evident in some teams, but the effect of this seems to be generally constructive rather than destructive.

If a permanent solution is to be found to the hierarchical arrangement of an instructional system team, a personnel and salary structure must be created with classification by rank or position, which can introduce order into school staffing. Also, there should be developed more highly specialized teaching assignments based on particular competences, personalities, or other important variables in the communication-learning process.

A common viewpoint among educators is that it is all right to have teacher aides or other types of assistance from nonteaching personnel as long as they are not permitted to teach. This questionable attitude carries with it the assumption that a teaching responsibility cannot be shared with anyone who is not a professional, certificated teacher. Lieberman points to situations in medical practice in which the difficult task is diagnostic, whereas the work after diagnosis may be as simple as giving a patient a pill.[11] On

---

[10] Judson Shaplin and Henry F. Olds, Jr. (eds.), *Team Teaching*. New York, Harper and Row, Publishers, Incorporated, 1964, p. 57.
[11] Myron Lieberman, *The Future of Public Education*. Chicago, The University of Chicago Press, 1960, pp. 99–100.

the other hand, there are situations in which the diagnosis is obvious even to a nurse but the action called for requires the highest levels of professional skill and judgment. In other words, one cannot say that the medical aides should never do any diagnosing or that they should never do any medicating. Lieberman draws an analogy to this situation by saying it might be very hard to diagnose a reading difficulty but relatively easy to supervise the remedial action needed once the diagnosis is clear. Obviously, whatever role a member of the instructional systems team is given, it must be appropriate to his education, experience, and skill.

part 3

background of
instructional media research

Introduction

Our purpose in Chapters 14 and 15 of this part is (1) to develop the institutional background of instructional media research, and (2) to review selected studies or research programs which, in the author's judgment, best illustrate certain historical phases of instructional media research. It is not within the scope of this book to analyze at length all those studies cited or to produce a comprehensive history of past or recent instructional media research. For this reason, many studies (perhaps most obviously a good part of the numerous investigations sponsored by the National Defense Education Act) have of necessity been excluded.

The third objective of this part is to analyze the problems and prospects of instructional technology (Chapter 16).

chapter 14

**beginnings of
instructional media research:
1918–1945**

Our purpose in this chapter is to indicate the general
background of instructional media research which has
been historically significant in the growth and development of instructional technology. Since this development
was influenced critically by instructional film and radio
research during the period 1918–1945, the focus of this
chapter will be on these areas.

Early instructional film research: prior to 1934

Although the first tests of films for instructional purposes were reported as early as 1912,[1] the first experimental studies on instructional films were those by D. R.

[1] One of the first tests was made at the Brooklyn Teachers Association. Films used were screenings of diverse theatrical subjects.

Sumstine [2] of the Pittsburgh public schools, reported in 1918, and by J. V. Lacy [3] in two New York City schools, reported in 1919. The primary value of these studies was to raise questions and stimulate further research. One notable pioneer experiment was Weber's [4] 1921 study of the comparative effectiveness of several visual aids, including the motion picture. Weber introduced pictorial tests in this study and thus became the first investigator to measure the results of learning by a pictorial medium rather than by purely verbal tests.

Thus instructional film research began in the United States near the end of World War I and has since advanced through a series of major studies subsidized by foundations, institutions of higher learning, and commercial organizations.

Johns Hopkins University Studies. The first large-scale instructional film research was undertaken in 1919 when a grant of $6,600 was made by the United States Interdepartmental Social Hygiene Board to the psychological laboratory of Johns Hopkins University "for the purpose of assisting the laboratory in investigating the informational and educative effect upon the public of certain motion pictures used in various campaigns for the control, repression and elimination of venereal diseases." [5] The study was conducted by Karl S. Lashley and John B. Watson under the supervision of an advisory board consisting of Adolph Meyer, S. I. Franz, and R. S. Woodworth.

The film selected for study was *Fit to Win*, a six-reel, 35-mm film prepared from the World War I version, *Fit to Fight*. In the experiment, the film was shown to approximately five thousand persons. Results were tested by questionnaires on the informational and emotional effects of the film and by interviews with thirty-five men, from six to eighteen months after the film showing. Pretests on venereal disease information were obtained from approximately 425 persons, and posttests were obtained from 1,230 persons of the various audiences to whom the film was shown in the experiment. The experimental population included a medical group, an executive and clerical group, a group of literary clubwomen, a mixed audience of male and female youths and adults, and separate groups of male streetcar company employees, merchant sailors, and soldiers.

Results indicated that the film was found to be effective in disseminating information on venereal disease, but they also indicated that a single film

[2] David R. Sumstine, "A Comparative Study of Visual Instruction in the High School," *School and Society*, vol. 7 (February, 1918), pp. 235–238.
[3] J. V. Lacy, "The Relative Value of Motion Pictures as an Educational Agency," *Teachers College Record*, vol. 20 (1919), pp. 452–465.
[4] Joseph J. Weber, "Comparative Effectiveness of Some Visual Aids in Seventh Grade Instruction," *Educational Screen*, vol. 1 (1922).
[5] K. S. Lashley and J. B. Watson, *A Psychological Study of Motion Pictures in Relation to Venereal Disease Campaigns*. Washington, D.C., U.S. Interdepartmental Social Hygiene Board, 1922, p. 3.

may not be effective in bringing about any basic changes in attitudes or behavior.

The Lashley-Watson study is a classic because it anticipated many of the conceptualizations rediscovered or formulated since. For example, the observation by Lashley and Watson that learning from films varies in amount with audience characteristics has only recently come to be appreciated. Moreover, their analytic study of the variables of film treatment antedate many of the theoretical formulations made in later years.

The University of Chicago Experiments.   The University of Chicago experiments (sometimes called the Freeman-Commonwealth research) was the first major instructional media program supported by an institution outside the mainstream of instructional technology.

The origin of the University of Chicago experiments can be traced to a 1920 conversation between Frank N. Freeman, professor of educational psychology at the University of Chicago, and F. Dean McClusky, a graduate student there. Freeman had been impressed by the possibilities of the film as an instructional medium and felt that a systematic study should be made to determine its educational potential. He suggested such a study to McClusky as a doctor's thesis. Freeman then approached the Society for Visual Education (a commercial instructional film production company established in Chicago in 1919) with the request that they assist the McClusky study by supplying some of their films for experimental purposes. Although the society supplied fourteen films, it soon became apparent that the McClusky proposal would warrant additional support. Therefore Freeman contacted the Commonwealth Fund of New York which, on April 1, 1922, granted $10,000 to the University of Chicago for the McClusky study and a series of additional studies, all of which became known as the Freeman-Commonwealth Study.

The University of Chicago experiments were conducted under the direction of Frank N. Freeman in eight school systems, involving over five thousand students, for a period of three years.[6] The final report, *Visual Education*, was published by the University of Chicago Press in 1924. The University of Chicago study "gives no support to the belief that pictures may be substituted for language. It does indicate, however, that they have a definite function to perform. This function is determined by the nature and purpose of the instruction."[7] Moreover, "the relative effectiveness of verbal instruction as contrasted with the various forms of concrete experience . . . depends on two major conditions: the nature of the instruction to be given, and the character of the pupils' previous acquaintance with the objects which are

[6] The investigators were F. Dean McClusky, H. W. James, E. H. Reeder, A. P. Hollis, Caroline Hoefer, Edna Keith, Howard Y. McClusky, E. C. Rolfe, Lena A. Shaw, D. E. Walker, Nina J. Beglinger, and Jean A. Thomas.
[7] Frank N. Freeman, *Visual Education*. Chicago, The University of Chicago Press, 1924, p. 79.

dealt with in the instruction." [8] These studies also showed that "the usefulness of motion pictures would be enhanced if they were so organized as to
confine themselves to their peculiar province. Their province seems to be the
exhibition of moving objects and particularly to facilitate the analysis of
motion. They are outside their province when they show still objects or when
they enter the field of abstract verbal discussion. They cannot compete, in
these respects, with still pictures and with the teacher." [9] Thus, it was recommended that "subject matter should not be included in educational films
which is not primarily the representation of motion or action" and "it is
probably desirable to have motion picture films in small units. [10] It is evident
from these and other concepts that the University of Chicago experiments
contributed some important theoretical insights concerning the function of
the instructional film. However, these insights were largely ignored and were
not rediscovered until almost two decades later (for example, the recent
development of the single-concept film).

The Eastman Experiment.   The history of the Eastman experiment began
with the establishment of the Judd Committee by the National Education
Association in 1922, for the purpose of collecting data on the production
and distribution of instructional films. We have seen that the Motion Picture
Producers and Distributors of America, Inc. (MPPDA), granted this com-
mittee $5,000 in 1923 to carry on the investigation under the chairmanship of
Charles H. Judd, chairman of the School of Education, University of
Chicago.

In the process of carrying out this investigation, the Judd Committee
applied to a number of film concerns, including the Eastman Kodak Company, for information about instructional films. Thus the Eastman Kodak
Company became aware of the interest of educators and decided to launch
their own investigation of the existing status of instructional films and the
probable market for new ones. Much of the data collected by F. Dean
McClusky in his 1923 national survey of visual education for the National
Education Association was utilized by Eastman, but they also conducted a
survey of their own. Simultaneously, Eastman began the production of a
few pilot instructional films.

The outcome of the Eastman investigation became known in February,
1926, when George Eastman wrote the following letter to Will H. Hays,
president of the Motion Picture Producers and Distributors Association of
America:

> For the last three years, the Eastman Kodak Company has been
> making a survey of the use of motion pictures in teaching as a supple-

[8] *Ibid.*, p. 69.
[9] *Ibid.*, pp. 77–78.
[10] *Ibid.*, p. 79.

ment to textbooks, to find out what has been done and what promise there was of future sound development. Such films were not practicable until an easily operated projector and economical films were available to schools. We believe that these two problems have been solved by the Kodascope and our new standard narrow width film.

The survey led us to the conclusion that very little had been accomplished in producing teaching films suitable for classroom use and that there was little prospect of any organization with the necessary resources attempting to solve the problem. Therefore, after full consideration, *the company has decided to approach the solution of this problem in an experimental way. It proposes to make a number of teaching films closely correlated with selected courses and in accordance with a definite educational plan. These films will be prepared with the advice and assistance of competent educators and will be put into a limited number of representative schools in different cities for trial in their classrooms* [italics mine]. As the work of production goes on, the company will thus have definite information as to whether the right sort of films are being made.

In making this announcement the company wants it to be clearly understood that it will have no apparatus or films for sale to schools during this experimental period, which will take about two years. Any future developments will be determined by the success of these experiments. The company leaves itself free to discontinue this undertaking if at any time it feels that there are unsurmountable obstacles to its success.[11]

In March, 1926, George Eastman invited a group of educators to Rochester, New York, for the purpose of revealing the details of his film production plans and to obtain their support.[12] A few months later, in September, 1926, Thomas E. Finegan, commissioner of public instruction for Pennsylvania, was asked by Eastman to become director of the instructional film production project.

When Finegan assumed his duties, a few more than twenty films were already under way. Ten were planned on geography, five each on health and general science, one on the life of a New England fisherman, and one to show the effect of iron on the industrial progress of the United States. In addition, more than thirty other instructional films were planned for the

[11] George Eastman, letter to Will H. Hays, Feb. 17, 1926.
[12] Those who attended the Eastman meeting were Thomas E. Finegan of Harrisburg, Pennsylvania; John H. Finley, of the *New York Times* and member of the board of directors of Harmon's Religious Film Foundation; Payson Smith, Massachusetts commissioner of education; Mary Pennell, Columbia University; Otis Caldwell, principal of Lincoln School of Teachers College, Columbia University, and member of the board of directors of the Society for Visual Education; William A. McAndrew, superintendent of Chicago public schools; Howard Burge, principal of Fredonia New York State Normal School; and from Rochester, Herbert S. West, superintendent of schools, Charles E. Finch, director of vocational schools, and Mabel Simpson, supervisor of primary grades.

fall of 1927. To prepare their content, selected teachers came to Rochester during the summer months to serve as consultants and to review each stage of the productions. The technical supervision of these films was done by Herford Tynes Cowling, well-known producer of travelogues.

By early 1928, the Eastman Kodak Company had produced the first comprehensive series of instructional silent films. Eastman Teaching Films, Inc., was established the same year with Thomas E. Finegan as president and general manager. Finegan remained with Eastman until he died in November, 1932.

In February, 1928, the experimental phase began. Ben D. Wood, director of the Bureau of Collegiate Educational Research, Columbia University, and Frank N. Freeman of the University of Chicago were asked to serve as codirectors of the Eastman teaching film experiment. The investigation was extensive: it included twelve cities in widely separated areas of the United States,[13] nearly eleven thousand students and two hundred teachers, in grade levels four to nine. From February to May of 1928, twenty instructional films were integrated into two 12-week units in geography and general science. The films and textbooks for these units were designed especially for the experiment. The units of instruction were carefully outlined and taught alike in similar classes; except for one control group of classes, the instruction utilized films. The teachers of the control groups were encouraged to use any other instructional media that seemed appropriate. The relative effectiveness of the two methods of instruction was measured by objective tests. Comprehensive examinations were given to all the students at the beginning and at the end of the experiment.

The general conclusion by members of the Eastman teaching film experiment was that the instructional film had an enormous educational potential in the classroom. Wood and Freeman emphasized that "the casual introduction of films into the curriculum without careful organization is of comparatively little value. Insofar as possible, a classroom film should always be used for some definite and particular purpose. It should be a necessary link in the chain of development of the subject. It should constitute the necessary basis for the understanding, by the pupil, of the phases of the topic which follow, and a clarifying of those that have preceded." [14] Wood and Freeman concluded, "If we examine the average gains made by the entire group of children in all cities and on topics taken together, we find that the X group excelled the C group by a substantial and significant margin." [15]

---

[13] The cities participating in the Eastman teaching film experiment were the following: Newton, Massachusetts; Rochester, New York; New York, New York; Winston-Salem, North Carolina; Atlanta, Georgia; Detroit, Michigan; Chicago, Illinois; Lincoln, Nebraska; Kansas City, Missouri; Denver, Colorado; Oakland, California; and San Diego, California.
[14] Ben D. Wood and Frank N. Freeman, *Motion Pictures in the Classroom*. Boston, Houghton Mifflin Company, 1929, p. 223.
[15] *Ibid.*, pp. 214–215.

An unpublished critique by McClusky makes this quite different assessment of the Eastman teaching film experiment:

> When I first approached this book [*Motion Pictures in the Classroom* by Ben D. Wood and Frank N. Freeman] it was with the belief that here was a new contribution to visual education. I have a genuine interest in the use of the motion picture in teaching and believe it has value and a place of worth in the educative process. Furthermore, the reviewer believes that the Eastman Kodak Company (has) done a service to education to show a concrete constructive interest in motion pictures for instruction. My first reading of *Motion Pictures in the Classroom* brought a feeling of anxious questioning, this later turned to disappointment. . . .
>
> A mistake has been made to attempt classroom experimentation for a few weeks on a "big" scale and to deal with mass statistics on the assumption that discrepancies in experimental technique may be ironed out in the general results. As an example of scientific experimentation in teaching this book will find a place as an illustration of how *not* to do research in education. . . .
>
> I feel that propaganda has no place in visual instruction or in any type of instruction dressed up in the clothes of experimental and statistical procedure. In the future, "research" of this sort should be avoided.[16]

Despite the questionable experimental procedures illustrated by the Eastman experiment, it did provide the impetus for the expanding use of the instructional film in many areas. For example, much of the initial stimulus of the audiovisual movement in California came from this experiment, with the San Diego County audiovisual agency as a concrete result.

Yale University Studies.   At about the same time that the Eastman Kodak Company was producing silent instructional films, Yale University was producing a series of silent instructional films known as the *Chronicles of America Photoplays.* Beginning in November, 1927, and ending in June, 1928, Daniel C. Knowlton and J. Warren Tilton, of the Yale faculty, undertook to discover whether these films could aid in the teaching of seventh-grade history. The plan of the experiment involved 15 classes, 521 pupils, and 6 teachers. In teaching the control group, the teachers used textbooks, maps, and other instructional media, with the exception of motion pictures. Objective tests were designed to show (1) the amount of time saved by the use of films; (2) the amount of factual historical knowledge obtained by the pupil; and (3) pupil attitudes toward the subject matter of history. Knowlton and Tilton's experimental design showed rare insight by including problems which involved a knowledge of time relationships, historical relationships, and the influence of personages on historical events. The design

[16] F. Dean McClusky, "An Experiment with School Films." Unpublished manuscript, 1929, p. 15.

also incorporated a rather rare experimental approach in which the effects of films on class discussion were investigated. Eight classes were selected for observation by three experienced observers who recorded the number of hands raised in response to teaching questions as well as the responses and questions of the pupils themselves. From three to seven months after the experimental instruction had been given in the various courses of study, delayed-recall tests were given.

The general results of this study were as follows:

1. The ten photoplays made a large contribution to the teaching of an enriched course of study, increasing the pupil's learning by about 19 per cent.
2. This contribution was of such magnitude that average children with the aid of photoplays learned as much as bright children did without them.
3. The increase in the total number of pupil participations attributable to the use of the photoplays was 10 per cent.[17]

In closing the account of their investigation, Knowlton and Tilton make this very important point:

> The ability of the pupils to grasp and appreciate these relationships was in no small degree determined by the teacher's own interest in them and the emphasis which she attached to them. However inherently effective the photoplays may be—and the evidence submitted here indicates the potentialities of such material—it will only attain its highest degree of effectiveness when accompanied by good teaching, based on the appreciation of the real goal to be attained and of the capacity of this material to contribute to its attainment. The teacher has at her command an instrument which, as these results indicate, will go far toward economizing her time and effort and stimulating her pupils to secure those abiding values inherent in this vital subject.[18]

While the Eastman experiment was extensive, the Knowlton and Tilton investigation was intensive. Also, in contrast to the Eastman experiment, Knowlton and Tilton devised more scientific methods for securing their basic data.[19]

Instructional Media Research to 1930. Weber summarized the instructional media research completed up to 1930 as follows:

> It should be pointed out that the usefulness of visual aids—films, slides, stereographs, and other realia—is specific: that is, the usefulness of any

[17] D. C. Knowlton and J. W. Tilton, *Motion Pictures in History Teaching.* New Haven, Conn., Yale University Press, 1929, p. 90.
[18] *Ibid.,* p. 91.
[19] Yale University sponsored another study based on the *Chronicles of America Photoplays* in 1938 which proved to be a valuable supplement to the Knowlton and Tilton studies. See H. A. Wise, *Motion Pictures as an Aid in Teaching American History.* New Haven, Conn., Yale University Press, 1939.

one visual aid varies with every topic or project. Visual aids are supplementary to actual experience, and both are fundamental to verbal instruction. Visual aids thus provide perceptual foundations where actual experience is lacking and enable verbal instruction to transmute these into conceptual products through the processes of interpretation, integration, and generalization. This truth being self-evident, there is no further need for experimentation of the kind discussed (over 30 experiments conducted during the 1920's). . . . Future research must progress into areas of specification and application.[20]

Weber went on to name a number of unsolved research problems. He suggested, for example, that research studies should be conducted to determine "the optimum length and content of informational films for the use of classroom teachers." [21] He would also have the researcher analyze and evaluate the factor of animation in motion pictures and have him "go into the problem of individual differences as well as into the matter of interrelationships between animation and other psychological factors." [22] In both of these suggestions for research it can be seen that Weber anticipated the contemporary approaches to instruction and the study of which media characteristics provide desirable conditions for learning.

Carnegie Foundation Study.   One of the first serious attempts to investigate the educational potential of sound instructional films was made by the Harvard Film Foundation and the Harvard Graduate School of Education under the sponsorship of the Carnegie Foundation for the Advancement of Teaching. This study, conducted by P. J. Rulon [23] in 1932, dealt with the contributions of films and textbooks which, except for two films, were specially designed and produced by the Harvard Film Foundation to include specific subject-matter content so as to meet specific instructional objectives.

The results of this study showed a significant increase in informational and conceptual learning when films are used in combination with textbooks.[24]

Payne Fund Studies.   The first comprehensive, careful studies which dealt with the effects of theatrical films on the cognitive and affective learning of children were the Payne Fund studies, made during a four-year period

[20] J. J. Weber, *Visual Aids in Education.* Valparaiso, Ind., Valparaiso University, 1930, p. 195.
[21] *Ibid.*, p. 209.
[22] *Ibid.*, p. 199.
[23] P. J. Rulon, *The Sound Motion Picture in Science Teaching.* Cambridge, Mass., Harvard University Press, 1933.
[24] Other notable studies of the instructional sound film made during the early thirties include the following: V. C. Arnspiger, *Measuring the Effectiveness of Sound Pictures as Teaching Aids,* Teachers College Contributions to Education, no. 565, New York, Teachers College Press, Columbia University, 1933; and C. C. Clark, *Sound Pictures as an Aid in Classroom Teachings.* Unpublished doctoral dissertation, New York University, New York, 1932.

(1929–1932). These studies, supervised by W. W. Charters of Ohio State University, were made by professors and their associates from several major institutions of higher learning.[25]

The history of the investigations is brief. In 1928 William H. Short, executive director of the Motion Picture Research Council (which had been formed in 1927 to gather factual evidence against the motion picture industry for the purpose of replacing the Hays Office), invited a group of behavioral scientists and educators to confer with the council about the possibility of discovering what effect theatrical motion pictures have on children. When these men proposed a research study, Short appealed to the Payne Fund for a grant. He found the foundation receptive because the Payne Fund itself had formed a National Committee for the Study of Social Values, in 1927, to secure factual data regarding motion pictures on the basis of which a national policy, socially constructive in character, could be formulated. Thus the proposal of Short gave the Payne Fund an opportunity to implement its stated policy with reference to theatrical motion pictures.

The distinctive technique used in the Payne Fund studies was to analyze a complex social problem into a series of subordinate problems, to select competent investigators to work on each of the subordinate projects, and to integrate the findings of all the investigators into a solution of the initial problem.

The basic approach used in these studies was to assemble data in answer to a series of questions. For example, the council asked, "What is the amount of knowledge gained and retained from motion pictures by children of various ages and the types of knowledge most likely to be thus gained and retained?"[26] The council also wanted to know "the extent to which motion pictures influence the conduct of children and youth either in desirable or undesirable directions and particularly in regard to patterns of sex behavior."[27] What effect motion pictures had on the attitudes of children toward significant social concepts and on the standards and ideals of children was also a matter of concern to the council. The council wished to know the effect of motion pictures on the emotions and health of children; the number and ages of children who attended motion picture theaters; the frequency with which they made their visits; and what could be done to teach children to discriminate between good and poor films. The council

[25] Members of the Committee on Educational Research were as follows: L. L. Thurstone, Frank N. Freeman, R. E. Park, Herbert Blumer, and Philip M. Hauser of the University of Chicago; George D. Stoddard, C. A. Ruckmick, P. W. Holaday, and Wendell Dysinger of the University of Iowa; Mark A. May and Frank K. Shuttleworth of Yale University; Frederick M. Thrasher and Paul G. Cressey of New York University; Charles C. Peters of Pennsylvania State College; Ben D. Wood of Columbia University; and Samuel Renshaw, Edgar Dale, and W. W. Charters of Ohio State University.
[26] W. W. Charters, *Motion Pictures and Youth.* New York, The Macmillan Company, 1935, p. vi.
[27] *Loc. cit.*

also raised a number of questions concerning the effect of theatrical films on the standards of American life. Finally, the investigators sought to find data, but could not, to prove that the onset of puberty is or is not affected by motion pictures.

The studies fell into two broad groups: one, to measure the effect of motion pictures, as such, on children and youth; the other, to study theatrical film content and children's attendance at commercial theaters. In measuring the effect of films on children, the studies were focused on five areas—information, attitudes, emotions, health, and conduct. On the basis of what was discovered to be the effect of motion pictures in these five areas, it became possible to measure the influence of theatrical motion pictures on children by ascertaining what they see when they attend the theaters and how often they go.

In reviewing the Payne Fund studies, Charters concluded the following:

> The motion picture, as such, is a potent medium of education. Children, even of the early age of eight, see half the facts in a picture and remember them for a surprisingly long time. A single exposure to a picture may produce a measurable change in attitude. Emotions are measurably stirred as the scenes of a drama unfold and this excitement may be recorded in deviations from the norm in sleep patterns, by visible gross evidences of bodily movement and by refined internal responses. They constitute patterns of conduct in daydreaming, phantasy, and action.
>
> Second, for children the content of current pictures is not good. There is too much sex and crime and love for a balanced diet for children.
>
> Third, the motion-picture situation is very complicated. It is one among many influences which mold the experience of children. How powerful this is in relation to the influence of the ideals taught in the home, in the school, and in the church, by street life and companions or by community customs, these studies have not canvassed.[28]

The Payne Fund studies are relevant today because many of the theatrical films evaluated in these studies, together with similar films, have now been shown repeatedly throughout the United States on television. In view of the massive evidence contained in the twelve-volume report of the Payne Fund studies, the contention by broadcast industry spokesmen that little is definitely known about the effects of television viewing on children is not justified, at least where old Hollywood films are concerned.

Although the Payne Fund studies stimulated a short-lived motion picture appreciation movement in the schools in the middle 1930s, they appear to have had little influence on the function and use of the theatrical motion picture in formal instruction. These studies were, however, a precursor to

[28] *Ibid.*, pp. 60–61.

modern communication research, constituting the first systematic studies of mass media tied to a concrete operational problem.

Motion Picture Project of the American Council on Education

Probably the most significant project in instructional technology during the 1930s was the Motion Picture Project of the American Council on Education. The experiences of this project generated insights and theories of instruction which pointed the way to instructional approaches and techniques that were to set, almost totally, the pattern for the instructional programs of the U.S. Office of Education and the Armed Forces during World War II.

Background.   The germinal concepts underlying the Motion Picture Project were first given expression when George F. Zook, United States Commissioner of Education, deeply impressed by the recent findings of the Payne Fund studies, decided there was a need to harness this powerful medium for the purposes of education. Zook knew that, despite the demonstrated power of film in influencing information, attitudes, conduct, and emotions of children and young adults, use of the motion picture had been unorganized and neglected in the nation's schools and in educational agencies. For example, Koon had reported in 1934 that less than 10 percent of the nation's public schools made systematic use of the motion picture for instruction. What is more, there was no responsible agency to which these schools could turn for accurate information on films, equipment, and allied questions; there was a lack of educationally worthwhile films; a comprehensive distribution system did not exist; and cumbersome, expensive, 35-mm silent projectors predominated.[29] It was true that some commercial organizations (the Eastman Kodak Company, for example) and a few educational organizations (Department of Visual Instruction of the NEA) had attempted to solve these problems; but they had failed either because they misunderstood the needs of educators, or because they had not sufficiently equipped themselves for the task, or for both reasons.

During the summer of 1933, the U.S. Office of Education was invited to report to, and participate in, the International Congress on Educational and Instructional Cinematography to be held in Rome in April, 1934, under the auspices of the International Institute of Educational Cinematography.[30] Soon after this invitation, Zook called a conference on September 25, 1933,

[29] Cline M. Koon, *Motion Pictures in Education in the United States.* U.S. Department of the Interior Bulletin 130, 1934, p. 43.
[30] The International Institute of Cinematography was founded in 1928 in Rome, Italy, by the Committee on Intellectual Cooperation of the League of Nations. Its principal activity was the publication of a periodical—*International Review of Educational Cinematography*, later called the *Intercine.*

of thirty-five representatives of universities, city school systems, motion picture producers and distributors, equipment manufacturers, educational organizations, and governmental agencies to consider whether the United States should participate in the Congress. It was agreed that the United States should make a report, and Cline M. Koon, Senior Specialist in Radio and Visual Education of the U.S. Office of Education, was given the task of compiling the so-called Rome report.

By reason of the intensified work being done in connection with the Rome report, Zook began to see the need for some type of national cooperative organization which could provide leadership in utilizing the full educational potential of the motion picture. About this time, Lorraine Noble, a Hollywood scenario writer and long-time advocate of the educational film who had also been strongly influenced by the Payne Fund studies, conferred with Zook and Koon and volunteered her services for the development of a national educational film institute. By January, 1934, Miss Noble had prepared the first outline for the institute.

Also, during March, 1934, Cline Koon completed the Rome report, now entitled *Motion Pictures in Education in the United States* and sent it to the International Institute of Educational Cinematography in Rome. The last two paragraphs of this report are significant:

(d)   A strong national film institute is needed in the United States.

In comparison with the theatrical motion picture, the non-theatrical picture in the past usually lacked technical excellence, is used comparatively little, and with varying regularity. Many agencies have pioneered in the development of the educational film, but the result in the United States today is chaotic and disorganized. The principal reasons for this condition seem to be the past policy of the Federal Government to leave to private industry and voluntary endeavor many activities that the typical European government would assume, and the educational system of the country which is not centralized in the Federal Government, but, in the main, is left to each of the 48 States. Private industry is dead-locked over the fact that producers cannot afford to make films until a sufficient number of projectors is sold to make the work profitable, and the projector concerns cannot sell their apparatus because there is no comprehensive library of suitable films available for their use.

Commendable efforts are being made in many places to overcome these difficulties, but there is a great need for a national film institution (1) to assemble, edit, classify, publicize, and catalog non-theatrical film material, and to set up a convenient and economical distribution system; and (2) to produce and stimulate the production and effective utilization of educational films. An entire nation seeks enlightenment—courage to look for-

ward and inspiration to work for the new social order wherein
every human being would have the chance to enjoy living and
working. The education of tomorrow should give a new appreciation of leisure and its usefulness and a new sense of citizen-
ship and cooperation. The vast potentialities of the use of motion
pictures in the nation's education are only beginning to be generally recognized.[31]

Shortly after the Koon report was published, Zook persuaded Secretary
of State Cordell Hull to appoint an American delegation to the Rome Congress. Thus for the first time in American history, the United States
officially participated in an international meeting concerned with instructional films.

The American delegation was active throughout the sessions of the
Rome Congress. W. W. Charters (director of the Payne Fund studies), as
vice-president of the Congress, helped shape its policies and projects; C. F.
Hoban, Sr., director, State Museum and Visual Education, Pennsylvania State
Department of Public Instruction, and Paul B. Mann, head of the biology
department, Evander Childs High School, New York City, made useful contributions concerning the school use of films; Chester A. Linstrom, associate
chief, Office of Motion Pictures, U.S. Department of Agriculture, contributed
to the discussions on the use of films in agricultural education; Carl E. Milliken, secretary of the Motion Picture Producers and Distributors of America,
Inc., assembled and delivered examples of American educational films; and
Cline M. Koon served as chairman of the American delegation and spoke
at the opening and closing sessions of the Congress.

The importance of the Congress for American instructional technology
was extremely significant. First of all, it gave the members of the American
delegation a tremendous insight into the production, distribution, and use of
instructional films in European countries. Second, it left the vivid impression
that the United States educational establishment was backward in its utilization of the film medium for instructional purposes and for influencing attitudes and behavior. In a letter to Secretary of State Cordell Hull, W. W.
Charters gave perhaps the clearest statement of the implications of the
Congress for instructional technology:

> The influence of both recreational and educational films is amaz-
> ing. In 30 years they have become more influential in distributing ideas,
> patterns of conduct and the like than printing has been able to achieve
> in 400 years. Their concreteness, dramatic power and simplicity of
> presentation make them understandable by the masses to a degree that
> reading can never attain. This conviction is based upon the research
> studies of the Payne Fund—and on the accumulated practical ex-

[31] Koon, *op. cit.*, pp. 43–44.

perience of European experts assembled at the Cinema Congress in Rome. . . .

That this power may be utilized equally in raising the ideals and culture of a nation or in debasing them is entirely clear. Attitudes toward races may be powerfully directed toward either a better understanding or increased hostility. Fact and error are indiscriminately accepted by audiences. . . .

The European peoples with their canny recognition of realities have caught the vision of the cultural and political possibilities of the motion picture. . . . in many European countries the educational film, which is indistinctly separated from the recreational film, has become the matter of persistent attention. This interest is widespread among twenty or more nations. . . .

People in the United States have not yet caught the vision of the place of the motion picture in American civilization. . . .

The United States should study authoritatively and in statesman-like fashion the place of motion pictures in our culture, formulate the factors to be considered and work toward solutions in accordance with the temperament of our people.

To this end I make the proposal that the Office of Education be given the responsibility of assembling persons under governmental auspices and representing the Government, the public, the university, the schools and other appropriate agencies to study the problem in all its bearings, and that to this end it secure preferably from Congress or possibly from a foundation, a modest appropriation to provide for meetings, a collection of necessary data and the publication of conclusions. . . .

The study herein proposed is merely the first step of a historical series.[32]

Meanwhile, Zook was also convinced that a study should be made but took no immediate action because he was leaving his position as United States Commissioner of Education to assume the presidency of the American Council on Education in June, 1934. In this new capacity, he went to work at once on the implications of the Charters report, visiting the British Film Institute in London, and conferring with representatives of the Swiss, French, and other European educational film organizations. On his return to the United States, Zook brought before the Problems and Plans Committee of the council a project which had as its objective the establishment of the most appropriate type of organization to act as a national clearing house for instructional films. In October, 1934, Zook was authorized to formulate a proposal for foundation financing which would result in the organization of a film institute. In the meantime, the Payne Fund made a grant to carry on the preliminary work and Zook asked Miss Noble to continue with her services in connection with this activity of the council.

[32] Quoted in *ibid.*, pp. 7–9.

Within the next few months, Zook called two conferences with selected educational leaders for the purpose of considering the establishment and organization of a national film institute.[33] At the first conference, held on December 4–5, 1934, at the American Council on Education in Washington, D.C., the following objectives were framed:

1. To develop a national appreciation of the potential contribution of the motion picture to the cultural life of America.
2. To collect and distribute significant information concerning motion pictures in education, at home and abroad.
3. To stimulate the production and use of motion pictures for educational purposes.
4. To promote the cooperation of all agencies interested in the production and use of motion pictures in education.
5. To initiate and promote research pertaining to motion pictures and allied visual and auditory aids in education.[34]

In addition, a number of activities were planned to be carried out by staff members of the council and cooperating groups. Among them were the following:

1. A budget was to be prepared for submission to a foundation.
2. A series of conferences with various motion picture industry groups was to be held; one with the equipment industry, another with producers, another with the representatives of the motion picture theaters.
3. All of the leading educational associations were to be interviewed.
4. The form or organization, the charter and constitution, were to be worked out.
5. A document describing the proposed institute and its aims was to be prepared.[35]

The entire direction of the project was left in the hands of George F. Zook, with Lorraine Noble as assistant director.

The second conference to consider a national film institute was held on February 28 and March 1, 1935, at the American Council on Education in Washington, D.C. More than one hundred educational organizations had

[33] Persons attending the first conference to consider a national film institute were the following: Chancellor S. P. Capen, University of Buffalo, Buffalo, New York; William P. Farnsworth, National Recovery Act Administrator, Washington, D.C.; Superintendent Vierling Kersey, California State Department of Education, Sacramento, California; Superintendent C. H. Lake, Cleveland public schools, Cleveland, Ohio; Mrs. B. F. Langsworthy, president, National Congress of Parents and Teachers; Cline M. Koon, U.S. Office of Education; Lorraine Noble, American Council on Education; Henry B. Ward, American Association for the Advancement of Science; W. W. Charters, professor of education, Ohio State University; and George F. Zook, president, American Council on Education.
[34] *Minutes of Conference to Consider Establishment of a National Film Institute*, Washington, D.C., Dec. 4–5, 1934.
[35] *Loc. cit.*

already been contacted by Miss Noble, and all opinions favored the establishment of a film institute. Thus it was decided that immediate steps should be taken for the organization and financing of the institute, and a committee was formed for the purpose which consisted of the following: W. W. Charters, Edgar Dale, C. F. Hoban, Sr., Cline M. Koon, Levering Tyson, and George F. Zook, ex-officio.[36]

After receiving the approval of the Problems and Plans Committee of the council, Zook submitted the first formal proposal for a national educational film institute to the General Education Board of the Rockefeller Foundation in May, 1935, for the purpose of obtaining a supporting grant.[37]

Initiation of Studies on the Use of Instructional Films.   While the council was awaiting the decision of the General Education Board concerning its application, it decided that the incorporation of the institute should be postponed until the most appropriate form for its organization became clearer. A number of ground-clearing projects were therefore presented to the General Education Board with the suggestion that these be carried to completion before the actual financing and launching of the film institute was undertaken. A document entitled "Proposed Studies Relating to the Use of Films in Education," calling for five "interim projects" and a budget of $12,500, was submitted to the General Education Board and a grant made for such projects in June, 1935.[38]

The first of the five interim projects began in the fall of 1935. Interim Project No. 1, dealing with sports films, was assigned to Gladys Palmer of Ohio State University.[39] Interim Project No. 2 resulted in the publication *Teaching with Motion Pictures: A Handbook of Administrative Practices* by Edgar Dale and Lloyd Ramseyer, in April, 1937.[40] Interim Project No. 3 was devoted to the preparation of a bibliography of literature in the instructional film field. The digest of this work was published by the H. W. Wilson Company in a volume entitled *Motion Pictures in Education.* Interim Project

---

[36] *Minutes of Second Conference to Consider Establishment of a National Film Institute,* Feb. 28 and Mar. 1, 1935, Washington, D.C.

[37] One of the first proposals for a national educational film institute was probably made by George A. Skinner in his 1925 Schoolmaster Plan. His plan called for (1) a thorough piece of research into the social value of the motion picture; (2) a noncommercial independent clearinghouse for the gathering and disseminating of information concerning the social and educational use of the motion picture; and (3) a commercial company operated solely for the production and distribution of the teaching film.

[38] An Interim Committee, consisting of George F. Zook, Edgar Dale, Cline M. Koon, Robert A. Kissack, Jr., and Lorraine Noble, was formed in July, 1935, for the purpose of supervising the studies under this grant.

[39] Gladys E. Palmer, "A Motion Picture Survey in the Field of Sports for College Women," *The Research Quarterly of the American Association for Health, Physical Education, and Recreation,* vol. 7 (March, 1936), pp. 166–167.

[40] Edgar Dale and Lloyd L. Ramseyer, *Teaching with Motion Pictures: A Handbook of Administrative Practices.* Washington, D.C., American Council on Education Studies, ser. 2, no. 2, April, 1937.

No. 4 resulted in the preparation of a catalog of instructional films. Interim Project No. 5 was a survey of audiovisual equipment in the public schools of the United States.

Interim Project No. 3 was originally started by Lorraine Noble, with the assistance of Fannie Dunn, Robert A. Kissack, Jr., Charles F. Hoban, Jr., and Alice Keliher. The intent was to build a central library in Washington, D.C., consisting of reference books and annotated literature concerned with instructional films. During the spring and summer of 1936, two lengthy volumes of digests, prepared mainly by Fannie Dunn and Etta Schneider, were issued in experimental form by the council. About five hundred of these two digests were distributed to educators throughout the country.[41]

Interim Project No. 4 was assigned to Lorraine Noble and developed in cooperation with the U.S. Office of Education and the H. W. Wilson Company (a publishing firm). More than eighteen hundred film sources were located and, for the first time, a large body of information on all existing educational films was collected in one central place. Moreover, for the first time a uniform system of film classification was developed.[42] As a result of this work, the first comprehensive educational film catalog was published in 1936.[43]

Interim Project No. 5 was first assigned to Robert A. Kissack, Jr., to be administered from the University of Minnesota, for the purpose of considering the problems of schools in relation to the purchase and use of various types of audiovisual equipment. However, the project was taken over by Cline M. Koon of the U.S. Office of Education, under the sponsorship of the council, when he presented a proposal for a national survey of visual instruction in the United States. In this study, printed questionnaires were sent to 21,000 superintendents of schools throughout the United States. Approximately 9,000 replies indicated the following equipment as owned by the schools reporting:

17,040 lantern slide projectors
3,007 stillfilm attachments
2,733 filmstrip projectors
2,073 micro-slide projectors
2,720 opaque projectors

[41] The H. W. Wilson Company published these digests in 1937.
[42] Credit for the development of the first uniform educational film classification system should go to the following: E. Winifred Crawford, director of visual instruction, Montclair, New Jersey; Marion Evans, director of the Visual Instruction Center, San Diego, California; and Annette Glick, director of the audiovisual department, Los Angeles, California.
[43] The first issue of the *Educational Film Catalog* was published in May, 1936, with credit given to the American Council on Education and the U.S. Office of Education, by the H. W. Wilson Company. The first volume, set up on a Dewey basis, listed 1,175 educational films. The first supplement to the catalog was published in January, 1937. The name of the catalog was changed to *Educational Film Guide* in 1945.

6,074 16 mm silent motion picture projectors
458 16 mm sound motion picture projectors
3,230 35 mm silent motion picture projectors
335 35 mm sound motion picture projectors
11,501 radio receiving sets
841 centralized radio-sound systems [44]

A direct result of this project was a conference of motion picture projector manufacturers in St. Louis, Missouri, in February, 1936, for the purpose of working out some plan for reducing the price of apparatus. Other by-products of this project were published educational film handbooks, film lists, directories, and newsletters.

Inasmuch as the initial application for a supporting grant for a national film institute had been withdrawn by the council a few weeks after it was first submitted to the General Education Board, a new proposal entitled "Proposed First Year Program of the American Film Institute" was presented to the board in March, 1936. When the council was told that approval of this proposal with a budget of $60,000 could not be expected, a revised proposal was prepared calling for $40,000. However, the General Education Board also rejected the second proposal, providing, instead, $25,000 to cover the completion of the interim projects to the end of June, 1937.

In view of the prevailing orientation and activities of the Rockefeller Foundation during the middle and late 1930s, it is difficult to understand why the council's request for the funding of a national educational film institute was refused by the General Education Board. We know, for example, that in 1935 the trustees of the Rockefeller Foundation decided to strike out experimentally in new fields, authorizing the officers to develop projects in the general area of libraries and museums, radio, drama, and the motion picture. The president of the Rockefeller Foundation later said:

> From being aristocratic and exclusive, culture is becoming democratic and inclusive. The conquest of illiteracy, the development of school facilities, the rise of public libraries and museums, the flood of books, the invention of the radio and the moving picture, the surge of new ideas—and above all, perhaps, the extension of leisure, once a privilege of the few—are giving culture in our age a broader base than earlier generations have known. . . . New interests are in the making—an adventurous reaching out for a fuller life by thousands to whom non-utilitarian values have hitherto been inaccessible. . . . Any program in the humanities must inevitably take account of this new renaissance of the human spirit.[45]

[44] Cline M. Koon and Allen W. Noble, *National Visual Education Directory*. Washington, D.C., American Council on Education, 1936, p. 9.
[45] R. B. Fosdick, *The Story of the Rockefeller Foundation*. New York, Harper & Row, Publishers, Incorporated, 1952, p. 45.

An exploratory beginning was made in 1935 in radio with a series of grants to the World Wide Broadcasing Foundation, which operated a short-wave station in Boston, to make possible experimentation with educational broadcasting on a worldwide scale. Another supporting grant was given the same year to a cooperative educational broadcasting experiment (University Broadcasting Council) in Chicago, involving the University of Chicago, Northwestern and De Paul Universities, the National Broadcasting Company, and the Columbia Broadcasting System. Still another 1935 grant for experimentation along regional lines laid the groundwork for the Rocky Mountain Radio Council, embracing the states of Colorado and Wyoming. And in the motion picture field, the Rockefeller Foundation in 1935 provided assistance to the Museum of Modern Art in New York City for the establishment of a film library, a repository for film literature, and a distribution center.

With this background in view, there seems to be no obvious reason why the Foundation should not have supported a national educational film institute—an organization whose functions seemed perfectly compatible with similar activities then being undertaken by the General Education Board.

Committee on Motion Pictures in Education. For whatever reasons the General Education Board rejected the council's proposal for a film institute, it was clear to Zook and the council that a new approach must now be taken. Therefore, Zook formed the Committee on Motion Pictures [46] in 1936 to set about developing a new foundation proposal for defining "the functions of motion pictures in general education" and for facilitating "the development of general education through the use of motion pictures." [47] In December, 1937, the General Education Board awarded a grant of $135,000 ($15,000 was added later) for a three-year study on the use of films in general education. Meanwhile, the Committee on Motion Pictures chose Charles F. Hoban, Jr., as director of the study, with Floyde E. Brooker as assistant director.

Film Evaluation Centers. We have seen that when the Motion Picture Project was inaugurated, a lack of basic information on available instructional films had constituted one of the chief obstacles to effective utilization of films in the classroom. Under the new Motion Picture Project grant of the General Education Board, it was decided that the films listed in the *Educational Film Catalog* produced by Interim Project #3 should be evaluated and that this evaluation should be made available to all teachers.

For three years, therefore, from 1938 to 1941, the Committee on Motion

---

[46] Members of this committee were the following: Ben G. Graham, chairman; W. W. Charters; Frank N. Freeman; Mrs. B. F. Langworthy; Mark A. May; J. C. Wardlaw; and George F. Zook, ex-officio.

[47] Charles F. Hoban, Jr., *Focus on Learning.* Washington, D.C.: American Council on Education, 1942, p. v.

Pictures in Education spent most of its time and effort evaluating instructional films. This was done in four key evaluation centers throughout the country. Hoban describes this program as follows:

> Four centers cooperated for two years in the extensive study of motion pictures in the curriculum: Tower Hill School, Wilmington, Delaware; and the public schools of Denver, Colorado, and of Santa Barbara, California. Each of these was engaged in the development of curriculum programs. Supplementing these centers during the second year of the evaluation program were the public schools of Minneapolis, Minnesota; Rochester, New York; and Pittsburgh, Pennsylvania; and a group of schools and colleges in the southeastern states, organized through the Division of General Extension of the University System of Georgia.[48]

The first evaluation center was established at Tower Hill School, Wilmington, Delaware, in the spring of 1938. Answers were sought to such questions as the following:

> What is the function of motion pictures in education? What educational objectives can specific films serve? What are the strengths and weaknesses of existing films? Is there one or are there several best ways of using films? Can the same film be used on different grade levels and on the same grade level for different purposes? Are reactions of children on these different levels the same or different?[49]

Answers to these questions were obtained from teachers and students on the basis of their experience with the actual use of films in normal activities of the school. Through arrangements made by the Motion Picture Project staff, films were made available by producers and distributors. Moreover, the study was purely descriptive. There was no experimental interruption of regular class activities and only anecdotal data were secured from students and teachers.

Beginning in 1938, a two-year study also began in the Santa Barbara (California) city schools.[50] Earlier this same year, the Santa Barbara schools

---

[48] *Ibid.*, p. 2.

[49] The Staff of Tower Hill School, Wilmington, Del., *A School Uses Motion Pictures.* Washington, D.C., American Council on Education Studies, ser. 2, vol. 4, no. 3, 1940, p. 10.

[50] Much of the credit for the selection of Santa Barbara as a film evaluation center belongs to Francis W. Noel, audiovisual director of the Santa Barbara city schools during this period. When, on an Eastern tour, Noel learned about Charles F. Hoban, Jr.'s plans to make an inspection trip West, he invited Hoban to Santa Barbara to observe its curriculum-revision program and consider it as a possible film evaluation center. Although Hoban had been considering Los Angeles and San Diego instead, he accepted Noel's invitation. Noel alerted Santa Barbara Superintendent Curtis Warren and they set about preparing the "right" activities for each classroom along the path designated for Hoban's observation. However, Noel's plans went slightly awry when Hoban inadvertently strolled off the planned path and entered the wrong room! Then it happened that a first-year teacher had even better activities in progress than those that had been planned. Hoban was so impressed that he remained in this classroom and never completed the tour planned for him. Francis W. Noel, interview, March 15, 1952.

had begun a curriculum-revision program with consultant aid from the School of Education, Stanford University. Over two hundred Santa Barbara teachers participated in the film evaluation program. The pattern was similar to that used in the Tower Hill evaluation center. For example, techniques used in film evaluation included teachers' and students' judgments, anecdotal records, stenographic records of class discussions, specimens of creative activities, interest inventories, and paper-and-pencil tests of pupil behavior.

Two departures from the film evaluation approach occurred in Denver and at the University of Minnesota. In Denver, a project was developed under the supervision of Floyde E. Brooker and Eugene Herrington [51] whereby it was demonstrated that schools could produce technically satisfactory motion pictures for their own use. At the General College of the University of Minnesota, a series of experimental studies on the influence of instructional films in biological and social science revealed that measures of functional information were not significantly different between film and nonfilm classes, but measures of interest between these groups showed a significant difference in interest in the subject of human biology in the film group over the nonfilm group. [52]

Results of the Motion Picture Project.   Lorraine Noble, assistant director of the Motion Picture Project during its first years (1934–1937), made the following assessment which she expressed to this writer:

> The original concept of a national film institute was the dominant motive of the Motion Picture Project when it began in 1934. The film institute was visualized as freewheeling, that it would be equally controlled by the schools, the motion picture industry, and government: *that it would operate without a profit motive and not become the creature of any organization* [italics mine]. When the film institute failed to materialize, a period of boondoggling began, and none of the projects finally undertaken was very vital. [53]

Charles F. Hoban, Jr., director of the Motion Picture Project during its final years (1937–1942), focused his assessment on the film evaluation program as follows:

> After three years of experience in the use of panel judgments and of teacher and student judgments based on classroom use, it is the conclusion of the staff of the Motion Picture Project that a combination of the three makes for well-roundedness of evaluation intended to assist the teacher in selecting the film appropriate to a given purpose and in

---

[51] Floyde E. Brooker and Eugene Herrington, *Students Make Motion Pictures.* Washington, D.C., American Council on Education Studies, ser. 2, vol. 5, no. 7, 1941.
[52] Reports of the Minnesota experiments were prepared in manuscript form by C. I. Potthoff, L. C. Larson, and D. O. Patterson (1940); E. C. Wilson, L. C. Larson, and F. Lord (1940). Unpublished. Project was under Robert Kissack.
[53] Lorraine Noble, interview, April 12, 1952.

assisting him to prepare for its most effective use. In other words, film evaluations based on teacher and student judgments help the teacher with no previous knowledge of specific films to select those which are most likely to serve the purposes intended.[54]

A number of publications resulted from the last, or film evaluation phase (1938–1941), of the Motion Picture Project. Probably the most important document was a descriptive encyclopedia of educational films titled *Selected Educational Motion Pictures* (1942).[55] This encyclopedia contains essential information on approximately five hundred 16-mm films which were judged by educators to be of value in the classroom. About fifty-five hundred teacher judgments and twelve thousand student judgments were collected and analyzed in this process. In addition, the previewing of all films included in the encyclopedia and the preparation of their content descriptions were supervised by Blake Cochran, Robert S. Sackett, and Floyde E. Brooker of the project staff, assisted by a group of Rockefeller fellows with the project.[56]

Although some of the activities of the Motion Picture Project cannot be considered very significant, the project did succeed in stimulating the classroom use of films and did call attention to the need to critically evaluate the relationship of film content to the school curriculum.

In the final analysis, the direction taken by the Motion Picture Project lay solely in the hands of the American Council on Education. In contrast to the Ford Foundation,[57] the Rockefeller Foundation had no specific program for education. It wished to explore the use of films for general education and therefore provided money for R & D (research and development), and for the education of personnel in this area. The responsibility for the merit or lack of merit of these studies rests entirely with those educators involved in the Motion Picture Project. Lorraine Noble suggested to the writer that the projects, in her opinion, were not very vital because "most educators did not know what they wanted."[58] There is no question, however, that the Motion Picture Project provided a rather unique training ground for many future leaders in instructional technology who were associated with it.

Some Final Considerations. When the early, unpublished documents of the Motion Picture Project (which were examined by this writer) are con-

---

[54] Hoban, *op. cit.*, p. 146.

[55] This publication is the historical antecedent of the *Educational Media Index*, begun in 1964 by the Educational Media Council.

[56] Rockefeller fellows involved in this project include the following: James D. Finn, Colorado College of Education; William H. Bowen, Jr., and James W. Brown, Virginia Board of Education; Abram VanderMeer, Laboratory School, University of Chicago.

[57] The Ford Foundation's usual policy is to develop a program and then set out to implement it with grants. For example, a current objective of the Ford Foundation is to automatize the classroom. Thus the Ford Foundation has not made grants for R & D unless they conform to this general goal.

[58] Lorraine Noble, interview, April 12, 1952.

sidered, a number of questions inevitably arise. Why, for example, was the "interim projects" proposal developed within a few days after the council had submitted a major proposal for its supposed primary area of interest— the national educational film institute? The official reason was that these projects would keep alive the interest already generated in the film institute. But if, in fact, the council had developed these interim projects for the purpose of sustaining interest in the film institute, why did the council withdraw the film institute proposal as soon as the interim projects grant was made? Did the council anticipate rejection of the film institute proposal by the Rockefeller Foundation for some reason and wished to avoid this rejection? Or did the council propose the interim projects as a face-saving retreat from the film institute plan because they realized they were not ready or able to implement it? This would explain why the council quickly withdrew its film institute proposal when a grant was made for the interim projects. Then again, why did the council decide to resubmit the film institute proposal almost a year later, and did this delay have any influence on the General Education Board's decision to reject it? If the primary goal of the council was to establish a film institute, why were no efforts made to approach other foundations for financing? Finally, was there any pressure from the theatrical motion picture industry on either the council or the Foundation, or both, which led to the ultimate failure of the film institute proposal or even doomed it to failure from its inception? Certainly there has been abundant evidence over the years that the motion picture industry has been persistently antagonistic to the idea that educators should produce their own films.

These questions remain unanswered for the writer, and it appears unlikely that satisfactory answers will be forthcoming. Nevertheless, they continue to generate provocative speculations.

Early instructional radio research: prior to 1937

The impetus for instructional radio research first came from commercial radio. Since radio did not have the convenient audience indexes available to the film (box-office returns) or print (circulation figures) media, commercial radio audience research was undertaken as early as 1927.

Assessment of Early Instructional Radio Research. Foundations have played an important role in instructional radio research just as they have in instructional film research. Much of the credit for this activity should go to John Marshall of the Rockefeller Foundation and to S. Howard Evans of the Payne Fund. Significant contributions have also been made by the Carnegie Corporation and by the Alfred P. Sloan Foundation.

An unfortunate aspect of instructional radio research is that few early studies have actually been published in detail. Many have been briefly summarized in the *Education on the Air* yearbooks which were published by the Institute for Education by Radio at Ohio State University. A number of these studies, constituting work for advanced degrees, have not been published in any form. As a result, many of their instructional implications have not been widely known.

An effort to coordinate radio research investigations was begun in 1931 by the Bureau of Educational Research at Ohio State University, with the help of the Payne Fund, by the publication of a bulletin entitled *Research Studies in Education by Radio—Cooperative Group.* W. W. Charters directed the activities of the bureau and F. M. Lumley directed radio research.

Many of the early radio projects were media comparison studies which presaged the now-familiar research pattern of "no significant differences" in instructional television research. A few provided more specific data on the effect of radio instruction on the learning process. Radio was usually found to be more effective for those subjects in which aural-verbal skills predominate.

Typical Early Instructional Radio Studies.   In order to suggest the nature of early instructional radio studies, a few typical ones are listed:

1   A survey of the use of radio in adult education was made by the American Association for Adult Education under the sponsorship of the Carnegie Foundation (1929).[59]

2   Ben H. Darrow and Cline M. Koon of the Ohio School of the Air made studies of the classroom use of the Ohio School of the Air broadcasts (1929).[60]

3   The Department of Rural Education, Teachers College, Columbia University, made a study of the classroom use of radio in 100 rural schools (1929).[61]

4   John Guy Fowlkes and H. L. Ewbank of the University of Wisconsin made a study of the effectiveness of radio in teaching music appreciation (1929).[62]

5   H. Cantril and Gordon Allport made a series of studies to determine the extent to which a personality could be judged from the voice; a comparison of listeners' attitudes toward male and female voices; a

[59] Frank E. Hill, *Listen and Learn.* New York, American Association for Adult Education, 1937, pp. 36–37.

[60] B. H. Darrow, *Radio Trailblazing.* Columbus, Ohio, College Book Company, 1940, pp. 39–40.

[61] Margaret Harrison, *Radio in Rural Schools.* Address given before Department of Rural Education of the Department of Superintendents at Atlantic City, Feb. 26, 1930. (Mimeographed.)

[62] John Guy Fowlkes and H. L. Ewbank, "The Radio in Wisconsin Rural Schools," *Elementary School Journal,* vol. 30 (May, 1930), pp. 642–643.

study of the differences between a radio lecture and a regular lecture; a comparison of the mental processes of an audience listening before a radio with the same audience in the presence of the broadcaster; a study of the conditions influencing the relative effectiveness of visual and auditory presentation; a determination of the most effective conditions for broadcasting; and a study of certain attitudes and preferences of radio listeners (1932).[63]

6   F. M. Lumley and Frank N. Stanton of Ohio State University did some of the first systematic work in radio measurement (1934).[64]

7   Merton E. Carver of Harvard University studied some of the conditions that influence the relative effectiveness of visual and auditory presentations of identical material (1934).[65]

Major instructional radio research projects

When the results of the Payne Fund studies became generally known between 1933 and 1935, the same storm that raged earlier over films now set the air waves reverberating. There were emotional thunderbursts from women's organizations over children's programs. The result was a repetition of the film experience: The Federal Radio Education Committee [66] of the Federal Communications Commission drew up a research program and submitted it to the Rockefeller Foundation. Out of this effort came the support of the General Education Board in the launching of three major radio projects —the Ohio Evaluation of School Broadcasts Project, the Princeton Project (which was the beginning of the Office of Radio Research), and the Wisconsin Research Project.

Ohio Evaluation of School Broadcasts Project.   The Evaluation of School Broadcasts Project was unique in scope and cost. It was "a research and service project engaged in analyzing the educational values of radio in schools and classrooms, and in studying the social and psychological effects of radio listening upon children and young people." [67] The project, started in the fall of 1937 and terminated in the spring of 1943, was directed by

[63] Hadley Cantril and Gordon W. Allport, *The Psychology of Radio.* New York, Harper and Brothers, 1935.

[64] F. M. Lumley, *Measurement in Radio.* Columbus, Ohio, Ohio State University Press, 1934.

[65] Merton E. Carver, "A Study of Conditions Influencing the Relative Effectiveness of Visual and Auditory Presentation." Doctoral Dissertation, Harvard University, Cambridge, Mass., 1934.

[66] The Federal Radio Education Committee was created in 1935 by the FCC to eliminate controversy and misunderstandings between industry and educators and to promote cooperative undertakings in educational broadcasting.

[67] Norman Woelfel and I. Keith Tyler, *Radio and the School.* Tarrytown-on-Hudson, New York, World Book Company, 1945, p. iii.

I. Keith Tyler of the Bureau of Educational Research of Ohio State University. The associate director was J. Wayne Wrightstone.

The actual work was carried on in centers located in Chicago, Detroit, New York City, and the San Francisco Bay region. In the fall of 1938, the Ohio School of the Air was added as a center. Also, certain advisory centers were located at Rochester, New York; Cleveland, Ohio; Madison, Wisconsin; Zanesville, Ohio; and the Nation's School of the Air at WLW, Cincinnati, Ohio.

After the selection of the centers, the major activities of the project staff during the years 1937–1940 were those of meeting with groups of teachers who were using radio in their classrooms and demonstrating its effective uses for instructional purposes. Two or three such meetings were held each year with teachers of English, music, science, and social studies from the Chicago, Detroit, and New York City areas. Between meetings, the teachers kept diaries of their schools' use of radio and prepared anecdotal records of pupils' behavior while listening to school broadcasts. Members of the project staff analyzed these records and observations and prepared a list of classified objectives and sample evaluation instruments. After these objectives had been critically evaluated by the teachers in subsequent meetings, they were published as a tentative form of a *Dictionary of Objectives*.[68] These objectives were later classified into the following categories: (1) attitudes and appreciations, (2) interests and self-motivation, (3) critical thinking and discrimination, (4) creative expression, (5) social behavior and personal-social integration, (6) skills and techniques, and (7) informational background. Furthermore, objectives were also stated for each of the four fields of music, social studies, English, and science.[69]

After this preliminary work, which consumed some eight months, the staff began the second phase of the study, directed toward the obtaining of research evidence regarding school broadcasts. Instruments of evaluation were developed in tentative form and tried out by some of the cooperating teachers. A much larger number of evaluation instruments was developed at summer workshops held at Bronxville, New York; Denver, Colorado; and Oakland, California, in cooperation with the General Education Board and the Progressive Education Association. Special fellowships were given by the General Education Board to thirty-seven persons who came to these workshops and worked closely with the project staff. In addition, special committees of the workshops prepared a manual on the utilization of broadcasts, a script series of school broadcasts, and outlines for work in radio program discrimination. By the fall of 1938, twenty-one exploratory studies of school broadcasting were in progress.

[68] *Tentative Report on Objectives*, Bulletin 1, Evaluation of School Broadcasts, Columbus, Ohio, Ohio State University, 1938.
[69] *Ibid.*, p. 33.

After the renewal of the original two-year grant in 1939, the results of the preliminary studies were used as a basis for planning more comprehensive research in the remaining three years.

The American School of the Air of the Columbia Broadcasting System was subjected to a thorough-going critical analysis during the 1940–1941 series by a selected group of teachers and members of the Evaluation of School Broadcasts staff. From these analyses, the conclusions were:

> *First:* Teachers who used the broadcasts in their classrooms sometimes found them extremely valuable in providing educational experiences not otherwise available to their students, in constituting interesting and worth-while curricular materials, in serving as integrative experiences in broad areas of subject matter, in stimulating students to engage in other educational activities, and in furnishing enjoyable classroom listening experiences to students. Of the three series, the "New Horizons" broadcasts were judged to be the most educationally worth while, and the "Americans at Work" boardcasts the least worth while.
>
> *Second:* Even though the broadcasts in general were educationally worth-while experiences to both teachers and students in classrooms, the three series contained various curricula defects and deficiencies, notably in the failure to define purposes sharply, to consider criteria governing the scope of the series and the sequence of the broadcasts, to recognize the major functions of education in American democracy, and to develop accurate printed aids to accompany the broadcasts.
>
> *Third:* Most of the broadcasts were clear and comprehensible to classroom listeners, but in the three series there were various minor errors in the selection of the content and in the form of presentation which, according to teachers, made the broadcasts at times and in spots extremely difficult for students to understand. By and large, these errors of content and production seemed attributable to a lack of knowledge concerning classroom listening conditions and to a lack of understanding of the social and educational backgrounds of pupils nine to fourteen years of age.
>
> *Fourth:* Most of the broadcasts were enjoyable classroom listening experiences for students, but in three series there were certain techniques used which made the radio programs less interesting to boys and girls than they might have been. Some of these errors were due to limitations of budget and personnel at the Columbia Broadcasting System, but others were due to a lack of understanding of the social maturity of students in grades four to nine.[70]

Studies in the effectiveness of recordings were also conducted by the Evaluation of School Broadcasts staff. A study made at Cicero, Illinois,[71]

---

[70] *Network School Broadcasts: Some Conclusions and Recommendations,* Bulletin 35, Evaluation of School Broadcasts, Columbus, Ohio, Ohio State University, 1941.

[71] See *Auditory Aids and the Teaching of Science: Two Experimental Studies,* Bulletin 57, Evaluation of School Broadcasts, Columbus, Ohio, Ohio State University, 1942.

showed that student interest in scientific information could be greatly stimulated through the use of recordings. Another study, made at Zanesville, Ohio,[72] revealed that recordings could be used effectively in the creation of desirable interests and attitudes. R. R. Lowdermilk,[73] in utilizing a series of transcriptions of *America's Town Meeting of the Air,* found that the classroom use of recordings possessed values superior to assigned home listening to live broadcasts. Furthermore, a study by Irving Robbins indicated that criteria of discrimination could be evolved and that recordings could be used as a stimulus for the discernment of such criteria.[74]

Perhaps the most significant study of recordings was the joint study conducted by the American Council on Education and the Evaluation of School Broadcasts Project at Ohio State University. For this, more than one thousand educational recordings were collected and listed by Emilie L. Haley for the Committee on Motion Pictures in Education of the American Council on Education. This report, made in January, 1939, and entitled a *Study of Recordings for General Education,* is divided into three parts: (a) a survey of the efforts that were being made to produce educational recordings, (b) an account of rulings of organizations affecting the release of recordings of broadcast programs for classroom use, and (c) a description of the methods used in recording programs, with a statement of comparative costs.[75] In commenting on the status of educational recordings in 1939, Miss Haley remarked that:

> It is unfortunate that recordings of the various Schools of the Air are not available. In some cases off-the-air recordings are made for reference and study purposes but no permanent recording is being done to date. It is advisable that a thorough analysis should be made of these off-the-air recordings to ascertain the programs that would be suitable for re-recording for general distribution to schools.
>
> The directors of the Schools of the Air, as well as the directors of civic educational broadcast programs, are willing to cooperate in making their programs available for recording if funds were provided.
>
> In a coast-to-coast survey conducted to discover available recordings, great enthusiasm was shown with reference to the acquisition of educational recordings to supplement classroom curricula.
>
> Expressions of interest and cooperation on the part of organizations affecting the recording of educational broadcast programs indicate complete accord towards the proposed project.[76]

---

[72] *Loc. cit.*

[73] *A Study of America's Town Meeting of the Air,* Bulletin 46, Evaluation of School Broadcasts, Columbus, Ohio, Ohio State University, 1942.

[74] Irving Robbins, *Teaching Radio Program Discrimination,* Bulletin 56, Evaluation of School Broadcasts, Columbus, Ohio, Ohio State University, 1942.

[75] *Study of Recordings for General Education,* Motion Picture Project, American Council on Education, January, 1939, p. i.

[76] *Loc. cit.*

Subsequently, these recordings were described and evaluated in *Recordings for School Use: A Catalog of Appraisals.*[77]

Without question, the Evaluation of School Broadcasts Project made a significant contribution to educational broadcasting and instructional technology. It provided many valuable by-products in the form of factual evidence and produced helpful materials designed to aid the educational broadcaster in the planning and effective utilization of instructional broadcasts.

Wisconsin Research Project.   In 1937, the Rockefeller Foundation also supported a study at the University of Wisconsin to test a number of fundamental assumptions concerning the strengths and limitations of radio as a medium of communication and instruction. The initial phases of this study concentrated on the planning of radio lessons in all subjects at all grade levels, and on the establishment of research designs involving different combinations of subject matter, educational objectives, and listening groups. The planning of each series of broadcasts was based on the cooperative efforts of classroom teachers, supervisors, and administrators, and the staff of the State Department of Public Instruction.

During the 1937–1939 period, the following programs were broadcast over the Wisconsin School of the Air to serve as the basis for comparative studies:

Music: Journeys in Music Land	grades 5 and 6
Nature Study: Afield with Ranger Mac	grades 7 and 8
Geography: Neighbors Round the World	grades 6 and 7
Social Studies: Community Living	grades 7 and 8
English: (1) English as You Like It	grades 10, 11, 12
(2) Good Books	grades 10, 11, 12
Speech: Good Speech	grades 10, 11, 12 [78]

In general, the results of these comparative studies showed "no significant differences." The comparisons consistently favored the radio groups only in the field of music, and even there, the differences were not large enough to be statistically significant.

Probably the most important results of the Wisconsin project were the training in radio research it afforded graduate students and the subsequent research it stimulated in other phases of instructional broadcasting.

Princeton Project.   The third major radio research project financed by the Rockefeller Foundation during this period began at Princeton University in

[77] J. Robert Miles, *Recordings for School Use: A Catalog of Appraisals.* Tarrytown-on-Hudson, New York, World Book Company, 1942.

[78] *Radio in the Classroom.* Report of the Wisconsin Research Project in School Broadcasting, Madison, Wis., The University of Wisconsin Press, 1942, p. 4.

the fall of 1937 with the establishment of an Office of Radio Research (part of the Federal Radio Education Committee) headed by Paul F. Lazarsfeld as director, and Frank N. Stanton and Hadley Cantril as associate directors.

The project attempted to answer such questions as these: What individuals and social groups listen to radio? How much do they listen and why? In what ways are they affected by their listening? Since the radio industry had already studied the size and distribution of its audience as prospective purchasers for products advertised over the air, the Princeton study began where industry left off.

In June, 1939, the first progress report summarized the principal findings as follows:

1. For listeners to the serious type of program, content of the program is more important than dramatic effects or personalities of the speakers.

2. People not likely to read for serious content are usually unlikely to listen for serious content.

3. Low-income families who read little are inclined to listen to the radio extensively and to seek the escape that comes with the non-serious content.

4. Higher-income families who have a wide variety of interests and available entertainment find most radio programs, which are commonly written for the listener with average ability and tastes, to be rather boring.[80]

As the work of the project progressed, field headquarters were established in New York City, and the Institute of Public Opinion at Princeton began to publish valuable materials in the field of radio. Eventually, however, it became apparent that the total research program would be considerably expedited if it were transferred to a university located in New York City. Therefore, in the spring of 1940, the project was moved to Columbia University.[81]

The Office of Radio Research at Columbia University extended the scope of research begun at Princeton. By collecting work done in the radio industry and in universities, the office created, in a series of publications, a

[80] Paul F. Lazarsfeld, *Radio and the Printed Page.* New York, Duell, Sloan & Pearce, Inc., 1940, p. vii.

[81] Out of the Princeton project grew another project which had wide public implications. In 1940, the Princeton School of Public and International Affairs, with the help of the Rockefeller Foundation, began to record and analyze shortwave broadcasts dealing with the war and beamed to America from Europe. At the same time, a similar station, located at Stanford University in California, began, also with the assistance of the Rockefeller Foundation, to monitor shortwave broadcasts from across the Pacific. Some of this broadcasting was news, much of it was propaganda. The results of the analysis in both institutions were made available in the form of bulletins and sent to students of communications and international affairs. When the United States entered the war, the Federal Communications Commission established at Washington the Foreign Broadcasting Monitoring Service, with the basic methods developed at Princeton and Stanford put into use.

body of techniques and data about the radio audience which held important educational implications. Its next major publication after *Radio and the Printed Page* was *Radio Research 1941.* In this volume, six studies were reported as representative of the range of problems that were being confronted. These included studies of foreign language broadcasts over local American stations, the popular music industry, the radio symphony, the problems of serious music broadcasting, radio and the press among young people, and the relation of the radio to the farmer.

Although World War II made it technically difficult to continue the publication of the radio research series begun in 1941, radio research expanded during World War II and the activities of the Office of Radio Research directly influenced the creation of the Radio Bureau in the Office of War Information.

Simultaneously, three trends in radio research became apparent. One development was a tendency toward an integration of a variety of approaches to the same problem. Another was one of innovation in research methodology. An example of this trend was the development of the Program Analyzer by Paul F. Lazarsfeld and Frank N. Stanton. The third trend was the study of technical problems in listener research. Examples can be found in the panel method of interviewing, in the detailed case studies of specific radio programs, and in the content analysis of enemy broadcasts carried through by the Research Project on Totalitarian Communication.

Indeed, it was becoming evident to Lazarsfeld and others at the office that radio research would ultimately merge with the study of other mass media to form the broad field of communications research. One of the first indications of this trend became manifest in the Office of Radio Research publication, *Radio Research 1942-1943.*[82] In this book, there was a report on the use of the Program Analyzer in the study of instructional films, and one on biographies in popular magazines.

In 1944, in recognition of the fact that the office was increasingly conducting research beyond the field of radio, it was reoriented toward the broad field of communications and renamed the Bureau of Applied Social Research. Under the brilliant leadership of Lazarsfeld, this organization has continued to contribute to historical advances in the field of communications research.

Status of instructional radio research: end of World War II

By the end of World War II, instructional radio research was still generally immature, inadequate, and incidental, mainly because, with the ex-

[82] Paul F. Lazarsfeld and Frank N. Stanton, *Radio Research 1942-1943.* New York, Duell, Sloan & Pearce, Inc., 1944.

ception of commercial radio surveys and the radio studies sponsored by the Rockefeller Foundation during the late thirties, no long-range systematic studies had been proposed or undertaken in many important unexplored areas of the teaching-learning process. In most instances, the results of the studies that had been conducted indicated that learning through the medium of radio is more effective than through print, especially among the not-too-well educated and not-too-intelligent. Moreover, the studies dealt largely with the characteristics of radio audiences or the effectiveness of radio as a medium of instruction of some specific subject matter. Although the content of radio broadcasts was analyzed and the relationships of program control and content were explored during World War II, instructional radio research had virtually ceased by the close of the war.

United States Army studies in World War II

The major instructional media research programs during World War II were conducted by the Army in the use of films. Three series of research studies were undertaken by various Army agencies. Two of these dealt with the effectiveness of films in achieving specific learning outcomes, and the third, with the organizational factors influencing the extent of film use in training situations.[83]

Experiments on Mass Communication.   Studies conducted by the Experimental Section, Research Branch, Information and Education Division of the War Department were reported by Hovland, Lumsdaine, and Sheffield in *Experiments on Mass Communication* (1949).[84] This report is of great historical value because it contains a comprehensive discussion of various hypotheses concerning the effectiveness of films, and contributes hypotheses offering suggestions for additional research.

Film Testing and Research.   Another phase of Army research in films during World War II was undertaken by the Psychological Test Film Unit of the Aviation Psychology Program of the Army Air Forces, located at Santa Ana Army Air Base, Santa Ana, California. The work of the Unit evolved out of its efforts to utilize the film medium for psychological testing and the classification of aircrews. In the process of this research, the Unit became involved with such problems as the representation of three-dimen-

[83] The third series of Army film research studies was conducted at the Signal Corps Photographic Center and dealt with patterns of film supply, print utilization, and film library administration. Results of these studies were incorporated in a report by C. F. Hoban, Jr., *Movies That Teach*. New York, The Dryden Press, Inc., 1946.
[84] C. I. Hovland, Arthur A. Lumsdaine, and F. D. Sheffield, *Experiments on Mass Communication*. Princeton, N.J., Princeton University Press, 1949.

sional space by pictures, perceptual learning, and problems associated with the projection of films and still pictures.[85]

By the end of World War II, it was evident that a new phase of instructional media research was at hand, a phase characterized by increasing scientific sophistication in the development of research designs and in the use of experimental procedures. The next chapter will introduce the reader to this phase of instructional media research.

[85] The work of the Psychological Test Film Unit was directed by J. J. Gibson. The report of the work of this Unit can be found in AAF Aviation Psychology Program Research Report no. 7, entitled *Motion Picture Testing and Research.*

chapter **15**

intensification of
instructional media research:
1945–1965

The period from 1945 to 1965 represents two decades of
intensive research on instructional media. Much of this
research was stimulated by a growing concern with education as a response to the forces of technological change
impinging on American society. Decisions to restructure
various branches of knowledge (e.g., physical sciences,
biological sciences, mathematics, foreign languages), to
improve instruction at all levels, and to improve the
preparation of teachers are all related to questions of what
to teach to whom and how to teach it in less time. During this period a number of new media formats and
modes of presenting instructional materials developed. A
major innovation was the systems approach to instruction,
an approach which moved closer to a scientific technology
of instruction. The systems approach, as we have seen,
raised questions of what media or combination of media,

should be used with specific subject matter and learners of specific characteristics for the most effective teaching-learning situations.

The great volume of instructional media research during the 1945–1965 period was made possible largely by unprecedented financial support from the United States Army, Navy, and Air Force in the late 1940s and the 1950s; by support for a series of studies and projects from the motion picture industry; by the assistance of several philanthropic foundations in the 1950s; and more recently, by the introduction of massive instructional media research programs by the federal government under Title VII of the National Defense Education Act (NDEA) of 1958 (Public Law 85-864). In addition, there was an almost steady stream of dissertation studies on instructional media research and projects conducted by individual researchers.

The great amount of instructional media research produced during this period brought with it new problems in the dissemination and diffusion of research data to educators. Thus, beginning in the early 1960s, the U.S. Office of Education took the lead in the exploration of an information indexing, storage, and retrieval system for research documents in the field of instructional technology.

Communication research

There has been a progressive development since the early 1940s of committees, institutes, departments, divisions, schools, colleges, and programs of communications in higher education throughout the United States. Although this movement has had comparatively little influence on educational practices, communication research has important implications for instructional technology.[1]

Lasswell has described the scope of communication research with reference to

> Who
> Says What
> In Which Channel
> To Whom
> With What Effect? [2]

"Who" is the study of communicators and the institutional or organizational background of the source of communications. "What" is the study of content,

[1] See, for example, Nelson B. Henry (ed.), *Mass Media and Education,* the Fifty-third Yearbook of the National Society for the Study of Education, part II. Chicago, The University of Chicago Press, 1954; and the Educational Policies Commission, *Mass Communications and Education.* Washington, D.C., NEA, 1958.

[2] Harold Lasswell, "The Structure and Function of Communication in Society," in Wilbur Schramm, *Mass Communications,* 2d ed. Urbana, Ill., The University of Illinois Press, 1960, p. 117.

ranging from content analysis to sample surveys. "Channel" refers to the study of different media. "Whom" refers to studies of the receiver—his characteristics, needs, perceptions, goals, etc. "Effect" has reference to communication effect on attitudes, values, and behavior.

Background of Communication Research. In the early 1930s, a small group of men began to realize the necessity of blending the diverse elements which had emerged in the various areas of the humanities and the social sciences. In 1931, the Social Science Research Council (organized in 1923 to correlate and stimulate research in the social sciences), under the leadership of David Stevens (professor of English at the University of Chicago and vice-president of the General Education Board of the Rockefeller Foundation), appointed an interdisciplinary committee for the study of communication. An important result of this committee's work was the publication of the first comprehensive, annotated bibliography of professional literature related to communication and mass media.[3]

In 1938, John Marshall of the Rockefeller Foundation organized a monthly seminar group.[4] The purpose of this seminar was twofold: first, to provide an integrated, philosophical approach to communication; and second, to construct a systematic pattern of communication research methodology.

An important early contribution to communication theory and research came from the political scientists. Other fields or disciplines might have been expected to provide this impetus, but they failed to do so for a number of reasons. Schools of journalism, business, and advertising did not provide the early interdisciplinary leadership because they were essentially trade schools on the periphery of academic scholarship. Schools of education had devised instructional approaches which had implications for communication research, but they never achieved a working relationship with the social science or humanities departments. Such fields as law, divinity, medicine, literature, history, linguistics, music, architecture, or any of the creative arts also might have given the initial stimulus to the communications movement, but they lacked the broad perspectives which were being developed by the political scientists.

The advent of readership and audience surveys, public opinion polls, and propaganda studies in the 1920s and 1930s resulted in the development of mass media research activity in institutions of higher learning and thus

[3] See Bruce Lannes Smith, Harold D. Lasswell, and Ralph D. Casey, *Propaganda and Promotional Activities: An Annotated Bibliography.* Minneapolis, The University of Minnesota Press, 1935.

[4] The regular participants of this seminar were as follows: Lyman Bryson, Teachers College, Columbia University; Douglas Waples, University of Chicago Library School; Harold Lasswell, University of Chicago; I. A. Richards, Cambridge University; and Charles Siepmann, BBC director of program planning, who had been invited by the Rockefeller Foundation to come to the United States to study the status of educational radio.

foreshadowed the later emergence of the university communication research center. Probably the Payne Fund studies, conducted by investigators from a number of universities between 1929 and 1933, provided the first important impetus to communication research. In 1933, George Gallup (who developed one of the first systematic techniques of public polling in 1928) conducted the first experimental readership survey while teaching psychology at Iowa State University. In 1937, Clyde Miller of Teachers College, Columbia University, and associates from other universities began the first systematic propaganda research with the establishment of the Institute for Propaganda Analysis in New York City. Other significant influences on the development of communication research during the 1930s came from the work of Paul F. Lazarsfeld and others at Princeton and later Columbia University (Office of Radio Research), and Gordon Allport and Hadley Cantril [5] in their studies of the psychology of radio at the Harvard Psychological Laboratory. Moreover, studies of why and how people read and what reading does to people first began at the University of Chicago Library School in 1930 with the work of Douglas Waples [6] and others. Meanwhile, Kurt Lewin [7] and his associates at the University of Iowa studied individual behavior under group pressures in a variety of experimental settings. Additional valuable sources of hypotheses for communication research have flowed from psychotherapy, advertising, semantic theory, and from the analysis of communication problems in industry.

Communication studies stimulated by World War II brought a significant impetus to communication research. From pioneer studies by Carl I. Hovland [8] and others for the Research Branch of the War Department's Information and Education Division came the widely accepted concepts of the psychological processes of communication and persuasion. Samuel A. Stouffer,[9] as Research Director for the Information and Education Branch of the Army during World War II, organized several hundred attitude surveys among soldiers all over the world. Robert K. Merton studied the effects of a World War II bond drive conducted as a marathon radio appeal by Kate Smith and provided one of the classic studies of communication process in his monograph *Mass Persuasion.*[10]

[5] Hadley Cantril and Gordon W. Allport, *The Psychology of Radio*. New York, Harper & Brothers, 1935.
[6] Douglas Waples and Ralph Tyler, *What People Want to Read about*. Chicago, The University of Chicago Press, 1931.
[7] Kurt Lewin, *Field Theory in Social Science*. New York, Harper & Row, Publishers, Incorporated, 1951.
[8] Carl I. Hovland, A. A. Lumsdaine, and Fred D. Sheffield, *Experiments on Mass Communications*. Princeton, N.J., Princeton University Press, 1949, vol. 3.
[9] Samuel A. Stouffer et al., *The American Soldier*. Princeton, N.J., Princeton University Press, 1949, vol. 1.
[10] Robert K. Merton, *Mass Persuasion*. New York, Harper & Row, Publishers, Incorporated, 1946.

In the following years, the momentum of war studies continued to stimulate communication research. A major influence on communication research came from cybernetics scholars like Norbert Wiener [11] and John Neuman, and from communications mathematicians like Claude Shannon and Warren Weaver.[12] Vital theoretical contributions to communication research have been made in recent years by Ernest Cassirer,[13] Colin Cherry,[14] George Gerbner,[15] Elihu Katz and Paul F. Lazarsfeld,[16] Susanne K. Langer,[17] Harold Lasswell,[18] Marshall McLuhan,[19] George A. Miller,[20] Jurgen Ruesch and Gregory Bateson,[21] and Wilbur Schramm.[22]

Communication research is still in its infancy despite its important strides in recent years. As yet, there is no integrated, generally acceptable theory of communication. Moreover, research is lacking in many vital areas and new research approaches and techniques are needed to understand a rapidly developing communication technology.[23]

---

[11] Norbert Wiener, *Cybernetics*. New York, John Wiley & Sons, Inc., 1948.

[12] Claude E. Shannon and Warren Weaver, *The Mathematical Theory of Communication*. Urbana, Ill., The University of Illinois Press, 1949.

[13] Ernest Cassirer, *The Philosophy of Symbolic Forms*. New Haven, Conn., Yale University Press, 1953.

[14] Colin Cherry, *On Human Communication*. New York, John Wiley & Sons, Inc., 1957.

[15] George Gerbner, "Toward a General Model of Communication," *AV Communication Review*, vol. 4 (Summer, 1956), pp. 171–199.

[16] Elihu Katz and Paul F. Lazarsfeld, *Personal Influence*. New York, The Free Press of Glencoe, 1955.

[17] Susanne K. Langer, *Philosophy in a New Key*. New York, New American Library of World Literature, Inc., 1948.

[18] Harold Lasswell, "The Structure and Function of Communication in Society," in Wilbur Schramm (ed.), *Mass Communications*, 2d ed. Urbana, Ill., The University of Illinois, 1960, p. 117.

[19] Marshall McLuhan, *Understanding Media*. New York, McGraw-Hill Book Company, 1964.

[20] George A. Miller, *Language and Communication*. New York, McGraw-Hill Book Company, 1951.

[21] Jurgen Ruesch and Gregory Bateson, *Communication: The Social Matrix of Psychiatry*. New York, W. W. Norton & Company, Inc., 1951.

[22] Wilbur Schramm, *The Process and Effects of Mass Communications*. Urbana, Ill., The University of Illinois Press, 1954.

[23] Joseph T. Klapper made a comprehensive examination of the mass media research literature in 1950 to find answers to these questions: Do the mass media raise or lower popular taste, and how? What are the comparative effects of books and each of the other media, including face-to-face discourse, and of multiple-media operations? What is the function and effect of "escapist" communication (best sellers, soap operas, etc.)? How is persuasion with regard to important civic attitudes carried on with greatest likelihood of effectiveness? In 1960, Klapper brought his earlier memorandum up to date and summed up twenty years of theory and research on mass communication effect. Klapper's orientation to communication research reflects a field theory of behavior. Rather than regarding mass communication as a cause of audience effects, his approach emphasizes the total communication situation, including such decisive factors as perception, cognition, attitudes, group values, and personal influence. See Joseph T. Klapper, *The Effects of Mass Communication*. New York, The Free Press of Glencoe, 1960.

Development of Communication Research Centers in Higher Education.
The University of Illinois, under the leadership of Wilbur Schramm, took the
lead in developing communication research centers in institutions of higher
learning after World War II. In January, 1948, the Institute of Communication Research, University of Illinois, sponsored one of the first national institutes of mass communications. This institute is of historic importance for
two main reasons: first, it marked the first formal beginning of mass communications research in higher education; second, it served as the first major
point of convergence of related disciplines.[24]

By the 1960s, over twenty institutions of higher learning in the United
States were using the communications label to describe their interdisciplinary
approach to the study of mass media and communication research. Moreover, schools, colleges, institutes, divisions, and departments were organized
with curricula leading to baccalaureate and graduate degrees in communications. Contributing areas making up the communications programs consisted
of the blending of such traditional areas as cinema, radio, television, journalism, speech, and audiovisual education. Supporting areas might include psychology, social psychology, social science, English, library science, and education. Leadership in the various communications programs is equally varied.
It comes from radio-television, education, journalism, the social sciences,
business, library science, English, or even speech.[25] According to Lasswell,
"No change in the academic world has been more characteristic of the age
than the discovery of communications as a field of research, teaching, and
professional employment."[26]

Today four primary strands of influence, represented by Paul F. Lazarsfeld[27] (the sample survey), Kurt Lewin[28] (small-group analysis), Harold
Laswell (propaganda analysis), and Carl Hovland[29] (experimental-psycho-
logical), are clearly evident in the United States. There is also an increasing
tendency for communication researchers to be eclectic, but a true blending
of the various disciplines still needs to be achieved and there is still a lack
of an integrated theory underlying communication research.

[24] Wilbur Schramm (ed.), *Communications in Modern Society.* Urbana, Ill., The University of Illinois Press, 1948.
[25] See Donald P. Ely, "Communications Programs in Higher Education," *AV Communication Review* (Winter, 1960), pp. 69–73.
[26] H. D. Lasswell, "Communications as an Emerging Discipline," *AV Communication
Review*, vol. 6 (Fall, 1958), p. 245.
[27] Paul Lazarsfeld, trained as a sociologist in Vienna, came to the United States in 1932
and became deeply interested in the audiences and effects of mass media of communication.
[28] Kurt Lewin was a cognitive-field psychologist from Germany who came to the United
States in the early 1930s.
[29] Hovland made one of the largest single contributions to communication theory during
the time he directed the Yale research program between 1950 and 1961.

Nebraska film program

The Nebraska Program of Educational Enrichment Through the Use of Motion Pictures (sponsored by the Carnegie Corporation and the Motion Picture Association of America through Teaching Film Custodians), was launched in September, 1946, under the joint direction of the University of Nebraska and the State Department of Public Instruction.

Background.　Nebraska's educational leaders had long recognized the educational deficiencies of small high schools located in villages and towns throughout the state. They were aware that the schools were hampered by poor or nonexistent library facilities, inadequate laboratories, and, in some cases, inadequately prepared teachers. Many educators were convinced because of the World War II educational program of the Armed Forces that films could prove useful in helping to solve some of these problems. Thus in the autumn of 1945, a group of educators [30] toured Nebraska to assess the instructional situations firsthand and to explore the possibilities of using films to improve the instructional program. The result was that Frank E. Sorenson, who had made the initial trip across Nebraska, completed a proposal entitled "The Nebraska Program of Educational Enrichment, a Four-Year Experimental Study Designed to Develop an Enriched Instructional Program in Nebraska Schools through the Use of Motion Pictures." This was submitted to the Carnegie Corporation of New York in April, 1946. After a grant was obtained in May, 1946,[31] Teaching Film Custodians provided an additional $5,000 for the acquisition of films the first year of the project, and supplied, without cost, films from its own stock.[32]

In July, 1946, an administrative committee was organized and Wesley C. Meierhenry, assistant professor of education, University of Nebraska, was selected to be the administrator of the program. In addition, an area film director was appointed in each of four state teachers colleges and in the University of Omaha and the University of Nebraska in order to:

1.　Give general direction and supervision to area programs of action designed to develop enriched instructional programs in schools through the use of motion pictures;

[30] The team was composed of Frank E. Sorenson, professor of secondary education, University of Nebraska; David B. McCulley, director of the department of audiovisual instruction, University of Nebraska; and Roger Albright, educational director of Teaching Film Custodians.
[31] Grants totaling $53,900 were made to the Nebraska Film Program over a four-year period.
[32] Teaching Film Custodians provided $10,857.44 over the four years to apply toward the cost of loans of prints from other distributors or producers.

2. Stimulate and assist with studies related to the program;
3. Work cooperatively with his own college and the high schools in developing and evaluating programs of action; and
4. Assist with the production of guides for teachers and pupils, program progress reports, and other essential publications.[33]

Since the Sorenson proposal defined the research study only in broad outline, work on the refining of the research design continued until the middle of October, 1946, with the final approval given for the recommended design by the administrative committee in November, 1946. The actual experimental phase of this study did not begin until January, 1947.

Overview of the Experiment. The Nebraska Film Program used with Nebraska public school children in grades nine through twelve was confined to courses most common in the Nebraska school curriculum. Each of the seventy secondary schools chosen for experimentation was selected jointly by the program administrator and the area directors.

One of the most important tasks was the selection of motion pictures to be used in the experimentation. Two basic criteria were used for selecting films. They were:

1. The motion picture had to show a real potential for enriching the course or activity in which it was to be used.
2. The motion picture had to be of such a nature that its integration into one or more of the courses chosen for experimentation might be readily accomplished.[34]

The general design of the study called for the use of standardized achievement tests and film tests. In addition, an intelligence test was administered and provisions were made for recording, observing, and reporting the experiences which gave evidences of changes in behavior as a result of motion pictures shown.

The main results of this study indicated that the experimental groups generally learned subject matter from the films that they would not have learned otherwise. The results also indicated that bright students profited more from films in terms of actual learning.

Motion Picture Association of America studies

Following World War II, the Motion Picture Association of America supported two important projects in instructional film research: (1) the

---

[33] Wesley C. Meierhenry, *Enriching the Curriculum through Motion Pictures.* Lincoln, Nebr., University of Nebraska Press, 1952, p. 28.
[34] *Ibid.*, p. 41.

Commission on Motion Pictures of the American Council on Education and (2) the Yale Motion Picture Research Project.

Background. The Commission on Motion Pictures and the Yale Motion Picture Project grew out of a series of joint conferences and committee meetings of educators and leaders of the motion picture industry held between April, 1943, and February, 1944. The purpose of these meetings, sponsored jointly by the American Council on Education and the Motion Picture Association of America (then the Motion Picture Producers and Distributors of America, Inc.), was to explore methods of developing a cooperative progam for the production and use of instructional films in the postwar period. The first conference, held in Los Angeles, California, on April 5, 1943, was attended by some twenty-five persons—about half from the motion picture industry and half invited by the American Council. The result was the general agreement that some cooperative effort should be undertaken by the motion picture industry and educators in the production of instructional films.

The second meeting of the motion picture industry representatives and the American Council was again held in Los Angeles on July 15, 1943. The chairman of the agenda committee, George F. Zook, president of the American Council, presented four questions for discussion:

1. Can major producers, in making feature pictures, include in them certain educational items or points which would reach the vast theatrical audiences?
2. Can the short subjects now distributed by Teaching Film Custodians within the United States be distributed to foreign countries, especially among our English-speaking allies?
3. Can the industry make certain new short subject films based on educational specifications, but also having sufficient entertainment value to repay their production costs by theatrical exhibition?
4. Can the industry afford to make more of the so-called "message" films (for example, *Wilson* and *One Foot in Heaven*)? [35]

In the ensuing discussion, a fifth question was introduced:

5. To what extent can the needs of the schools for new films be met by so-called "industrial," or advertising, films sponsored by private companies?

In response to the first question the producers were generally negative and asserted that theater audiences pay primarily to be amused and entertained, rather than to be educated or informed. The answer to the second question was in the affirmative. The third question was left open for further exploration. In regard to the fourth question, there was agreement that more

[35] Mark A. May, *Planning Films for Schools: The Final Report of the Commission on Motion Pictures.* Washington, D.C., American Council on Education, 1949, p. 5.

"message" pictures should be made, but this raised the further question of what the educational leaders could do to stimulate attendance at the showing of such films. Discussion of the fifth question focused on the possibilities of producing industrial films with sufficiently high educational standards. At the close of the meeting it was agreed that a joint committee should be appointed to formulate a plan of cooperation between educators and the motion picture industry. The industry representatives on this committee were: N. Peter Rathvon (RKO), chairman; Joseph Hazen (Warner Brothers); and J. Robert Rubin (MGM); representatives from the American Council were George F. Zook, George D. Stoddard, and Mark A. May.

After a series of meetings and discussions the joint committee, composed of representatives of the Motion Picture Association of America (MPAA) and the American Council on Education, recommended the following broad cooperative program:

1. A survey of the needs of the schools for new pictures, particularly in the field of international understanding, and the preparation of curricular materials for filming.
2. The production of certain needed films.
3. The experimental evaluation of existing educational films and of new films as they are produced.
4. Promotion, including the demonstration to schools and colleges of the values and possible uses of teaching films.[36]

It was obvious that this program revived many of the notions embodied in the proposal for a national film institute developed by the American Council as far back as 1934. We have seen that the council, at that time, failed to receive foundation support for a number of obscure reasons, among them the possible intervention of some members of the motion picture industry. Since the council could not hope to secure sufficient financial support for this new program from foundations, there was some hope that the MPAA itself would be willing to underwrite the financing of a program which it had participated in developing. However, the MPAA indicated that it was not ready to undertake the financing of an educational film institute. Instead the MPAA agreed to recommend that the motion picture industry provide funds for that part of the program which had to do with the selection of film topics and the preparation of educational specifications for these films. It was also made clear by the MPAA that this would be done through an outright gift to the American Council and that the materials prepared would be made freely available to all member companies of MPAA. Moreover, MPAA did not commit itself to the production of any of the materials prepared by the council. As a result, the council accepted the conditions of this offer and appointed a Commission on Motion Pictures, in February, 1944, to survey

[36] *Ibid.*, pp. 6–7.

the requirements of schools and develop a series of educational specifications for needed films.

Meanwhile, when Eric Johnston became president of MPAA in 1945, a new policy was adopted with reference to the production of educational films. In March, 1946, the board of directors of MPAA, on the recommendation of the MPAA's Committee on Educational Matters,[37] appropriated $100,000 for the production of several experimental films with the purpose of gaining information on procedures, processes, and costs of producing effective instructional films. Although only three pilot films were produced in this project, they were of historical significance because they anticipated to a large extent the single-concept film developed in the early 1960s and because they represented the first attempt of the MPAA to produce a genuine instructional film. The entire production of these experimental films was under the general management of Arthur L. Mayer of New York City and was cooridinated by Roger Albright, director of the newly created Division of Educational Services of the MPAA. Two of the three pilot films, *Seasons* and *Osmosis*, were produced in cooperation with the Macmillan Company and Henry Holt and Company, Inc.[38]

Meanwhile, Mark A. May,[39] chairman and director of research of Teaching Film Custodians (a film distribution organization of the MPAA), organized the Yale Motion Picture Research Project, secured its financing from the MPAA, and served as general director from its beginning in 1946 to its end in 1954. Its stated purpose was to discover, through controlled experimental studies, methods of improving the teaching effectiveness of educational films.[40] Thus we come full circle from similar objectives first stated in 1934 as part of a proposal for a national film institute by the American Council on Education. However, there were two important differences: First, there was adequate financial support to conduct such experimentation; second, there was wholehearted psychological support and cooperation from the motion picture industry.

Commission on Motion Pictures.[41]   The commission's main tasks were (1) to study the needs of schools for teaching films, particularly for pictures

[37] The members of this committee were: N. Peter Rathvon, J. Robert Rubin, and Joseph Hazen, the same men who had represented the motion picture industry on the joint committee of MPAA and the American Council in 1943.

[38] The script of *Seasons* was written by Philip Knowlton, elementary school textbooks editor for Macmillan. The script of *Osmosis* was written with the technical advice of Milton Hopkins, science editor for Henry Holt and Company, Inc.

[39] Mark A. May, professor of educational psychology and director of the Institute of Human Relations at Yale University.

[40] Mark A. May, "Educational Projects," *Educational Screen*, vol. 26, no. 4 (April, 1947), p. 201.

[41] The original members of the Commission on Motion Pictures, appointed by the American Council on Education in February, 1944, were: Edmund E. Day, president, Cornell University; Monsignor George Johnson, director, Department of Education, National Cath-

that would help meet the opportunities and challenges presented by problems of the postwar period, (2) to write educational specifications for the production of needed films and to select and organize content materials, and (3) when possible and feasible, to prepare film treatments and scripts.[42]

The commission, basing its assessment of film needs to a large extent on the Seaton survey [43] of teacher opinion concerning films, selected five general areas of instruction—geography, problems of democracy, mathematics, music, and art. Plans for 141 films in these areas were prepared, but the commission actually released to producers the materials for a total of only 117 films. Work on preliminary treatments for films in problems of democracy for senior high schools was carried on by a committee under the general chairmanship of George S. Counts, Teachers College, Columbia University. Late in 1946, the commission employed George F. Kneller as general editor of the series.[44] On the basis of criticisms received from readers, the commission finally selected fifteen treatments and released them to producers.

About a year before the commission was organized, President W. W. Atwood, Clark University, and F. Dean McClusky, headmaster of the Scarborough School, Scarsdale-on-Hudson, New York, had received a grant of $10,000 from RKO Pictures, Inc., to develop an outline for a series of films on global geography. Their completed outline, entitled *Widening Our Horizons,* was first presented in a commission meeting in April, 1944, by N. Peter Rathvon, president of RKO. Following a series of meetings, discussions, and outline revisions, a committee consisting of Atwood, McClusky, and Gardner L. Hart, director of the commission, was appointed to select ten key topics in the outline and to write detailed specifications for the production of these films, including scripts. This decision, however, raised a question of policy as to the function of the commission. Prior to this time the commission had not engaged in the writing of shooting scripts and had confined itself to the preparation of educational specifications and an outline of film content. Some

---

olic Welfare Conference; Willard E. Givens, executive secretary, National Education Association; George S. Counts, director, Division of the Foundations of Education, Teachers College, Columbia University; Mark A. May, director, Institute of Human Relations, Yale University, chairman; and George F. Zook, president, American Council on Education, ex-officio. George N. Shuster, president, Hunter College, replaced Monsignor Johnson when he died in May, 1944. Four more members were added later: A. L. Threlkeld, superintendent of schools, Montclair, New Jersey; W. W. Atwood, president, Clark University; Mary D. Barnes, principal, William Livingston School, Elizabeth, New Jersey; and Frank N. Freeman, dean, School of Education, University of California. Edmund E. Day resigned in 1947 because of other commitments.

[42] May, *Planning Films for Schools,* p. 1.

[43] See Helen Hardt Seaton, *A Measure for Audio-Visual Programs in Schools.* Washington, D.C., American Council on Education, 1944.

[44] Kneller found that it was difficult to find individuals who had a talent for dramatic writing and who could at the same time stay within the bounds of historical accuracy. The result was that all the research material collected and organized was not put into the form of film treatments.

members felt that scriptwriting belonged more to production and should be left to commercial producers. Nevertheless, with Atwood insisting that the film materials could and should be carried to the script stage, the commission agreed to engage a scriptwriter and authorized Atwood to find a producer for the series. The result was that a contract was made with Louis de Rochemont Associates, Inc., for the production of thirty-six films and Atwood was engaged as an educational consultant.

In getting the mathematics film treatments started, Gardner Hart first consulted W. D. Reeve, Teachers College, Columbia University, who was then editing a yearbook prepared by the Multi-Sensory Aids Committee of the National Council of Teachers of Mathematics. When Reeve recommended that this committee would be especially well qualified to plan for needed films in mathematics, his suggestion was accepted by the commission. Harold L. Walton, general research associate of the commission, was placed in charge of the development of the mathematics material and educational specifications were developed for seven films on algebra and nine on geometry.

The work of the commission in the field of art grew out of an exchange of letters among Stanley A. Czurles, director of art education, New York State College for Teachers, Buffalo; Mark A. May, the commission's chairman; and Gardner L. Hart, its director. Czurles volunteered to prepare a report for the commission entitled *Outline for Motion Pictures to Teach the Basic Skills and Techniques in Art*, which was presented to a meeting of the commission in October, 1945. As a result of this presentation, the commission voted to establish an art committee to develop plans for art films and appointed a member of the commission, A. L. Threlkeld, superintendent of the Montclair, New Jersey, public schools, as chairman. The materials prepared and released by the art committee included educational specifications for twenty-one films on art.[45]

The commission set up a music committee at its meeting in March, 1947. Since this was the last committee of the commission to be organized, the group benefited from the problems encountered by other committees, particularly in determining the format of the materials to be developed. The committee worked in cooperation with the Music Research Council of the Music Educators National Conference, headed by William Sur, Michigan State College. The materials prepared by the music committee were unique; they included two special reports covering the fields of music reading and music listening, in addition to specifications for a number of different music films. Plans were developed for a series of fifteen films on music.[46]

[45] The members of the commission staff assigned to this project were Gardner Hart, R. S. Hadsell, and H. L. Walton.
[46] R. S. Hadsell and H. L. Walton were the commission staff members assigned to this project.

The work of the commission has been variously evaluated. There is no question that it represents a significant cooperative endeavor between educators and the motion picture industry. Unfortunately, however, much of the work of this commission has yet to prove useful—if ever it will. With the one single exception of the geography series sponsored at the initiative of Rathvon of RKO, before the commission itself was organized, none of the film treatments prepared by the commission have been produced to date. Since the original, comprehensive, mimeographed film treatments and outlines for these 117 films are in the sole possession and control of the MPAA, it is unlikely that the work of the commission will ever come to fruition.

Yale Motion Picture Research Project.   The financial support for this project, beginning in 1946 and ending in 1954, came from Teaching Film Custodians, Inc., a film distribution organization affiliated with the MPAA. The initial grant was for the purpose of experimentally evaluating certain pilot teaching films that were being produced under the sponsorship of the MPAA (the Mayer film production activities already referred to in the background portion of this section). The work of the project, however, was soon expanded to include exploratory experimental studies of problems associated with instructional film production and utilization.[47] Thus the project came to be focused on two broad objectives: first, to discover principles of effective production and utilization of instructional films; and second, to explore the uses and limitations of existing types of films for instructional purposes and to find out why teachers were not making a wider use of films and graphic presentations in the classroom. The series of studies conducted in this project compared the effects of alternate ways of utilizing a finished film product and measured the learning of factual information, the acquisition of skills, and the modification of interests, attitudes, and opinions. However, these studies were generally devoid of theoretical orientation and uneven in meth-

[47] This project was carried out under the general direction of Mark A. May, director of the Motion Picture Research Project and of the Institute of Human Relations, Yale University. Other staff members included: Arthur A. Lumsdaine, associate director from 1946 to 1949; R. S. Hadsell, assistant director from 1950 to 1954 and director of the Commission on Motion Pictures in Education during the years 1948 to 1950; Arthur I. Gladstone, member of the staff for the year 1948–1949; John J. Howell, part-time member of the staff while a graduate student in the Department of Education at Yale University from 1950 to 1954; Mary C. Arnold, secretary, research assistant, and office manager of the project from 1946 to 1949; Gardner Hart, director of the Commission on Motion Pictures in Education from 1945 to 1948, staff member of the project from 1946 to 1948; Edna Kauffman, part-time staff member from 1947 to 1949 while a graduate student in psychology, Yale University; A. J. North, part-time staff member while a graduate student in psychology, Yale University; Harold Walton, member of the staff for the year 1948–1949; and J. J. Wulff, a part-time member of the staff while a graduate student in psychology, Yale University. The testing program was conducted in the public schools of New Haven, West Haven, East Haven, and Hamden, Connecticut; in St. Louis, Missouri; and in New York City.

odology. Teaching Film Custodians developed the film materials used to test experimental variables, but as far as can be determined, these films were completely unaffected by theory or the findings of past film research. The common attitude of MPAA was that successful entertainment films could be edited, or modified, and transformed into effective instructional films. Since the researchers in the project had little or no control over the basic structure of films produced for this experiment, they could hardly be expected to test complex experimental variables in any systematic or penetrating fashion. It is regrettable that this lengthy project did not produce results which could have significantly influenced the production and utilization of instructional films.[48]

Major military film research programs

The immediate postwar years saw the initiation of two major film research programs by military sponsors. The United States Navy, in collaboration with the United States Army, supported a series of studies by Pennsylvania State University beginning in 1947 and ending in 1955. A counterpart film research program was organized by the United States Air Force from 1950 to 1957. Both of these programs were primarily planned to meet a national emergency in which there would be a serious shortage of time, instructional facilities, and instructors.

Instructional Film Research Program. This project, conducted by the Division of Academic Research and Services at Pennsylvania State University under the direction of C. R. Carpenter, involved over eighty individual research studies resulting in some 155 publications. It was probably the most extensive single program of experimentation dealing with instructional films ever conducted.

The basic experimental approach used in the Instructional Film Research Program was to produce special versions of films, incorporating defined variables, and then to compare the effects of these versions on appropriate groups of learners under controlled conditions.

In order to carry on these experiments, a response system called the Classroom Communicator was designed and built in the early 1950s to do the following: (1) provide a means by which individuals in a classroom could signal their choice of answer from five choices given with a question; (2) provide a means to record the responses of the individuals in such a manner that the data could be collected and subjected to analysis; and (3)

---

[48] For a complete report of the Yale Motion Picture Research Project, see Mark A. May et al., *Learning from Films.* New Haven, Conn., Yale University Press, 1958.

provide a means to inform each individual as to whether or not his choice was correct or what the correct response should have been. It can be seen that the Classroom Communicator was the early prototype of contemporary response systems.

The general conclusions reached in these studies indicate the following:

1. Well-produced films, either used singly or in a series, can be employed as the sole means of teaching some types of performance skills and conveying some kinds of factual data.
2. Postviewing tests will increase learning when students have been told what to look for in the film and that a test on the film content would be given.
3. Students will learn more if they are given study guides for each film used.
4. Note-taking by students during the showing of a film should be discouraged because it distracts them from the film itself.
5. Successive showings of a given film can increase learning.
6. Short films can be spliced end-to-end in a loop and are beneficial in practice or drill situations.
7. Students can watch motion pictures for one hour without reduction in training effectiveness.
8. The effectiveness of film learning should be evaluated by tests.
9. After a film has been shown, its major points should be summarized and discussed lest students form misconceptions.
10. Follow-up activities should be encouraged to provide carryover of generalizations.[49]

Another section of this summary provides these guidelines for instructional film makers:

1. *Camera angle.* Show a performance on the screen the way the learner would see it if he were doing the job himself.
2. *Rate of development.* Keep the rate of development of a film slow enough to permit the learner to grasp the material as it is shown.
3. *Succinct treatment.* Do not present only the bare essentials or cover subject matter too rapidly.
4. *Introductions.* Present relevant information in the introduction and tell the viewer what he is expected to learn from the film.
5. *Summary.* Summarize important points in the film in a clear, concise manner. Summaries probably do not significantly improve learning unless they are complete enough to serve as repetition and review.
6. *Concentration of ideas.* Present ideas or concepts at a rate appropriate to the ability of the audience.

[49] C. R. Carpenter and L. P. Greenhill, *Instructional Film Research Reports*, vol. 2. Technical Report 269-7-61, NAVEXOS P1543, Port Washington, N.Y., Special Devices Center, 1956.

7. *Commentary.* Don't "pack" the sound track: the number of words (per minute of film) in the commentary has a definite effect on learning.
8. *Special effects.* Avoid the use of special effects as attention-getting devices; it has no positive influence on learning.
9. *Color.* Experimentation has not yet demonstrated any general over-all increase in learning as a result of using color in instructional films.
10. *Music.* Preliminary experimentation suggests that music does not add to the instructional effectiveness of an informational film.[50]

Most of the studies conducted in this film research program are bound together in two volumes (*Instructional Film Research Reports,* and *Instructional Film Research Reports, Vol. II*) and are available from the Office of Technical Services, U.S. Department of Commerce. In addition, a valuable by-product of this project was a report summarizing more than two hundred instructional film studies conducted between 1918 and 1950.[51]

In 1954, the Instructional Film Research Program was reorganized and new objectives were formulated. Since there seemed to be similarities between instructional sound films and instructional television, it was decided that a more integrated research program should be initiated. Therefore, a general agreement was reached with the Fund for the Advancement of Education (subsidiary of the Ford Foundation) that a closed-circuit instructional television research project would be conducted on an exploratory basis during the 1954–1955 period by part of the Instructional Film Research Program staff in cooperation with the departments of chemistry and psychology of Pennsylvania State University. After the completion of preliminary work during the first year, the Fund agreed to continue the television project and the Instructional Film Research Program was terminated.

Air Force Film Research Program.   During the period 1950–1957, the Research and Development Command of the United States Air Force conducted, under the direction of Arthur A. Lumsdaine (former assistant director of the Yale Motion Picture Research Project), a series of research studies on instructional films as well as other forms of instructional media. From 1950 to 1953, there was a rather intensive focus on instructional film research. All of the studies in the Air Force film research program involved the manipulation of film variables and techniques for eliciting and/or guiding overt responses during a course of instruction. These studies were conducted by a number of individuals at different locations over an extended period of time. Reports on this program have been largely confined to

[50] *Ibid.*
[51] See C. F. Hoban, Jr., and E. B. Van Ormer, *Instructional Film Research 1918–1950.* Technical Report SDC 269-7-19, Port Washington, N.Y., U.S. Naval Training Devices Center, December, 1950.

mimeographed reports of a limited circulation. The largest collection of the main studies in this program appeared in the book *Student Response in Programmed Instruction.*[52]

Although it is impossible within the space of this book to summarize adequately the results of the many studies in the Air Force program, it is clear from the available studies that they hold significant implications for the use and design of instructional films and related media. However, we are simultaneously confronted with the puzzling fact that this extensive Air Force program failed to influence the film production techniques employed while these studies were in progress. Moreover, it is even more baffling when we find that none of the results of the hundred or more studies flowing from both the Army-Navy Pennsylvania State University program and the Air Force program have yet to be implemented in the instructional films produced by the Armed Forces. One explanation for this paradox may lie in the almost complete isolation of researchers from film production personnel which occurred in the joint Army-Navy studies as well as in the Air Force studies. Kanner suggests that film production personnel attitudes toward researchers who attempt to influence the film-making process typically reflect resentment.[53] In addition, he describes the prevailing perception by film production personnel that "anyone who could make a successful entertainment film could readily adapt to making a training film—a kind of film often described as a minor subspecies where a homely mixture of 'motivation,' humor, and animation could carry the teaching message." It is clear from the history of both of the military studies we have discussed here that there is a need for a close working relationship between research and film production personnel and that some effective methods of dissemination and innovation must be devised whereby the results of media research can be readily put into effect.

Instructional television research

Practically all of the studies of instructional television have been conducted since 1950, and particularly during the decade 1954–1964. The Armed Forces were the first to experiment with television as an instructional medium because of its promise in meeting the mass instruction requirements demanded by military training. As early as 1950, the Navy began some of the first studies of the instructional effectiveness of television. Shortly after-

[52] A. A. Lumsdaine (ed.), *Student Response in Programmed Instruction.* Washington, D.C., National Academy of Sciences, National Research Council, 1961.
[53] J. H. Kanner, "The Development and Role of Teaching Aids in the Armed Forces," in *New Teaching Aids for the American Classroom.* Stanford, Calif., The Institute for Communication Research, 1960, pp. 123–124.

wards, the Human Resources Research Office, George Washington University, conducted for the Army a study comparing television with conventional instruction in teaching effectiveness. It was not until 1955 or 1956 that full-scale instructional television research began in schools and colleges with financial support from the Ford Foundation. The National Defense Education Act of 1958 provided financial grants through Title VII which spurred the development of instructional television research in the late 1950s and the early 1960s.

Pennsylvania State University Closed-circuit Television Project. As we have seen, the Fund for the Advancement of Education began its support for a closed-circuit instructional television project at Pennsylvania State University in 1954. Subsequently, the Fund agreed to finance the project until 1959, with the University increasing its contribution each year and eventually assuming the entire expense of regular operation of the instructional television system.

The experimental phase of this project was carried out during the spring semester of 1955 and the fall semester of 1956–1957. Since 1957 there has been a steady expansion of instructional television at Pennsylvania State University. By 1958, 3,700 (out of a total of 14,000) students were taking one or more of thirteen television courses offered. The initial experiments of this closed-circuit television project, under the direction of C. R. Carpenter and L. P. Greenhill, were designed to determine whether television could be used effectively in regular undergraduate courses and what its effects would be on instructors, students, and on the institution itself. In one phase of experimentation, a course taught in the traditional manner was compared with the same course taught by an instructor over television. New courses and materials were prepared for further comparisons. The primary focus was on extending the influence of superior teachers in those introductory courses attended by large numbers of students, which were usually taught by the lecture or lecture-demonstration method. When the students were tested at the end of the courses, it was found that there were no significant differences in achievement. It also appeared that teachers and students did not like television very much, although most instructors were willing to experiment with it and most students preferred it to live presentations in very large classes. These studies did demonstrate, however, that the influence of outstanding teachers could be extended to large groups of students without measurable loss of learning and that television could be economically feasible if the type of equipment chosen is appropriate to the task and if the system is used for a sufficiently large group (several courses involving 300 to 400 students).

The results of the Pennsylvania State University closed-circuit television project proved a bitter blow to those who thought that television instruction would revolutionize education. In addition, accumulating evidence from the majority of similar studies also revealed "no significant differences" between televised instruction and direct instruction. Thus it became apparent to some researchers that new experimental approaches were needed to replace the stereotyped instructional media comparisons design in order to understand and develop the potential of instructional television.[54]

Washington County. Closed-circuit Educational Television Project.   We have seen that one of the largest single experiments in the use of closed-circuit television for instruction started in 1956 in Hagerstown, Washington County, Maryland. The Washington County Board of Education had first considered using television in the schools in 1954. Although the Board was unaware of it then, the Ford Foundation's Fund for the Advancement of Education, and the Electronic Industries Association, had formed a joint committee for the purpose of starting a large-scale project in instructional television—a model program that would provide for regular, direct instruction by television rather than for a supplemental use of it. On the basis of the Washington County Board of Education's proposal to use television for instruction at all grade levels and in basic subject areas, as well as for teacher education, the Fund chose Washington County as the site for its first comprehensive test of instructional television in the public schools.

The project extended over a period of five years (1956–1961), starting in the summer of 1956 when approximately one hundred teachers and administrators gathered at a workshop for the purpose of planning the new instructional television program. Simultaneously, engineers began stringing cable for the television network. The first instructional telecasts were beamed to eight schools in the fall of 1956, and by the end of the project in 1961, every public school in Washington County was linked to the television circuit.[55]

This project cannot be considered a formal experiment, for it was largely exploratory. As it developed, television came into use at all grade levels and in most subject areas. One of the most interesting aspects of this project was the successful application of television within a district-wide guidance program. In brief, the results of this study showed that television produced substantial increases in achievement and indicated that this gain was statistically significant in some course areas. For example, in fifth-grade arithmetic, pupils made almost two years' growth in arithmetic—from five

---

[54] See, for example, L. Siegel and L. C. Siegel, "The Instructional Gestalt: A Conceptual Framework and Design for Educational Research," *AV Communication Review*, vol. 12, no. 1 (Spring, 1964), pp. 16–45.
[55] Throughout the five years of the project, the Washington County school system received support from two major sources—the Electronic Industries Association and the Fund for the Advancement of Education. Seventy-five manufacturers donated the equipment valued at $300,000, and the Fund contributed about $200,000 each year.

months below grade level to four months above it.[56] Although the project staff did not claim that television per se was totally responsible for learner achievement, they saw educational value in television because:

1. It focused attention on problems in a way never before possible.
2. It stimulated team work and planning.
3. It created interest in curriculum development and teaching procedures.
4. It required pupils to assume more responsibility.
5. Parents took a greater interest than formerly in the school program and in the progress of their children.[57]

Much of the success of the Washington County project was a direct result of the way television was introduced into the system. During the five-year experiment, summer workshops were continued, frequently supplemented during the regular school terms with consultant service, as well as field trips. Also, there was no lack of emphasis on the fact that the teacher in the classroom, who followed the instructional telecasts, was the key person in the teaching team.[58]

Instructional Television Research to 1960.   By 1960 there was no longer any doubt that students could learn effectively from instructional television. It had been demonstrated—in approximately four hundred quantitative

[56] Washington County Board of Education, *Washington County Closed-circuit Television Report.* Hagerstown, Md., 1963, pp. 47–53.

[57] *Ibid.*, p. 73.

[58] Since the Fund for the Advancement of Education considered the Washington County Closed-circuit Educational Television Project a success, funds were provided in 1957 to launch a nationwide experiment in instructional television known as The National Program in the Use of Television in the Public Schools. The main thesis of *Schools for Tomorrow*, a report by Alexander J. Stoddard of the Fund, was that television is an effective medium of instruction for the teaching of large groups. In an effort to test this hypothesis, the Fund involved over two hundred thousand students in more than eight hundred elementary and secondary schools throughout the country. Public school systems participating in this program were the following: Anaheim, California; Atlanta, Georgia; Buena Vista No. 9 School District, Saginaw, Michigan; Cincinnati, Ohio; Dade County (Miami), Florida; Detroit, Michigan; Jefferson County, Kentucky; Milwaukee, Wisconsin; Norfolk, Virginia; Oklahoma City, Oklahoma; Philadelphia, Pennsylvania; and Wichita, Kansas, as well as schools in central Michigan; the Columbus, Ohio, area; Evansville and vicinity; western Florida; Des Moines, Iowa; and Kansas City, Missouri. During the first two years of the national program, the participating schools made many comparisons between achievement of television students and conventionally taught students. In the second year of the experiment, the number of comparisons favoring television students was more than twice the number of comparisons favoring control groups, while the number of significant differences favoring television was more than three times the number favoring conventional teaching. The most obvious thing was the large number of *no significant difference* results. However, the difference between the results for the younger and older students was highly significant, showing that television has been a more effective medium for younger students than for older. See *Teaching by Television.* New York, Ford Foundation and Fund for the Advancement of Education, 1961.

studies in which television instruction was compared to conventional instruction—that students in some cases will learn more, and in some, less. However, the overall conclusion was that there was "no significant difference." Relative to this conclusion is the evidence presented by Kumata as follows:

> In the United States, we have put most of our bets on the discovery of some effect which is directly attributable to the means of message transmission and hundreds of similar studies have been conducted. Almost all of them say that it makes no difference whether television is present or absent. They say that if you ignore audience variables, the nature of the student; if you ignore the nature of the source, those who put on the program; and if you look just at the media of transmission, you will get rather ambiguous results.
>
> We have been insisting that perhaps we should look at television instruction as part of a general communication process and that we may get some valuable hints from other research which has been done in the communications field.
>
> If we were to characterize the research done, I think four points would stand out. First, *no particular theoretical framework has been apparent in most of the studies* [italics mine]. Almost all of the studies have been of an applied nature. . . . Further there has been very little dependence on prior research. Second, the overwhelming majority of these studies have been what we call "comparability" studies, and almost all of these have been comparisons of television versus face-to-face instruction. Very few studies have been done as comparisons of radio, film, and television. Third, almost all of the main dependent variables in these investigations have been some measure of students' information gain. . . . Most examinations have been in the nature of requests for students to reproduce information previously supplied by the instructor. Fourth, most research in instructional television has been done in the classroom situation, with regularly enrolled students. In other words, research has concentrated upon the captive audience aspects of educational television.[59]

The implication for the researcher and the educator is that areas of new research must be conceived and that the emphasis should be shifted to the totality of the teaching-learning process. When Carpenter,[60] for example, talks about instructional television research as systems research, he is, in effect, asking that we determine the place of television within an instructional system or within the context of a technology of instruction.

[59] Report presented at the International Seminar on Instructional Television, Oct. 8–18, 1961, at Purdue University, Lafayette, Ind. From *History and Progress of Instructional Television Research in the United States* by Hideya Kumata.
[60] C. R. Carpenter, "Approaches to Promising Areas of Research in Field of Instructional Television," in *New Teaching Aids for the American Classroom.* Pp. 73–94.

The Denver-Stanford Project.   One of the first extensive research projects which attempted to measure combinations of instructional media, as well as combinations of related activities with television, was conducted jointly over a three-and-one-half-year period (1960–1964) by the Denver public schools and the Institute for Communication Research at Stanford University. When it became apparent that there was need for an investigation of the context of instructional television, in late 1959, the National Educational Television and Radio Center brought together representatives of the Denver public schools and Stanford's Institute for Communication Research. From this meeting emerged a proposal for a joint project financed under Title VII (NDEA), and funds were granted. The project was officially titled "Four Years of Research on the Context of Instructional Television," but it has come to be known as the Denver-Stanford Project.

Beginning with the 1960–1961 school year, the Denver public schools made foreign language mandatory for all fifth and sixth graders, and pupils were permitted to choose between Spanish and French. Since some 80 percent chose Spanish and since there was a shortage of elementary teachers qualified to teach Spanish, the problem of the study was how to introduce and teach Spanish most effectively in elementary school under the conditions pertaining at Denver. In more general terms, the problem was to determine the kind of teaching and learning context that would make for maximum learning from instructional television. This is what Denver and Stanford were working on from 1960 to the beginning of 1964.

Field research was conducted for three full years. Fifth-grade pupils were involved all three years, and sixth graders were involved the last two. Instructional open-circuit telecasts, each fifteen minutes in length, provided the basic instruction for all pupils, but fifth graders had forty-five minutes of television instruction each week, and sixth graders had thirty minutes. All television instruction was audiolingual, but half the sixth graders had a full thirty-minute period each week the first semester while the other half had further audiolingual instruction. All sixth graders took reading and writing the second semester. What is more, reading and writing were begun at different times to determine what effects they would have on listening and speaking skills. In still another variation, children studied reading and writing in two ways: by the traditional teacher-directed approach and by the programed instruction method. Furthermore, in the last year of the research, fifth-grade activities were designed to evaluate classroom practice on the basis of a second viewing of the television lessons, of electronic media with and without feedback, and of parent participation in the instructional process.

It is emphasized in the Denver-Stanford Summary Report that the object of this study was not to test the audiolingual method against any other method of language teaching. The purpose of this test was, therefore, not of the method but of how the most effective course could be built, given an accepted method. Moreover, the goal of this project was not to prepare every teacher to be an expert in teaching a course in Spanish by the audiolingual method but to make every teacher more expert in developing learning activities in connection with television. In the Denver schools, the concept was that a team consisting of the expert language teacher on television, the classroom teacher who manages the things that would integrate with television, and the parents who assist at home should all combine to teach elementary school Spanish. This project was essentially the devising of experiments to find the most effective combinations of activities and instructional media for the teaching team.

The findings of the Denver-Stanford Project showed that the most effective context for instructional television in the audiolingual year was provided by classroom teacher-conducted practice plus practice with an electronic aid, such as a dual-channel tape recorder. In general, an eclectic method including structure drill, dialogue drill, and narrative drill proved effective. The most effective classroom combination for the second year of the language—the sixth-grade audiolingual-reading-writing year—proved to be teacher-directed practice, programed instruction in school, and a Spanish corner for individual use in the classroom. A striking relationship was noted between pupil performance and the preparation of the teacher. It was found, for example, that a pupil could work independently with programed instruction, extending reading, etc., to the extent that the teacher was prepared and experienced. Another finding was that for teacher-directed activities, small classes tended to perform better, but for individual activities like programed instruction, large classes tended to perform better. Timing was also found to be an important factor. Reading and writing should start at least by the beginning of the second year of instruction—in this case, the sixth grade. It was found that for most pupils programed instruction was better started in the second semester when the pupils had a better command of the spoken language and were more apt to work independently on reading and writing. Also, results showed that programed instruction was not capable of carrying the complete instructional load, as many of its proponents have suggested.

The aspect of the Denver-Stanford Project which has attracted the most interest has been the direct involvement of parents in the instructional process. In all three years of the project, parents were invited to help their children learn Spanish, a practice which ran contrary to the trend of public school methods over the last fifty years. This part of the project was administered through the local PTA. The PTA secured the volunteers, instructed them in the procedures they were to follow, supplied them with special materials, and provided them with the information needed to evaluate their procedures. The best school performance in Spanish was associated with high amounts of practice and viewing by parents and children. Attitudes were associated with participation. When family participation was high, favorable parental attitudes made relatively little difference in the learner's school performance; but when family participation was low, favorable parental attitudes made a significant difference in how well the child did in school. Thus, if these results hold true generally, parents constitute an important instructional resource which has been largely overlooked. It seems certain that some of the characteristics of the Denver context will reappear when instructional television is used effectively as part of an integrated technology of instruction.[61]

Future Instructional Television Research.　　Research findings make it clear that instructional television's ultimate value will be judged on what it can or cannot do as compared to other media or techniques. Future instructional television research is likely to be focused on the discovery and solution of limitations to teaching by television. A representative approach to this general problem was carried out by Gropper and Lumsdaine [62] in their study of the use of student responses to improve televised instruction. Another hopeful area of research concerns the combination of other media with television. A study by Carpenter and Greenhill [63] illustrates an effort in this direction. Their study involved the programing of entire courses in mathematics and English grammar and the comparison of different methods and media for presenting programed materials, with special emphasis on closed-circuit television.

One of the fundamental problems of instructional media research, and of instructional television research in particular, is the lack of a theoretical framework for testing hypotheses. For example, in the four hundred or more experiments comparing conventional instruction with televised instruction, there is little theoretical evidence underlying the bulk of these studies. It seems clear that much work needs to be done by researchers in developing a theoretical structure for their experiments before educators can begin to develop a scientific technology of instruction.[64]

---

[61] See Denver Public Schools–Stanford University, *The Context of Instructional Television—Summary Report of Research Findings 1960–1964.* NDEA Title VII Project 354, U.S. Office of Education, June, 1964.

[62] G. L. Gropper and A. A. Lumsdaine, *The Use of Student Response to Improve Televised Instruction: An Overview.* Report no. 7 (summary of six prior reports), *Studies in Televised Instruction*, Pittsburgh, Pa., American Institute for Research, Report no. AIR-C13-61-FR-245 (VII), 1961.

[63] C. R. Carpenter and L. P. Greenhill, *Comparative Research on Methods and Media for Presenting Programed Courses in Mathematics and English.* Pennsylvania State University Report under USOE grant no. 736116, University Park, Pa., March, 1963.

[64] See Ernest R. Hilgard, "Perspective on the Relationship between Learning Theory and Educational Practices," in E. R. Hilgard (ed.), *Theories of Learning and Instruction,* The Sixty-third Yearbook of the National Society for the Study of Education, part I. Chicago, The University of Chicago Press, 1964, pp. 402–415.

Programed instruction research

Programed instruction research, in contrast to research in other instructional media, has been linked to a greater extent with basic and applied research. Such research can be classified into two broad categories: (1) field-study experiments involving the use of programed materials in actual classroom situations or (2) laboratory studies in which relatively small groups of experimental subjects have been given programed materials outside of classroom situations. In the laboratory experiments, two different versions of a program might be written and each version given to a different group of subjects. Their relative achievement scores would then be compared. Or these studies might involve such theoretical problems as the comparison of different response modes and of different prompting and confirmation methods, ways of eliciting desired responses, or adapting programs to individual differences.

It is our purpose in this section to focus on a very few studies selected as representative of the types of problems which have been investigated most frequently.

Effectiveness of Programed Instruction.   More than three-fourths of all the research on programed instruction has been undertaken since 1960. What is more, no method of instruction has ever been subjected to so much research activity in such a short period of time. However, the general conclusion from all this research was that no significant difference was found among treatment comparisons, and when significant differences were obtained, they seldom agreed with other findings on the same problem.

Research has disclosed that self-instructional approaches in the form of lineal and branching programs promote learning. Numerous other studies comparing programed instruction with so-called conventional teaching procedures have demonstrated that students learn from programed instruction. But the basic question—how well do they learn from programs, as compared to how well they learn from other methods of instruction—has produced no definitive answers. Silberman has reported, for example,[65] that in fifteen field-study comparisons of programed and conventional instruction, nine favored the programs with respect to criterion scores and six showed no significant differences. All fifteen comparisons showed that programed instruction took less time. This general pattern of results has been reflected in most recent research, although the results of some studies have favored conventional instruction.

Concern with evaluative criteria for assessing the quality of programed

[65] H. F. Silberman, "Characteristics of Some Recent Studies of Instructional Methods," in J. E. Coulson (ed.), *Programmed Learning and Computer-based Instruction.* New York, John Wiley & Sons, Inc., 1962, pp. 13–24.

materials was primarily responsible for the formation in 1961 of the Joint Committee on Programed Instruction (JCPI), representing the American Educational Research Association (AERA), the American Psychological Association (APA), and the Department of Audiovisual Instruction (DAVI) of the National Education Association (NEA). In 1964, the JCPI made the following three general recommendations about the reporting of evidence on a program's effectiveness:

> First: Evidence for the effectiveness of a program should be based on a carefully conducted study which shows what the program's use accomplished under specified conditions.

> Second: The results of the evaluation study should be carefully documented in a technical report prepared in keeping with accepted standards of scientific reporting.

> Third: All claims or statements about the effectiveness of a program should be supported by specific reference to the evidence contained in the technical report.[66]

The substance of the committee's further recommendations, made in 1965, indicates that prospective purchasers or users should evaluate each program on its own merits and determine the suitability of the program for their own purposes. Moreover, the prospective user was advised to ignore all claims for the effectiveness of a program which were not supported by appropriate data that had been subjected to competent evaluation. Other comprehensive recommendations were offered by the JCPI to program publishers, reviewers, producers, and technical advisers.[67]

Pressey Studies. Some of the earliest investigations of programed instruction were made in the 1920s by Sidney L. Pressey at Ohio State University as part of a course in educational psychology. These studies were designed to show that automated instruction facilitated learning by providing for immediate reinforcement, individual pace setting, and active responding.

The technique Pressey developed was to expose a question to a student and permit him to answer by pressing a key, by inserting his pencil tip in a punchboard, or by means of chemically treated paper. In addition, the student was referred to a specific textbook for supplementary information or his error was discussed with the instructor.

---

[66] American Educational Research Association, American Psychological Association, Department of Audiovisual Instruction, National Education Association: Joint Committee on Programed Instruction and Teaching Machines, *Recommendations for Reporting of Information on the Performance Characteristics of Programmed Learning Materials: Third Interim Report.* (Preliminary edition.) Berkeley, University of California Press, 1964.
[67] For further details on the effectiveness of programs, the reader may wish to consult Arthur A. Lumsdaine, "Assessing the Effectiveness of Instructional Programs," in Robert Glaser (ed.), *Teaching Machines and Programed Learning, II: Data and Directions.* Washington, D.C., NEA, 1965, pp. 267–320.

Pressey reported that his experimental students learned new material successfully from these automated programs and demonstrated significant reductions in errors when the same programs were taken a second time. He also found that the subject matter was learned faster and retained longer from his multiple-choice programs than from textbook reading.[68]

The Roanoke Experiment.[69]   One of the first extensive field tests of programed instruction was conducted in the Roanoke (Virginia) city schools in 1960. The Roanoke Experiment began as a result of an invitation by Allen Calvin, a psychologist at Hollins College, to Edward Rushton, Roanoke's superintendent. Calvin, who had earlier become interested in programed instruction, had applied for and received a grant from the Carnegie Foundation to develop an experiment utilizing an automatic teaching device to assess the possibilities of programed instruction. Soon after, Encyclopedia Britannica Films, Inc., became interested in his work and established, first at Hollins College and later in Palo Alto, California, its Center for Studies in Learning and Motivation.

EBF also worked with the Roanoke schools in the Roanoke Experiment. The arrangement was that Roanoke would set up the demonstration class and that EBF and Hollins College would provide Roanoke with teaching machines, the programed course, and consultation services. In February, 1960, eighth-grade students, working at their own speed and receiving no help from the teacher, worked directly with ninth-grade algebra programed materials, using lightweight Foringer teaching machines. The results of this pilot study were favorable, and in the fall of 1960 some nine hundred ninth graders in all of the Roanoke secondary schools participated in a field test of three mathematics programs, Algebra I and II and Plane Geometry. Classes were conducted in three ways. The so-called conventional class was taught as usual except that the students were told they would be part of an experiment. In the second, the programed material was used with no help from the teacher except to discuss examination results. In the third, the programed material was used with help from the teacher. The experimental classes had no homework but the conventional classes had homework as usual.

No definite conclusions were drawn from this study inasmuch as the study had a number of uncontrolled variables (for example, one teacher who failed 30 percent of the program group was described as hostile), and the data are not entirely consistent. Nevertheless, Roanoke decided that student and teacher attitudes warranted the continued use of programed instruction.

---

[68] S. L. Pressey, "Development and Appraisal of Devices Providing Immediate Automatic Scoring of Objective Tests and Concomitant Self-instruction," *Journal of Psychology*, vol. 29 (1950), pp. 417–447.
[69] E. W. Rushton, *Programmed Learning: The Roanoke Experiment.* Chicago, Encyclopedia Britannica, Inc., 1965.

Klaus and Lumsdaine Study.[70]   Another early large-scale field study designed to test the effectiveness of programed instruction was conducted by Klaus and Lumsdaine in the Pittsburgh (Pennsylvania) secondary schools, with 450 students. This study, however, compared programed instruction and conventional instruction in a somewhat different way. Of fifteen physics classes which were receiving regular instruction by lectures, viewing televised Harvey E. White physics films, using a textbook, and carrying out laboratory exercises, some were given, in addition, self-instructional programs in physics for six weeks. Although the use of these programed materials was not required, the classes in which they were used showed a substantial increase in test scores when compared with those classes without programs. There was no significant difference in achievement between students who received programed instruction and those who had lectures by their regular teachers. This suggests the possibility of substituting programed instruction for the lecture aspects of instruction and releasing teachers for more creative instructional tasks.

Teaching Machines versus Programed Texts.   In the early years of the programed instruction movement, many assumptions were made about how best to present material in a self-instructional program, but experimental studies have given little support to these judgments, demonstrating that programing is still more an art than a science.

One common early assumption was that the machine was the superior learning mode. However, the current dominant conception, supported by research, is that the teaching machine is less important than the program.[71] Moreover, studies involving linear programs indicate there are no significant differences between the two presentation modes of devices and texts.[72] But as we indicated earlier, the current conception of teaching machines may be inadequate and premature in light of the anticipated development of more sophisticated, computer-based instructional systems. For example, the recent development of the Edison Responsive Environment instrument (ERE) described by Gotkin [73] may point to a monistic rather than a dualistic view of teaching machines and their relationship to the teaching process.

---

[70] David J. Klaus and A. A. Lumsdaine, *An Experimental Field Test of the Value of Self-tutoring Materials in High School Physics,* an interim report of progress and findings. Pittsburgh, Pa., American Institute for Research, 1960.
[71] L. S. Goldstein and L. G. Gotkin, "A Review of Research: Teaching Machines vs. Programed Textbooks as Presentation Modes," *Journal of Programed Instruction,* vol. 1 (1962), pp. 29–36.
[72] Research on the techniques of programing has been largely concentrated on linear Skinnerian programs. It is interesting to find that only a few experiments have made use of other kinds of programing, such as the "intrinsic" kind of Norman Crowder, the "adjunct" type of Sidney L. Pressey, or the adaptive programing of Pask and others.
[73] L. G. Gotkin, "Teaching Machines and Programed Instruction," *AV Communication Review,* vol. 14, no. 2 (Summer, 1966), pp. 221–241.

Small Step versus Large Step. One programing variable which has been frequently investigated is size of step. An early study by Evans, Glaser, and Homme,[74] using four alternate versions of a program, found that graduate students with 51 and 68 steps did significantly better than other students using programs containing 30 or 40 steps, on the basis of posttest criteria. However, Smith and Moore [75] found no significant differences in the rates of learning to spell when pupils were taught 166 words by means of programs of 1, 128, and 546 steps, respectively. Weiss, Maccoby, and Sheffield [76] found that more learning came from gradually increasing the step size than from maintaining either very short or very long steps. They also discovered that when the learner was permitted to select his own size of step before practice, he chose a gradually increasing length. Those who were permitted to practice only short steps were negatively affected in their level of performance.

Overt versus Covert Responses. The experimental comparison of overt and covert responses in programed instruction has been investigated in a number of studies, but the basic difficulty, as with so many other programing variables, has been a lack of precise, careful definition. For example, the overt-covert response mode issue is further confused because of the inadequate definition of what constitutes an overt or covert response. Although the great majority of the studies find no significant differences between the amount of learning from overt or covert responses, results from other studies indicate overt responding may not be necessary in some situations or it may be very helpful in certain programed situations.[77]

Immediate Knowledge of Results. The majority of the studies in programed instruction support the general assumption that immediate knowledge of results contributes to learning. On the other hand, a few studies found no significant differences attributable to knowledge of results.[78]

[74] J. L. Evans, R. Glaser, and L. E. Homme, "A Preliminary Investigation of Variations in the Properties of Verbal Learning Sequences of the 'Teaching Machine' Type," in Arthur A. Lumsdaine and Robert Glaser (eds.), *Teaching Machines and Programed Learning: A Source Book.* Washington, D.C., Department of Audiovisual Instruction, NEA, 1960, pp. 446–451.

[75] Wendell Smith and J. William Moore, *Size-of-step and Achievement in Programed Spelling.* Lewisburg, Pa., Bucknell University, 1961.

[76] Walter Weiss, Nathan Maccoby, and Fred D. Sheffield, "Combining Practice with Demonstration in Teaching Complex Sentences: Serial Learning of a Geometric-Construction Task," in A. A. Lumsdaine (ed.), *Student Response in Programmed Instruction.* Washington, D.C., National Academy of Sciences, National Research Council, 1961, pp. 55–76.

[77] George L. Gropper and A. A. Lumsdaine, *An Investigation of the Role of Selected Variables in Programed TV Instruction. Studies in Televised Instruction, Report no. 4.* Pittsburgh, Pa., Metropolitan Pittsburgh Educational Television Stations WQED-WQEX and American Institute for Research, 1961.

[78] See, for example, J. William Moore and Wendell I. Smith, "Knowledge of Results in Self-teaching Spelling," *Psychological Reports,* vol. 9 (1961), pp. 717–726.

Learner Pacing.   Somewhat surprisingly, studies have not demonstrated any significant advantage for individual learner pacing. For example, Carpenter and Greenhill [79] compared an externally paced television program with self-paced teaching-machine programs in three experiments, and externally paced films with a self-paced programed text in another. In each instance they found no significant difference related to pacing.

The Problem of Reinforcement.   The attempt to reduce all learning to the reinforcement (or operant conditioning) model of Skinner has found many in disagreement and considerable contradictory experimental evidence. One line of evidence, for example, casting doubt on the reinforcement interpretation, indicates that linear programs, if prolonged, induce boredom.[80] Snygg's [81] analysis of reinforcement theory showed it to be relatively useless for two reasons: First, the basic problem of how to get the learner to elicit the desired response for the first time is neither posed nor answered; and second, the reinforcement theory offers no guide for predicting what will be reinforcing to learners. Clearly, Skinner was prematurely optimistic when he claimed that "the basic processes and relations which give verbal behavior its special characteristics are now fairly well understood." [82]

It is obvious that programed instruction and research is still in an embryonic stage and that any final assessment of it as a technology of instruction must await its future development. Perhaps the next revolution of programed instruction will come from the applications and research directions offered by the computer to problems of instructional technology.[83]

Impact of federal aid on instructional media research

Whether or not the National Defense Education Act (NDEA) of 1958 was inspired by the orbiting of the first Russian Sputnik, there can be little question that it supplied a historic stimulus to an unprecedented, massive instructional media research program throughout the country.[84] Under Title

[79] Carpenter and Greenhill, *Comparative Research on Methods and Media for Presenting Programed Courses in Mathematics and English.*

[80] See, for example, J. W. Rigney and E. B. Fry, "Current Teaching-machine Programs and Programming Techniques," *AV Communication Review,* vol. 9, no. 3, supplement 3 (May–June, 1961).

[81] D. Snygg, "The Tortuous Path of Learning Theory," *Audiovisual Instruction,* vol. 7 (1962), pp. 8–12.

[82] B. F. Skinner, *Verbal Behavior.* New York, Appleton-Century-Crofts, Inc., 1957, p. 3.

[83] See Don D. Bushnell, *The Computer in American Education.* New York, John Wiley & Sons, Inc., 1967.

[84] The selection of science, mathematics, and foreign languages for special emphasis in the 1958 provisions of the National Defense Education Act showed that Congress considered education to be an instrument of national policy. The amendments of 1964, under the "special projects" approach, resulted in the appropriation of $76.6 million for the improvement of instruction in elementary and secondary schools in the fields of history,

VII of this act, funds were provided for the support of "research and experimentation in more effective utilization of television, radio, motion pictures, and related media for educational purposes." Shortly after the enactment of NDEA, the U.S. Office of Education established an Educational Media Branch to administer the research and development program included under Title VII.[85]

From September, 1958, to June 3, 1963, for example, 277 projects were initiated under Title VII, Part A (for research), and 160 under Part B (for dissemination of information). One of the notable accomplishments of the Media Branch during this period was the unique partnership arrangement between government and industry (McGraw-Hill) in the planning and publication of the Educational Media Index.[86]

In 1965, Francis Keppel, Commissioner of Education, reorganized the U.S. Office of Education and in the process eliminated the Educational Media Branch, separating its functions under Title VII, Parts A and B, within a larger administrative unit known as the Bureau of Research. It remains to be seen whether this resulting fragmentation will have a negative effect on the quantity and quality of instructional media research.[87]

Educational Research Information Center (ERIC)

As a result of the considerable instructional media research generated by the National Defense Education Act of 1958, there has been an increasing concern in recent years with improving the storage and dissemination of information about instructional media research. A series of studies have been made by a number of institutions and individuals for the purpose of develop-

---

civics, geography, English, and reading, as well as in science, mathematics, and foreign languages. The funds made available were used for a variety of purposes: to redesign classrooms and laboratories, to purchase various types of instructional materials, and to improve programs of teacher education, state supervision, and administration. The Economic Opportunity Act of 1964 and the Elementary and Secondary Education Act of 1965 represented further extensions of the NDEA. In addition, the Higher Education Act of 1965 provided expanded assistance to institutions of higher education.

[85] See Malcolm S. Maclean, Jr., *Research Abstracts and Analytical Review of Completed Projects: National Defense Education Act, Title VII,* Installment 4, May–June, 1962, Dept. of Health, Education and Welfare, U.S. Office of Education, for a critical analysis of early Title VII research studies.

[86] *The Educational Media Index* was first published in 1964. This index provides classified, annotated descriptions of instructional materials in subindex form. Items described include educational films and kinescopes; charts, maps, and graphs (in sets); filmstrips; flat pictures (in sets); models and mockups; phonodiscs; phonotapes; programed materials; slides and transparencies; and video tapes. Available from McGraw-Hill Book Company, 330 West 42d Street, New York, New York, 10036.

[87] See James D. Finn, "The Marginal Media Man, Part I: The Great Paradox," *Audiovisual Instruction,* vol. 10, no. 10 (December, 1965), pp. 762–765.

ing an indexing system (or thesaurus of educational terms) designed for an electronic storage and retrieval system. In 1964, the U.S. Office of Education established the Educational Research Information Center (ERIC) to serve two functions: first, to operate as an educational research documentation and information center; and second, to provide a decentralized, nationwide network of information clearinghouses or research documentation centers. In this network, some centers are located at regional educational laboratories; others at research and development centers; and still others are at affiliated colleges and universities, state departments of education, or other professional organizations. Some are partially supported by the Office of Education research funds; others are affiliated with ERIC on the basis of cooperative agreements. The key to indexing documents for storage and retrieval is a thesaurus of educational terms. Each center sends to the central ERIC unit résumés and full texts of documents having the greatest research significance. Copies of the documents may be obtained at nominal cost, either on microfilm or hardcopy, through the ERIC Document Reproduction Service.[88] Thus ERIC promises to meet a long and urgent need in the field of instructional technology.

Educational Products Information Exchange (EPIE)

A significant contribution to the field of instructional technology occurred in September, 1966, when a group of educators established the Educational Products Information Exchange (EPIE) in New York City. This noncommercial, professional organization (financially supported by the U.S. Office of Education) has begun to meet a long need for a central agency to evaluate, codify, and disseminate reliable information about instructional media and instrumentation. Its stated objectives were:

1. To improve the educator's ability to select wisely among the increasingly numerous and complex products of the education industry.
2. To increase the exchange of information between users and producers of instructional materials, equipment, and systems, with the objectives of improving their design, development, and use.
3. To encourage educational innovation by calling attention to new products and innovative uses of familiar products.
4. To contribute to the humanistic use of technology in education.[89]

---

[88] The ERIC Document Reproduction Service is operated under an Office of Education contract by Micro Photo Division, Bell and Howell Company, Cleveland, Ohio.
[89] *EPIE Prospectus.* New York, Educational Products Information Exchange, 1967, p. 3.

To further these objectives, EPIE began by publishing a periodical called *The EPIE Forum* in 1967, by sponsoring workshops dealing with product analysis, by providing consultant services to schools, and by initiating studies on the use of media in all subject-matter areas and all grade levels.[90] For example, a school asking for help from EPIE would first of all be expected to define its instructional setting. Then in response, EPIE would identify the instructional materials available and those materials which seem most likely to meet the needs of that school. Similarly, a producer will eventually be able to obtain from EPIE data on the performance of, for example, a newly issued product in a wide range of instructional settings, as reported by schools across the country. These data can therefore become an important factor in the design and development of instructional materials for particular systems of instruction.

[90] The first pilot study of the EPIE began in the fall of 1967 with the investigation of the use of overhead projectors in elementary school science in a limited geographical area (Delaware, New Jersey, New York, and Pennsylvania). This study is being conducted with the cooperation of the national and local chapters of the National Science Teachers Association (NSTA), the Division of Educational Technology, NEA, the four state departments of education, and two regional educational laboratories—the Eastern Regional Institute for Education (ERIE) and Research for Better Schools, Inc. (RBS). The results of all EPIE pilot studies will be reviewed by an advisory council composed of representatives of cooperating associations and organizations. Only information judged to be dependable in the course of the pilot studies will be disseminated publicly—through *The EPIE Forum* and other means.

instructional technology:
problems and prospects

Our purpose in this concluding chapter is threefold: (1) to examine the response of instructional technology to the forces of social-cultural change, (2) to analyze the major problems growing out of this response, and (3) to speculate about the future directions of instructional technology.

Response to a changing society

If it is true that we can discern something of the future by observing the present, an analysis of the present response of instructional technology to the forces of a changing society may provide some insight into its future development. The major characteristics of the social-cultural revolution through which we are passing have been commented on at great length elsewhere, and there is no need for a lengthy exposition here.[1] There are, however, two general trends that relate to current developments in instructional technology. These are (1) the accelerating rate of change occurring throughout our society and (2) the so-called explosion of knowledge.

Recent incipient changes in instructional technology, developing as a kind of mirror reflection of the larger revolution in our society, are clearly evident. For example, since about 1957,[2] a curriculum-reform movement involving the restructuring of subject matter as well as the developing and refining of methodology and instructional materials has been under way, abundantly supported by the National Science Foundation, the U.S. Office of Education, and several foundations. The primary leadership for the current curriculum-reform movement has come from scholars in various academic disciplines, acting either as individuals or through their learned societies, outside the mainstream of the "educational establishment."[3] It has come neither from educational practitioners in the schools nor from professors of education who have traditionally contributed to the professional preparation of teachers. In fact, with few exceptions, professors of education have either been isolated or bypassed in this movement.

Typically, a group of academic scholars reviewed the needs for a precollegiate change in their field and then invited secondary school teachers to join them in planning course content and materials. The result was "new" courses and integrated instructional packages for secondary school mathematics, physics, chemistry, economics, geography, anthropology, English and the foreign languages.[4] At the elementary school level, curriculum reform has been generally confined to mathematics, science, and social studies.[5]

---

[1] Such forces as rapid population growth, changes in job requirements, automation and unemployment, the civil rights movement, and revolutionary advances in transportation, communication, and science are examples of great societal forces and ideas reshaping our society. See David A. Goslin, *The School in Contemporary Society*. Chicago, Scott, Foresman and Company, 1965.

[2] The beginnings of the curriculum-reform movement are commonly dated from the launching of the first Russian satellite in the fall of 1957. However, it is possible to trace the roots of this movement back to the organization of the University of Illinois Committee on School Mathematics (UICSM) in 1951.

[3] Conant has identified the "educational establishment" as that group of educators made up of state department of education personnel, school superintendents, principals, teachers, and professors of education. See James B. Conant, *The Education of American Teachers*. New York, McGraw-Hill Book Company, 1963.

[4] References to "new" courses in such subject fields as mathematics, physics, and biology are commonplace today. However, the "new" label may no longer be appropriate. In some fields, notably mathematics, the first "new" mathematics is to be followed by a "new" new mathematics.

[5] Men like Zacharias, Suppes, Begle, and Karpus were among the scholars who supplied much of the leadership in this development. Jerrold R. Zacharias, professor of physics at Massachusetts Institute of Technology, headed the Physical Science Study Committee (PSSC) and has served as chairman on the Panel on Educational Research and Development for the President's Science Advisory Committee. Patrick C. Suppes of Stanford University has developed mathematics programs for young children. E. G. Begle has headed

The basic assumption underlying these developments is that understanding the primary structural elements of a discipline (rather than memorizing facts) will enable a learner to discover meaningful relationships and to solve new problems relative to them. Simultaneously, this resurgence of interest in cognitive processes has stimulated new instructional approaches for the purpose of producing what has come to be widely known as discovery learning. Bruner says, for example, that:

> Mastery of the fundamental ideas of a field involves not only the grasping of general principles, but also the development of an attitude toward learning and inquiry, toward guessing and hunches, toward the possibility of solving problems on one's own. . . . To instill such attitudes by teaching requires something more than the mere presentation of fundamental ideas . . . it would seem that an important ingredient is a sense of excitement about discovery of regularities of previously unrecognized relations and similarities between ideas, with a resulting sense of self-confidence in one's abilities.[6]

In addition, some venerable beliefs about cognitive behaviors have been seriously challenged. One of these, that cognitive learning must proceed from the concrete to the abstract, from the simple to the complex, was subjected to closer scrutiny when Bruner asserted "that any subject matter can be taught to anybody at any age in some form that is honest."[7] Suppes introduced nonmetric geometry, then set theory, and finally mathematical logic into the primary grades.[8]

Social problems such as changes in job requirements; unemployment; rapid growth of school population; shortage of well-trained teachers; rising rate of secondary school dropouts (or pushouts); movement to integrate the schools racially; and attention to the long-neglected needs of the gifted, retarded, and educationally disadvantaged learners have all found some measure of response in instructional technology in recent years. These responses have been reflected primarily in a number of plans for school reorganization providing for team teaching, nongrading, flexible scheduling and grouping, and for teacher specialization so as to deploy teachers and learners for the improvement of instruction.

Societal forces are also having a direct impact on school organization with regard to new instructional media. For example, the team teaching

---

the School Mathematics Group, first at Yale and then at Stanford. Robert Karpus has experimented with new approaches to science for young children in his Science Curriculum Improvement Study.

[6] Jerome S. Bruner, *The Process of Education*. New York, Vintage Books, 1963, p. 20.
[7] See Jerome S. Bruner, "The Course of Cognitive Growth," *American Psychologist*, vol. 19 (1964), pp. 1–15.
[8] P. Suppes, "Modern Learning Theory and the Elementary School Curriculum," *Journal of Educational Research*, vol. 1 (1964), pp. 79–93.

scheme typically makes extensive use of such new media as television, video-tapes, and teaching machines. It is difficult to realize the scope of the communications and technological revolution which will offer expanded applications to instruction in the future. New media such as computer-based instruction are already affecting school organization, curriculum content, teacher deployment, and building design.[9]

An appraisal of recent developments and the relationship of the modes of thinking to future developments in instructional technology

The basic responses of instructional technology to the aforementioned forces of social change have reflected, primarily, a concern with technical accomplishment. Relatively little substantial progress has been made toward providing adequate solutions to the whole set of problems involving what to teach, to whom, and how. In the opinion of this author, this situation is closely related to two of the basic problems underlying the future development of instructional technology—that of changing the dominant physical science concept of instructional technology to a behavioral science concept, and that of changing the prevailing mode of thinking among educational practitioners as to how professional knowledge is produced and how it should be evaluated.[10] Unless these problems are recognized and solved, instructional technology may be unable to cope with the educational challenge of the present or the future.

Central to changing the prevailing mode of thinking is resolution of the conflict between what Conant has called the theoretical-deductive and the empirical-inductive modes of thought,[11] or what Snow has described from another viewpoint as the dichotomy between "the two cultures," the literary and the scientific.[12] The theoretical-deductive is best represented by mathematical thinking, particularly as applied in physics. Other forms of it may

[9] In recent years, a number of developments have indicated a concern for a more effective utilization of teaching and learning spaces, particularly in the employment of new media. Of particular note have been developments in the use of television and programed instruction; the growth of language laboratories; the development of facilities for the automatic playback of lectures in both audio and video form, using remote-control telephone dials or push-button systems; and the development of new teaching auditoriums, which often combine facilities for daylight, rear-screen, and multiple-screen projection, video- and audiotape presentations, various types of filmslides and other graphic materials, and student response stations for immediate feedback analyses of student learning. Moreover, there have been developments in the use of learning resources centers and in the use of computers for instruction and administrative purposes.

[10] For a distinction between the physical science concept and the behavioral science concept of instructional technology, see Chapter 1 of this book.

[11] See James Bryant Conant, *Two Modes of Thoughts: My Encounters with Science and Education.* New York, Trident Press, 1964.

[12] C. P. Snow, *The Two Cultures: And a Second Look,* 2d ed. London, Cambridge University Press, 1964.

be found in theology, philosophy, law, economics, and political science. The other mode, the empirical-inductive is best represented in the natural sciences and in such applications as medicine. Both modes have produced a vast body of scientific and technological knowledge and both have influenced the teaching of these bodies of knowledge. Lawyers are more likely to use the theoretical-deductive mode; engineers and medical doctors the empirical-inductive mode.

Educational researchers and other behavioral scientists investigating the teaching-learning process make the empirical-inductive mode of thinking their characteristic approach to problems of instruction. We know from research studies that teachers, in contrast, tend to reject the validity and utility of the empirical mode, preferring the theoretical-deductive mode even when it is clearly inappropriate or inadequate.[13] Why is this so? At the root, perhaps, is the educational practitioner's own education: The mode of thought prevailing in most teacher education institutions is theoretical-deductive.

This is not to say that training in the theoretical-deductive mode cannot be a powerful analytical and descriptive tool in the development of a science of instruction. However, it has no practical value if it does not lead to deductions which may be tested empirically, even though the method of testing may not be immediately available. Since methods courses in teacher education have consisted largely of deductions whose value rests on the assumed validity of theories rather than on deductions tested empirically, they are not practical in the sense of that term. At best, they are good theory courses. And as a consequence, the typical educational practitioner neither generates nor seeks theories of instruction, nor is he committed to the testing of hypotheses or to the design of experiments concerning the instructional process. He does not create theories because he has difficulty seeing how theory relates to practice. When he does theorize, he tends to accept his deductions as valid because they follow logically from the accepted premises of his theory.

An interesting example of the dominance of the theoretical-deductive mode may also be found in the curriculum study groups led by the academic subject-matter specialists. Curriculum study groups, such as the School Mathematics Study Group (SMSG), Physical Science Study Group (PSSG), the Biological Sciences Curriculum Study (BSCS), the Chemical Educational Materials Study (CHEMS), focus on content *per se* rather than on the learning of content. Such groups have had very general conceptions of learning and have been totally convinced of the theoretical value of their respective approaches before they began. Thus far, initial assumptions have been restated and there has been a reluctance to submit their systems to experimental verification.

---

[13] See, for example, Bruce J. Biddle and William J. Ellena (eds.), *Contemporary Research on Teacher Effectiveness*. New York, Holt, Rinehart and Winston, Inc., 1964.

One of the prevailing naïve assumptions held by these groups is the notion that the ends and means of instruction are derived primarily from the subject-matter discipline and only secondarily from the learning and developmental processes of learners. To date, much of the restructuring of subject matter has been a process of trial and error, lacking experimental testing. Empirical investigations and empirically oriented, inductive theorizing, such as that provided by Bruner [14] and other behavioral scientists, have sometimes followed, but only after the programs had been determined and were well under way. In most instances, original deductions have been refined rather than tested in practice, and instructional innovations have been characterized by evaluations of the validity of effective accomplishment rather than by the validity of what was being attempted.

Further, the beginning of the reform movement in the secondary rather than in the elementary level of instruction has resulted in planning from the top down. It has also tended to focus on separate disciplines already established in the curriculum and to ignore or give scant attention to the developmental processes of learners or to their social or cultural backgrounds. Goodlad's analysis,[15] for example, points to the fact that the current curriculum reform is a middle- and upper middle-class movement and that the new curricula do not even come close to doing what we should be doing.

The revision of subject-matter content by academic scholars has been closely tied to school reorganization plans proposed by educationists in recent years. These plans propose new solutions to a number of persistent problems involving learner grouping, advancement, scheduling, use of space and equipment, and teacher deployment. In addition, there have been many proposals to educate slow learners, the academically talented, the culturally disadvantaged, and the physically handicapped. However, when one searches for psychological theories underlying most of these proposals or innovations, it is evident that no clearly tested psychological principles do, in fact, exist. Most of the innovations appear to have arisen from social and political pressures rather than from empirical investigation. The type of sensitivity to the needs of learners which we have seen in the work of Comenius, Pestalozzi, and Montessori, for example, is frequently missing in many contemporary developments. Too often the assumption seems to be that the adoption of new content, new organizational plans, new instructional media, or new designs for facilities and buildings are, in themselves, sufficient for instructional improvement. It is interesting to note that the great bulk of research studies of nongrading, team teaching, and flexible scheduling undertaken thus far have yielded no significant results favoring these plans. This is not

[14] See, for example, Bruner et al., *Studies in Cognitive Growth*. New York, John Wiley & Sons, Inc., 1966.
[15] See John I. Goodlad, *School Curriculum Reform in the United States*. New York, The Fund for the Advancement of Education, 1964.

to say that an excellent rationale cannot be formulated for them; however, it is most important to recognize that most bear only a slight relationship to a basic improvement in the quality of instruction. For example, one rarely encounters any mention of, or effort to implement, reflective learning—learning which flows from a problematic situation about which a learner centers his thinking and research.[16]

To date, implementation of new organization plans has been hasty and superficial, with inadequate provisions for the total instructional system in terms of procedures, materials, media, and required staff. Some so-called nongraded classrooms, for example, have simply erased grade labels but have failed to provide authentic nongraded instruction. Teachers who have never individualized instruction in their graded classrooms can hardly be expected to know exactly how to individualize instruction in nongraded classrooms. Moreover, many educational practitioners have confused the concept of homogeneous grouping with continuous progress.[17]

It is the author's opinion that much of the foregoing failure to cope with the present challenge on an empirical basis stems from the adherence to the theoretical-deductive mode of thinking about instruction. Many educational practitioners bear the responsibility for creating and jumping on a bandwagon without the benefit of empirical-inductive examination. It is also clear that academic specialists involved in curriculum projects can be charged with neglecting the empirical-inductive mode of thinking in their approach to curriculum reform.

This may seem surprising since a major function of the university is to conduct research. In order to understand why these scholars have not generally engaged in the experimental verification of their systems, it must be realized that most have been traditionally contemptuous of "educationists," and that any activity dealing with problems of learning and teaching in the lower schools has not been considered academically respectable. In fact, there has been no place inside the academic departmental structure of a university where elementary or secondary course revision could take place. Curriculum-development projects, therefore, have had to be established outside formal university departments, or in nonprofit organizations, or in colleges. Scholars participating in these projects (usually for short periods of time) often maintained their academic ties, with little hope of enhancing their scholarly reputation while so engaged.

Why, then, did they become involved in the first place? A precise answer is not easy. However, it seems clear that as a few scholars, particularly in the

[16] For a discussion of the reflective method of learning, see H. Gordon Hullfish and Philip G. Smith, *Reflective Thinking: The Method of Education.* New York, Dodd, Mead & Company, Inc., 1961.
[17] John I. Goodlad and Robert H. Anderson, "Educational Practices in Nongraded Schools: A Survey of Perceptions," *The Elementary School Journal,* vol. 63 (October, 1962), p. 38.

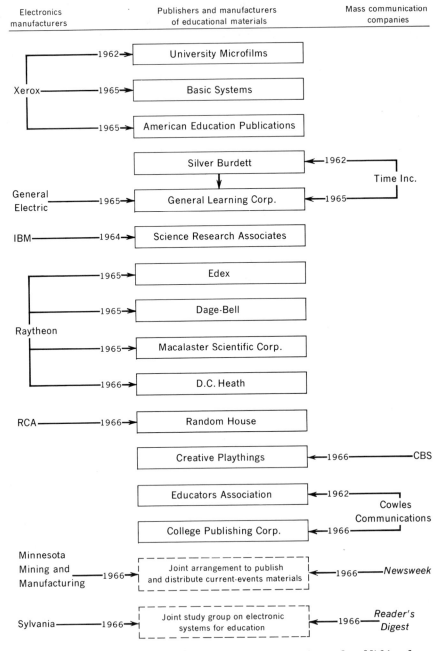

THE EDUCATION MARKET'S NEW FAMILY TREE

Mergers, Acquisitions, and Joint Ventures since 1962

Electronics manufacturers | Publishers and manufacturers of educational materials | Mass communication companies

- Xerox —1962→ University Microfilms
- Xerox —1965→ Basic Systems
- Xerox —1965→ American Education Publications
- Silver Burdett ←1962— Time Inc.
- General Electric —1965→ General Learning Corp. ←1965— Time Inc.
- IBM —1964→ Science Research Associates
- Raytheon —1965→ Edex
- Raytheon —1965→ Dage-Bell
- Raytheon —1965→ Macalaster Scientific Corp.
- Raytheon —1966→ D.C. Heath
- RCA —1966→ Random House
- Creative Playthings ←1966— CBS
- Educators Association ←1962— Cowles Communications
- College Publishing Corp. ←1966— Cowles Communications
- Minnesota Mining and Manufacturing —1966→ Joint arrangement to publish and distribute current-events materials ←1966— Newsweek
- Sylvania —1966→ Joint study group on electronic systems for education ←1966— Reader's Digest

Fig. 16.1   *Diagram showing recent mergers of electronics and publishing houses.* (*From Fortune, August, 1966.*)

sciences, became acutely aware in the early 1950s of the scientific and mathematical shortcomings of secondary school graduates, they felt obligated to involve themselves in the updating and reorganization of precollegiate courses. Meanwhile, the launching of Sputnik I by the Soviet Union in 1957 triggered a general movement of curriculum reform involving other university scholars.

Another recent movement offers prospects of continuing the alienation between the two modes of approach, further entrenching the physical science concept of instructional technology. We are referring to the development in the mid-sixties of a series of commercial mergers, principally involving electronics companies and publishing houses, for the purpose of designing complete instructional systems which provide for integrated materials and supporting equipment, for the training of teachers in their use, and for the testing of the learners. School districts purchasing such instructional systems or materials literally "buy" the educational objectives and instructional techniques built into them. Can we reasonably expect the developers of these systems to produce empirically tested instructional systems, materials, and techniques when most educational practitioners and academic specialists have failed to do so? The answer probably is that we cannot unless the present conditions change. For one thing, they work in a competitive market, and few, if any, commercial producers can afford large sums for empirical demonstration of the effectiveness of their materials. Moreover, since the educational practitioner usually relies on intuitive judgments rather than on empirical data, the commercial producer needs to produce materials which meet other standards of judgment. However, in the foreseeable future, published instructional materials and devices supplied by industry may be increasingly submitted to experimental verification, as a result of a recent U.S. Office of Education policy which awards research and development contracts—hitherto reserved for colleges and universities—to business and industry. Hopefully, too, this development may increase the sophistication of the educational practitioner in his use of criteria for evaluating these materials.

Prospects for the development of a behavioral science concept of instructional technology

If our foregoing analysis of the dichotomy between the typical approach of the educational practitioner and the behavioral scientist is valid, and if this same alienation in the modes of approach to problems of learning and instruction is seen to prevail among the academic scholars and the "educational businessmen," it then becomes clear that the estrangement between the theoretical-deductive and the empirical-inductive modes of thought will have to be resolved before we may move toward a behavioral science concept of instructional technology. Unless we do this, it seems unlikely that we will be able to solve the educational problems created by a changing society.

Although this author looks forward to the eventual development of an instructional technology based on the behavioral sciences and related interdisciplinary fields, he hesitates to set a timetable for such a transition, nor can he express great optimism about its early prospects. It appears to him that barring some remarkable unforeseen development, the emergence of a scientific technology of instruction will proceed at an evolutionary pace rather than in a revolutionary fashion as some have suggested. However, there is a wide range of possibilities on the horizon which hold much promise for uniting the theoretical-deductive and the empirical-inductive modes in a fruitful application of behavioral science research to instruction.

Although a behavioral science concept of instructional technology hardly exists today, we will examine in this final section some promising trends and speculate briefly about the approaches which seem vital in the realization of a mutually interacting relationship between the behavioral sciences and instructional practice. No attempt is made here to present a complete method for implementing a behavioral science concept of instructional technology.

Teachers of Teachers and Teacher Education.   Before we can develop a behavioral science concept of instructional technology, the schools, colleges, and departments of education which prepare teachers will have to shift their emphasis from the didactic, theoretic-deductive mode of disseminating knowledge to the hypotheses-creating-and-testing mode. Although a thorough analysis of this problem is not within the scope of this book, we shall consider a few of the implications of such a shift in approach.

The curriculum-reform movement has not become an integral part of teacher preparation programs either for teachers or teachers of teachers. What is needed, we believe, is to bring professors of education and academic specialists together so that they might teach each other and both learn to make the empirical-inductive mode their characteristic approach to problems of learning and instruction. For many years, subject-matter specialists have cut themselves off from a useful body of educational knowledge regarding the learning and developmental processes of learners while the educationists, in turn, have been generally separated from the mainstream of curriculum reform. It is essential, therefore, that the basic competencies of both the subject-matter specialists and the educationists be applied to problems of instruction. Some type of arrangement will need to be made whereby a continuing dialogue can take place. Perhaps a resultant mutual respect and understanding, traditionally lacking between these two groups, will ripen into a new, productive working relationship.[18]

If we make the assumption that the teachers of teachers will ultimately adopt the empirical-inductive mode as their typical approach to problems of instruction, we shall expect this to be reflected in a redesigned teacher education program. This will make it possible for the beginning practitioner to engage in some form of research activity while he is training for teaching. This does not imply additional courses in statistics or research design. Rather, the object will be to get the beginning practitioner to do some hypothesis-making and testing. Such a teacher education program might also include experienced teachers in cooperating neighbor schools who would work with beginning students on specific instructional problems. Both the experienced teacher and the beginning student might be aided by a subject-matter specialist and an experienced investigator from the college or university. Similarly, local institutes might be established in which behavioral scientists (including professors of education) and academic specialists would assist teachers in formulating ideas and in carrying out research projects. In this way a public school system, in cooperation with a college or university, could prepare future teachers as well as reeducate experienced practitioners in the empirical-inductive approach to instruction.

Research and Development Centers.   A recent development which promises to provide a solution to the prevailing dichotomy between the theoretical-deductive and the empirical-inductive modes of thought in educational practice is the establishment of regional Educational Research and Development Centers or Laboratories under the financial sponsorship of the U.S. Office of Education.[19] For the first time in the history of instructional technology, these Centers will test theories or hypotheses in a systematic manner before they are put into instructional practice. Furthermore, as increasing knowledge is accumulated in the behavioral sciences, a base can be laid for the development of a behavioral science concept of instructional technology. Whether the R and D Centers will actually provide a model of the research process and set the pace for a scientific and technological foundation of instructional practice will depend largely on the quality of the staffs selected and on the policies and programs they adopt. The basic problem, in our view, as described, is to change the prevalent mode of thinking among both educationists and academic subject-matter specialists about the teaching-

[18] This task might well be appropriate for a research and development center of the kind now being financed through the U.S. Office of Education.
[19] Regional research and development centers and laboratories are funded by the Office of Education under the Elementary and Secondary Education Act of 1965, P.L. 89–10, Title IV.

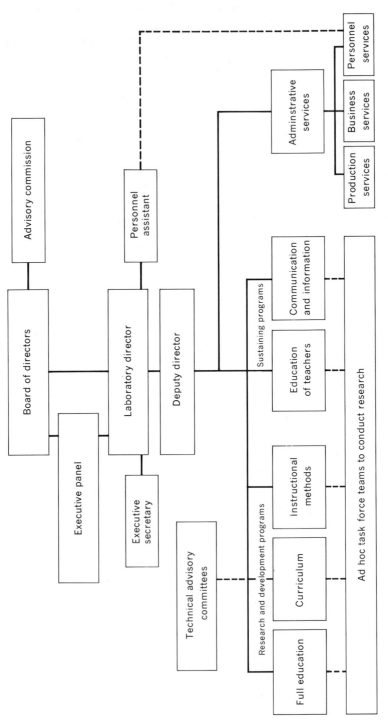

Fig. 16.2   Organization plan of Far West Laboratory for Educational Research and Development.

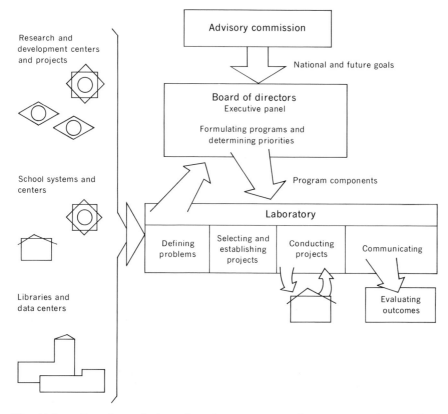

Fig. 16.3   Functions relations chart for Far West Laboratory for Educational Research and Development.

learning process. If the R and D Centers cannot solve that problem, they may prove to be nothing more than so much "sound and fury."

How, then, can the R and D Centers or Laboratories help to bring about such a change in the mode of thought? A fundamental way envisioned by the author is through the establishment of true laboratory schools under R and D Center control.[20] The primary function of these laboratory schools would be neither demonstration, dissemination, nor field testing, but research

---

[20] Although a little more than two hundred college- and university-controlled laboratory schools exist in the United States, few have demonstrated a commitment to the empirical mode of thinking. They appear, instead, to be committed to maintaining the *status quo* rather than advancing instructional theory and practice. One of the clearest expressions of the failure of the laboratory school is probably to be found in Brickell's recent survey, *Organizing New York State for Educational Change,* Albany, N.Y., State Education Department, 1961. He recommended that "the eleven campus schools at the State University Colleges should be closed and their elementary and secondary students returned to the public schools."

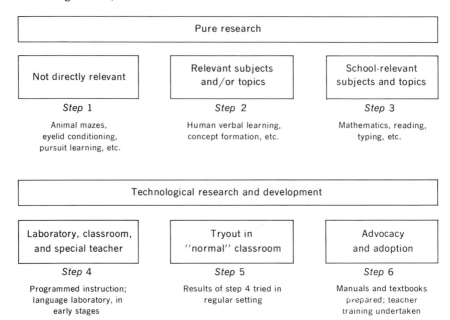

*Fig. 16.4   Steps in research on learning—pure research to technological development.
(From Ernest Hilgard.)*

and experimentation. They would provide the direction and impetus for innovation and diffusion and for the reeducation of teachers of teachers, educational administrators, subject-matter specialists, and experienced teachers by involving them in some phases of the research process—or what is usually called developmental research. In such experimental laboratory schools, representatives of all these groups would work together on bridging the gap between theoretical ideas and instructional practice and could develop mutual respect for each other.

Hilgard [21] has provided a model for developmental research which might be used by an R and D Center in conjunction with a laboratory school program. He breaks the research process into six phases or steps, beginning with pure research on learning, and terminating with technological research and development and with the innovation of new instructional practices in the public schools. The first three steps are pure-science research and often arise from theoretical issues having little or no relevance to application. The first of the last three steps is a small tryout with a few students and a highly trained teacher—a feasibility test. This is followed by a tryout in a more

[21] Ernest R. Hilgard, "A Perspective on the Relationship between Learning Theory and Educational Practices," in E. R. Hilgard (ed.), *Theories of Learning and Instruction,* The Sixty-third Yearbook of the National Society for the Study of Education, part I. Chicago, The University of Chicago Press, 1964, pp. 402–415.

typical classroom. Finally, the procedure is initiated on a larger scale, and studies are made of strategies of innovation and diffusion, or how new procedures can be adopted by those who have not participated in the experimentation.

The experimental laboratory schools which the author envisions, financed by the federal government and operated by the R and D Centers, would be implemented with the cooperation of school systems, colleges and universities, state departments of education, and private organizations within the geographical region served by the Center. It is not our purpose here to develop a method for the organization and operation of such R and D Center–controlled laboratory schools. We can only suggest that a good start might be made with the selection of high quality personnel (educational administrators, classroom teachers, subject-matter specialists, and teachers of teachers) who would become involved, for at least one year or longer, in developmental research on the teaching-learning process, in close cooperation with behavioral science investigators of the Center. For their work in research or teaching, or in both, they would avail themselves of all the R and D Center's facilities, such as research assistants, statistical and computer services, production services, and work space. When their period of activity at the R and D Center had been completed, they would return to their own districts and schools to provide leadership in innovations which had been experimentally verified.

Although each laboratory school would be relatively small, the student enrollment would be carefully controlled and highly diversified in terms of social and racial background, abilities, interests, ages, and a host of individual differences. Here atypical instructional procedures would be the rule, with the support of those cooperating rather than with the threat of interference. It would also be a place for extended observation and testing, where creative experimental treatments could be employed over a relatively long period of time. For example, one laboratory school might adopt an experimental theme such as Bruner's cognitive approach to learning; another, Skinner's operant conditioning approach. Other schools might derive their themes from techniques, goals, or values. Some schools could focus on individualization of instruction while others could concentrate on the development of creativity. Thus the R and D Center–controlled laboratory school could provide an ideal experimental setting which the public schools are unable to offer.

It is obvious that we know very little about the complex motivations and conditions involved in instructional innovation and diffusion. The existing literature reveals a paucity of empirical evidence on how to accelerate the change process or what strategy of innovation to employ. We do know that we cannot anticipate significant changes in instructional technology merely through the dissemination of research reports or by providing for demonstrations. Although the researcher naturally believes that he has fulfilled his responsibility as a researcher when he disseminates information on his research, we know that, unfortunately, research and instructional innovation are rarely found together. The same gap may continue to exist if those in the new R and D Centers produce research articles and disseminate information and material in the conventional manner. (We know, for example, that many teachers and administrators ignore good research because it was not done in their district or classroom.) Thus, an important function of the R and D Centers will be to take a creative approach to communication while studying the problem of dissemination and innovation.

We see the proposed R and D Center laboratory schools as unique institutions where behavioral scientists, teachers of teachers, educational administrators, classroom teachers, academic subject-matter specialists, and media specialists could join in a fruitful attack on problems of learning and instruction in a realistic setting. The resulting cross-fertilization of knowledge and skills should ultimately advance instructional technology to the status of a profession in which the behavioral sciences would provide the underlying foundation and essential nourishment.

The Future Challenge to Instructional Technology. In a talk entitled "Education's Challenge in the Future," James E. Russell, Secretary of the Educational Policies Commission, used these words:

> In that deep distant future people will face situations which are novel. If they are to succeed in establishing the conditions in which they can earn their own dignity, they will have to learn how to make responses which we do not today know how to make. When they meet novel situations that arise in their own lives, they will not be able to look to us for guidance. We do not have the knowledge required. They will not be able to consult the experience of our forefathers or even the accumulated experience of mankind. Whether they are good citizens about it will not make much difference. Whether they have ethical character will not help. Whether they perceive or are sensitive to its aesthetic significance will make no difference. They will not be able to ignore what is in front of them. It will do them no good to panic or retreat in confusion. It will not even be enough to pray. *They will have to think. Our job then is to teach them to think* [italics mine].[22]

According to Russell, we will have to redefine the goals of education, and this means overcoming what he calls the twentieth-century fallacy [23]— the idea that educational goals should be defined in terms of overt behaviors which all children can perform. Russell's viewpoint is that the whole of edu-

[22] James E. Russell, speech before the national convention of the Department of Audiovisual Instruction, NEA, San Diego, Calif., Apr. 25, 1966.
[23] See James E. Russell, *Change and Challenge in American Education.* Boston, Houghton Mifflin Company, 1965, pp. 40–48.

cation can be redefined with reference to the rational tradition.[24] But if we are to bring these goals to reality, it will require the blending of philosophical insights with psychological and technological insights. There is a bridge, Russell says, from philosophy to psychology and a bridge from both to technology, and someone, somewhere, somehow, is going to discover the footwork that will enable him to cross these bridges.

Furthermore, says Russell,

> The man who will cross our bridge is one who is at home in two widely disparate fields. One is conventional pedagogy. He will need to know much about learning, about human development, about the world of education as we know it. On the other side, he will need to be sure-footed in the world of advancing science and technology. Computer development, electronic games, new forms of circuitry, the character of DNA and RNA, neurological research—a lot of fields of pure science must also be his preserve, buttressed by skill in the gadgetry that goes with them.[25]

Where should we look for this man or men of the future? Is it not necessary that they be in education now? Wherever they are, they must perceive that the crucial instructional problem of our time is to improve and develop a science and technology of instruction. It may well be that the men who will cross the bridge from philosophy to psychology to technology will be catalytic agents of a kind, perhaps called instructional technologists or educational designers, who will bring about the needed cross-fertilization of the knowledge and skills of educational practitioners, subject-matter scholars, and behavioral scientists. There is high hope that some men have already taken the first steps across the bridge, but the crossing will be long and will require great daring and insight. Yet when it has been done, we may enter an exciting and rewarding era in instructional technology.

[24] The values of the rational tradition have been listed by Russell as follows: (1) the longing to know and understand; (2) the tendency to question; (3) the search for data and their meaning; (4) the demand for verification; (5) respect for logic; (6) consideration of premises; and (7) consideration of consequences.

[25] Russell, *Change and Challenge in American Education.*

Selected Bibliography

The following references provide a working bibliography for further reading or investigation. Selection has been made on the basis of general value, availability, or special interest.

chapter 1

BERELSON, BERNARD (ed.). *The Behavioral Sciences Today*. New York, Harper & Row, Publishers, Incorporated, 1964.

BROWN, JAMES W., RICHARD B. LEWIS, AND FRED HARCLEROAD. *A-V Instruction: Materials and Methods*, 2d ed. New York, McGraw-Hill Book Company, 1964.

———— AND KENNETH D. NORBERG. *Administering Educational Media*. New York, McGraw-Hill Book Company, 1965.

ELY, DONALD P. (ed.). "The Changing Role of the Audiovisual Process in Education: A Definition and a Glossary of Related Terms," *AV Communication Review*, vol. 11, no. 1, supplement 6 (January–February, 1963).

FINN, JAMES D. "Technology and the Instructional Process," *AV Communication Review*, vol. 8 (Winter, 1960).

GAGNE, R. (ed.). *Psychological Principles in System Development*. New York, Holt, Rinehart and Winston, Inc., 1962.

GERLACH, VERNON S. "The Professional Education of the Media Specialist," *AV Communication Review*, vol. 14 (Summer, 1966), pp. 185–201.

GLASER, R. (ed.). *Training Research and Education*. Pittsburgh, The University of Pittsburgh Press, 1962.

HARCLEROAD, FRED F. "The Education of the AV Communications Specialist," *AV Communication Review*, vol. 8 (September–October, 1960), pp. 3–96.

LUMSDAINE, A. A. "Educational Technology, Programmed Learning, and Instructional Science," in E. R. Hilgard (ed.), *Theories of Learning and Instruction*, The Sixty-third Yearbook of the National Society for the Study of Education, part I. Chicago, The University of Chicago Press, 1964, pp. 371–401.

SMITH, KARL U., AND MARGARET F. SMITH. *Cybernetic Principles of Learning and Educational Design.* New York, Holt, Rinehart and Winston, Inc., 1966.

TROW, WILLIAM C. *Teacher and Technology.* New York, Appleton-Century-Crofts, Inc., 1963.

chapter 2

BROUDY, HARRY S., AND JOHN R. PALMER. *Exemplars of Teaching Method.* Chicago, Rand McNally & Company, 1965.

HAVELOCK, ERIC A. *The Liberal Temper in Greek Politics.* New Haven, Conn., Yale University Press, 1957.

JAEGER, WERNER. *Paideia: The Ideals of Greek Culture,* tr. from the 2d German ed. by Gilbert Highet. Fair Lawn, N.J., Oxford University Press, 1939, vol. I.

SNOW, C. P. *The Two Cultures and the Scientific Revolution.* New York, Cambridge University Press, 1959.

WATKINS, MARK HANNA. "The West African 'Bush School,'" *American Journal of Sociology,* vol. 48, no. 6 (1943), pp. 666–675.

chapter 3

BARNARD, HENRY. *Connecticut Common School Journal,* vol. 3 (Dec. 15, 1840), p. 61.

BESTOR, ARTHUR E. *Educational Wastelands.* Urbana, Ill., The University of Illinois Press, 1953.

BOURNE, WILLIAM OLAND. *History of the Public School Society of New York City.* New York, Wood and Company, 1870.

BURTON, WARREN. *The District School as It Was,* ed. by Clifton Johnson. New York, Thomas Y. Crowell Company, 1928.

BUTLER, NICHOLAS MURRAY. *Education in the United States.* New York, American Book Company, 1900.

DEARBORN, NED H. *Oswego Movement.* New York, Teachers College Press, Columbia University, 1925.

ELIOT, CHARLES W. *The Tendency to the Concrete and Practical in Modern Education.* Boston, Houghton Mifflin Company, 1913.

GILL, JOHN. *Systems of Education.* Boston, D. C. Heath and Company, 1887.

GORDY, J. P. The Rise and Growth of the Normal-school Idea in the United States. U.S. Bureau of Education Circular of Information 8, 1891, p. 24.

KOERNER, JAMES D. *The Case for Basic Education.* Boston, Little, Brown and Company, 1959.

PAGE, DAVID P. *Theory and Practice of Teaching.* New York, A. S. Barnes and Co., Inc., 1893.

PATRIDGE, LELIA E. *The Quincy Methods Illustrated.* New York, E. L. Kellogg and Company, 1886.

PESTALOZZI, J. H. *How Gertrude Teaches Her Children,* tr. by L. E. Holland and F. C. Swan. Syracuse, N.Y., Bardeen's Inc., 1874.

RICKOVER, H. G. *Education and Freedom.* New York, E. P. Dutton & Co., Inc., 1959.

SALMON, DAVID. *Joseph Lancaster.* New York, Longmans, Green & Co., Inc., 1904.

chapter 4

BOBBITT, FRANKLIN. *How to Make a Curriculum.* Boston, Houghton Mifflin Company, 1924.

BRADFORD, H. ARNOLD. *Intuitive Concepts in Elementary Topology.* Englewood Cliffs, N.J., Prentice-Hall, Inc., 1962.

CURTI, MERLE. *The Social Ideas of American Educators.* Paterson, N.J., Pageant Books, Inc., 1959.

DEWEY, JOHN. "The Reflex Arc Concept in Psychology," *Psychological Review,* vol. 3 (1896), pp. 357–370.

GILBERT, THOMAS F. "A Structure for a Coordinated Research and Development Laboratory," in Robert Glaser (ed.), *Training Research and Education.* Pittsburgh, The University of Pittsburgh Press, 1962, pp. 559–578.

HILGARD, ERNEST R. *Theories of Learning,* 3d ed. New York, Appleton-Century-Crofts, Inc., 1966.

HUNT, J. MC V. "Motivation Inherent in Information Processing and Action," in O. J. Harvey (ed.), *Motivation and Social Interaction: Cognitive Determinants.* New York, The Ronald Press Company, 1963.

———. *Introduction* in Montessori, Maria. *The Montessori Method.* New York, Schocken Books, 1964.

KILPATRICK, WILLIAM H. *The Montessori System Examined.* Boston, Houghton Mifflin Company, 1914.

———. *Foundations of Method.* New York, The Macmillan Company, 1926.

LEWIN, KURT. "Formalization and Progress in Psychology," *University of Iowa Studies in Child Welfare,* vol. 16, no. 3 (1940), p. 16.

———. *Field Theory in Social Science.* New York, Harper & Row, Publishers, Incorporated, 1951.

MAYHEW, KATHERINE CAMP, AND ANNA CAMP EDWARDS. *The Dewey School.* New York, D. Appleton-Century Company, Inc. 1936.

MONTESSORI, MARIA. *The Montessori Method,* tr. by A. E. George. Philadelphia, J. B. Lippincott Company, 1912.

MORRISON, HENRY C. *The Practice of Teaching in the Secondary School.* Chicago, The University of Chicago Press, 1931.

PARKHURST, H. H. *Education on the Dalton Plan.* London, G. Bell & Sons, Ltd., 1922.

SEARCH, P. W. *An Ideal School.* New York, D. Appleton & Company, Inc., 1901.

SKINNER, B. F. *Science and Behavior.* New York, The Macmillan Company, 1953.

———. "The Science of Learning and the Art of Teaching," *Harvard Educational Review,* vol. 24 (1954), pp. 86–97.

———. "Teaching Machines," *Science,* vol. 128 (Oct. 24, 1958), pp. 969–977.

THORNDIKE, EDWARD L. *Education.* New York, The Macmillan Company, 1912.

———. *Educational Psychology,* vol. I, *The Original Nature of Man.* New York, Teachers College Press, Columbia University, 1913.

————. *Educational Psychology*, vol. II, *The Psychology of Learning*. New York, Teachers College Press, Columbia University, 1913.

———— AND R. S. WOODWORTH. "The Influence of Improvement in One Mental Function upon the Efficiency of Other Functions," *Psychological Review*, vol. 8 (May, 1901), pp. 247–261; (July, 1901), pp. 384–395; (November, 1901), pp. 553–564.

TRAVERS, ROBERT M. W. "A Study of the Relationship of Psychological Research to Educational Practice," in Robert Glaser (ed.), *Training Research and Education*. Pittsburgh, The University of Pittsburgh Press, 1962, pp. 525–558.

WASHBURNE, CARLETON W., AND SIDNEY P. MARLAND. *Winnetka: The History and Significance of an Educational Experiment*. Englewood Cliffs, N.J., Prentice-Hall, Inc., 1963.

chapter 5

RAMSEY, GRACE FISHER. *Educational Work in Museums of the United States*. New York, The H. W. Wilson Company, 1938.

RATHMANN, CARL G. *Educational Museum of St. Louis Public Schools*. U.S. Bureau of Education Bulletin 48, 1915, p. 11.

SIGMAN, JAMES G. "Origin and Development of Visual Education in the Philadelphia Public Schools." Unpublished doctoral dissertation presented to School of Education, Temple University, Philadelphia, Pa., 1933.

SKINNER, CHARLES E. "Museums and Visual Education," *Educational Screen*, vol. 3 (October, 1924), p. 308.

TOOTHACKER, CHARLES R. *The Educational Work of the Commercial Museum of Philadelphia*. U.S. Bureau of Education Bulletin 13, 1920, p. 16.

chapter 6

ELLIS, DON CARLOS, AND LAURA THORNBOROUGH. *Motion Pictures in Education*. New York, Thomas Y. Crowell Company, 1923.

GREGORY, W. M. "Problems concerning the Educational Motion Picture," *Moving Picture Age*, vol. 5, no. 1 (January, 1922), p. 20.

HARTSHORNE, HUGH, AND MARK A. MAY. *Studies in Deceit*. New York, The Macmillan Company, 1928.

KNOWLTON, D. C., AND J. W. TILTON. *Motion Pictures in History Teaching*. New Haven, Conn., Yale University Press, 1929.

KROWS, ARTHUR E. "Motion Pictures—Not for Theaters," *Educational Screen*, vol. 21 (March, 1942), pp. 104–106.

LEWIN, WILLIAM. *Photoplay Appreciation in American High Schools*. New York, D. Appleton-Century Company, Inc., 1934.

Visual Instruction. Curriculum Committee on Visual Education, Course of Study Monographs, no. 7, Berkeley, Calif., The Berkeley Public Schools, 1923.

WEBER, JOSEPH J. *Visual Aids in Education*. Valparaiso, Ind., Valparaiso University, 1930. (Mimeographed.)

WOOD, BEN D., AND FRANK N. FREEMAN. *Motion Pictures in the Classroom*. Boston, Houghton Mifflin Company, 1929.

chapter 7

ADAMS, JOHN. *Exposition and Illustration*. New York, The Macmillan Company, 1910.

ANKENEY, J. V. "Report of Committee on Teacher Training in Visual Instruction," *Educational Screen*, no. 5 (October, 1926), pp. 489–491.

AUGHINBAUGH, B. A. "Outline for Course in Visual Instruction," *Educational Screen*, no. 8 (December, 1929), pp. 307–308.

CARROLL, JOHN S. *Teacher Education and Visual Education for the Modern School*. San Diego, Calif., Office of Superintendent of Schools, 1948.

COOK, KATHERINE M., AND FLORENCE E. REYNOLDS. *Opportunities for the Preparation of Teachers in the Use of Visual Aids in Instruction*. Federal Security Agency, U.S. Office of Education, Pamphlet 89, 1940.

DALE, EDGAR, FANNIE W. DUNN, CHARLES F. HOBAN, JR., AND ETTA SCHNEIDER. *Motion Pictures in Education*. New York, The H. W. Wilson Company, 1937.

DORRIS, ANNA V. *Visual Instruction in the Public Schools*. Boston, Ginn and Company, 1928.

DUDLEY, W. H. *Organization for Visual Instruction*. U.S. Bureau of Education Bulletin 7, 1921.

HENDERSON, H. A. "What Should a Course in Visual Instruction Include?" *Educational Screen*, vol. 11, no. 2 (June, 1932).

HUTCHINSON, J. RAYMOND. "Fundamentals of Visual Education," *School Executive*, no. 55 (January, 1936), pp. 186–188.

INGLIS, RUTH A. *Freedom of the Movies*. Chicago, The University of Chicago Press, 1947.

chapter 8

BROOKER, FLOYDE E. *Training Films for Industry*. Federal Security Agency, U.S. Office of Education Bulletin 13, 1946.

———. "Communication in the Modern World," *Audio-Visual Materials of Instruction*. The Forty-eighth Yearbook of the National Society for the Study of Education, part I. Chicago, The University of Chicago Press, 1949.

EXTON, WILLIAM, JR. *Audiovisual Aids to Instruction*. New York, McGraw-Hill Book Company, 1947.

GOLDNER, ORVILLE. "Films in the Armed Services," in Godfrey M. Elliott (ed.), *Film and Education*. New York, Philosophical Library, Inc., 1948, p. 395.

HOBAN, CHARLES F., JR. *Movies That Teach*. New York, The Dryden Press, Inc., 1946.

MILES, JOHN R., AND CHARLES R. SPAIN. *Audio-Visual Aids in the Armed Services.* Washington, D.C., American Council on Education, 1947.

THOMPSON, GEORGE R., D. R. HARRIS, PAULINE M. OAKES, AND DULANY TERRETT. *The Signal Corps: The Test.* Office of the Chief of Military History, Department of the Army, 1957.

chapter 9

ALLEN, WILLIAM H. *Audio-Visual Communication Research.* Santa Monica, Calif., System Development Corporation, 1958.

BROWN, JAMES W. *The Virginia Plan for Audio-Visual Education.* Chicago, The University of Chicago Press, 1947.

———— AND JAMES W. THORNTON, JR. (eds.) *New Media in Higher Education.* Washington, D.C., Association for Higher Education and Department of Audiovisual Instruction, NEA, 1963.

BUSHNELL, DONALD. *The Computer in Education.* New York, John Wiley & Sons, Inc., 1967.

"The Changing Role of the Audiovisual Process in Education: A Definition and a Glossary of Related Terms," *AV Communication Review,* supplement 6 (January–February, 1963).

CONNELLY, JOHN W., JR. *Report of State Laws on Audio-Visual Media of Instruction in Public Schools and on Establishment of Educational Television Stations.* U.S. Office of Education, 1962.

CREMIN, LAWRENCE A. *The Transformation of the Schools: Progressivism in American Education, 1876–1957.* New York, Alfred A. Knopf, Inc., 1961.

FINN, JAMES D., DONALD G. PERRIN, AND LEE E. CAMPION. *Studies in the Growth of Instructional Technology, I: Audio-Visual Instrumentation for Instruction in the Public Schools, 1930–1960. A Basis for Take-off.* Washington, D.C., NEA Technological Development Project, 1963.

———— AND ————. *Teaching Machines and Programed Learning, 1962: A Survey of the Industry.* Washington, D.C., NEA Technological Development Project, 1962.

GIBSON, JAMES J. "A Theory of Pictorial Perception," *AV Communication Review,* vol. 2 (Winter, 1954), pp. 3–23.

"Learning Theory and AV Utilization," *AV Communication Review,* supplement 4 (September–October, 1961).

MILLER, NEAL E., et al. "Graphic Communication and the Crisis in Education," *AV Communication Review,* vol. 5, special supplement (Summer, 1957), p. 3.

MORRIS, BARRY (ed.). "The Function of Media in the Public Schools," *Audiovisual Instruction,* vol. 8 (January, 1963), p. 11.

NOEL, FRANCIS W., et al. *Practices of State Departments of Education in New Educational Media/Audiovisual Education during 1960–61.* Los Angeles, University of Southern California Press, 1963.

RUFSVOLD, MARGARET. *Audio-Visual School Library Service.* Chicago, American Association of School Librarians, ALA, 1949.

SAETTLER, PAUL. *History of Instructional Technology, II: The Technical Develop-*

ment of the New Media. Washington, D.C., NEA Technological Development Project, 1961.

SCHWARTZ, JOHN C. *Evaluative Criteria for an Audio-Visual Instructional Program*. Dubuque, Iowa, William C. Brown Company, 1950.

chapter 10

Education by Radio, vol. 1, no. 1, The National Committee on Education by Radio (Feb. 12, 1931).

Education by Radio, vol. 1, no. 7, The National Committee on Education by Radio (Mar. 26, 1931).

Education by Radio, vol. 11, no. 4, The National Committee on Education by Radio (Fourth Quarter, 1941).

EVANS, S. HOWARD. "The Rocky Mountain Radio Council," *Education by Radio*, vol. 10, no. 7 (Second Quarter, 1940).

Four Years of Network Broadcasting. A Report by the Committee on Civic Education by Radio of the National Advisory Council on Radio in Education and the American Political Science Association, reprinted from *Radio and Education*. Chicago, University of Chicago Press, 1936.

FROST, S. E., JR. *Is American Radio Democratic?* Chicago, The University of Chicago Press, 1937.

———. *Education's Own Stations*. Chicago, The University of Chicago Press, 1937.

GRIFFITH, W. I. Copy of a resolution included in report of the Fourth National Radio Conference, Washington, D.C., Nov. 12, 1925.

HILL, FRANK ERNEST. *Listen and Learn*. New York, American Association for Adult Education, 1937.

———. *Tune in for Education*. New York, National Committee on Education by Radio, 1942.

HILL, HAROLD E. *The National Association of Educational Broadcasters: A History*. Urbana, Ill., The National Association of Educational Broadcasters, 1954.

HUDSON, ROBERT B. "Allerton House, 1949, 1950," *Hollywood Quarterly*, vol. 5 (Spring, 1951), p. 239.

LEVENSON, WILLIAM B., AND EDWARD STASHEFF. *Teaching through Radio and Television*. New York, Rinehart & Company, Inc., 1952.

SELDES, GILBERT. *The Great Audience*. New York, The Viking Press, Inc., 1950.

TYLER, TRACY F. *An Appraisal of Radio Broadcasting in the Land-grant Colleges and State Universities*. Prepared under the direction of the Joint Radio Survey Committee on Education by Radio. Washington, D.C., The National Committee on Education by Radio, 1933.

———. *National Advisory Council on Radio in Education, Inc.* Information Series no. 1, Bulletin. New York, 1936.

chapter 11

ERICKSON, CLIFFORD G., AND HYMAN M. CHAUSOW. *Chicago's TV College*. Chicago, Chicago City Junior College, August, 1960.

GITLIN, IRVING. "A Commercial Broadcaster on ETV Programs," in *Educational Television: The Next Ten Years*. Stanford, Calif., The Institute for Communication Research, Stanford University, 1962.

HEAD, SYDNEY W. "A Friendly Critic on ETV Programs," in *Educational Television: The Next Ten Years*. Stanford, Calif., The Institute for Communication Research, Stanford University, 1962.

HERRINGHAUS, EARLY G. *An Investigation of Television Teaching*. St. Louis Public Schools, 1957.

HUDSON, ROBERT B. "How the National Program Center Sees the Outlook," in *Educational Television: The Next Ten Years*. Stanford, Calif., The Institute for Communication Research, Stanford University, 1962.

LEWIS, PHILIP. *Educational Television Guidebook*. New York, McGraw-Hill Book Company, 1961.

MERCER, JOHN, AND SAM BECKER. "The Disenchantment of Educational Television," *AV Communication Review*, vol. 3 (Spring, 1955), pp. 173–182.

NELSON, LYLE M. "The Financing of Educational Television," in *Educational Television: The Next Ten Years*. Stanford, Calif., The Institute for Communication Research, Stanford University, 1962.

POWELL, JOHN WALKER. *Channels of Learning*. Washington, D.C., Public Affairs Press, 1962.

STODDARD, ALEXANDER J. *Schools for Tomorrow: An Educator's Blueprint*. New York, The Fund for the Advancement of Education, 1957.

Teaching by Television. A Report from the Ford Foundation and the Fund for the Advancement of Education. New York, Ford Foundation, 1959, pp. 37–39.

Television in Education. A Summary Report, reprinted from the complete proceedings of the Educational Television Programs Institute held at Pennsylvania State College, Apr. 20–24, 1952. Washington, D.C., American Council on Education, 1952.

Washington County Closed-circuit Television Report. Washington County Board of Education. Hagerstown, Md., 1963.

chapter 12

CROWDER, N. A. "Automatic Tutoring by Intrinsic Programming," in Arthur A. Lumsdaine and Robert Glaser (eds.), *Teaching Machines and Programmed Learning: A Source Book*. Washington, D.C., Department of Audiovisual Instruction, NEA, 1960, pp. 286–298.

EIGEN, L. D., AND P. K. KOMOSKI. *Research Summary No. 1 of the Collegiate School Automated Teaching Project*. New York, Center for Programed Instruction, 1960.

EVANS, J. L., R. GLASER, AND L. E. HOMME. "An Investigation of 'Teaching Machine' Variables Using Learning Programs in Symbolic Logic," *Journal of Educational Research*, vol. 55 (June–July, 1962), pp. 433–450.

FINN, JAMES D., AND DONALD G. PERRIN. *Teaching Machines and Programed Learning, 1962: A Survey of the Industry*. Washington, D.C., NEA Technological Development Project, 1962.

GLASER, R., J. H. REYNOLDS, AND MARGARET C. FULLICK. *Programed Instruction in the Intact Classroom.* Pittsburgh, Learning Research and Development Center, University of Pittsburgh, 1963.

HOLLAND, JAMES G. "A Teaching Machine Program in Psychology," in E. Galanter (ed.), *Automatic Teaching: The State of the Art.* New York, John Wiley & Sons, Inc., 1959.

LEWIS, BRIAN N., AND GORDON PASK. "The Theory and Practice of Adaptive Teaching Systems," in Robert Glaser (ed.), *Teaching Machines and Programed Learning, II, Data and Directions.* Washington, D.C., Department of Audiovisual Instruction, NEA, 1965.

LITTLE, JAMES K. "Results of Use of Machines for Testing and for Drill upon Learning in Educational Psychology," *Journal of Experimental Education,* vol. 3, (September, 1934), pp. 59–65.

MONTESSORI, MARIA. *The Montessori Method,* tr. by A. E. George. Philadelphia, J. B. Lippincott Company, 1912.

MOORE, O. K. "Autotelic Response Environments and Exceptional Children," *Special Children in Century 21.* Seattle, Wash., Special Child Publications, 1964.

PASK, GORDON. "Interaction between a Group of Subjects and an Adaptive Automaton to Produce a Self-organizing System for Decision-making," in M. C. Yovits, G. T. Jacobi, and G. D. Goldstein (eds.), *Self-organizing Systems—1962.* Washington, D.C., Spartan Books, 1962.

PORTER, DOUGLAS. *An Application of Reinforcement Principles to Classroom Teaching.* Cambridge, Mass., Graduate School of Education, Harvard University, May, 1961.

PRESSEY, SIDNEY L. "A Third and Fourth Contribution toward the Coming 'Industrial Revolution' in Education," *School and Society,* vol. 36 (1932), pp. 1–5.

———. "Teaching Machine (and Learning Theory) Crisis," *Journal of Applied Psychology,* vol. 47 (February, 1963), pp. 1–6.

———. "Autoinstruction: Perspectives, Problems, Potentials," in E. R. Hilgard (ed.), *Theories of Learning and Instruction,* The Sixty-third Yearbook of the National Society for the Study of Education, part I. Chicago, The University of Chicago Press, 1964.

RUSHTON, E. *The Roanoke Story.* Chicago, Encyclopedia Britannica, Inc., 1963.

SCHRAMM, WILBUR (ed.). *Four Cases of Programed Instruction.* New York, Fund for the Advancement of Education, 1964.

SKINNER, B. F. "The Science of Learning and the Art of Teaching," in Arthur A. Lumsdaine and Robert Glaser (eds.), *Teaching Machines and Programmed Learning.* Washington, D.C., Department of Audiovisual Instruction, NEA, 1960.

SMITH, KARL U., AND MARGARET F. SMITH. *Cybernetic Principles of Learning and Educational Design.* New York, Holt, Rinehart and Winston, Inc., 1966.

THELEN, HERBERT A. "Programed Instruction: Insight vs. Conditioning," *Education,* vol. 83 (March, 1963), pp. 416–420.

———. "Programed Materials Today: Critique and Proposal," *The Elementary School Journal,* vol. 64 (1963), pp. 189–196.

The Use of Programed Instruction in U.S. Schools. Center for Programed Instruction. Washington, D.C., 1965.

chapter 13

ALLPORT, F. H. *Theories of Perception and the Concept of Structure*. New York, John Wiley & Sons, Inc., 1955.

GAGNE, ROBERT M. (ed.). *Psychological Principles in System Development*. New York, Holt, Rinehart and Winston, Inc., 1962.

GLASER, ROBERT (ed.). *Training Research and Education*. Pittsburgh, Pa., The University of Pittsburgh Press, 1962.

GOODLAD, JOHN, et al. *Computers and Information Systems in Education*. New York, Harcourt, Brace & World, Inc., 1966.

LAUGHARY, JOHN W. *Man-Machine Systems in Education*. New York, Harper & Row, Publishers, Incorporated, 1966.

TROW, WILLIAM CLARK. *Teacher and Technology: New Design for Learning*. New York, Appleton-Century-Crofts, Inc., 1963.

VON BERTALANFFY, LUDWIG. *Problems of Life: An Evaluation of Modern Biological Thought*. New York, John Wiley & Sons, Inc., 1952.

chapter 14

ARNSPIGER, V. C. *Measuring the Effectiveness of Sound Pictures as Teaching Aids*. Teachers College Contributions to Education, no. 565. New York, Teachers College Press, Columbia University, 1933.

Auditory Aids and the Teaching of Science: Two Experimental Studies. Bulletin 57, Evaluation of School Broadcasts, Columbus, Ohio, Ohio State University, 1942.

BROOKER, FLOYDE E., AND EUGENE HERRINGTON. *Students Make Motion Pictures*. Washington, D.C., American Council on Education Studies, ser. 2, vol. 5, no. 7, 1941.

CANTRIL, HADLEY, AND GORDON W. ALLPORT. *The Psychology of Radio*. New York, Harper and Brothers, 1935.

CHARTERS, W. W. *Motion Pictures and Youth*. New York, The Macmillan Company, 1935.

DALE, EDGAR, AND LLOYD L. RAMSEYER. *Teaching with Motion Pictures: A Handbook of Administrative Practices*. Washington, D.C., American Council on Education Studies, ser. 2, no. 2, April, 1937.

DARROW, B. H. *Radio Trailblazing*. Columbus, Ohio, College Book Company, 1940.

FREEMAN, FRANK N. *Visual Education*. Chicago, The University of Chicago Press, 1924.

HILL, FRANK E. *Listen and Learn*. New York, American Association for Adult Education, 1937.

HOBAN, CHARLES F., JR. *Focus on Learning*. Washington, D.C., American Council on Education, 1942.

———. *Movies That Teach*. New York, The Dryden Press, Inc., 1946.

HOVLAND, C. I., A. A. LUMSDAINE, AND F. D. SHEFFIELD. *Experiments on Mass Communication*. Princeton, N.J., Princeton University Press, 1949.

KNOWLTON, D. C., AND J. W. TILTON. *Motion Pictures in History Teaching*. New Haven, Conn., Yale University Press, 1929.

KOON, CLINE M. *Motion Pictures in Education in the United States.* U.S. Department of the Interior Bulletin 130, 1934, p. 43.

―――― AND ALLEN W. NOBLE. *National Visual Education Directory.* Washington, D.C., American Council on Education, 1936, p. 9.

LAZARSFELD, PAUL F. *Radio and the Printed Page.* New York, Duell, Sloan & Pearce, Inc., 1940.

―――― AND FRANK N. STANTON. *Radio Research 1942–1943.* New York, Duell, Sloan & Pearce, Inc., 1944.

LUMLEY, F. M. *Measurement in Radio.* Columbus, Ohio, Ohio State University Press, 1934.

A School Uses Motion Pictures. The Staff of Tower Hill School, Wilmington, Del. Washington, D.C., American Council on Education Studies, ser. 2, vol. 4, no. 3, 1940.

WEBER, J. J. *Visual Aids in Education.* Valparaiso, Ind., Valparaiso University, 1930.

WISE, H. A. *Motion Pictures as an Aid in Teaching American History.* New Haven, Conn., Yale University Press, 1939.

WOELFEL, NORMAN, AND I. KEITH TYLER. *Radio and the School.* Tarrytown-on-Hudson, New York, World Book Company, 1945.

WOOD, BEN D., AND FRANK N. FREEMAN. *Motion Pictures in the Classroom.* Boston, Houghton Mifflin Company, 1929.

chapter 15

BUSHNELL, DON D. *The Computer in American Education.* New York, John Wiley & Sons, Inc., 1967.

CANTRILL, HADLEY, AND GORDON W. ALLPORT. *The Psychology of Radio.* New York, Harper and Brothers, 1935.

CASSIRER, ERNEST. *The Philosophy of Symbolic Forms.* New Haven, Conn., Yale University Press, 1953.

CHERRY, COLIN. *On Human Communication.* New York, John Wiley & Sons, Inc., 1966.

ELY, DONALD P. "Communications Programs in Higher Education," *AV Communication Review* (Winter, 1960), pp. 69–73.

EVANS, J. L., R. GLASER, AND L. E. HOMME. "A Preliminary Investigation of Variations in the Properties of Verbal Learning Sequences of the 'Teaching Machine' Type," in Arthur A. Lumsdaine and Robert Glaser (eds.), *Teaching Machines and Programed Learning: A Source Book.* Washington, D.C., Department of Audiovisual Instruction, NEA, 1960.

FINN, JAMES D. "The Marginal Media Man, Part I: The Great Paradox," *Audiovisual Instruction*, vol. 10, no. 10 (December, 1965), pp. 762–765.

GOLDSTEIN, L. S., AND L. G. GOTKIN. "A Review of Research: Teaching Machines vs. Programed Textbooks as Presentation Modes," *Journal of Programed Instruction*, vol. 1 (1962), pp. 29–36.

GOTKIN, L. G. "Teaching Machines and Programed Instruction," *AV Communication Review*, vol. 14, no. 2 (Summer, 1966), pp. 221–241.

GROPPER, GEORGE L., AND A. A. LUMSDAINE. *An Investigation of the Role of Selected Variables in Programed TV Instruction,* Studies in Televised Instruction, Report 4. Pittsburgh, Pa., Metropolitan Pittsburgh Educational Television Stations WQED-WQEX and American Institute for Research, 1961.

——— AND ——— . *The Use of Student Response to Improve Televised Instruction: An Overview.* Report 7 (Summary of six prior reports). Studies in Televised Instruction. Pittsburgh, Pa., American Institute for Research Report AIR-C13-61-FR-245 (VII), 1961.

HENRY, NELSON B. (ed.). *Mass Media and Education,* The Fifty-third Yearbook of the National Society for the Study of Education, part II. Chicago, The University of Chicago Press, 1954.

HILGARD, ERNEST R. "Perspective on the Relationship between Learning Theory and Educational Practices," in E. R. Hilgard (ed.), *Theories of Learning and Instruction,* The Sixty-third Yearbook of the National Society for the Study of Education, part I. Chicago, The University of Chicago Press, 1964.

HOBAN, C. F., AND E. B. VAN ORMER. *Instructional Film Research 1918–1950.* Technical Report SDC 269-7-19, Port Washington, N.Y., U.S. Naval Training Devices Center, December, 1950.

HOVLAND, CARL I., A. A. LUMSDAINE, AND FRED D. SHEFFIELD. *Experiments on Mass Communications,* vol. 3. Princeton, N.J., Princeton University Press, 1949.

KANNER, J. H. "The Development and Role of Teaching Aids in the Armed Forces," in *New Teaching Aids for the American Classroom.* Stanford, Calif., The Institute for Communication Research, 1960.

KATZ, ELIHU, AND PAUL F. LAZARSFELD. *Personal Influence.* New York, The Free Press of Glencoe, 1955.

KLAPPER, JOSEPH T. *The Effects of Mass Communication.* New York, The Free Press of Glencoe, 1960.

KUMATA, HIDEYA. *History and Progress of Instructional Television Research in the United States.* Report presented at the International Seminar on Instructional Television, Oct. 8–18, 1961, at Purdue University, Lafayette, Ind.

LANGER, SUSANNE K. *Philosophy in a New Key.* New York, New American Library of World Literature, Inc., 1948.

LASSWELL, H. D. "Communications as an Emerging Discipline," *AV Communication Review,* vol. 6 (Fall, 1958), p. 245.

———. "The Structure and Function of Communication in Society," in Wilbur Schramm (ed.), *Mass Communications,* 2d ed. Urbana, Ill., University of Illinois Press, 1960.

LEWIN, KURT. *Field Theory in Social Science.* New York, Harper & Row, Publishers, Incorporated, 1951.

LUMSDAINE, A. A. (ed.). *Student Response in Programmed Instruction.* Washington, D.C., National Academy of Sciences, National Research Council, 1961.

LUMSDAINE, ARTHUR A. "Assessing the Effectiveness of Instructional Programs," in Robert Glaser (ed.), *Teaching Machines and Programed Learning, II: Data and Directions.* Washington, D.C., NEA, 1965.

MAY, MARK A., et al. *Learning from Films.* New Haven, Conn. Yale University Press, 1958.

MCLUHAN, MARSHALL. *Understanding Media.* New York, McGraw-Hill Book Company, 1964.

MEIRHENRY, WESLEY C. *Enriching the Curriculum through Motion Pictures*. Lincoln, Nebr., University of Nebraska Press, 1952.

MERTON, ROBERT K. *Mass Persuasion*. New York, Harper & Row, Publishers, Incorporated, 1946.

MILLER, GEORGE A. *Language and Communication*. New York, McGraw-Hill Book Company, 1951.

MOORE, J. WILLIAM, AND WENDELL I. SMITH. "Knowledge of Results in Self-teaching Spelling," *Psychological Reports*, vol. 9 (1961), pp. 717–726.

PRESSEY, S. L. "Development and Appraisal of Devices Providing Immediate Automatic Scoring of Objective Tests and Concomitant Self-instruction," *Journal of Psychology*, vol. 29 (1950), pp. 417–447.

RUESCH, JURGEN, AND GREGORY BATESON. *Communication: The Social Matrix of Psychiatry*. New York, W. W. Norton & Company, Inc., 1951.

RUSHTON, E. W. *Programmed Learning: The Roanoke Experiment*. Chicago, Encyclopedia Britannica, Inc., 1965.

SCHRAMM, WILBUR (ed.). *Communications in Modern Society*. Urbana, Ill., The University of Illinois Press, 1948.

SCHRAMM, WILBUR. *The Process and Effects of Mass Communications*. Urbana, Ill., The University of Illinois Press, 1954.

SEATON, HELEN HARDT. *A Measure for Audio-Visual Programs in Schools*. Washington, D.C., American Council on Education, 1944.

SHANNON, CLAUDE E., AND WARREN WEAVER. *The Mathematical Theory of Communication*. Urbana, Ill., The University of Illinois Press, 1949.

SIEGEL, L., AND L. C. SIEGEL. "The Instructional Gestalt: A Conceptual Framework and Design for Educational Research," *AV Communication Review*, vol. 12, no. 1 (Spring, 1964), pp. 16–45.

SILVERMAN, H. F. "Characteristics of Some Recent Studies of Instructional Methods," in J. E. Coulson (ed.), *Programmed Learning and Computer-based Instruction*. New York, John Wiley & Sons, Inc., 1962.

SKINNER, B. F. *Verbal Behavior*. New York, Appleton-Century-Crofts, Inc., 1957.

SMITH, BRUCE LANNES, HAROLD D. LASSWELL, AND RALPH D. CASEY. *Propaganda and Promotional Activities: An Annotated Bibliography*. Minneapolis, The University of Minnesota Press, 1935.

SMITH, WENDELL, AND J. WILLIAM MOORE. *Size-of-step and Achievement in Programed Spelling*. Lewisburg, Pa., Bucknell University, 1961.

SNYGG, D. "The Tortuous Path of Learning Theory," *Audiovisual Instruction*, vol. 7 (1962), pp. 8–12.

STOUFFER, SAMUEL A., et al. *The American Soldier*. Princeton, N.J., Princeton University Press, 1949, vol. 1.

Teaching by Television. New York, Ford Foundation and Fund for the Advancement of Education, 1961.

WAPLES, DOUGLAS, AND RALPH TYLER. *What People Want to Read About*. Chicago, The University of Chicago Press, 1931.

WEISS, WALTER, NATHAN MACCOBY, AND FRED D. SHEFFIELD, "Combining Practice with Demonstration in Teaching Complex Sentences: Serial Learning of a Geometric-construction Task," in A. A. Lumsdaine (ed.), *Student Response*

in *Programmed Instruction*. Washington, D.C., National Academy of Sciences, National Research Council, 1961.
WIENER, NORBERT. *Cybernetics*. New York, John Wiley & Sons, Inc., 1948.

chapter 16

BIDDLE, BRUCE J., AND WILLIAM J. ELLENA (eds.), *Contemporary Research on Teacher Effectiveness*. New York, Holt, Rinehart and Winston, Inc., 1964.
BRUNER, JEROME S. *The Process of Education*. New York, Vintage Books, 1963.
———. "The Course of Cognitive Growth," *American Psychologist*, vol. 19 (1964).
———, et al. *Studies in Cognitive Growth*. New York, John Wiley & Sons, Inc., 1966.
CONANT, JAMES B. *The Education of American Teachers*. New York, McGraw-Hill Book Company, 1963.
———. *Two Modes of Thoughts: My Encounters with Science and Education*. New York, Trident Press, 1964.
GOODLAD, JOHN I. *School Curriculum Reform in the United States*. New York, The Fund for the Advancement of Education, 1964.
——— AND ROBERT H. ANDERSON. "Educational Practices in Nongraded Schools: A Survey of Perceptions," *The Elementary School Journal*, vol. 63 (October, 1962).
GOSLIN, DAVID A. *The School in Contemporary Society*. Chicago, Scott, Foresman and Company, 1965.
HILGARD, ERNEST R. "A Perspective on the Relationship between Learning Theory and Educational Practices," in E. R. Hilgard (ed.), *Theories of Learning and Instruction*, The Sixty-third Yearbook of the National Society for the Study of Education, part I. Chicago, The University of Chicago Press, 1964.
HULLFISH, H. GORDON, AND PHILIP G. SMITH. *Reflective Thinking: The Method of Education*. New York, Dodd, Mead & Company, Inc., 1961.
RUSSELL, JAMES E. *Change and Challenge in American Education*. Boston, Houghton Mifflin Company, 1965.
SNOW, C. P. *The Two Cultures: And a Second Look*, 2d ed. London, Cambridge University Press, 1964.

index